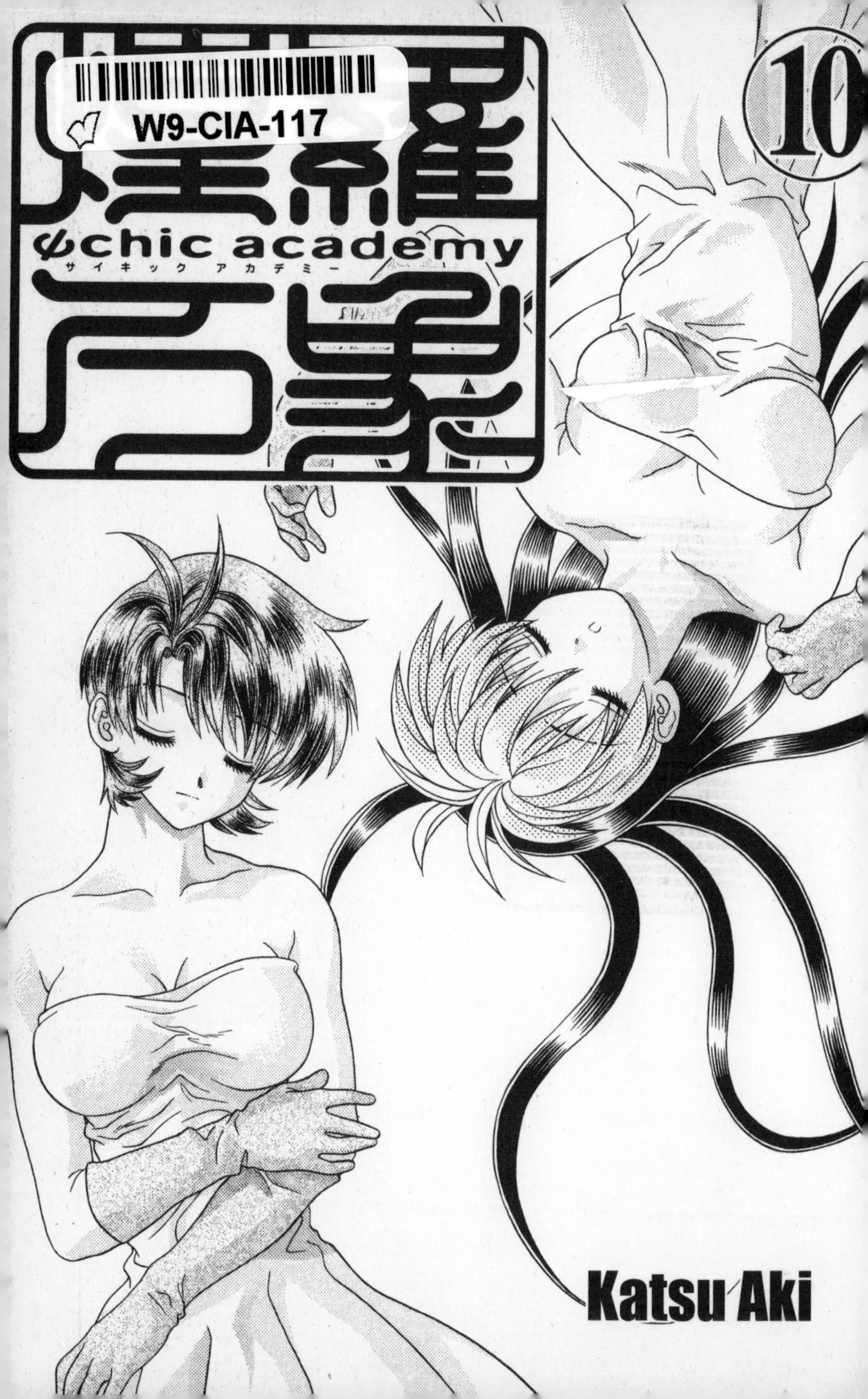

煌羅
ψchic academy
サイキック アカデミー
万象
10
Katsu Aki

PSYCHIC ACADEMY

VOLUME 10

By
KATSU AKI

TOKYOPOP®

HAMBURG // LONDON // LOS ANGELES // TOKYO

Psychic Academy Vol. 10
Created by Katsu Aki

Translation -	Yuki N. Johnson
English Adaptation -	Nathan Johnson
Retouch and Lettering -	Lucas Rivera
Production Artist -	Rafael Najarian
Cover Design -	Seth Cable
Editor -	Aaron Suhr
Digital Imaging Manager -	Chris Buford
Production Managers -	Jennifer Miller and Mutsumi Miyazaki
Managing Editor -	Lindsey Johnston
VP of Production -	Ron Klamert
Publisher and E.I.C. -	Mike Kiley
President and C.O.O. -	John Parker
C.E.O. -	Stuart Levy

A  Manga

TOKYOPOP Inc.
5900 Wilshire Blvd. Suite 2000
Los Angeles, CA 90036

E-mail: info@TOKYOPOP.com
Come visit us online at www.TOKYOPOP.com

ISBN: 1-59532-429-1
First TOKYOPOP printing: December 2005
10 9 8 7 6 5 4 3 2 1
Printed in the USA

Story Thus Far...

PSYCHIC ACADEMY

Zerodyme Kyupura Pa Azalraku Vairu Rua Darogu (a.k.a. Zero) stopped the evil demon lord with his incredible psychic ability, thereby saving the world from destruction and garnering the honorable and highly imaginative title "The Vanquisher of the Dark Overlord." Now he has accepted a position as teacher at Psychic Academy, a school for gifted psychokinetic youngsters who have demonstrated incredible raw psychic powers and desire to learn how to hone their abilities. Among the student body is young Ai Shiomi, Zero's little brother, a somewhat meek boy who, despite his parents' prodding and his fraternal reputation, feels that his limited skills hardly warrant enrollment at the prestigious academy. However, everyone else is convinced that he, too, is destined for greatness--a lot of pressure for a boy just entering adolescence.

Tokimitsu is back, and he's desperate for Ai to join the ADC. Tokimitsu believes that by sparring with Ai, his own powers will intensify. In the heat of battle, things look grim for Ai--until Mew arrives on the scene. The fight quickly turns in Ai's favor, and he once again questions his relationship with Orina...Ever since the Para dream, Ai can't seem to get his mind off Mew. Has their relationship passed the turning point?

C O N T E N T S

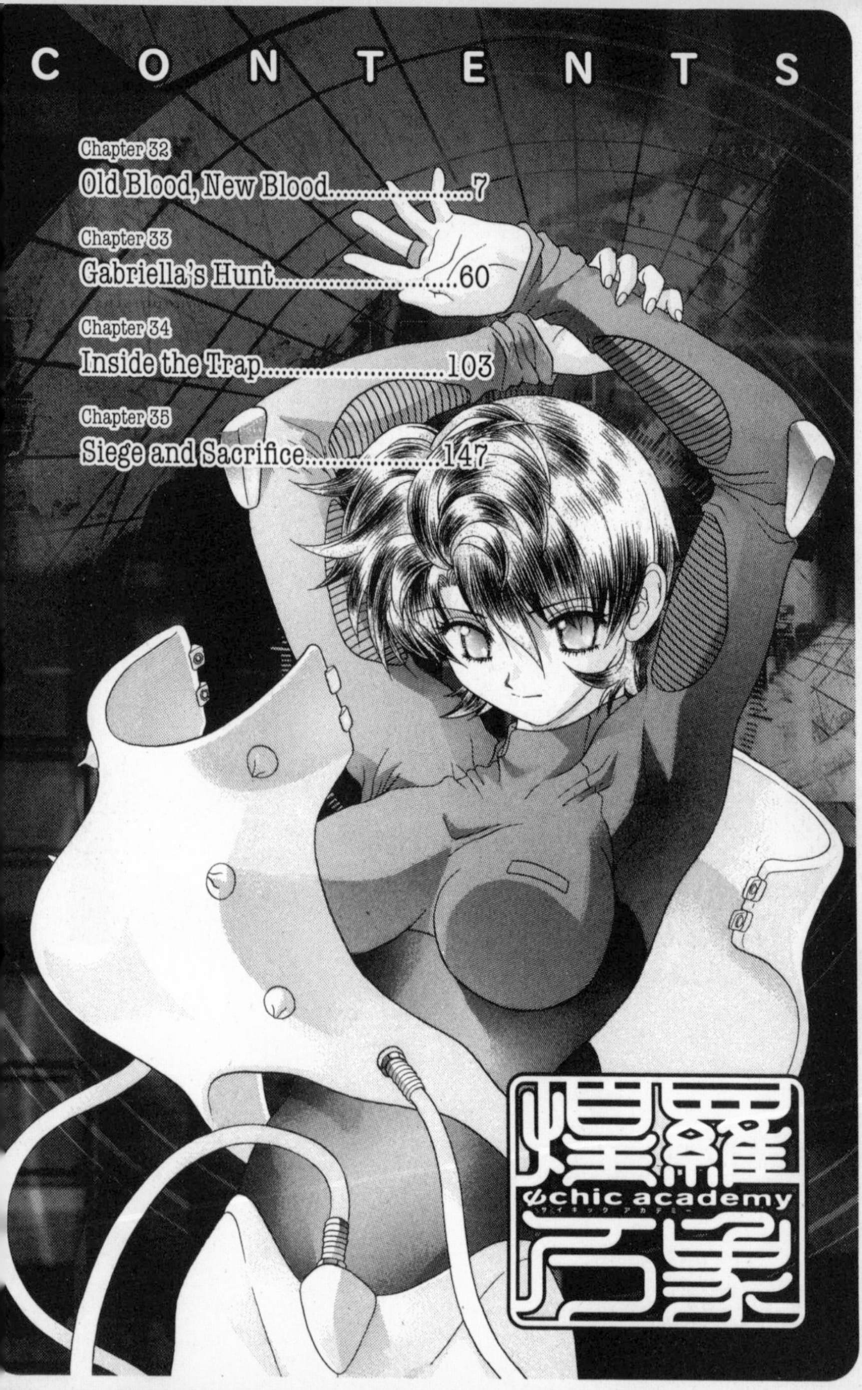

ψchic academy

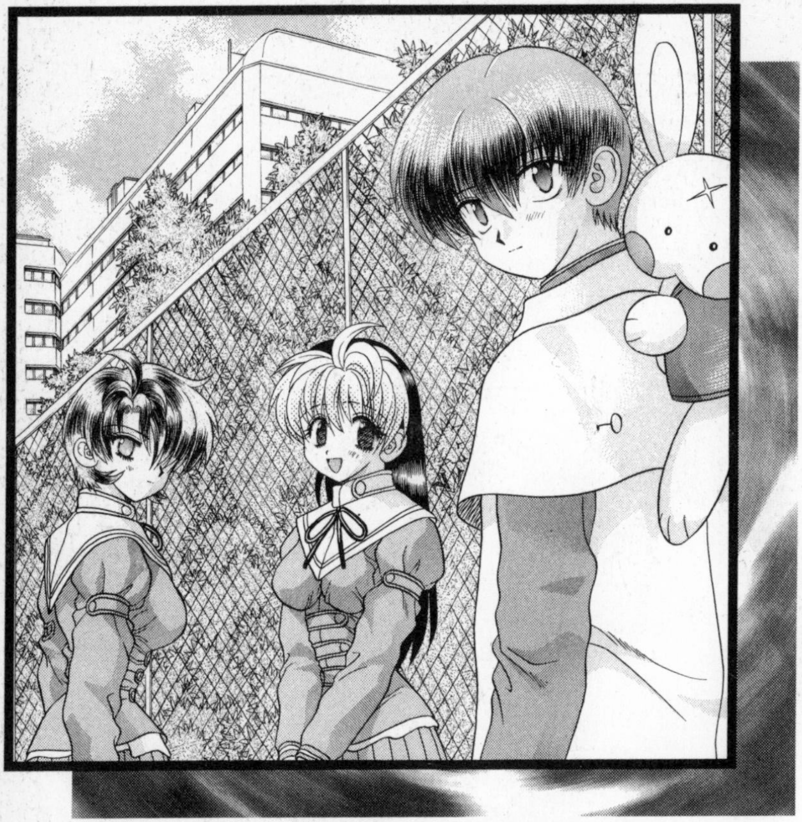

Chapter 32 Old Blood, New Blood

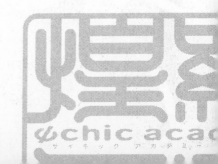

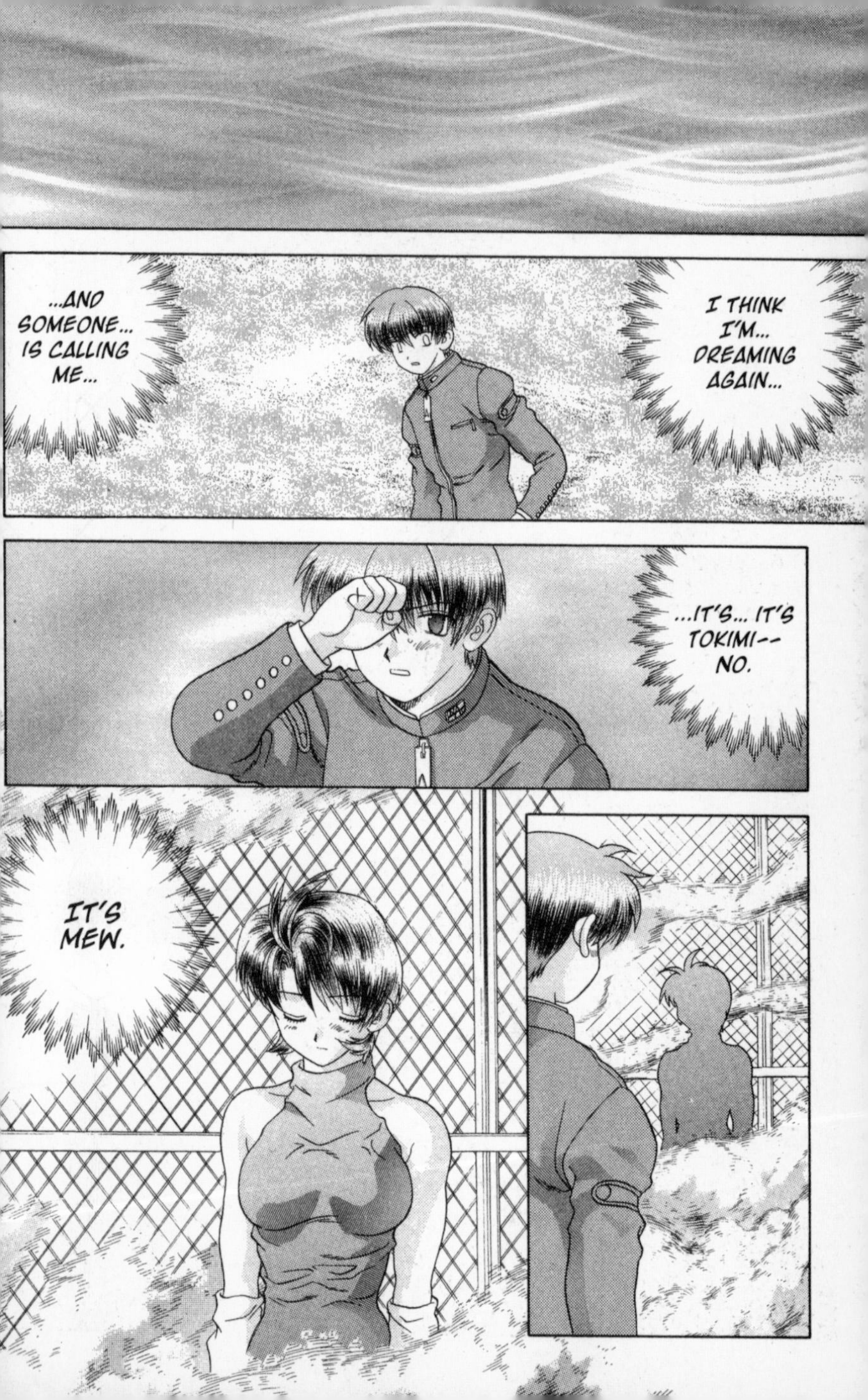
I THINK I'M... DREAMING AGAIN...
...AND SOMEONE... IS CALLING ME...
...IT'S... IT'S TOKIMI-- NO.
IT'S MEW.

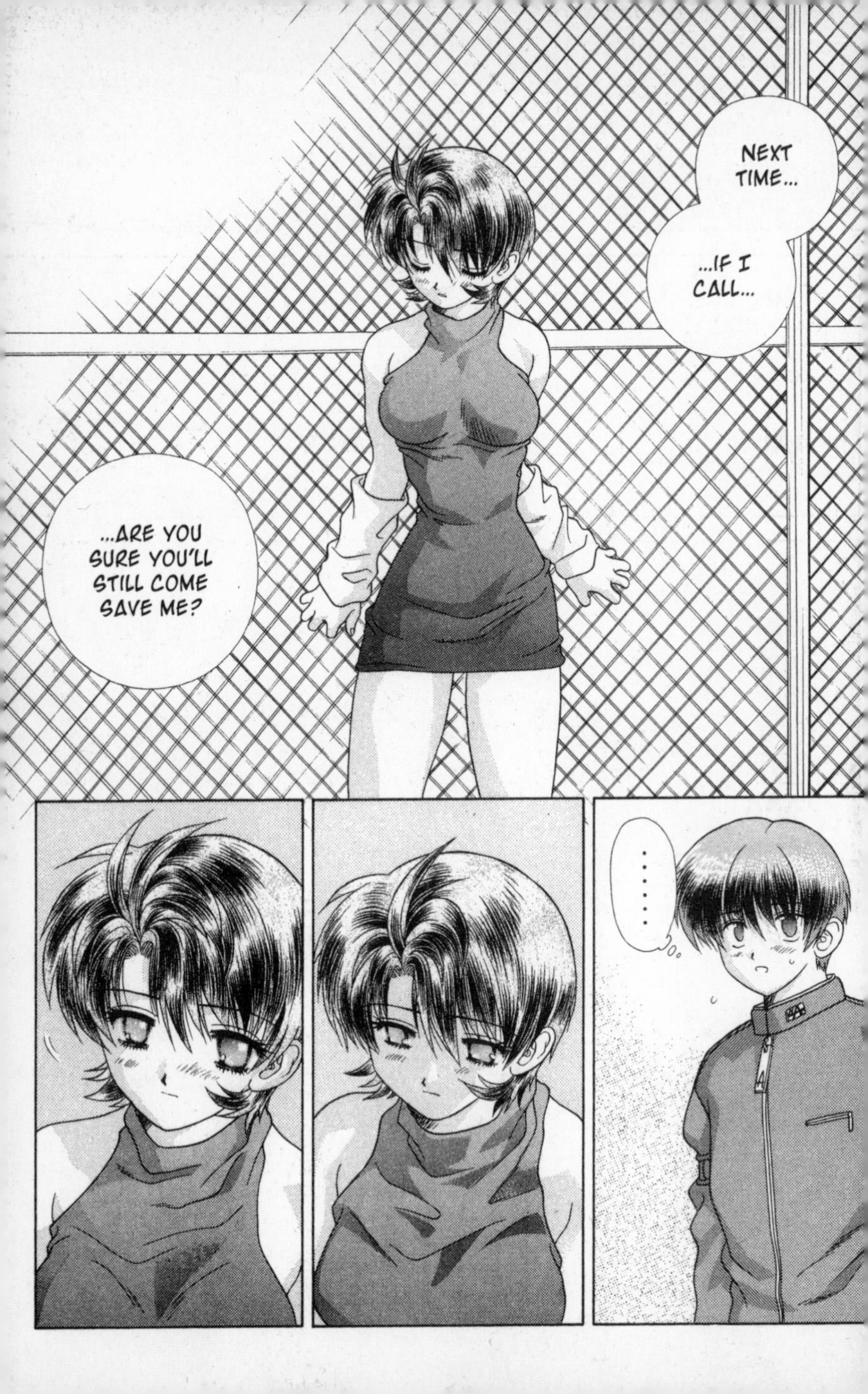
NEXT TIME...
...IF I CALL...
...ARE YOU SURE YOU'LL STILL COME SAVE ME?
......

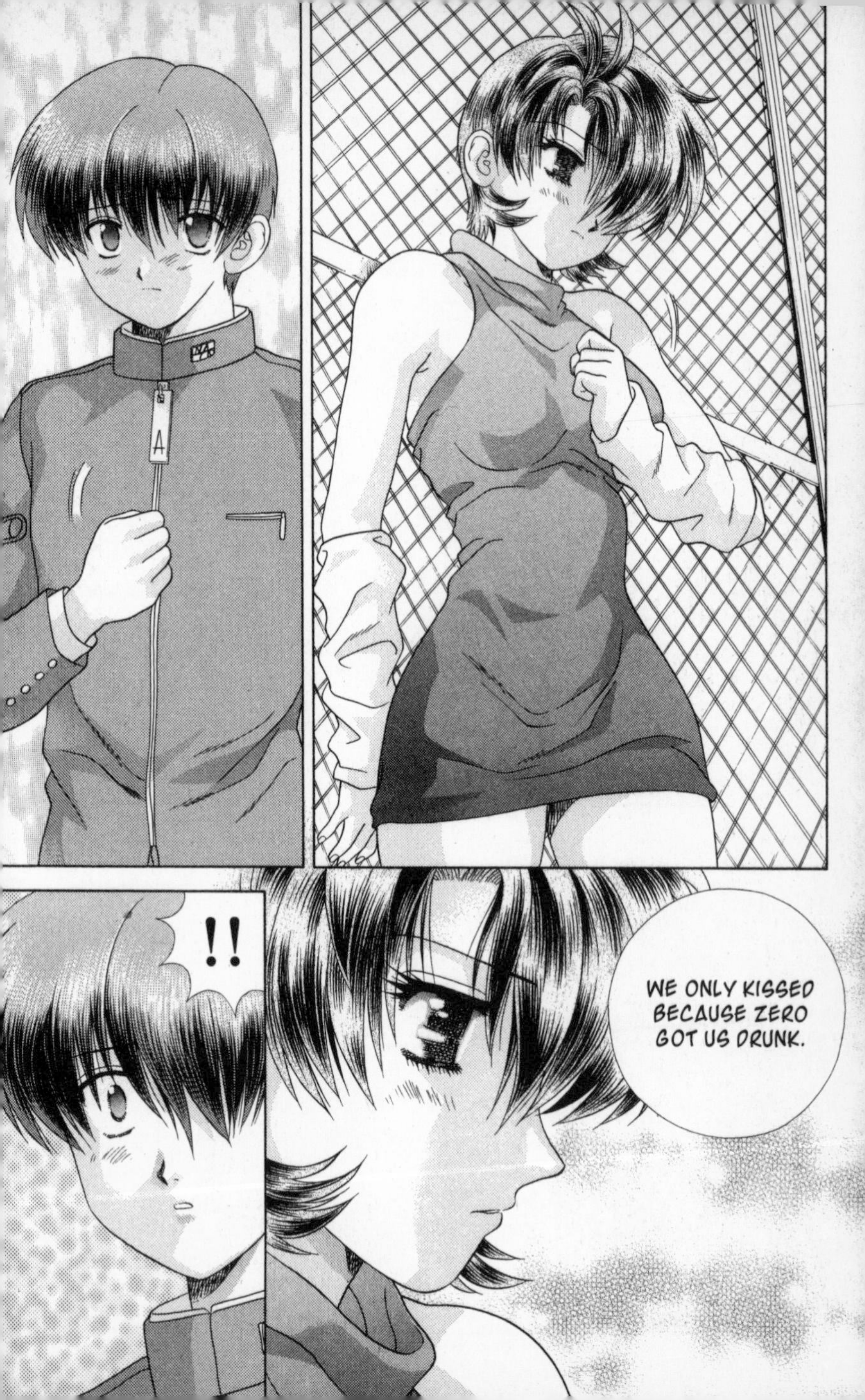
WE ONLY KISSED BECAUSE ZERO GOT US DRUNK.
!!

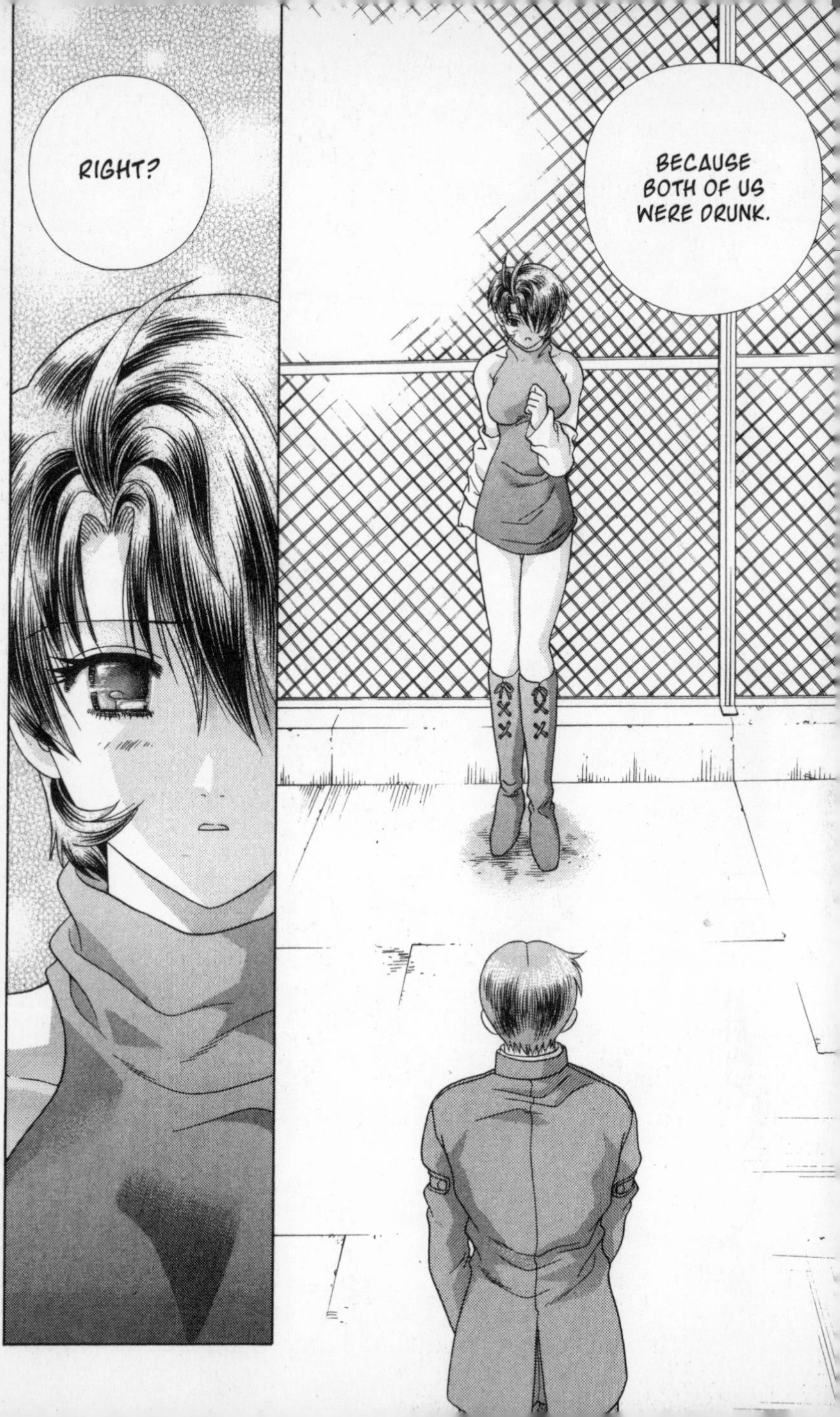
BECAUSE BOTH OF US WERE DRUNK.
RIGHT?

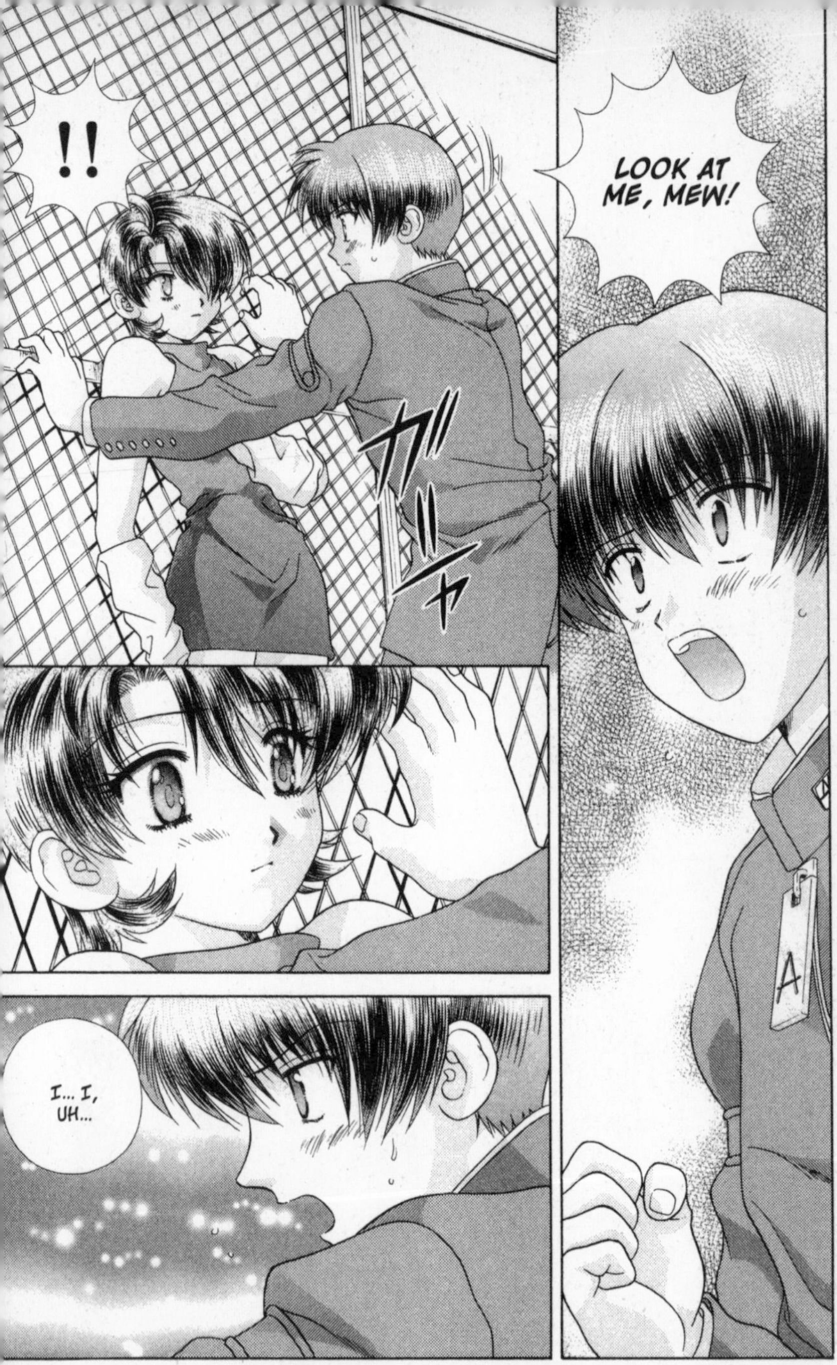
LOOK AT ME, MEW!
!!
ガシャ
I... I, UH...

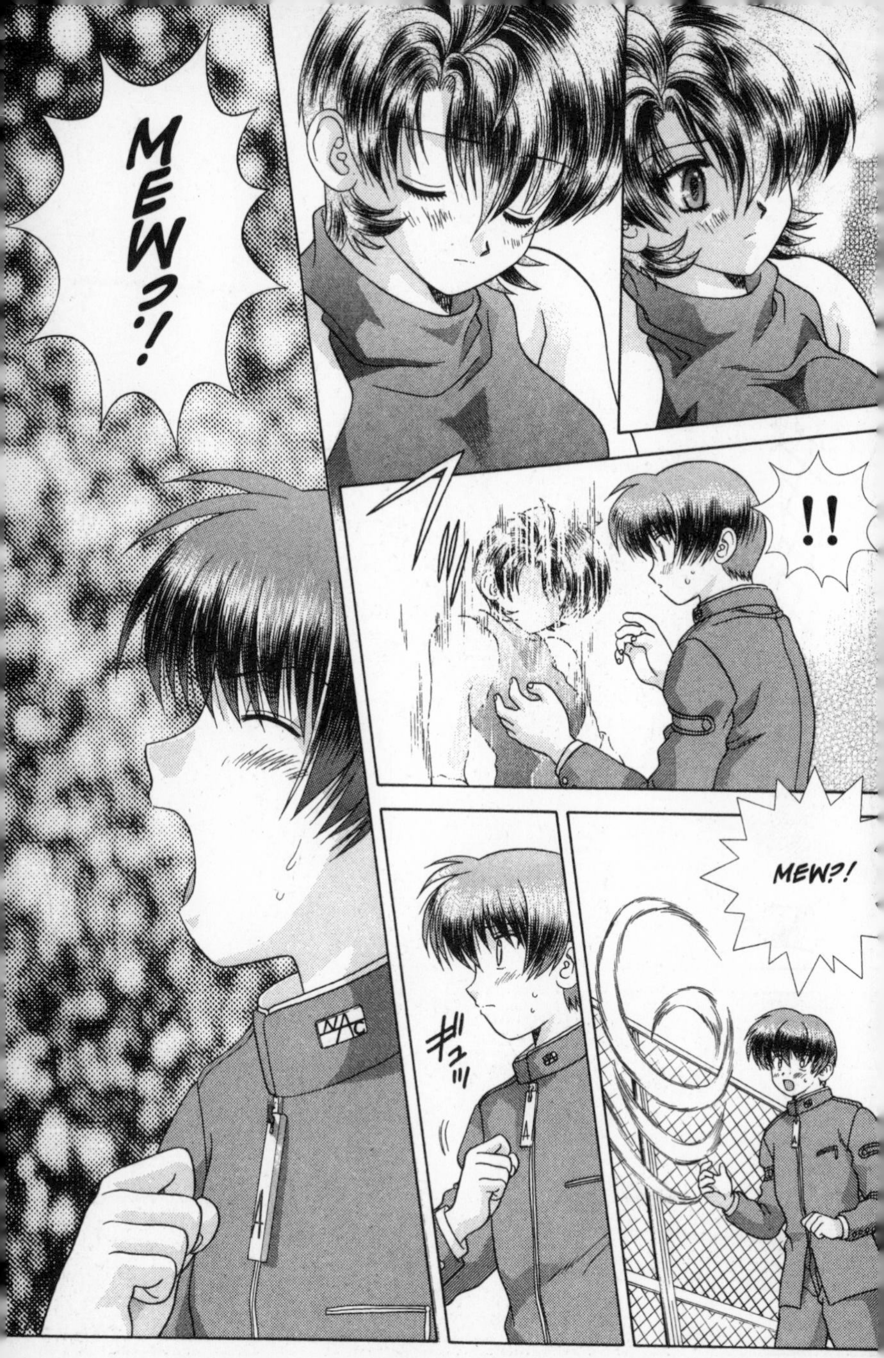
!!
MEW?!
ギュッ
MEW?!

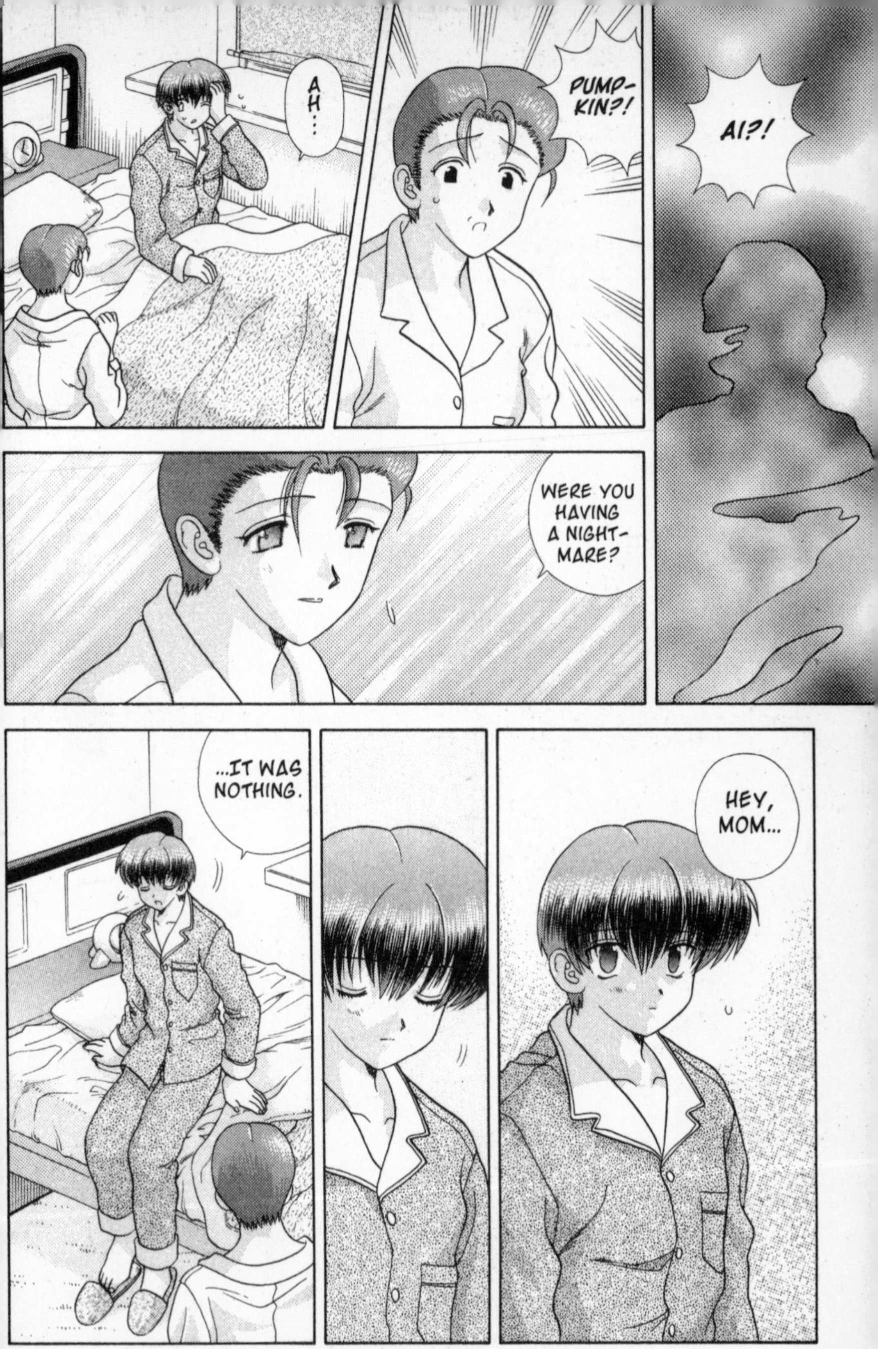
AI?!
PUMP-KIN?!
AH...
WERE YOU HAVING A NIGHT-MARE?
HEY, MOM...
...IT WAS NOTHING.

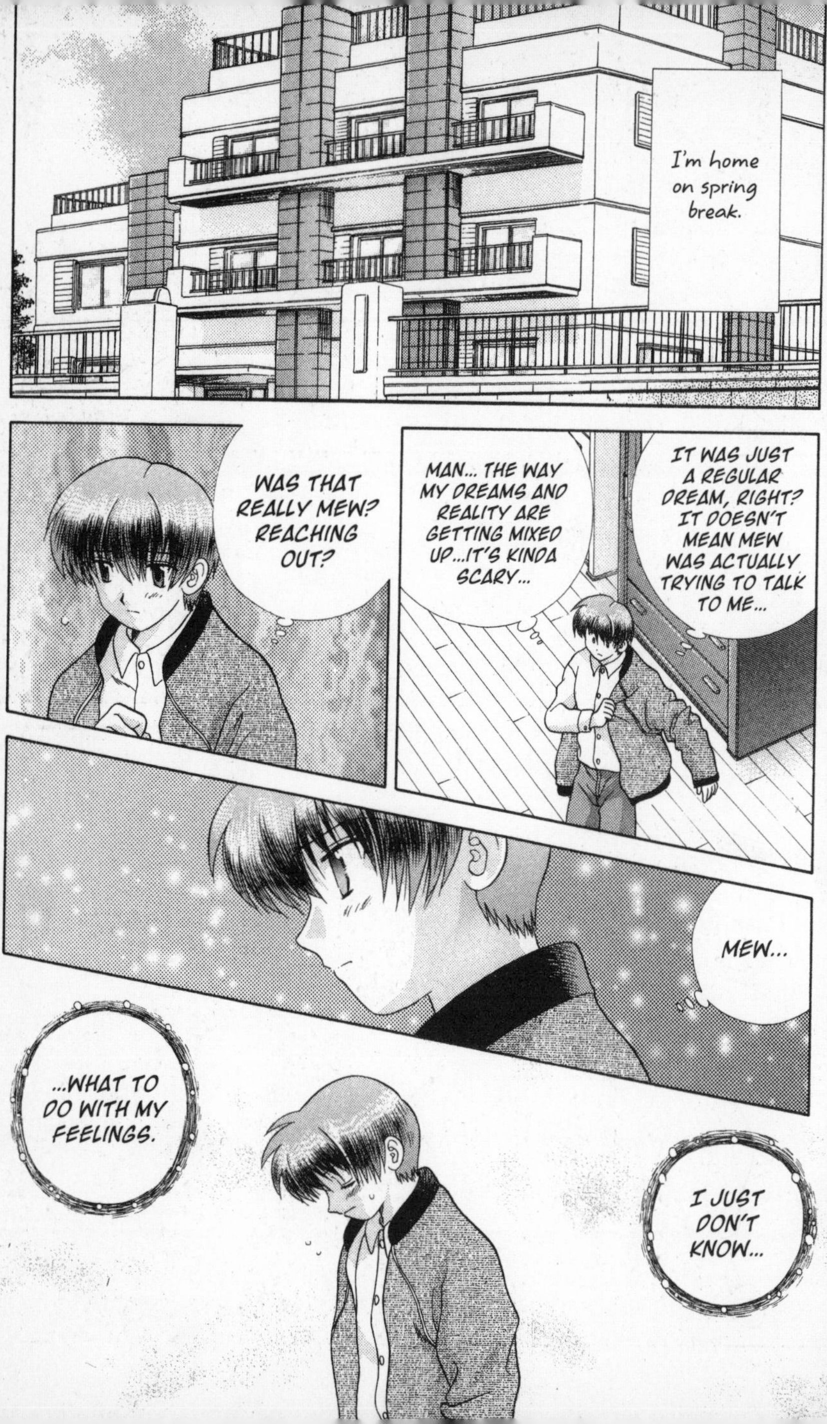
I'm home on spring break.
IT WAS JUST A REGULAR DREAM, RIGHT? IT DOESN'T MEAN MEW WAS ACTUALLY TRYING TO TALK TO ME...
MAN... THE WAY MY DREAMS AND REALITY ARE GETTING MIXED UP...IT'S KINDA SCARY...
WAS THAT REALLY MEW? REACHING OUT?
MEW...
I JUST DON'T KNOW...
...WHAT TO DO WITH MY FEELINGS.

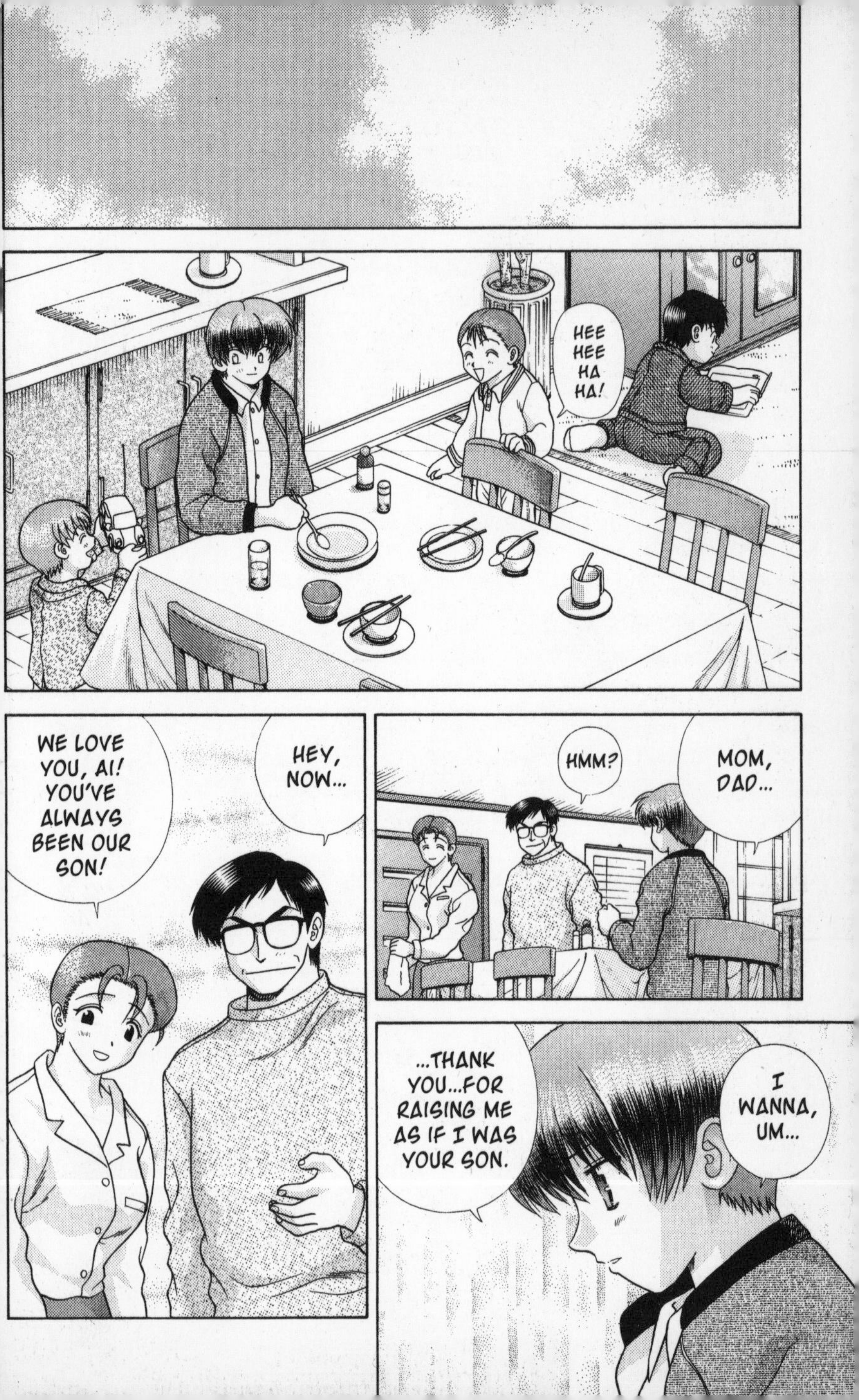
HEE HEE HA HA!
MOM, DAD...
HMM?
I WANNA, UM...
...THANK YOU...FOR RAISING ME AS IF I WAS YOUR SON.
HEY, NOW...
WE LOVE YOU, AI! YOU'VE ALWAYS BEEN OUR SON!

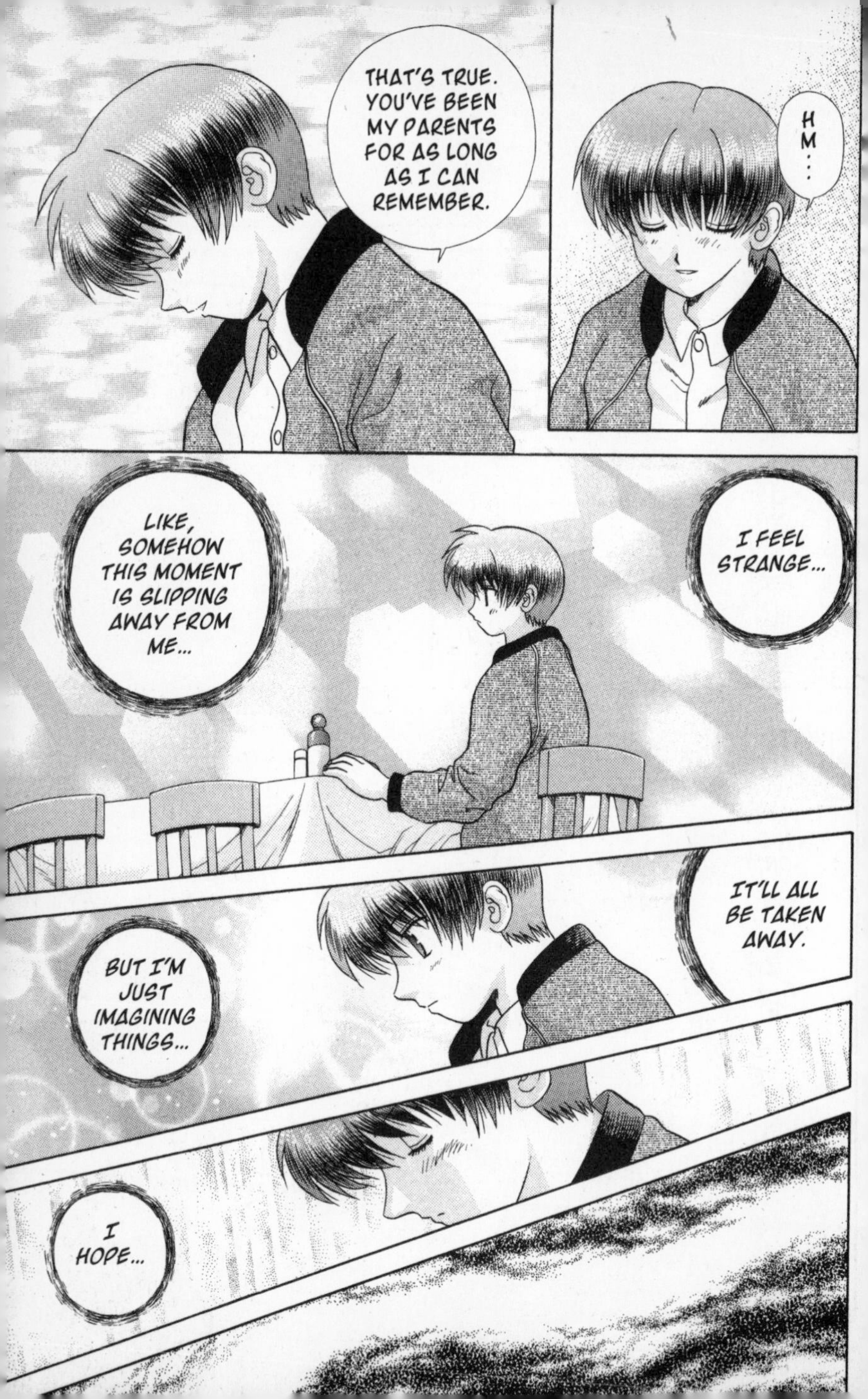
HM...
THAT'S TRUE. YOU'VE BEEN MY PARENTS FOR AS LONG AS I CAN REMEMBER.
I FEEL STRANGE...
LIKE, SOMEHOW THIS MOMENT IS SLIPPING AWAY FROM ME...
IT'LL ALL BE TAKEN AWAY.
BUT I'M JUST IMAGINING THINGS...
I HOPE...

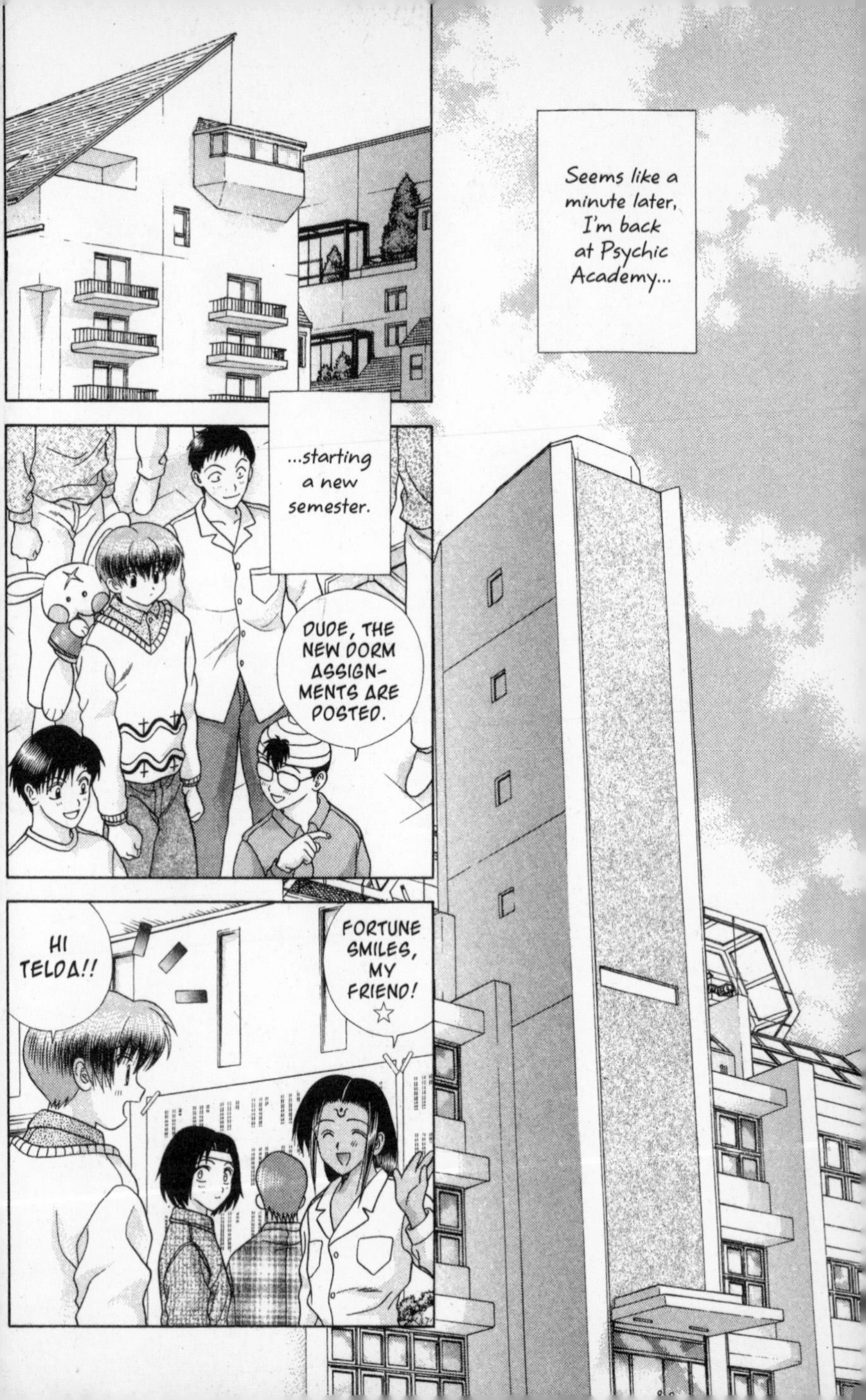
Seems like a minute later, I'm back at Psychic Academy...
...starting a new semester.
DUDE, THE NEW DORM ASSIGNMENTS ARE POSTED.
FORTUNE SMILES, MY FRIEND! ☆
HI TELDA!!

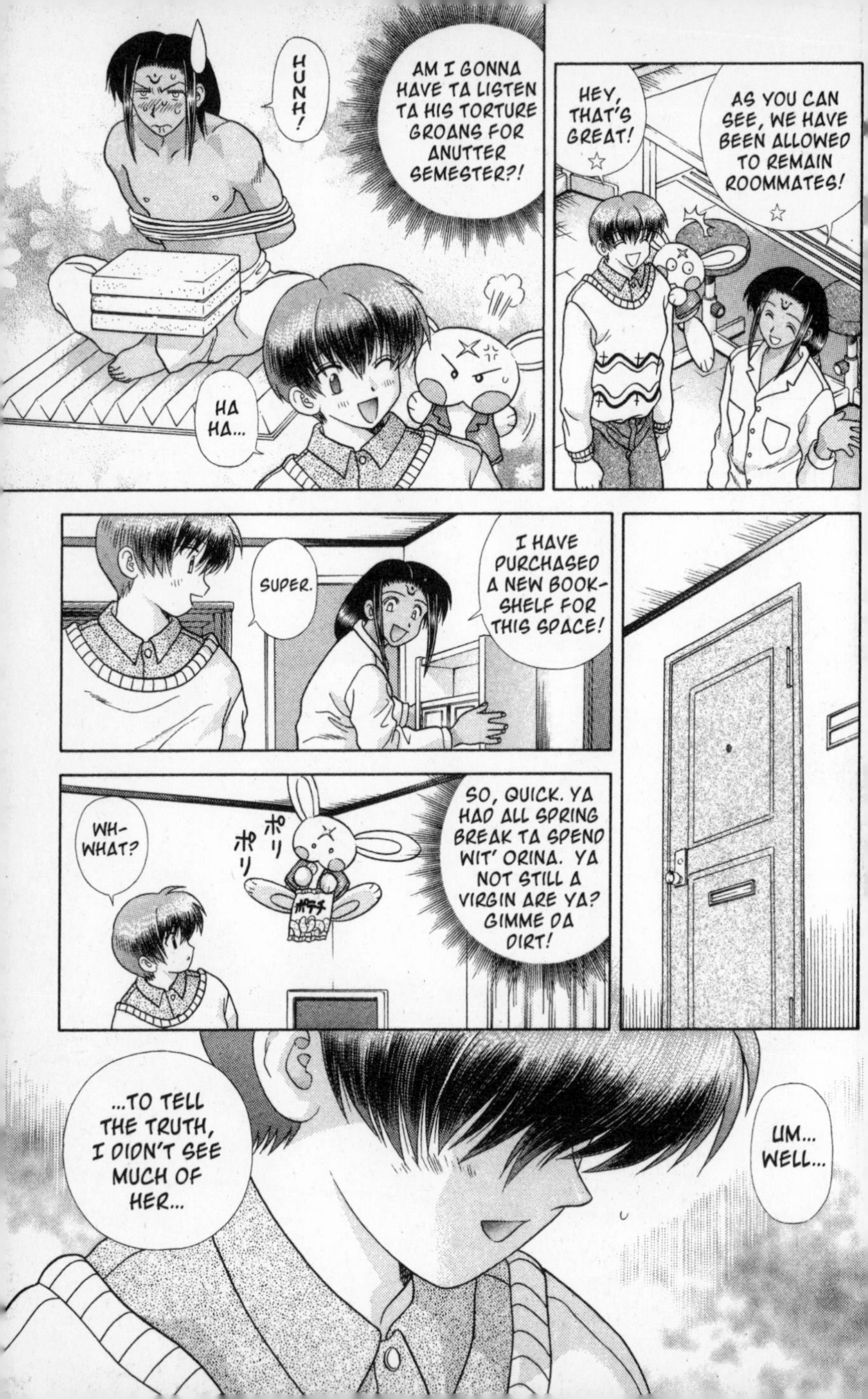
AS YOU CAN SEE, WE HAVE BEEN ALLOWED TO REMAIN ROOMMATES!
HEY, THAT'S GREAT!
AM I GONNA HAVE TA LISTEN TA HIS TORTURE GROANS FOR ANUTTER SEMESTER?!
HUNH!
HA HA...
I HAVE PURCHASED A NEW BOOK-SHELF FOR THIS SPACE!
SUPER.
SO, QUICK. YA HAD ALL SPRING BREAK TA SPEND WIT' ORINA. YA NOT STILL A VIRGIN ARE YA? GIMME DA DIRT!
ポリ
ポリ
ポテチ
WH-WHAT?
UM... WELL...
...TO TELL THE TRUTH, I DIDN'T SEE MUCH OF HER...

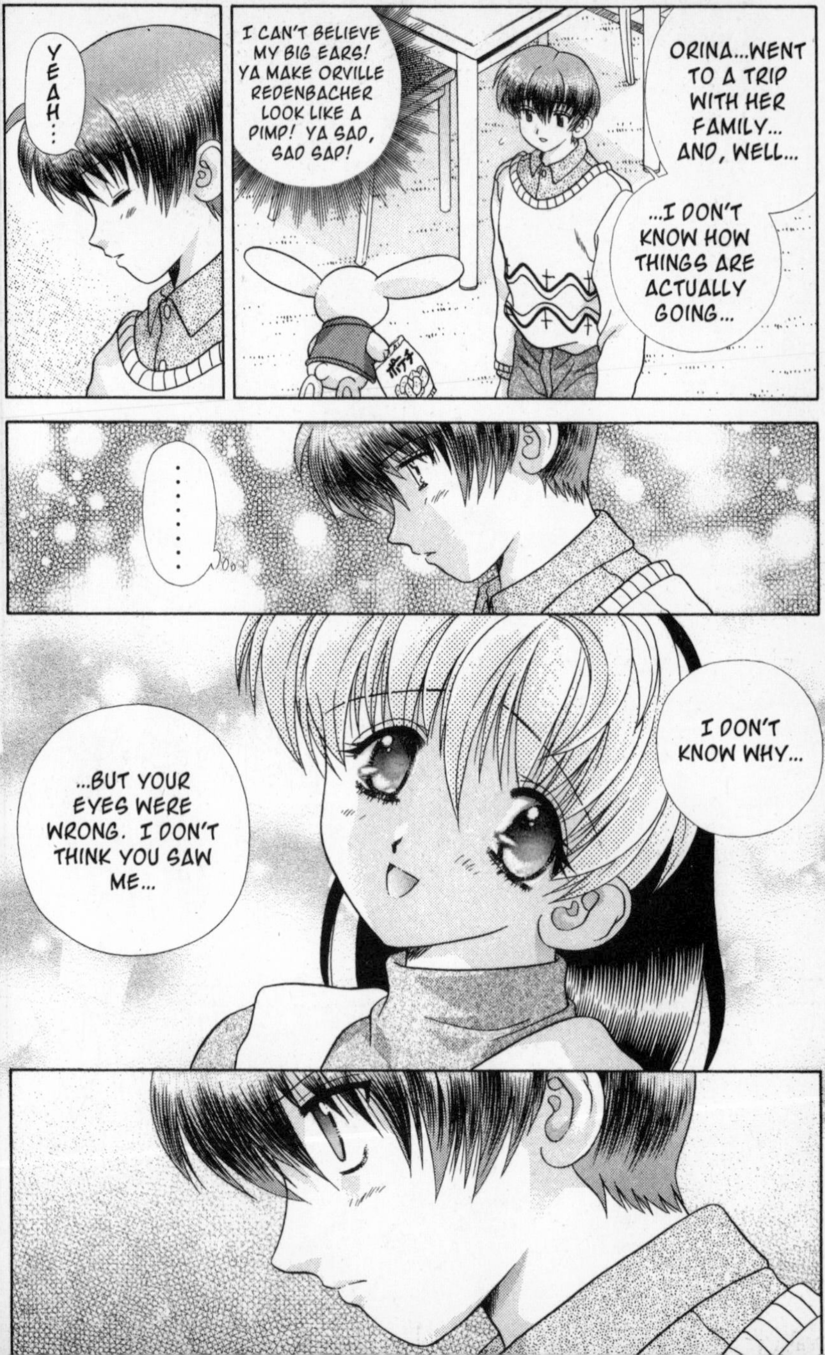
ORINA...WENT TO A TRIP WITH HER FAMILY... AND, WELL...
...I DON'T KNOW HOW THINGS ARE ACTUALLY GOING...
I CAN'T BELIEVE MY BIG EARS! YA MAKE ORVILLE REDENBACHER LOOK LIKE A PIMP! YA SAD, SAD SAP!
YEAH...
....
I DON'T KNOW WHY...
...BUT YOUR EYES WERE WRONG. I DON'T THINK YOU SAW ME...

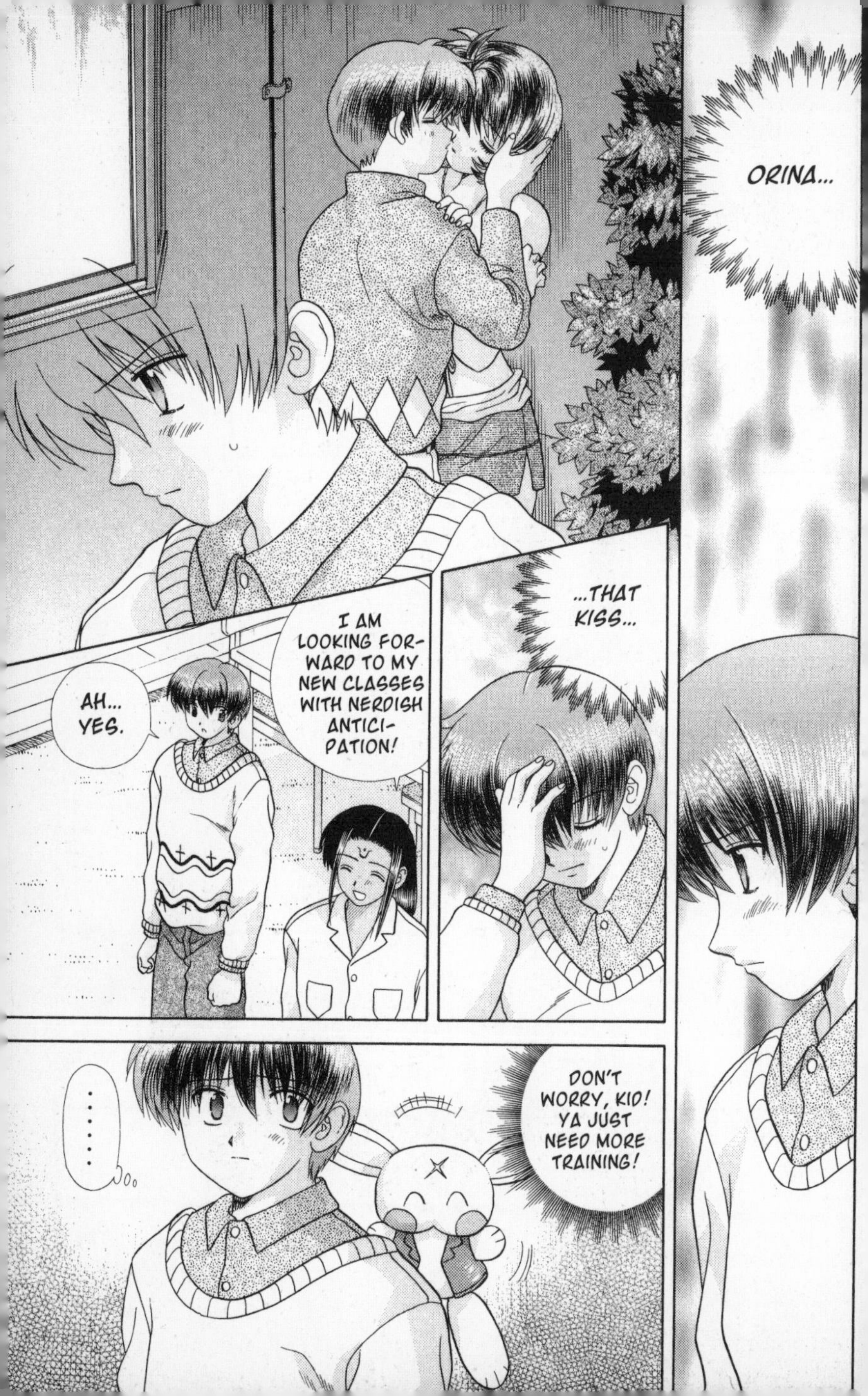
ORINA...
...THAT KISS...
I AM LOOKING FOR-WARD TO MY NEW CLASSES WITH NERDISH ANTICI-PATION!
AH... YES.
DON'T WORRY, KID! YA JUST NEED MORE TRAINING!
......

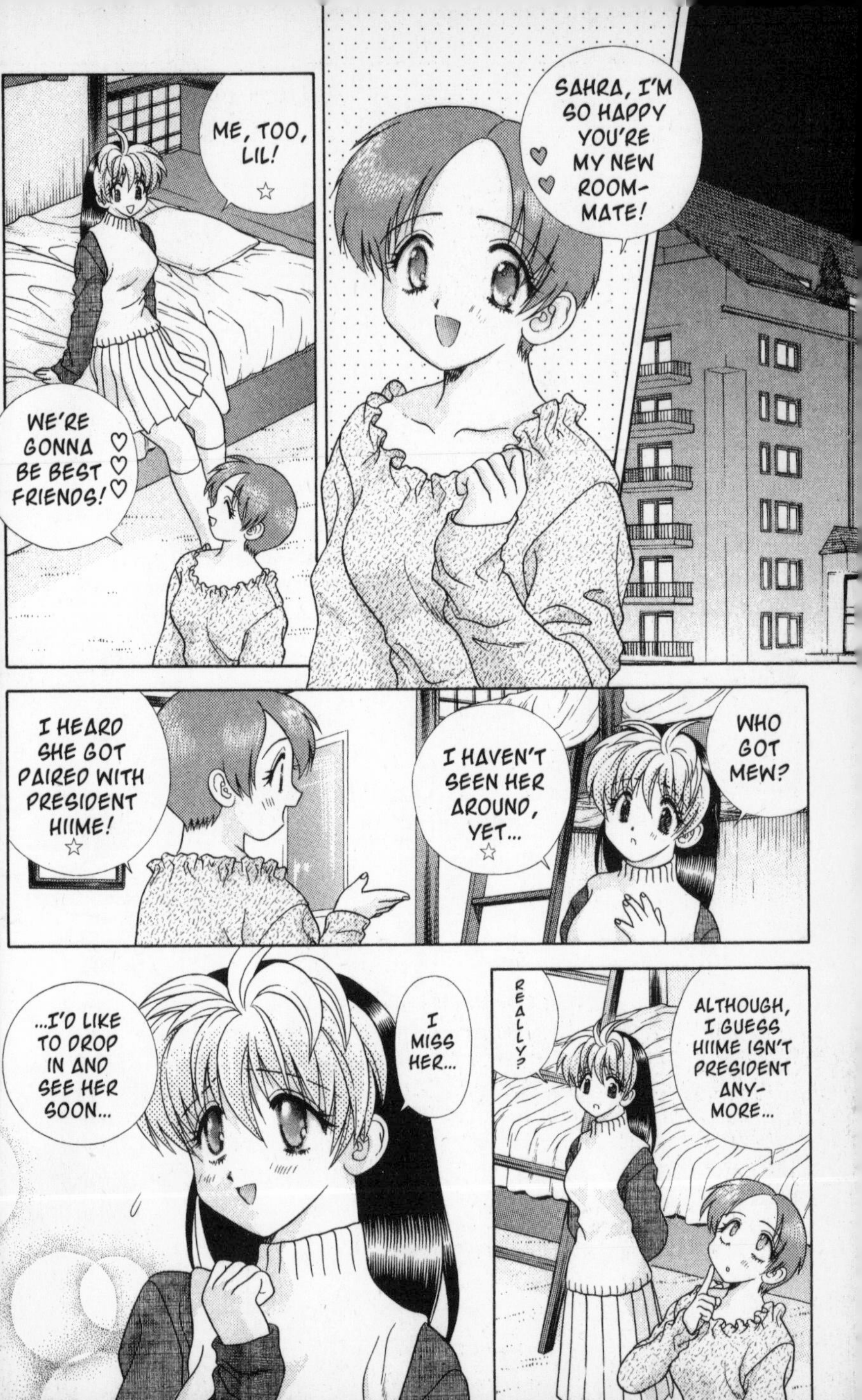
SAHRA, I'M SO HAPPY YOU'RE MY NEW ROOM-MATE! ♡ ♡
ME, TOO, LIL! ☆
WE'RE GONNA BE BEST FRIENDS! ♡♡♡
WHO GOT MEW?
I HAVEN'T SEEN HER AROUND, YET... ☆
I HEARD SHE GOT PAIRED WITH PRESIDENT HIIME! ☆
ALTHOUGH, I GUESS HIIME ISN'T PRESIDENT ANY-MORE...
REALLY?
I MISS HER...
...I'D LIKE TO DROP IN AND SEE HER SOON...

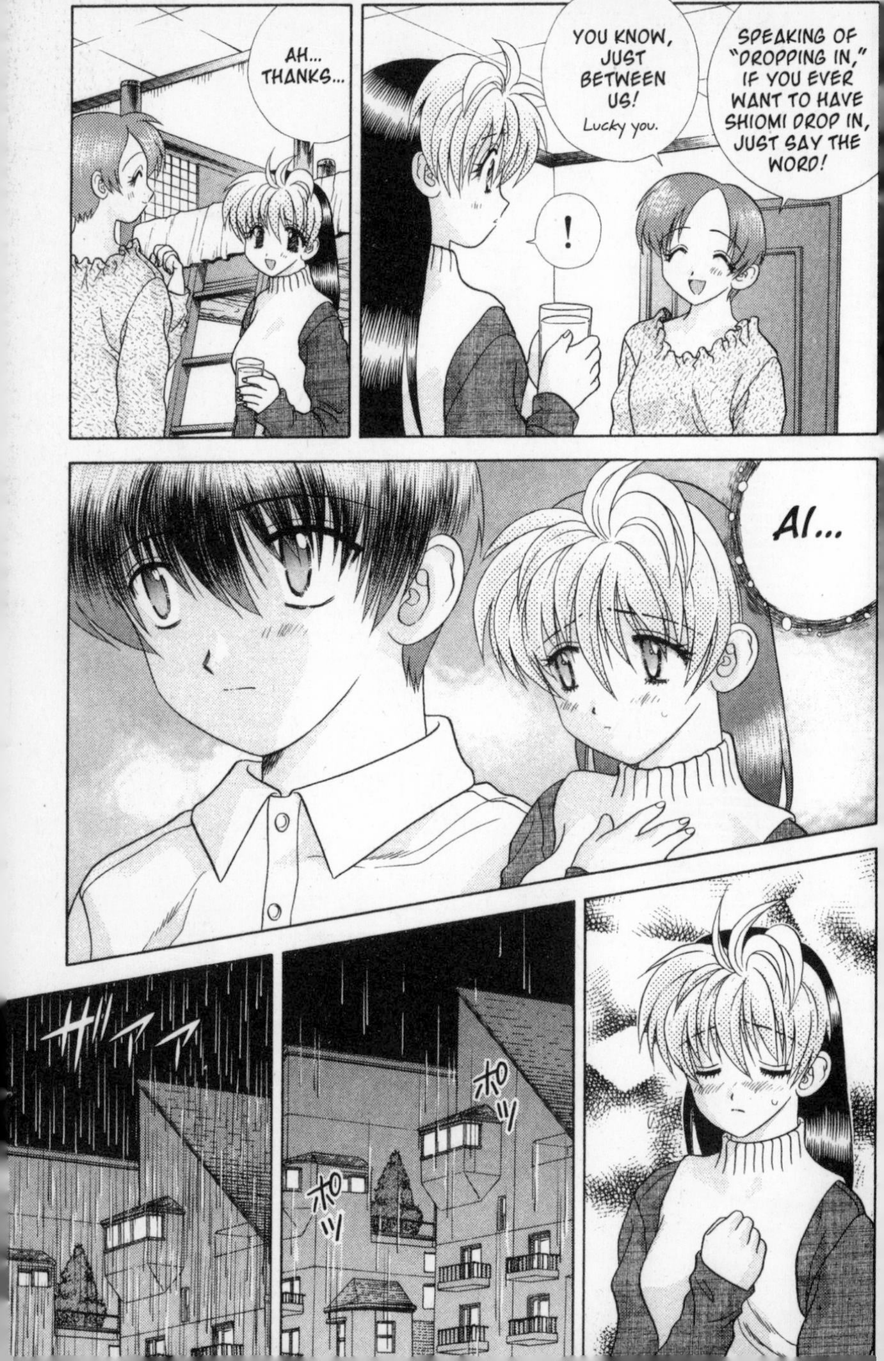
SPEAKING OF "DROPPING IN," IF YOU EVER WANT TO HAVE SHIOMI DROP IN, JUST SAY THE WORD!
YOU KNOW, JUST BETWEEN US!
Lucky you.
!
AH... THANKS...
AI...
ポッ
ポッ
ザァァ

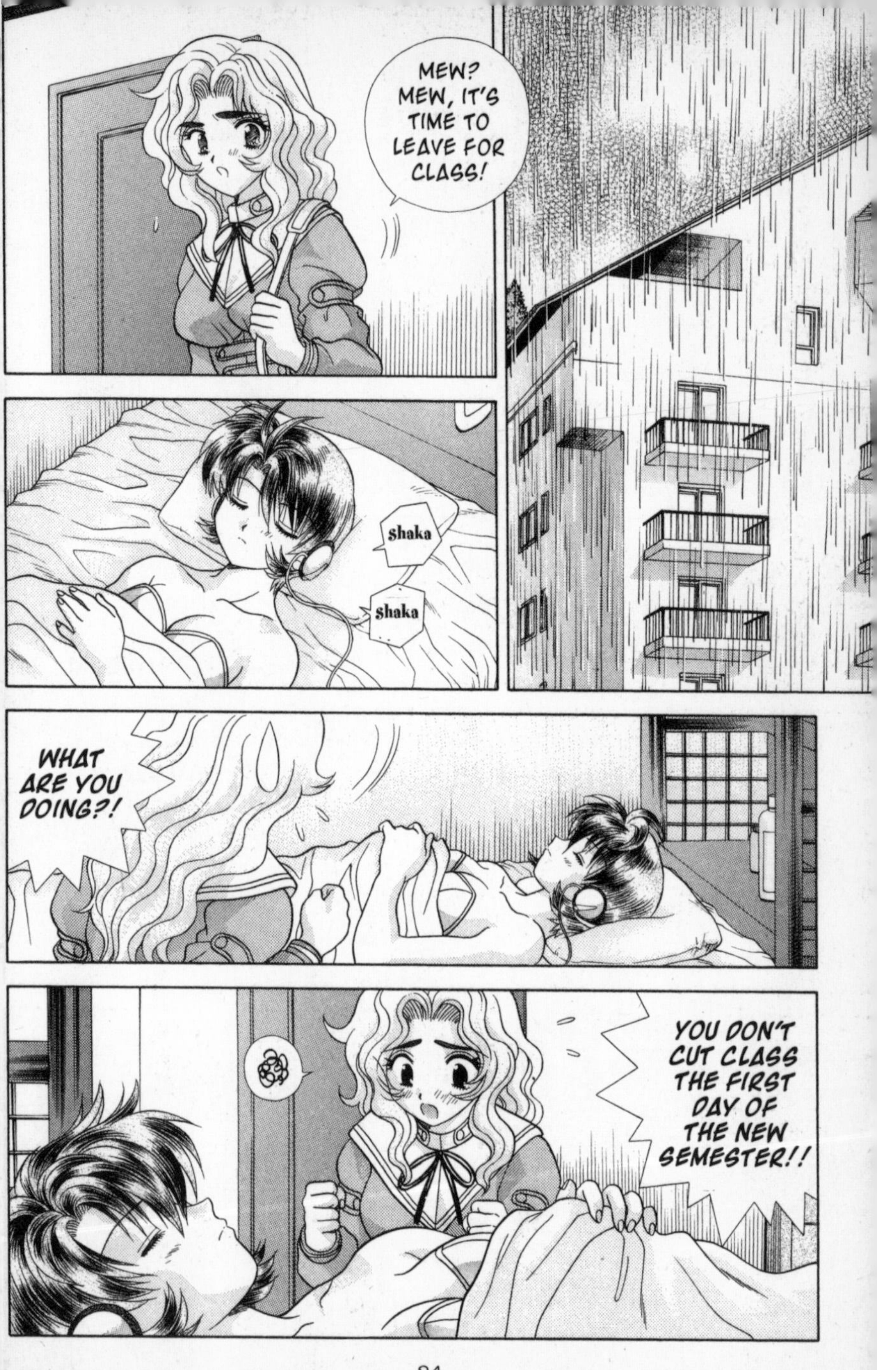
MEW? MEW, IT'S TIME TO LEAVE FOR CLASS!
Shaka
Shaka
WHAT ARE YOU DOING?!
YOU DON'T CUT CLASS THE FIRST DAY OF THE NEW SEMESTER!!

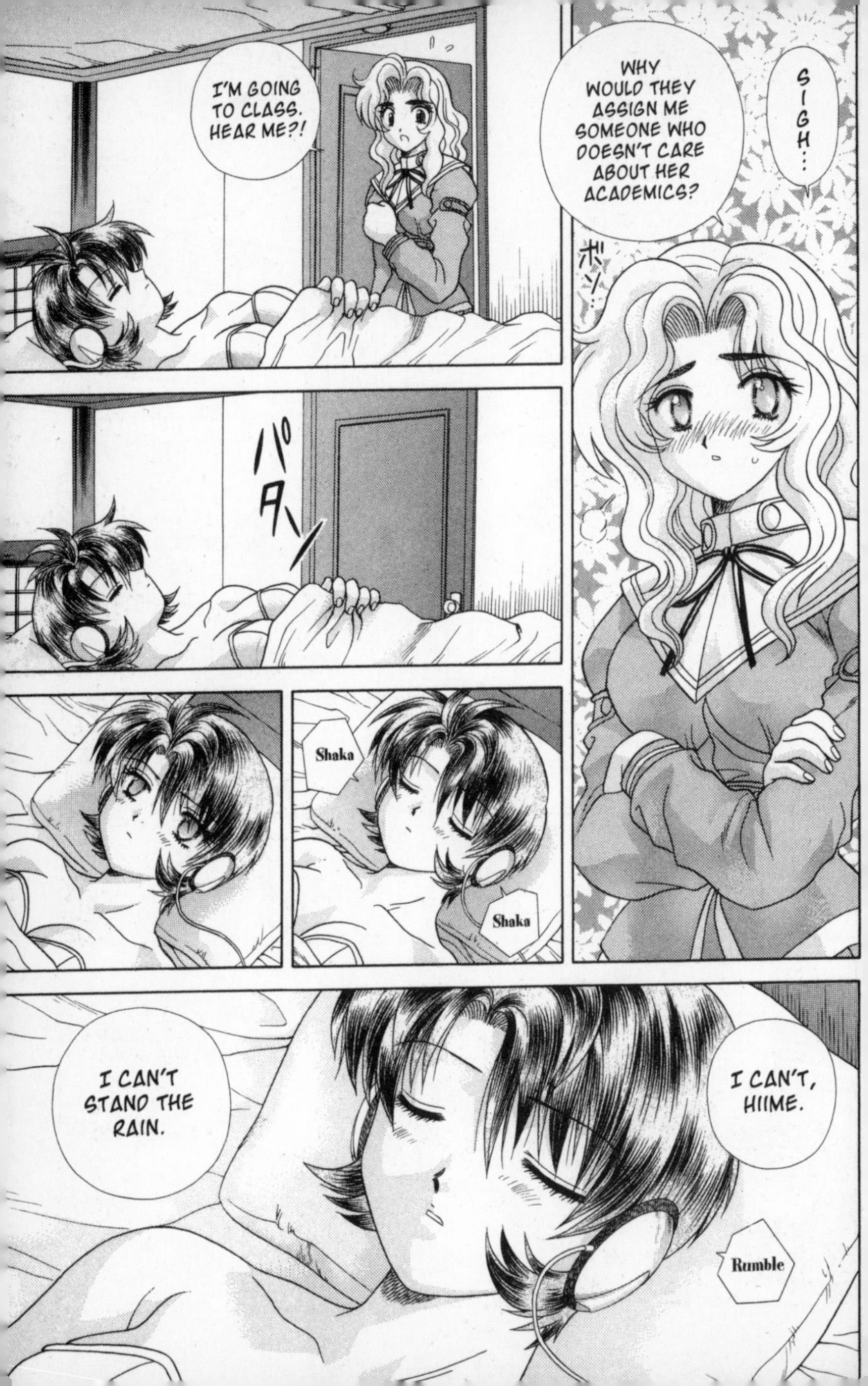

SIGH…
WHY WOULD THEY ASSIGN ME SOMEONE WHO DOESN'T CARE ABOUT HER ACADEMICS?
ボン…
I'M GOING TO CLASS. HEAR ME?!
パタン
Shaka
Shaka
I CAN'T, HIIME.
I CAN'T STAND THE RAIN.
Rumble

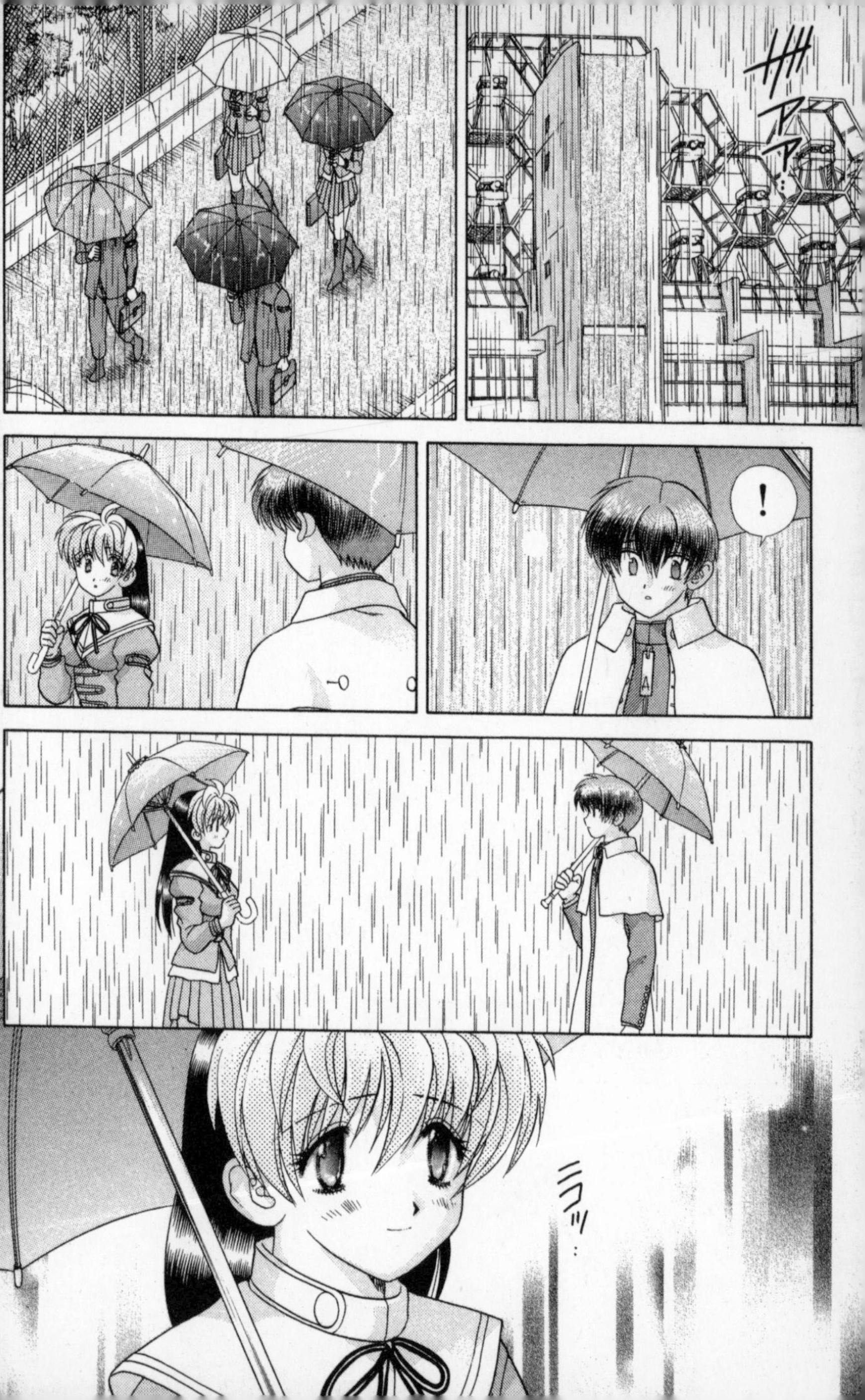
ザァァ…
!
ニコッ…

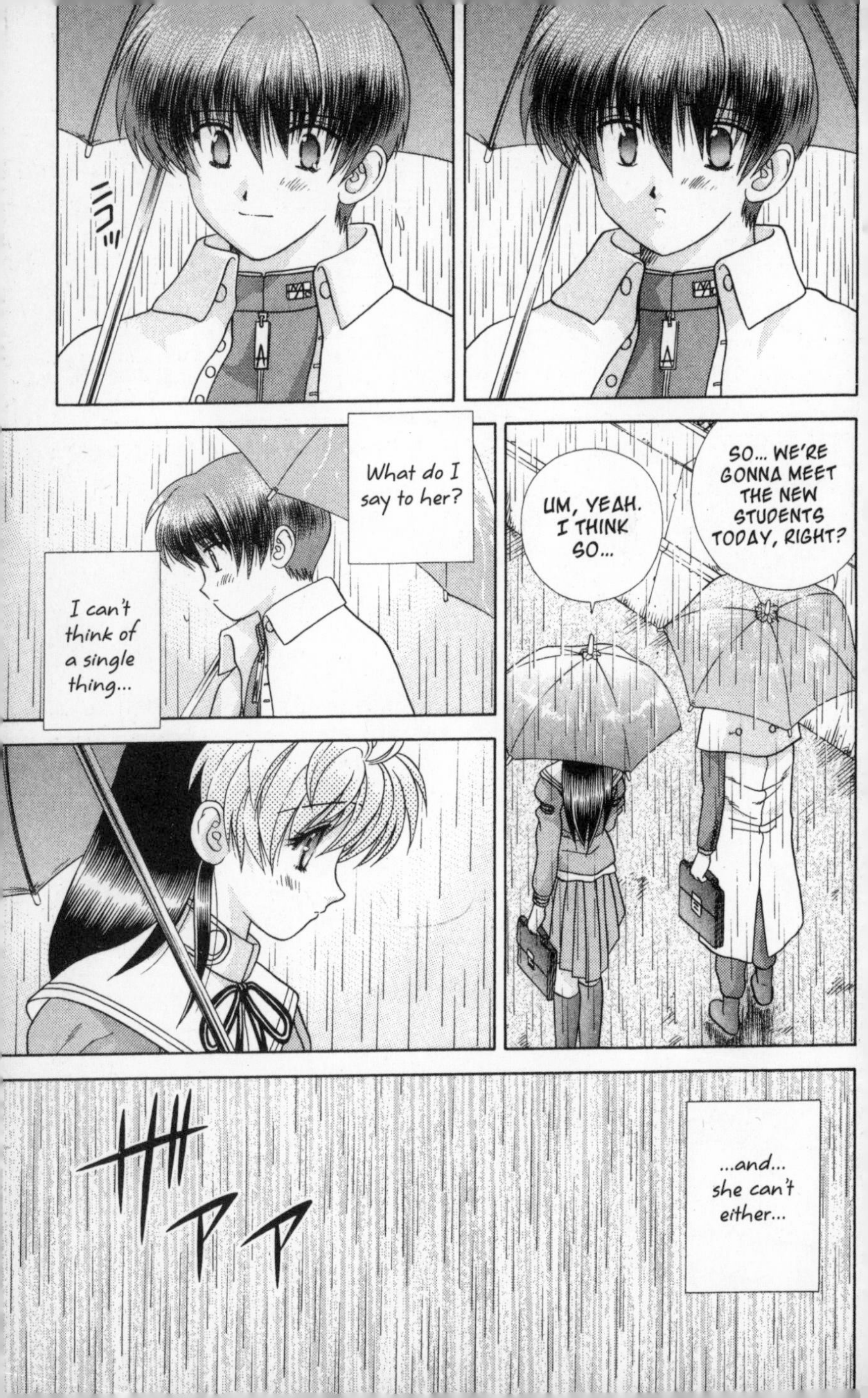
ニコッ
SO... WE'RE GONNA MEET THE NEW STUDENTS TODAY, RIGHT?
UM, YEAH. I THINK SO...
What do I say to her?
I can't think of a single thing...
...and... she can't either...
ザァァ

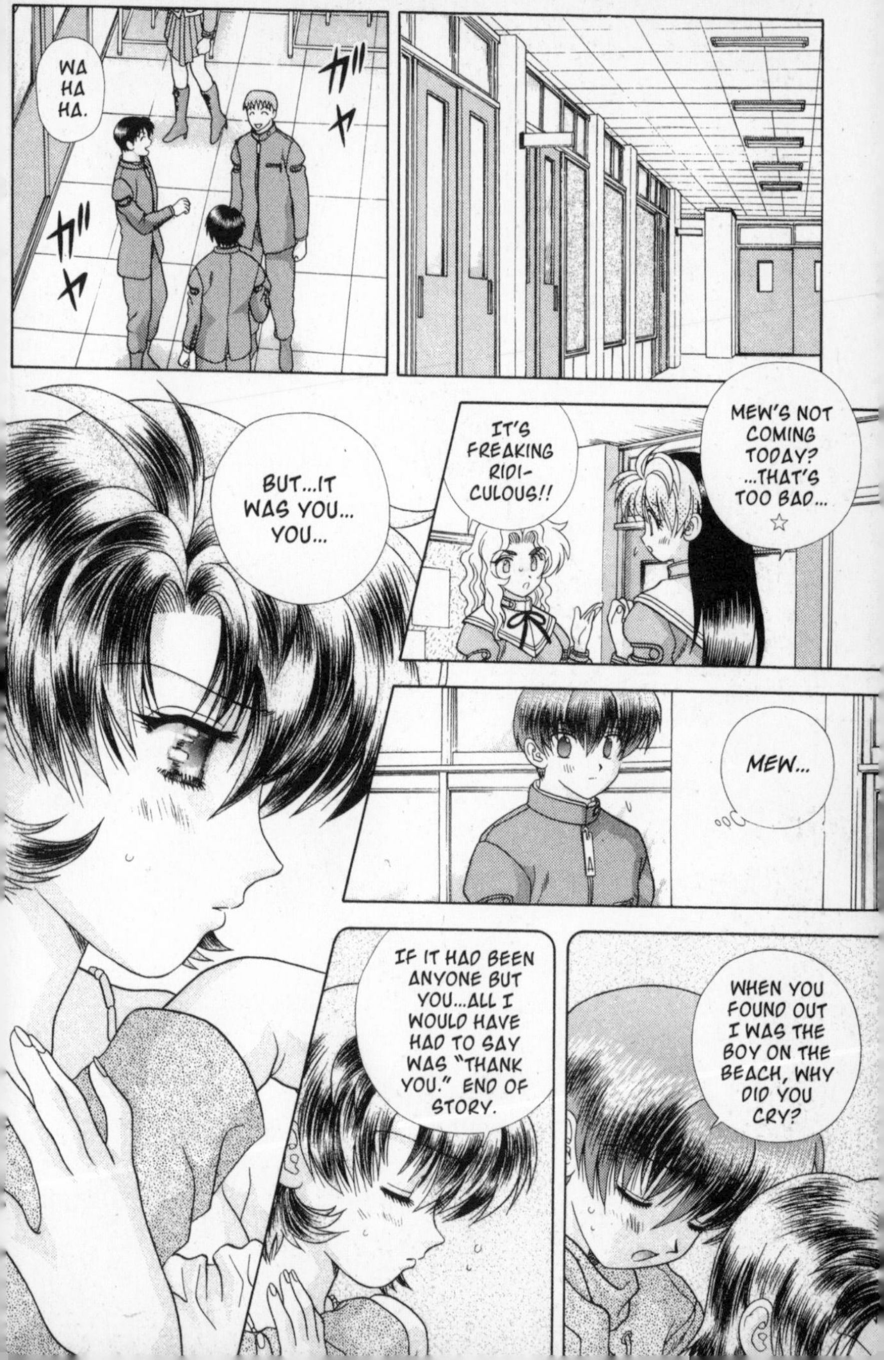
ガヤ
ガヤ
WA HA HA.
MEW'S NOT COMING TODAY? ...THAT'S TOO BAD... ☆
IT'S FREAKING RIDI-CULOUS!!
MEW...
WHEN YOU FOUND OUT I WAS THE BOY ON THE BEACH, WHY DID YOU CRY?
IF IT HAD BEEN ANYONE BUT YOU...ALL I WOULD HAVE HAD TO SAY WAS "THANK YOU." END OF STORY.
BUT...IT WAS YOU... YOU...

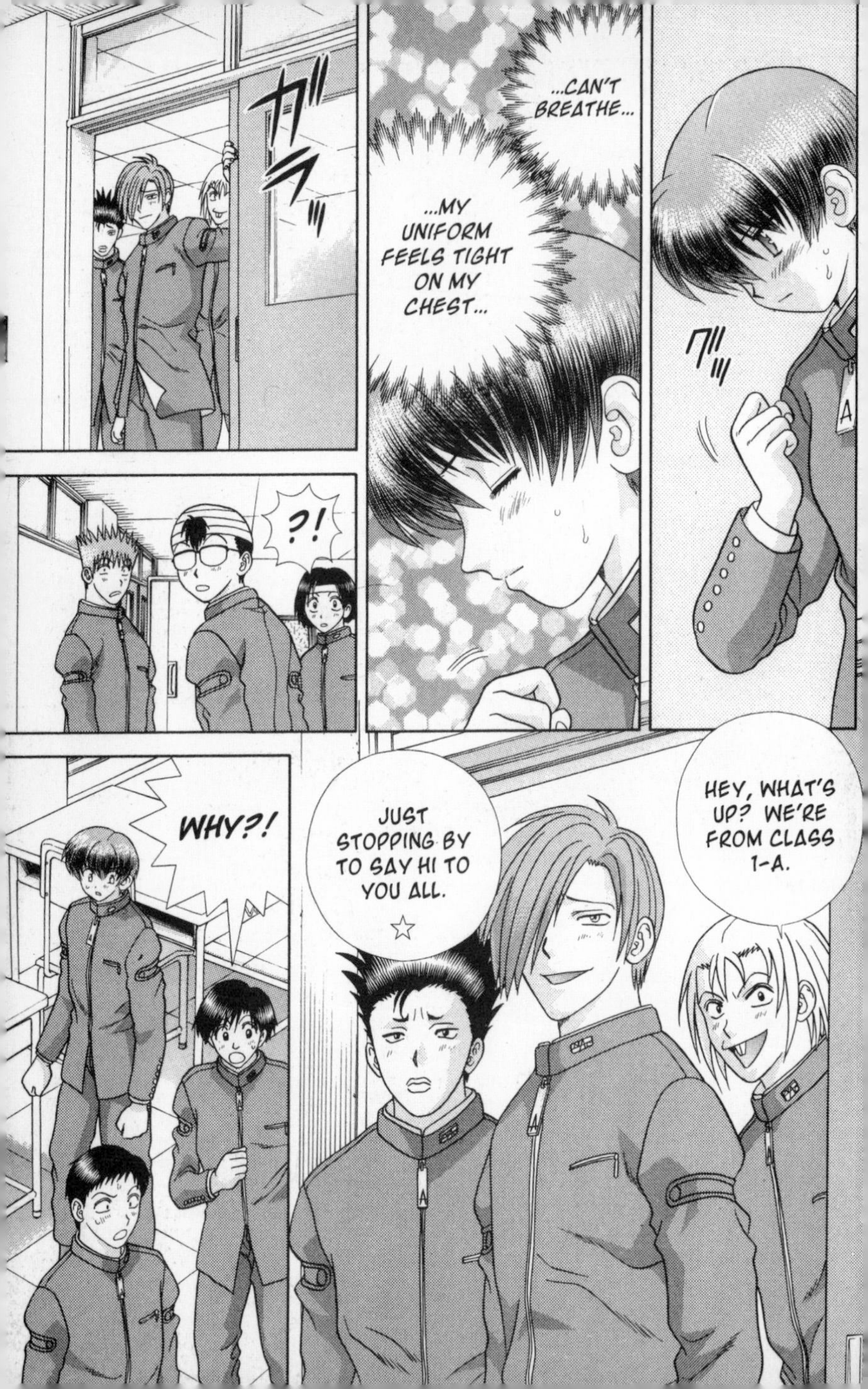
...CAN'T BREATHE...
...MY UNIFORM FEELS TIGHT ON MY CHEST...
?!
HEY, WHAT'S UP? WE'RE FROM CLASS 1-A.
JUST STOPPING BY TO SAY HI TO YOU ALL. ☆
WHY?!

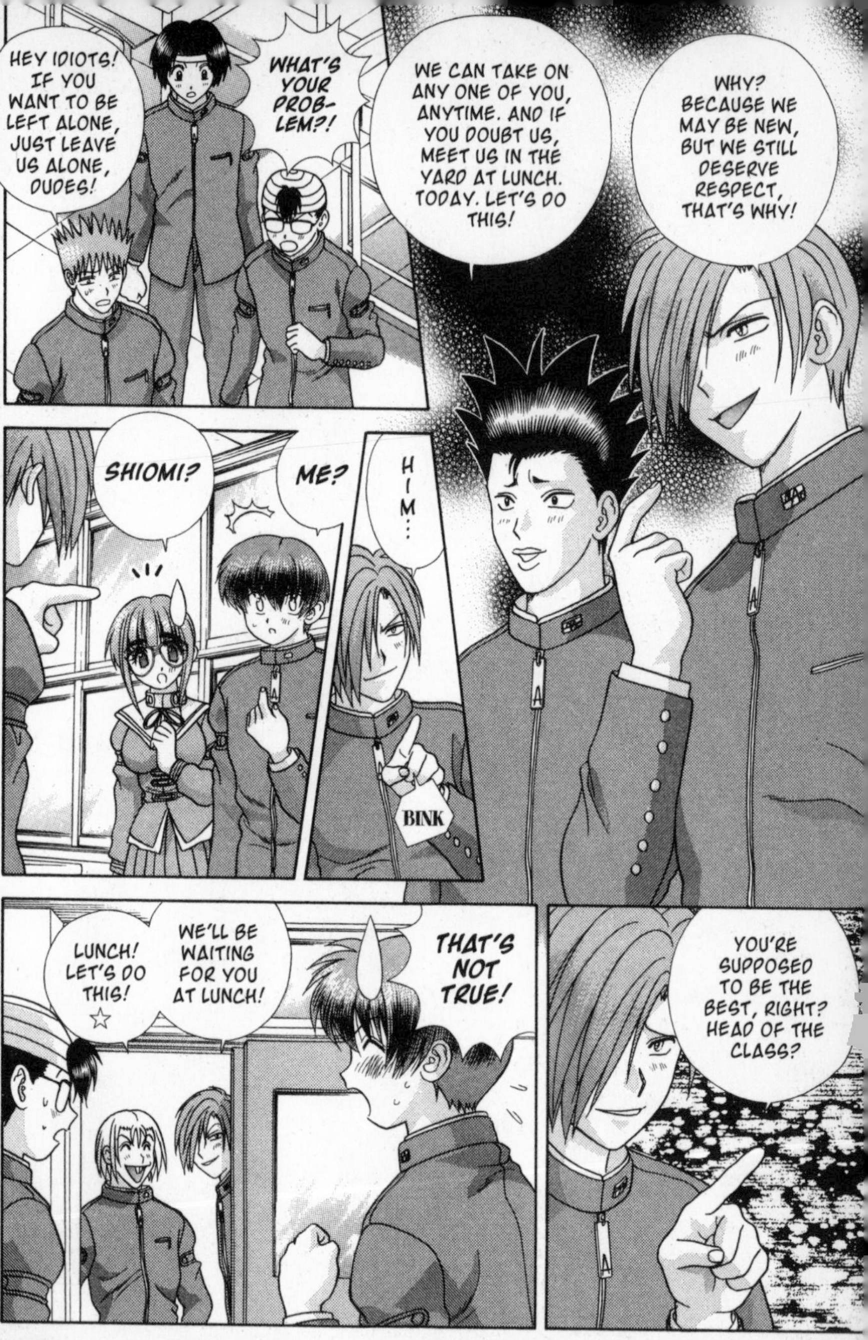
WHY? BECAUSE WE MAY BE NEW, BUT WE STILL DESERVE RESPECT, THAT'S WHY!
WE CAN TAKE ON ANY ONE OF YOU, ANYTIME. AND IF YOU DOUBT US, MEET US IN THE YARD AT LUNCH. TODAY. LET'S DO THIS!
WHAT'S YOUR PROB-LEM?!
HEY IDIOTS! IF YOU WANT TO BE LEFT ALONE, JUST LEAVE US ALONE, DUDES!
HIM...
BINK
ME?
SHIOMI?
YOU'RE SUPPOSED TO BE THE BEST, RIGHT? HEAD OF THE CLASS?
THAT'S NOT TRUE!
WE'LL BE WAITING FOR YOU AT LUNCH!
LUNCH! LET'S DO THIS! ☆

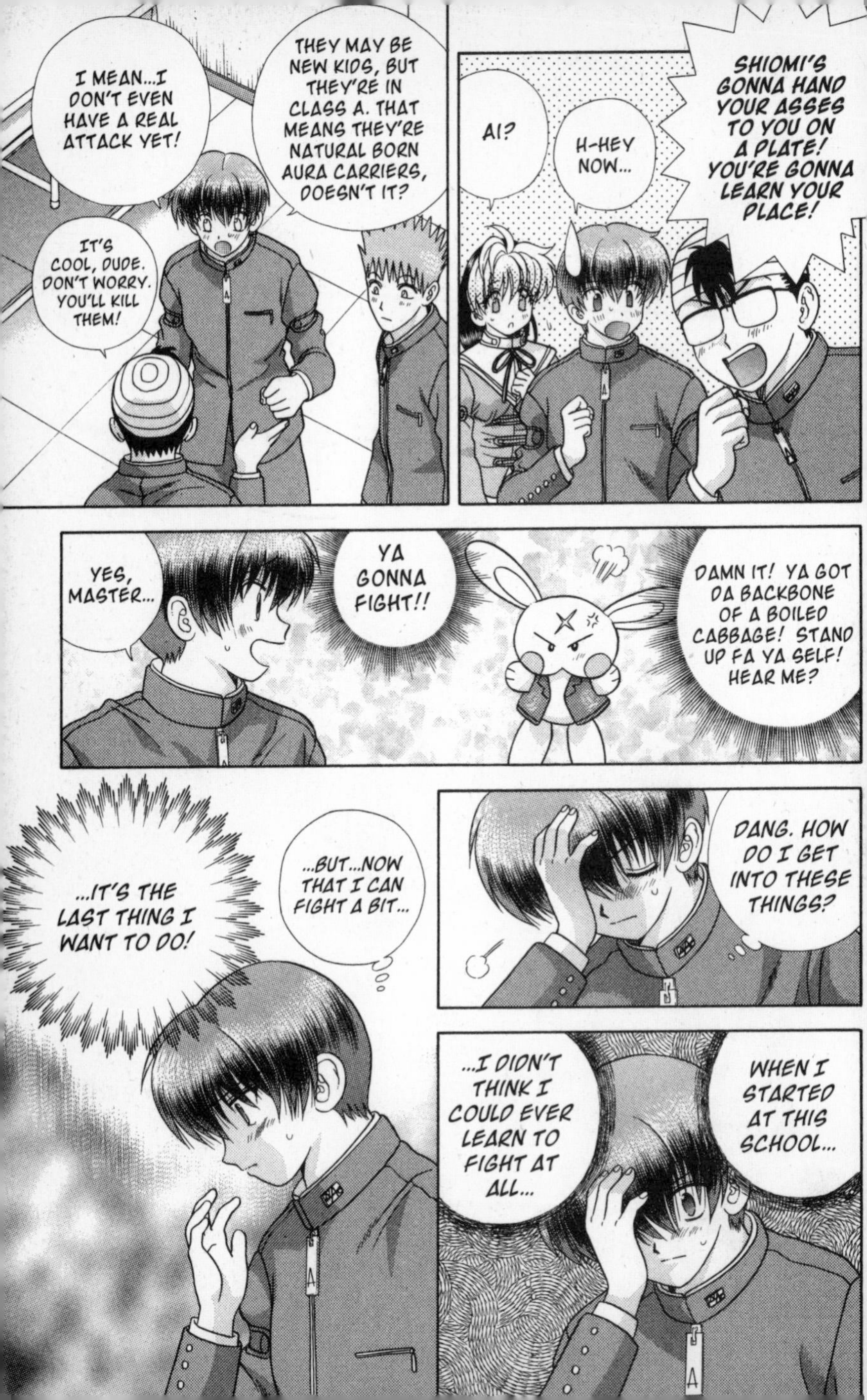
SHIOMI'S GONNA HAND YOUR ASSES TO YOU ON A PLATE! YOU'RE GONNA LEARN YOUR PLACE!
H-HEY NOW...
AI?
THEY MAY BE NEW KIDS, BUT THEY'RE IN CLASS A. THAT MEANS THEY'RE NATURAL BORN AURA CARRIERS, DOESN'T IT?
I MEAN...I DON'T EVEN HAVE A REAL ATTACK YET!
IT'S COOL, DUDE. DON'T WORRY. YOU'LL KILL THEM!
DAMN IT! YA GOT DA BACKBONE OF A BOILED CABBAGE! STAND UP FA YA SELF! HEAR ME?
YA GONNA FIGHT!!
YES, MASTER...
DANG. HOW DO I GET INTO THESE THINGS?
WHEN I STARTED AT THIS SCHOOL...
...I DIDN'T THINK I COULD EVER LEARN TO FIGHT AT ALL...
...BUT...NOW THAT I CAN FIGHT A BIT...
...IT'S THE LAST THING I WANT TO DO!

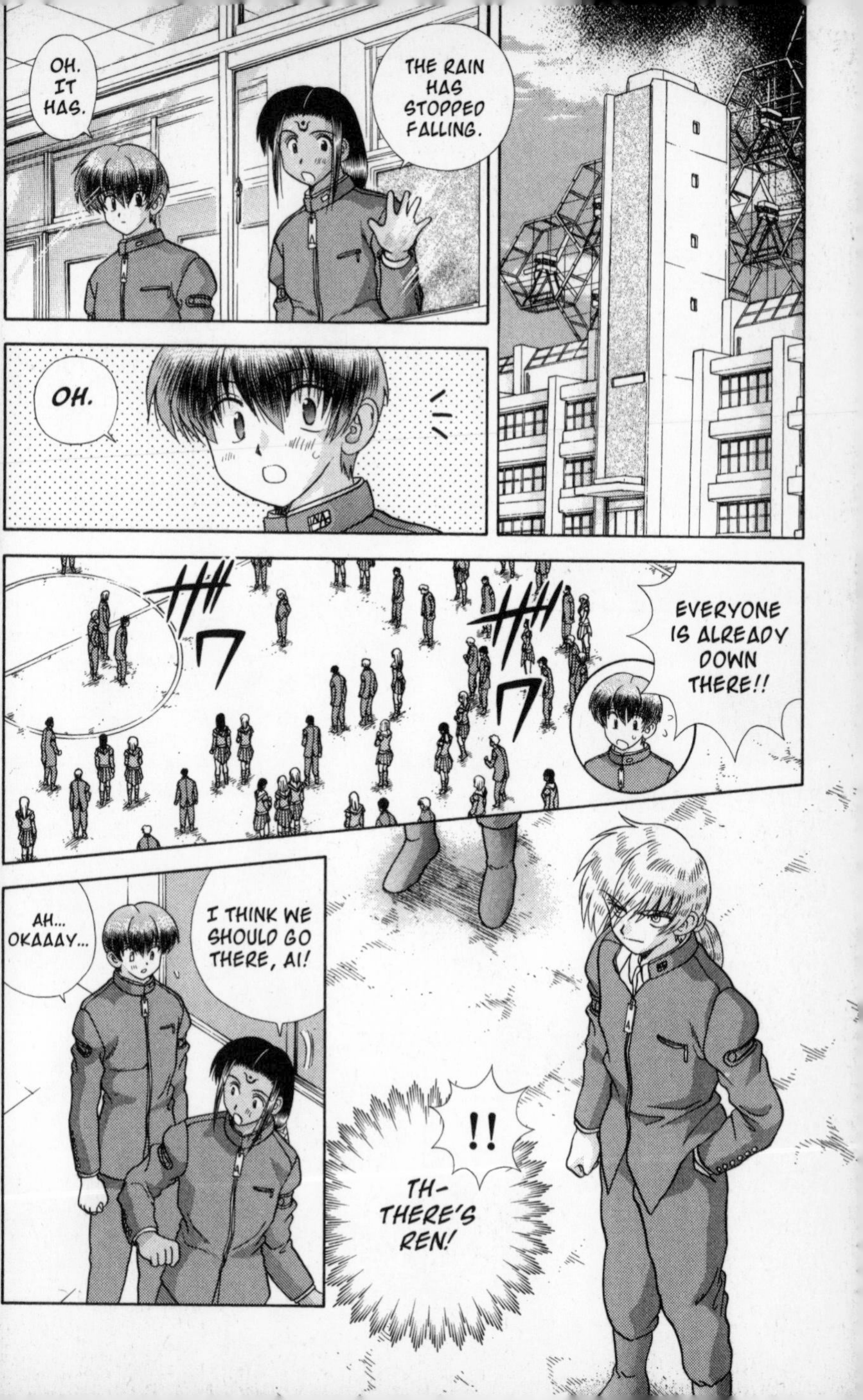
THE RAIN HAS STOPPED FALLING.
OH. IT HAS.
OH.
EVERYONE IS ALREADY DOWN THERE!!
ザワ
ザワ
!!
TH-THERE'S REN!
I THINK WE SHOULD GO THERE, AI!
AH... OKAAAY...

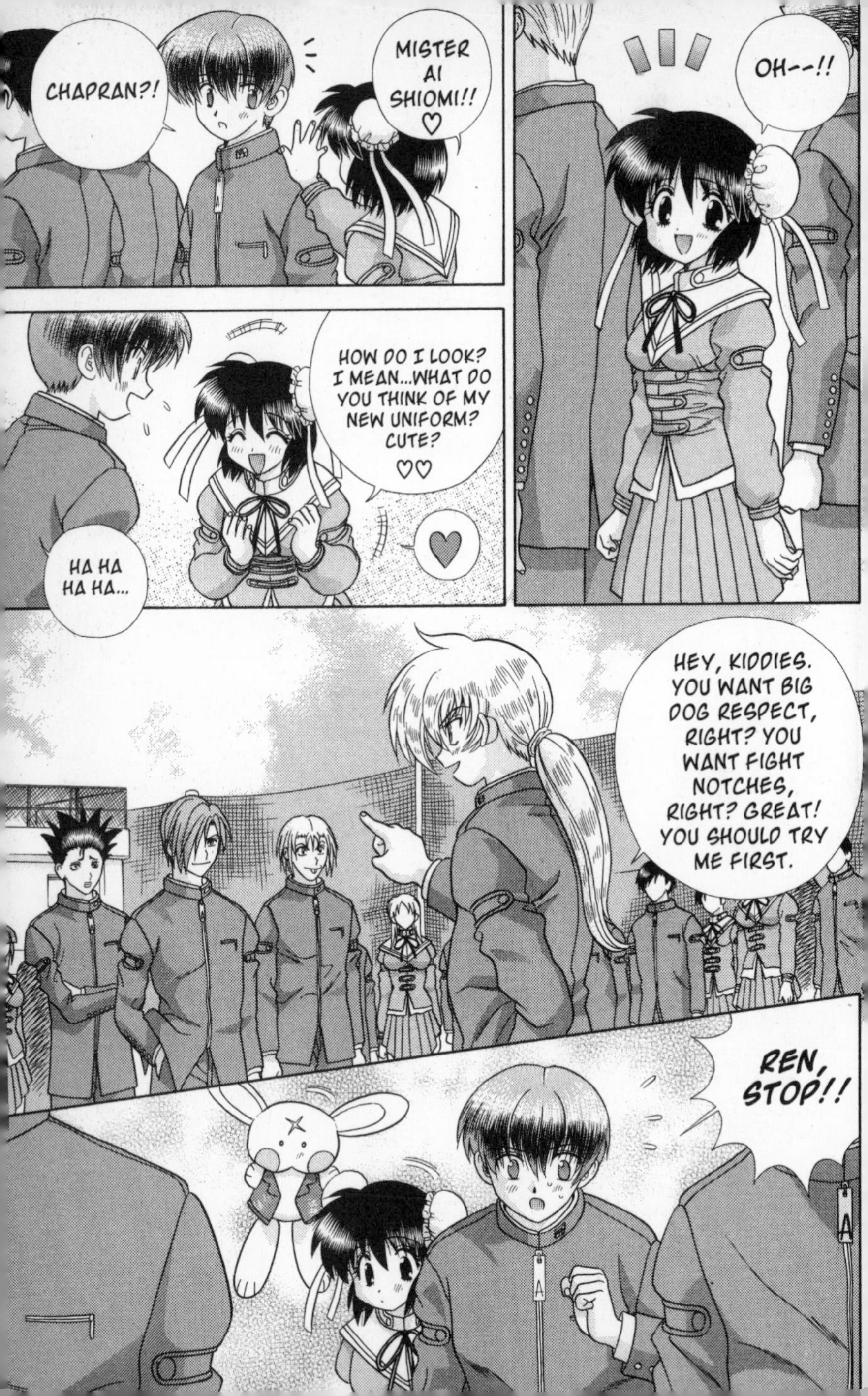
OH--!!
MISTER AI SHIOMI!! ♡
CHAPRAN?!
HOW DO I LOOK? I MEAN...WHAT DO YOU THINK OF MY NEW UNIFORM? CUTE? ♡♡
HA HA HA HA...
HEY, KIDDIES. YOU WANT BIG DOG RESPECT, RIGHT? YOU WANT FIGHT NOTCHES, RIGHT? GREAT! YOU SHOULD TRY ME FIRST.
REN, STOP!!

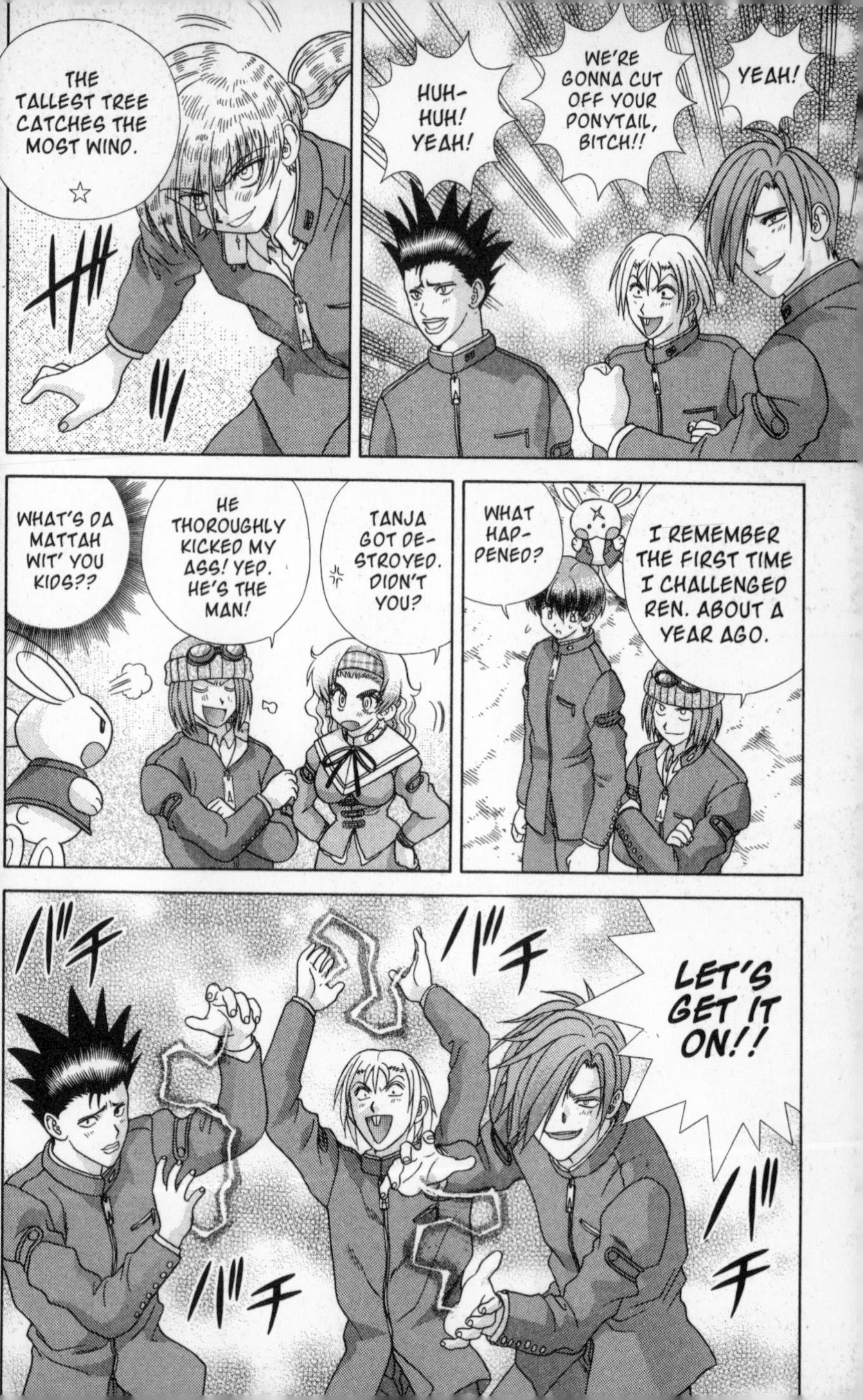
YEAH!
WE'RE GONNA CUT OFF YOUR PONYTAIL, BITCH!!
HUH-HUH! YEAH!
THE TALLEST TREE CATCHES THE MOST WIND. ☆
I REMEMBER THE FIRST TIME I CHALLENGED REN. ABOUT A YEAR AGO.
WHAT HAPPENED?
TANJA GOT DE-STROYED. DIDN'T YOU?
HE THOROUGHLY KICKED MY ASS! YEP. HE'S THE MAN!
WHAT'S DA MATTAH WIT' YOU KIDS??
バチ
LET'S GET IT ON!!
バチ
バチ
バチ

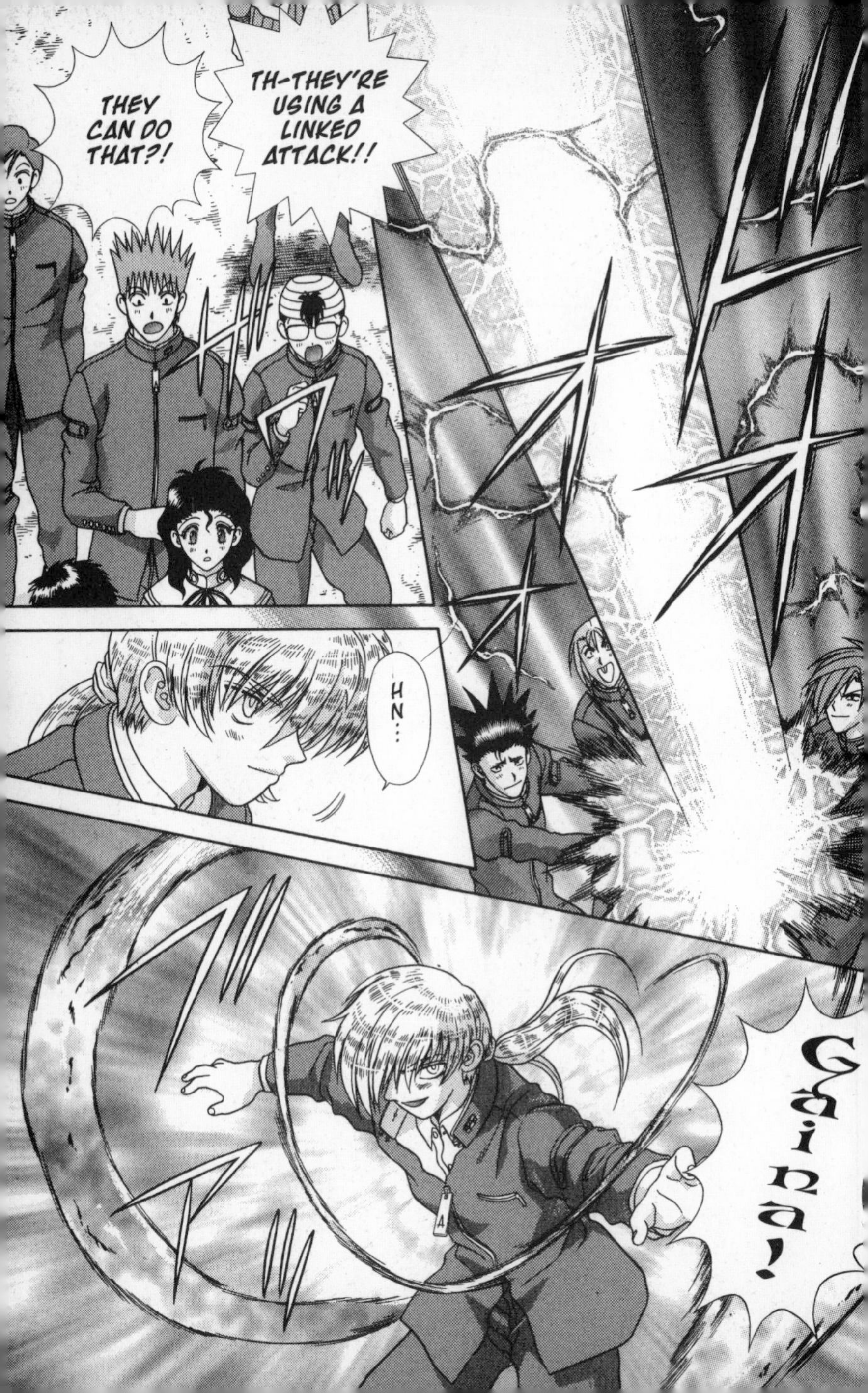
TH-THEY'RE USING A LINKED ATTACK!!
THEY CAN DO THAT?!
HN...
Gaina!

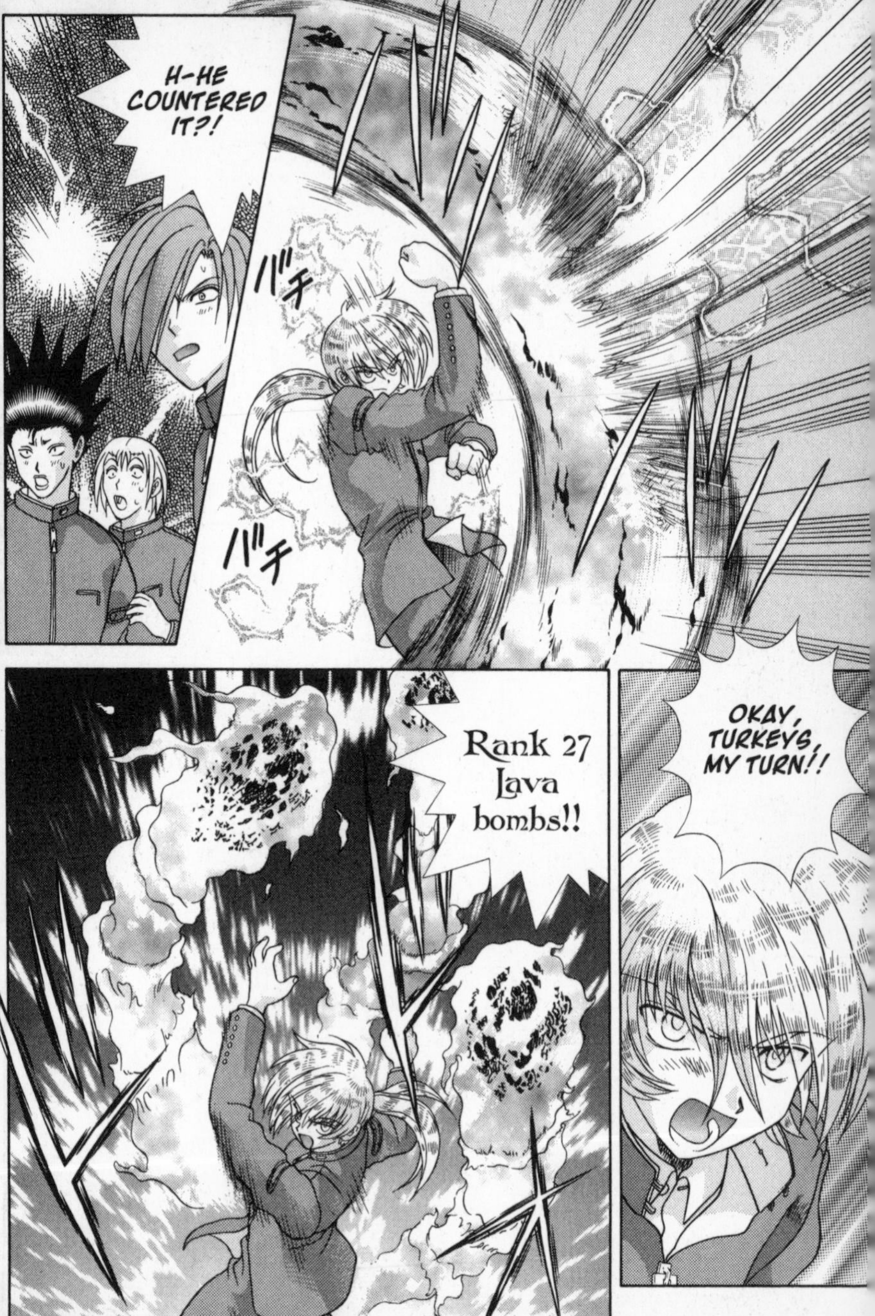
H-HE COUNTERED IT?!
バチ
バチ
OKAY, TURKEYS, MY TURN!!
Rank 27 Lava bombs!!

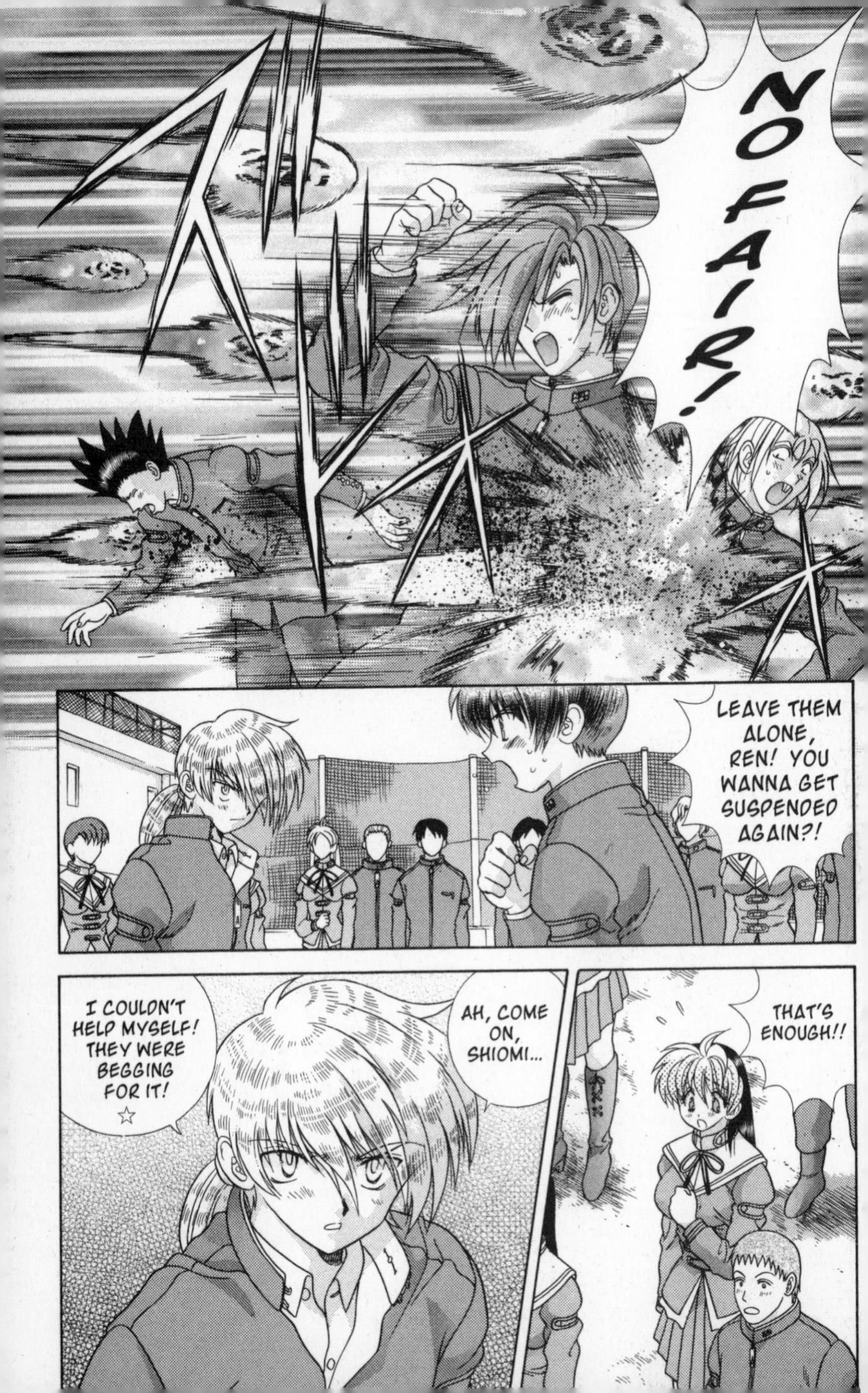
NO FAIR!
LEAVE THEM ALONE, REN! YOU WANNA GET SUSPENDED AGAIN?!
THAT'S ENOUGH!!
AH, COME ON, SHIOMI...
I COULDN'T HELP MYSELF! THEY WERE BEGGING FOR IT! ☆

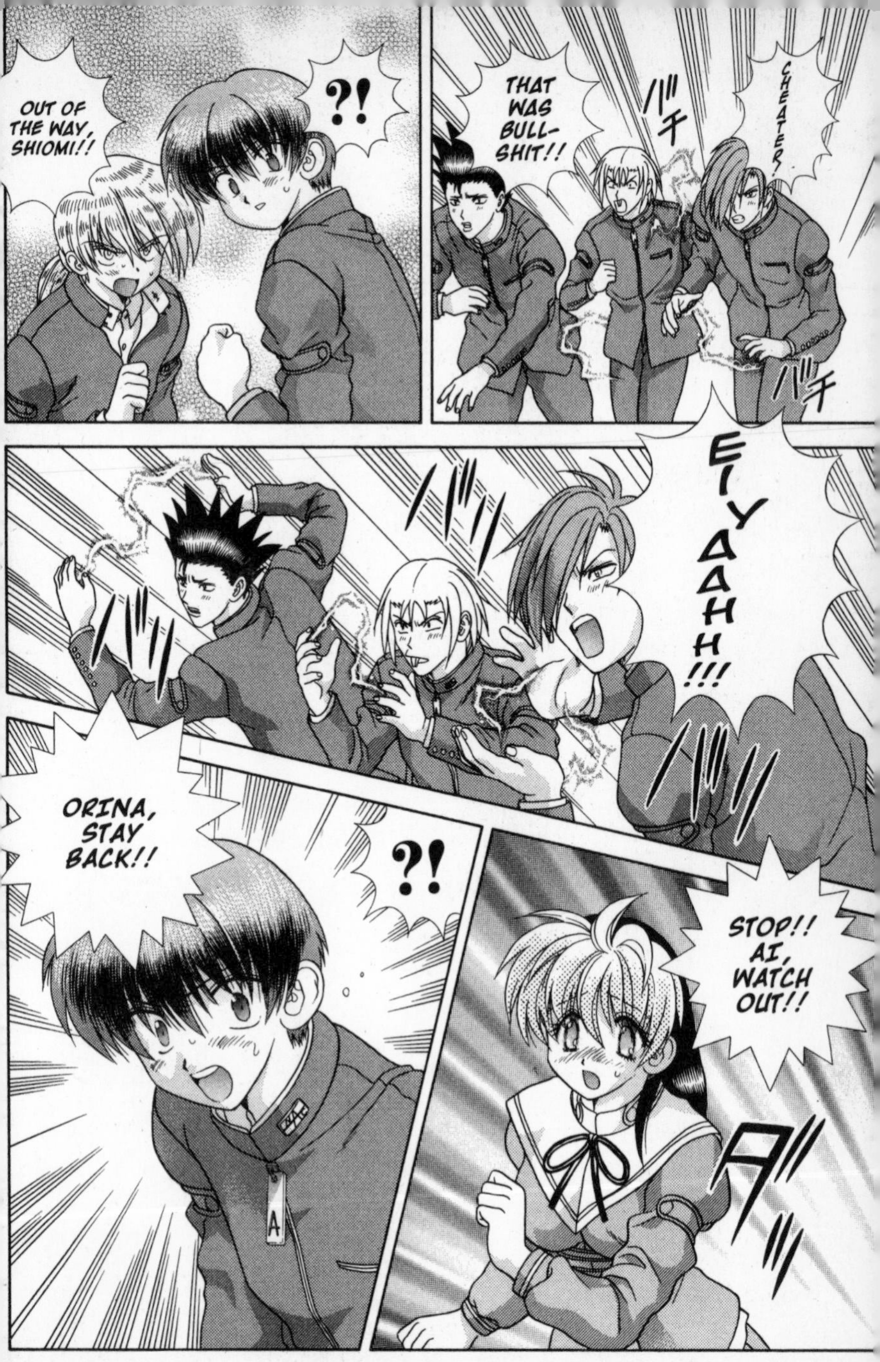
THAT WAS BULL-SHIT!!
バチ
CHEATER!
バチ
?!
OUT OF THE WAY, SHIOMI!!
EIYAAHH!!!
STOP!! AI, WATCH OUT!!
?!
ORINA, STAY BACK!!

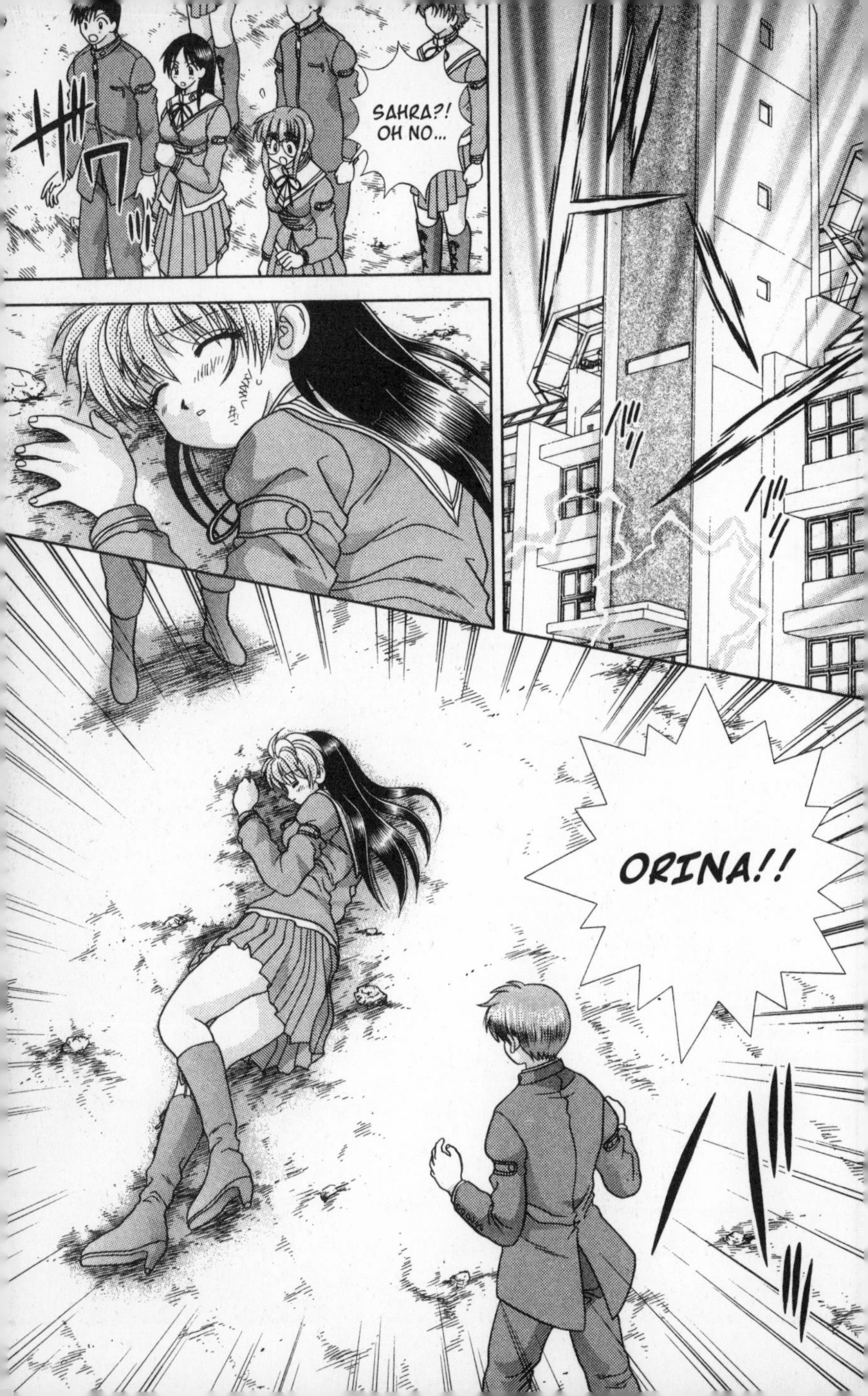
SAHRA?! OH NO...
ORINA!!

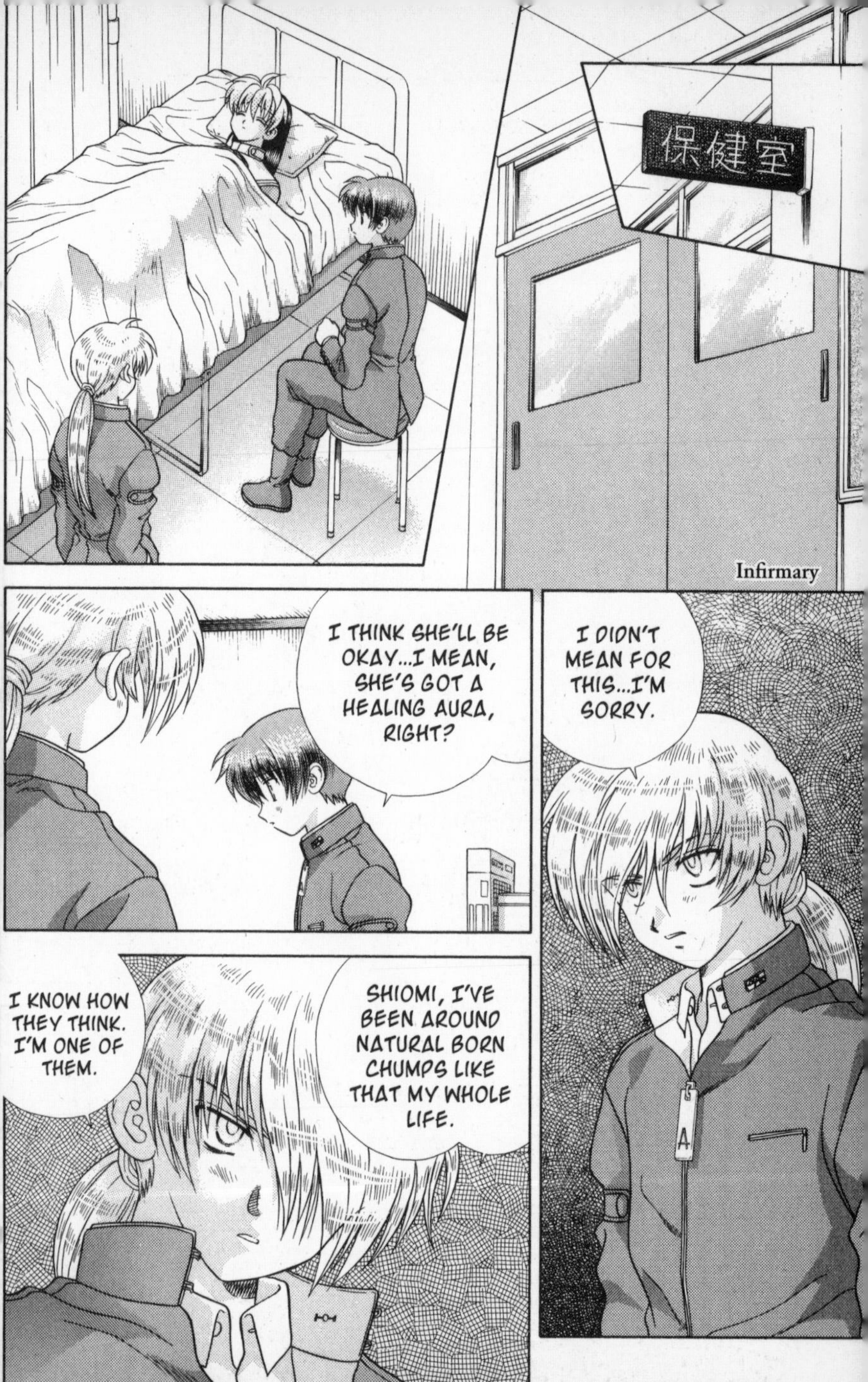
保健室
Infirmary
I DIDN'T MEAN FOR THIS...I'M SORRY.
I THINK SHE'LL BE OKAY...I MEAN, SHE'S GOT A HEALING AURA, RIGHT?
SHIOMI, I'VE BEEN AROUND NATURAL BORN CHUMPS LIKE THAT MY WHOLE LIFE.
I KNOW HOW THEY THINK. I'M ONE OF THEM.

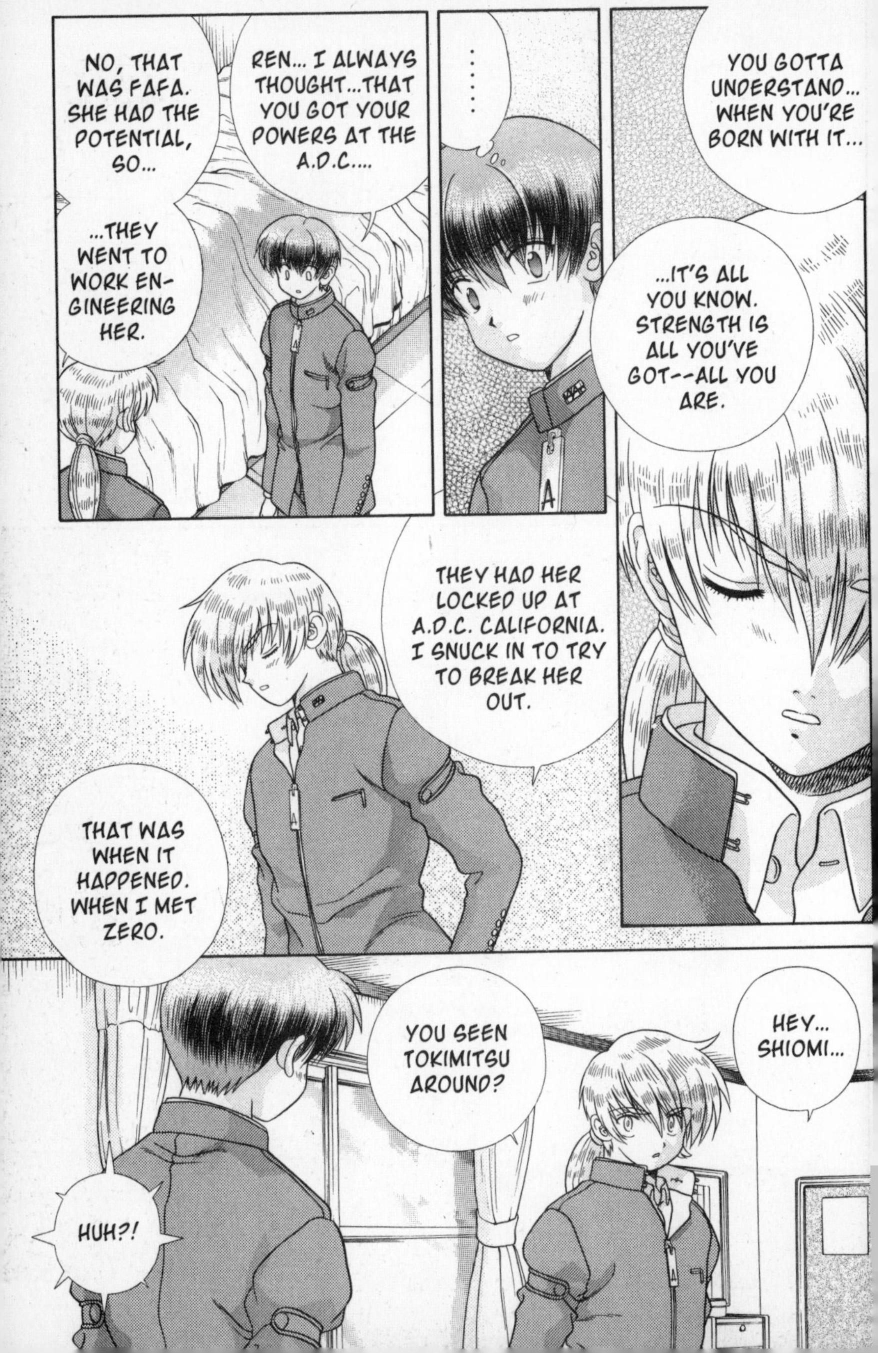
YOU GOTTA UNDERSTAND... WHEN YOU'RE BORN WITH IT...
...IT'S ALL YOU KNOW. STRENGTH IS ALL YOU'VE GOT--ALL YOU ARE.
......
REN... I ALWAYS THOUGHT...THAT YOU GOT YOUR POWERS AT THE A.D.C....
NO, THAT WAS FAFA. SHE HAD THE POTENTIAL, SO...
...THEY WENT TO WORK EN-GINEERING HER.
THEY HAD HER LOCKED UP AT A.D.C. CALIFORNIA. I SNUCK IN TO TRY TO BREAK HER OUT.
THAT WAS WHEN IT HAPPENED. WHEN I MET ZERO.
HEY... SHIOMI...
YOU SEEN TOKIMITSU AROUND?
HUH?!

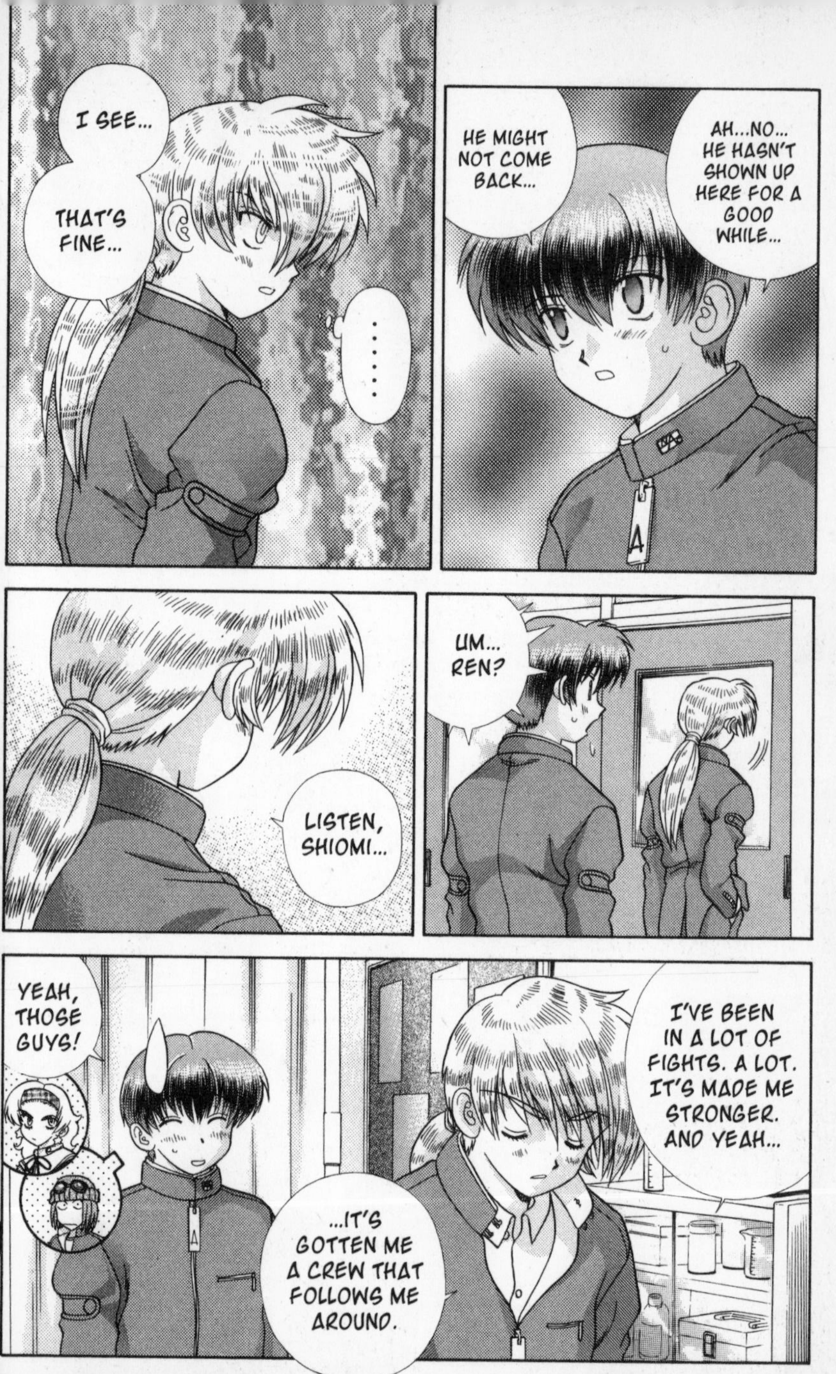
AH...NO... HE HASN'T SHOWN UP HERE FOR A GOOD WHILE...
HE MIGHT NOT COME BACK...
I SEE...
THAT'S FINE...
......
UM... REN?
LISTEN, SHIOMI...
I'VE BEEN IN A LOT OF FIGHTS. A LOT. IT'S MADE ME STRONGER. AND YEAH...
...IT'S GOTTEN ME A CREW THAT FOLLOWS ME AROUND.
YEAH, THOSE GUYS!

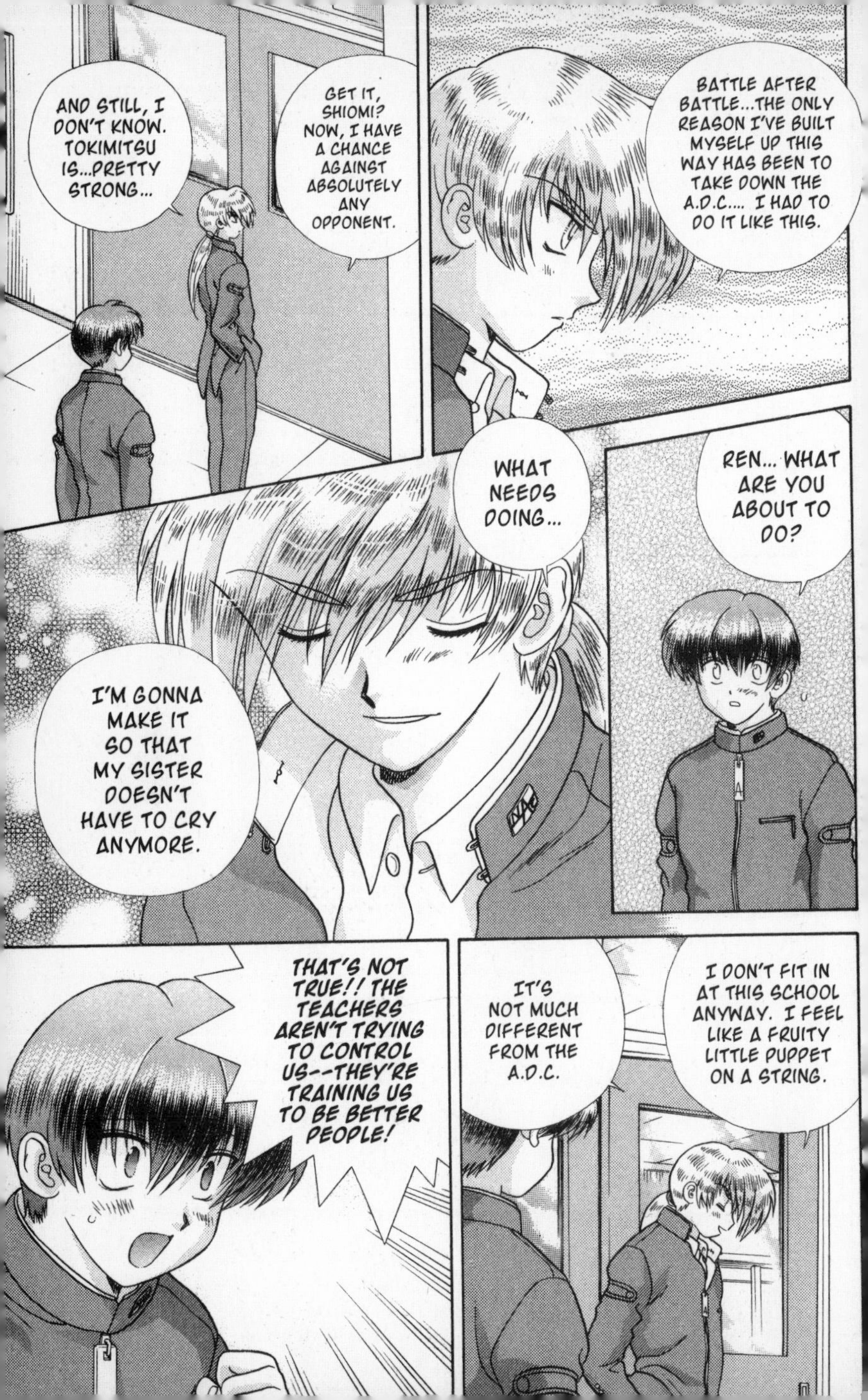
BATTLE AFTER BATTLE...THE ONLY REASON I'VE BUILT MYSELF UP THIS WAY HAS BEEN TO TAKE DOWN THE A.D.C.... I HAD TO DO IT LIKE THIS.
GET IT, SHIOMI? NOW, I HAVE A CHANCE AGAINST ABSOLUTELY ANY OPPONENT.
AND STILL, I DON'T KNOW. TOKIMITSU IS...PRETTY STRONG...
REN... WHAT ARE YOU ABOUT TO DO?
WHAT NEEDS DOING...
I'M GONNA MAKE IT SO THAT MY SISTER DOESN'T HAVE TO CRY ANYMORE.
I DON'T FIT IN AT THIS SCHOOL ANYWAY. I FEEL LIKE A FRUITY LITTLE PUPPET ON A STRING.
IT'S NOT MUCH DIFFERENT FROM THE A.D.C.
THAT'S NOT TRUE!! THE TEACHERS AREN'T TRYING TO CONTROL US--THEY'RE TRAINING US TO BE BETTER PEOPLE!

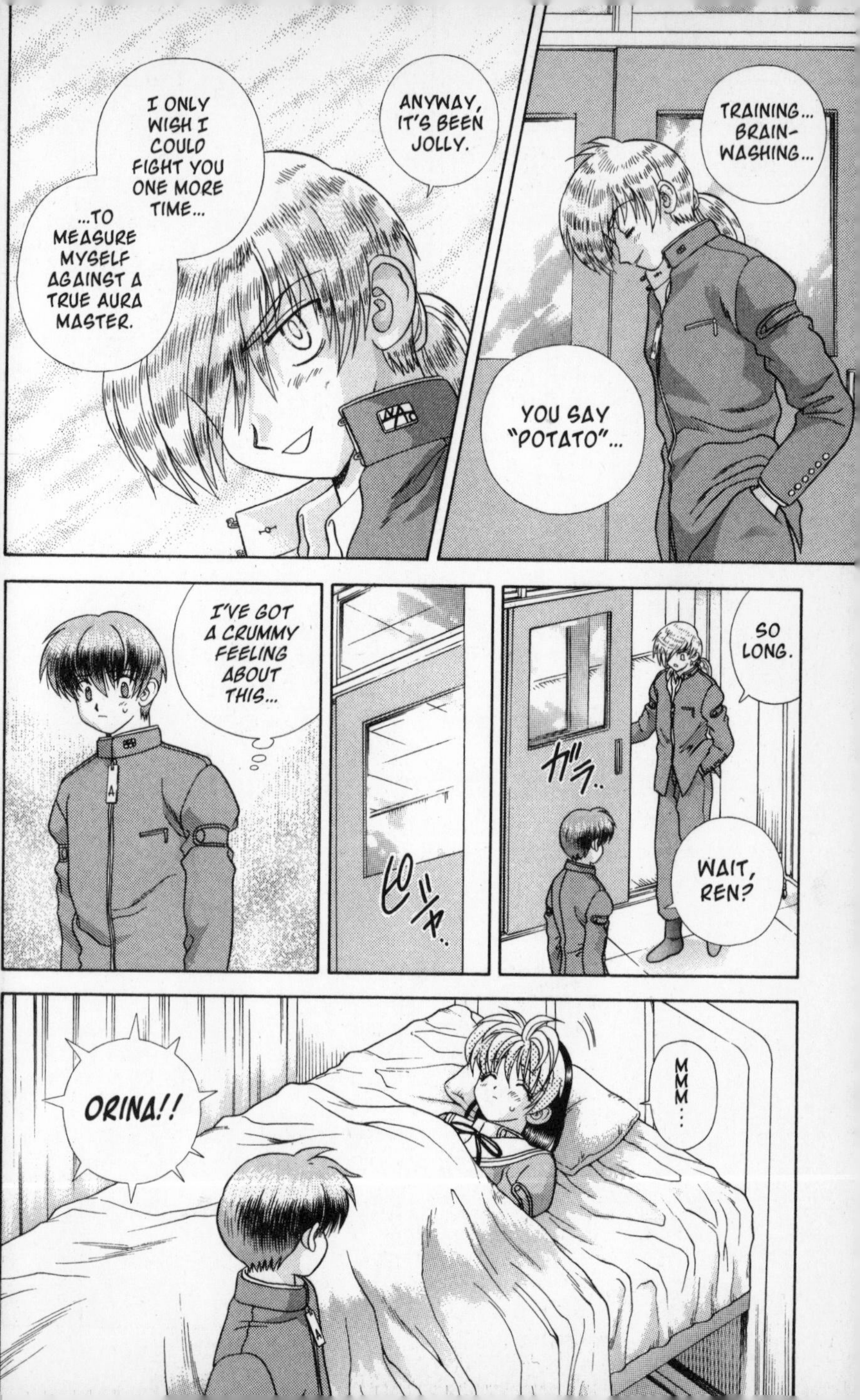
TRAINING... BRAIN-WASHING...
YOU SAY "POTATO"...
ANYWAY, IT'S BEEN JOLLY.
I ONLY WISH I COULD FIGHT YOU ONE MORE TIME...
...TO MEASURE MYSELF AGAINST A TRUE AURA MASTER.
SO LONG.
ガラ..
WAIT, REN?
ピシャ..
I'VE GOT A CRUMMY FEELING ABOUT THIS...
MMM...
ORINA!!

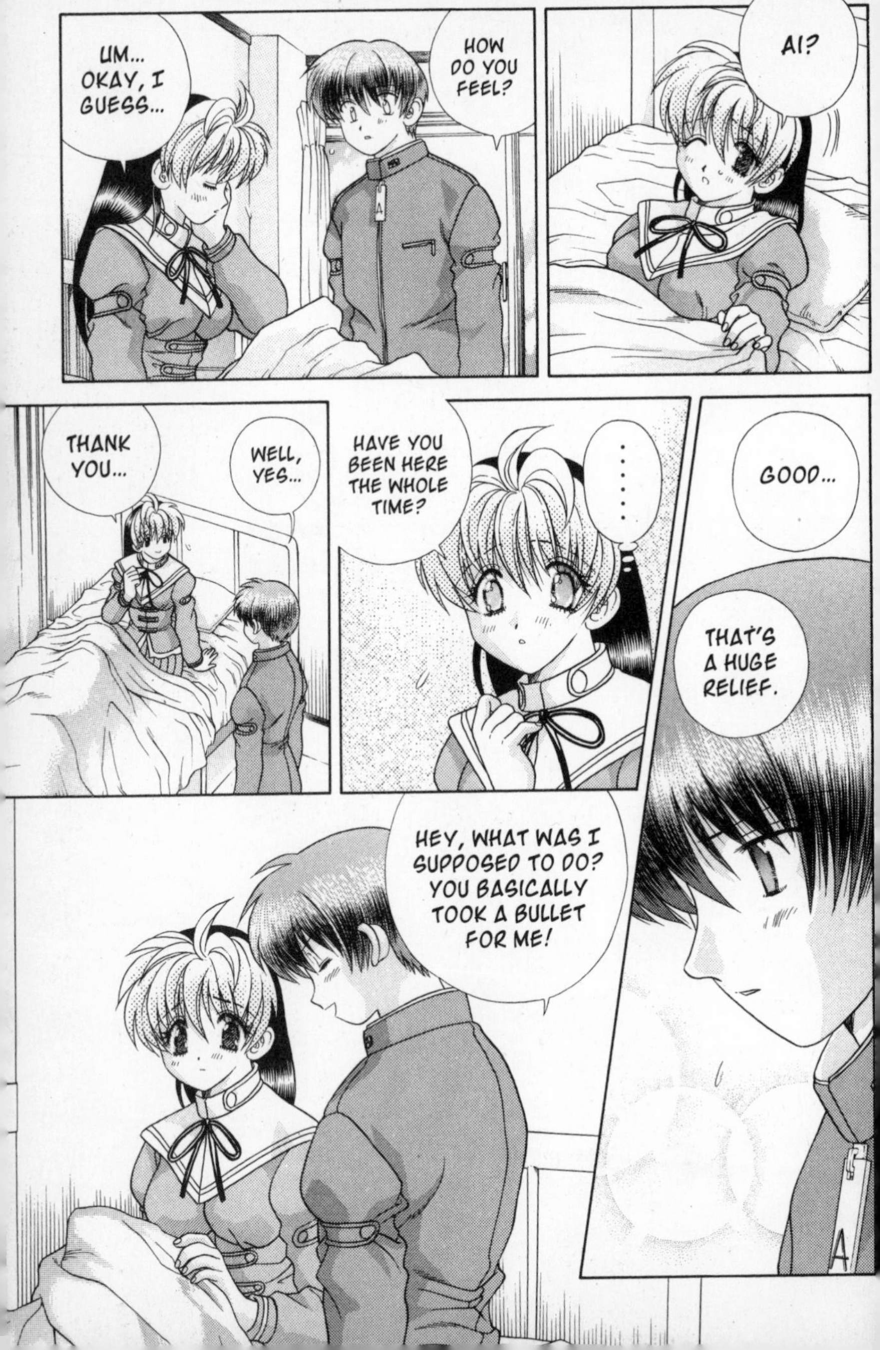
AI?
HOW DO YOU FEEL?
UM... OKAY, I GUESS...
GOOD...
THAT'S A HUGE RELIEF.
......
HAVE YOU BEEN HERE THE WHOLE TIME?
WELL, YES...
THANK YOU...
HEY, WHAT WAS I SUPPOSED TO DO? YOU BASICALLY TOOK A BULLET FOR ME!

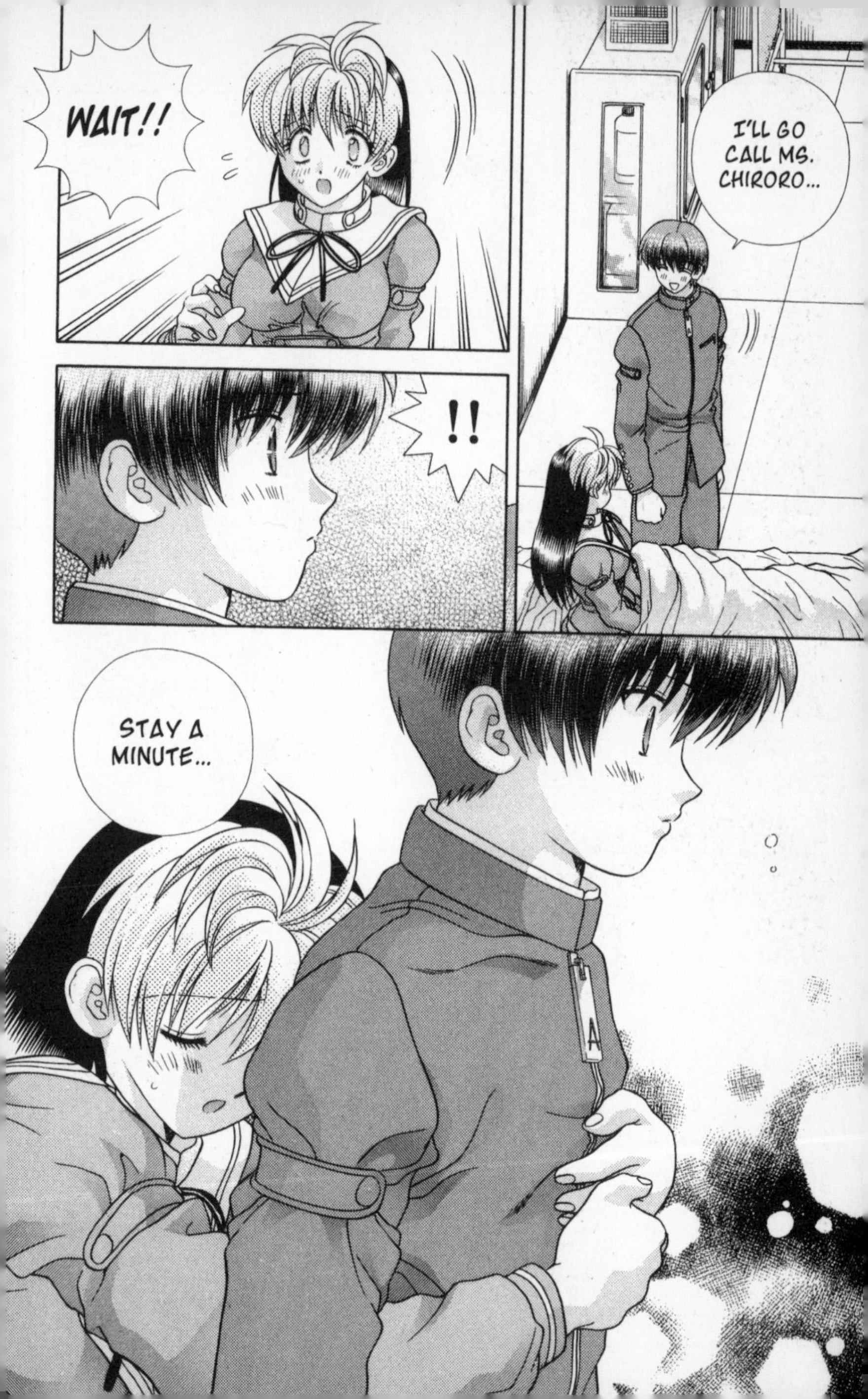
I'LL GO CALL MS. CHIRORO...
WAIT!!
!!
STAY A MINUTE...

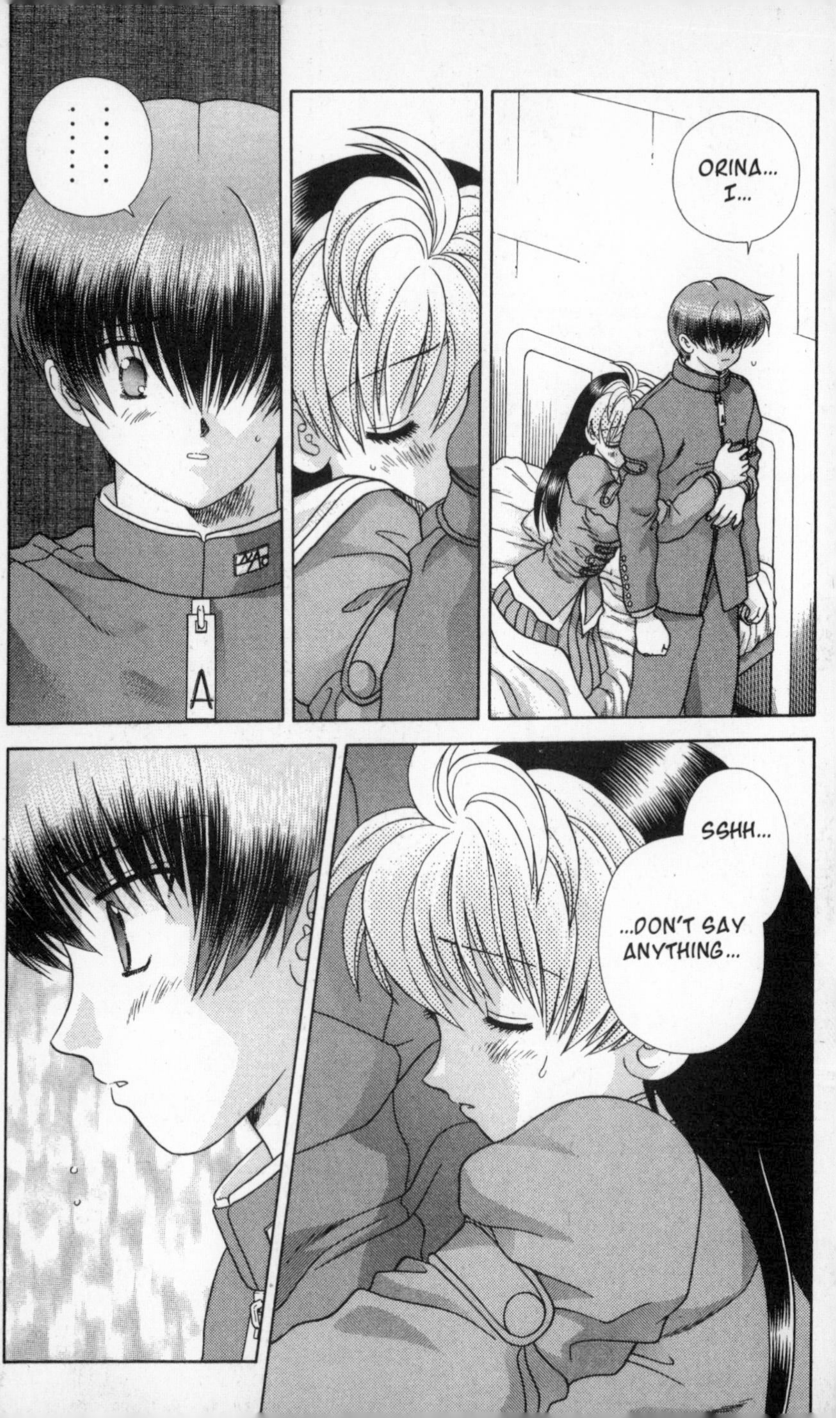
ORINA... I...
......
SSHH...
...DON'T SAY ANYTHING...

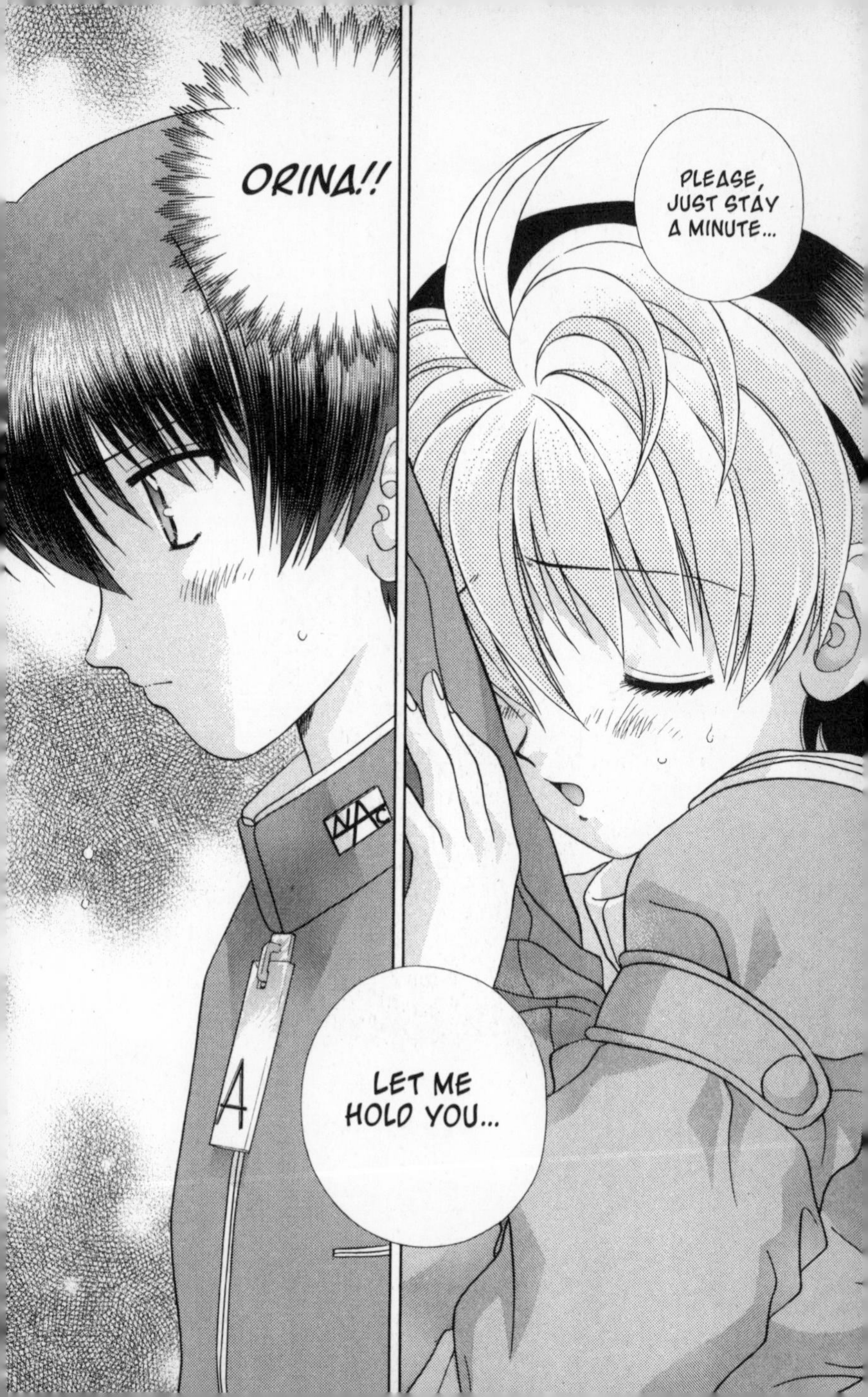
PLEASE, JUST STAY A MINUTE...
ORINA!!
LET ME HOLD YOU...

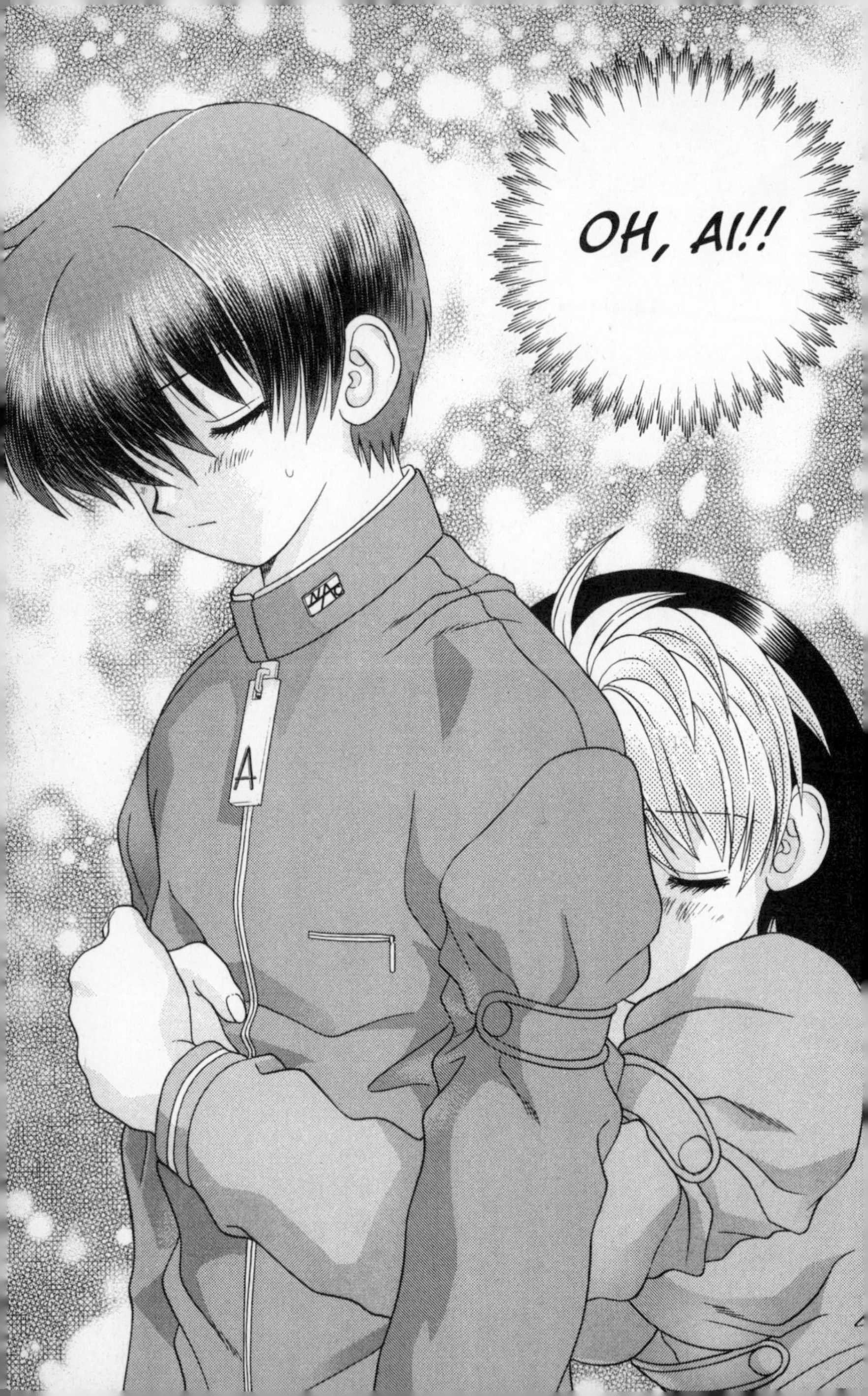
OH, AI!!

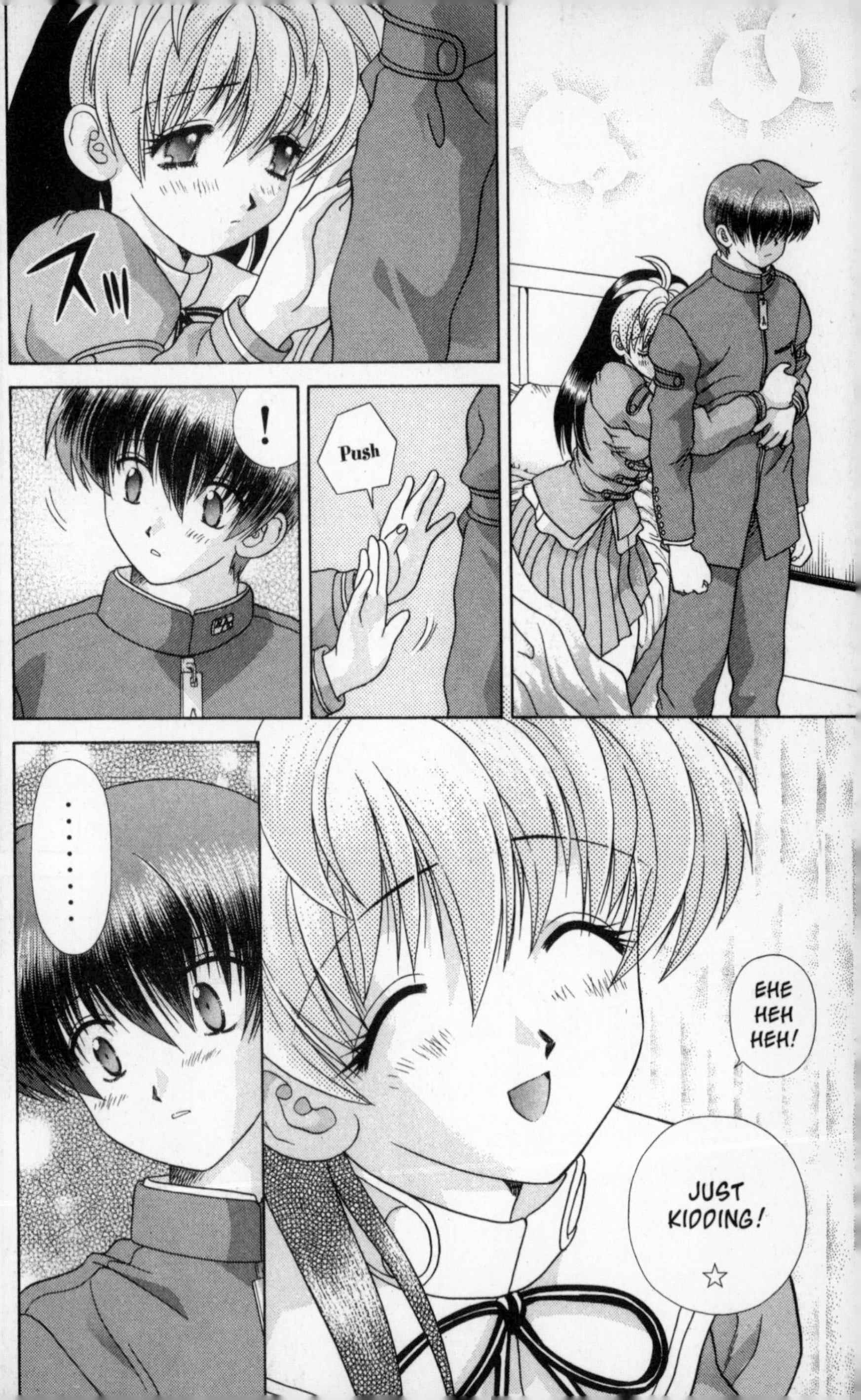

ス
Push
!
EHE HEH HEH!
JUST KIDDING! ☆
....

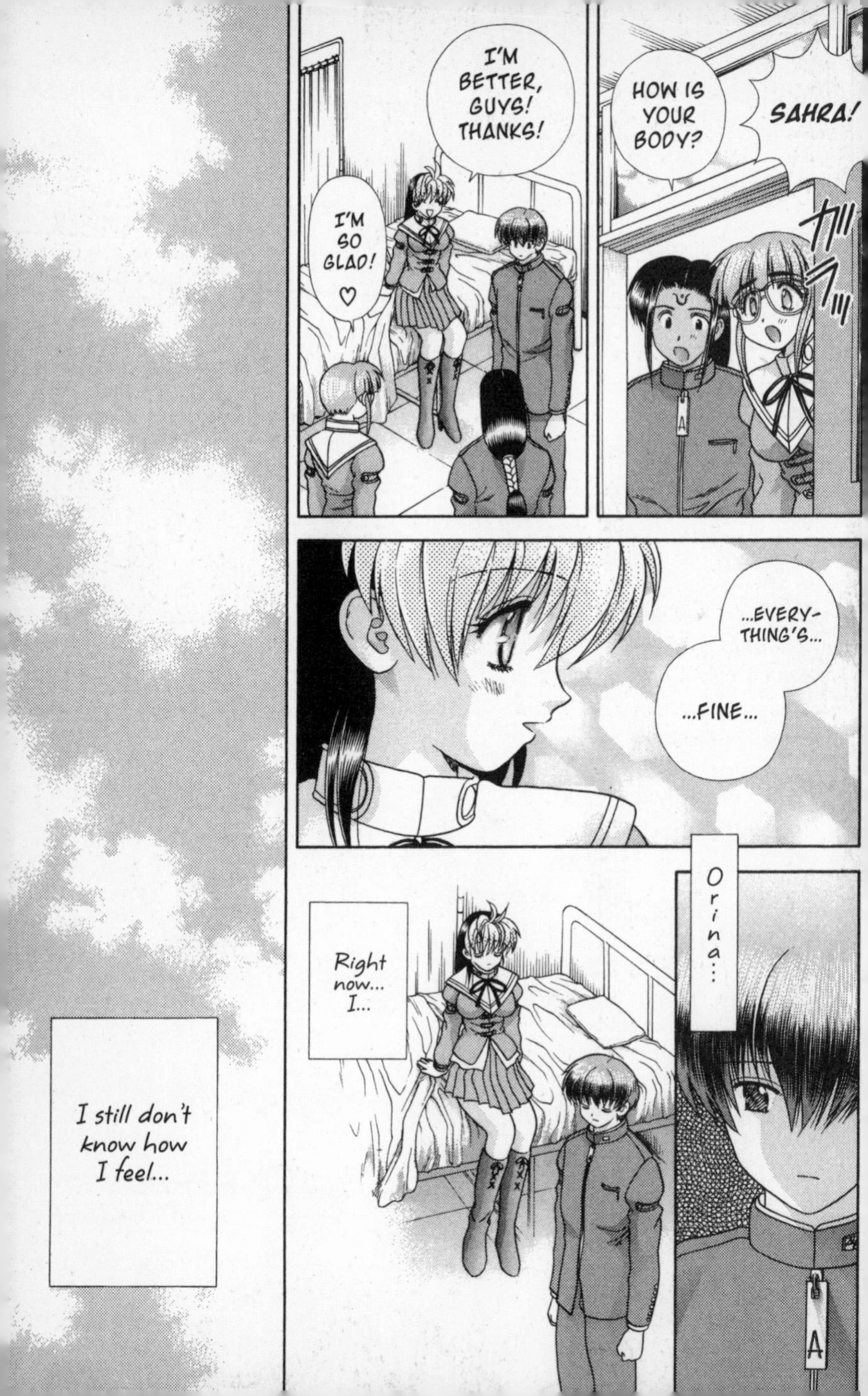
SAHRA!
ガラッ
HOW IS YOUR BODY?
I'M BETTER, GUYS! THANKS!
I'M SO GLAD! ♡
...EVERY-THING'S...
...FINE...
Orina...
Right now... I...
I still don't know how I feel...

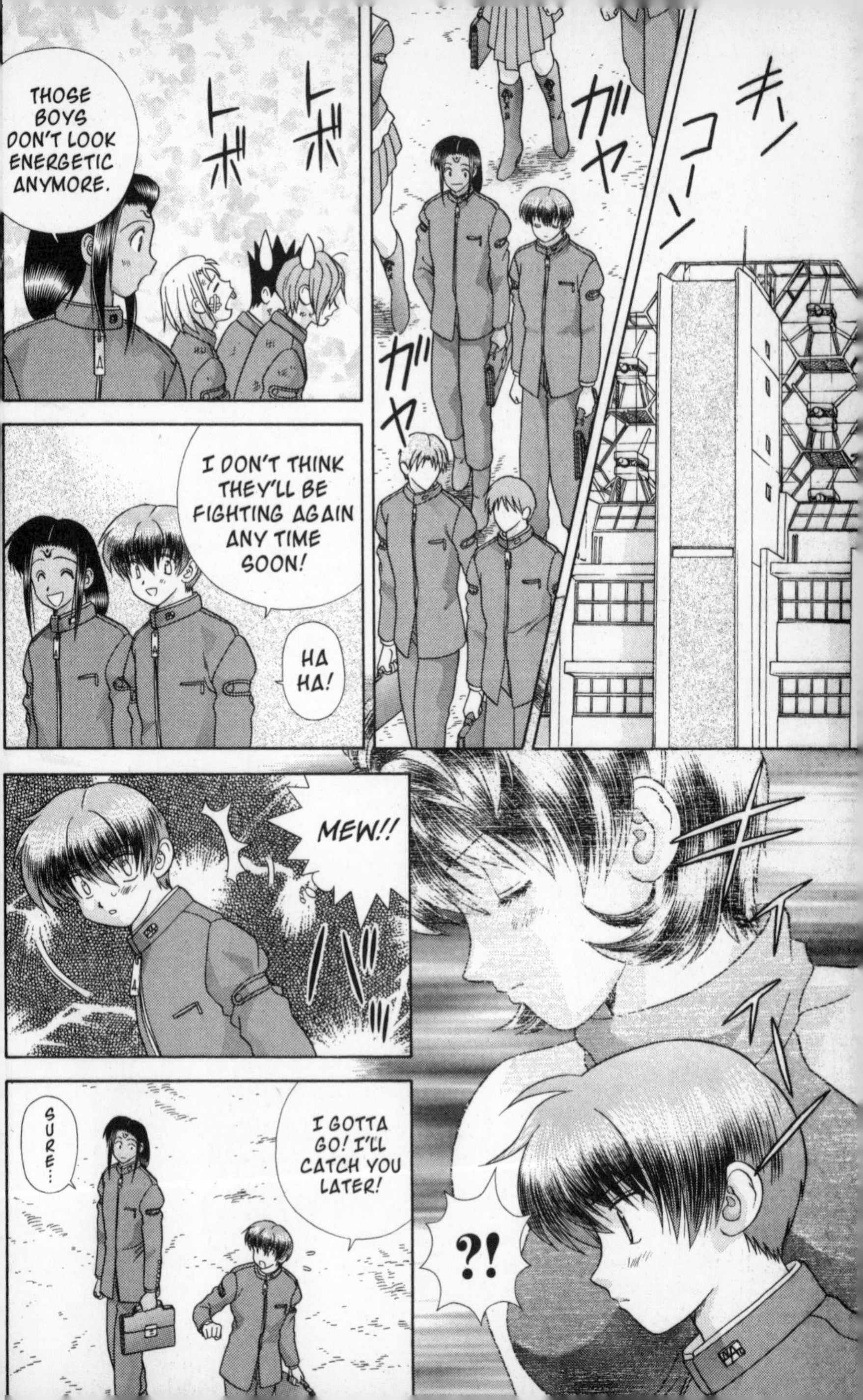

キンコーン
ガヤ
ガヤ
トボ
トボ
THOSE BOYS DON'T LOOK ENERGETIC ANYMORE.
I DON'T THINK THEY'LL BE FIGHTING AGAIN ANY TIME SOON!
HA HA!
キイイイ
?!
MEW!!
バ
I GOTTA GO! I'LL CATCH YOU LATER!
SURE...

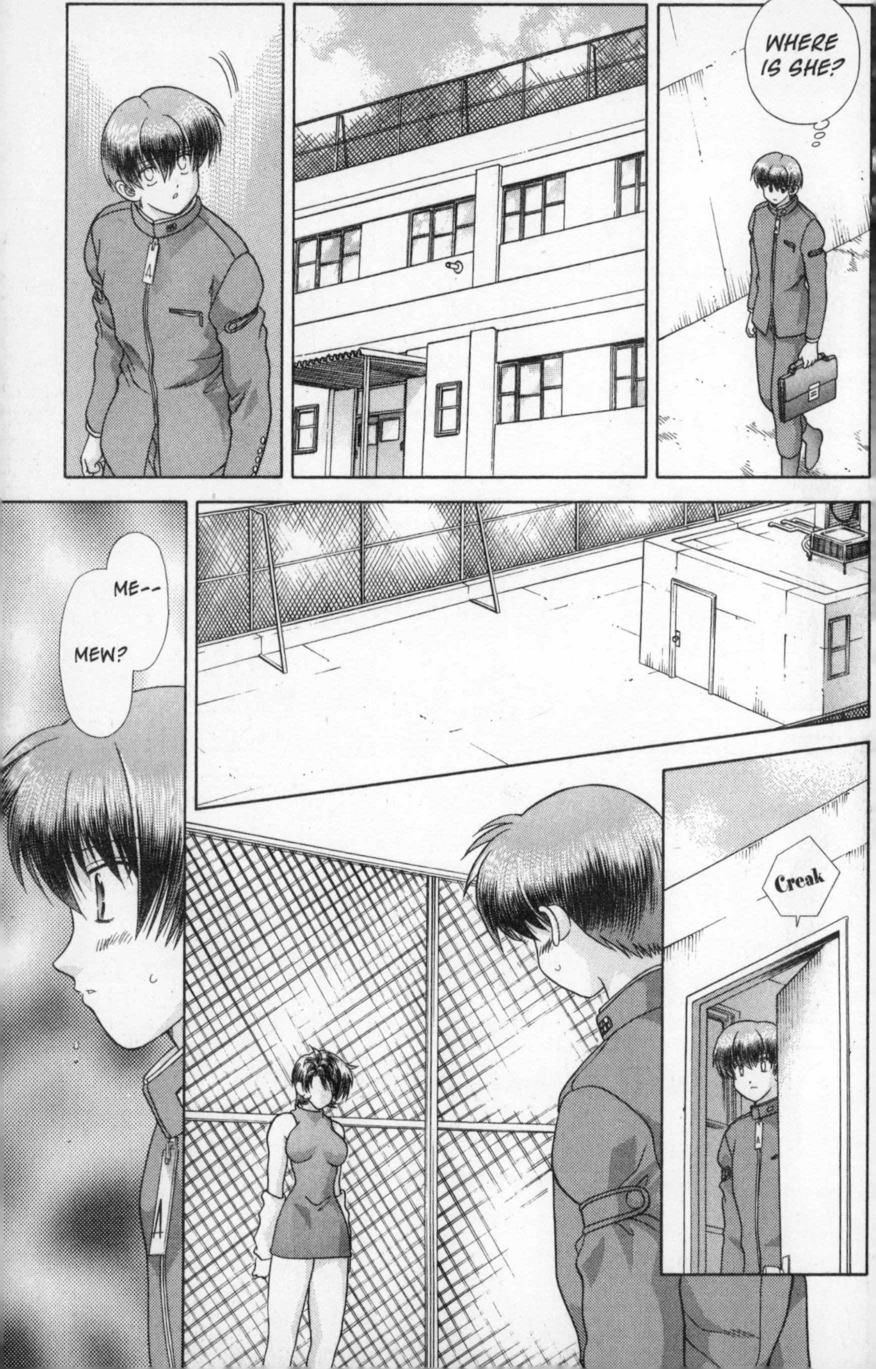
WHERE IS SHE?
Creak
ME--
MEW?

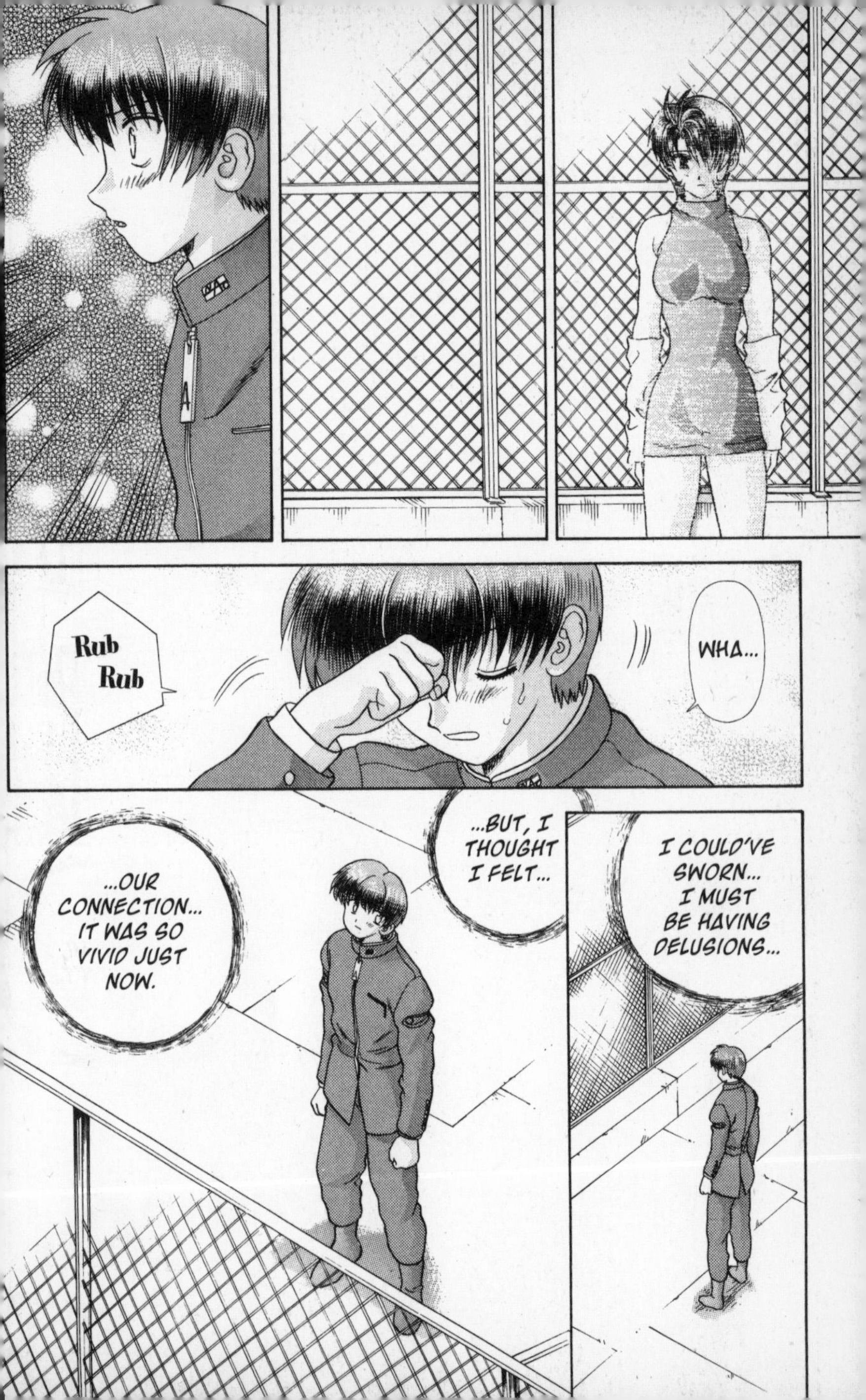
WHA...
Rub Rub
I COULD'VE SWORN... I MUST BE HAVING DELUSIONS...
...BUT, I THOUGHT I FELT...
...OUR CONNECTION... IT WAS SO VIVID JUST NOW.

MEW!!

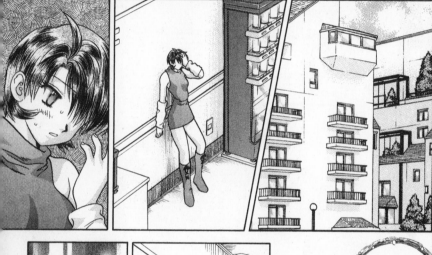

I...

SHIOMI, I
CAN'T.

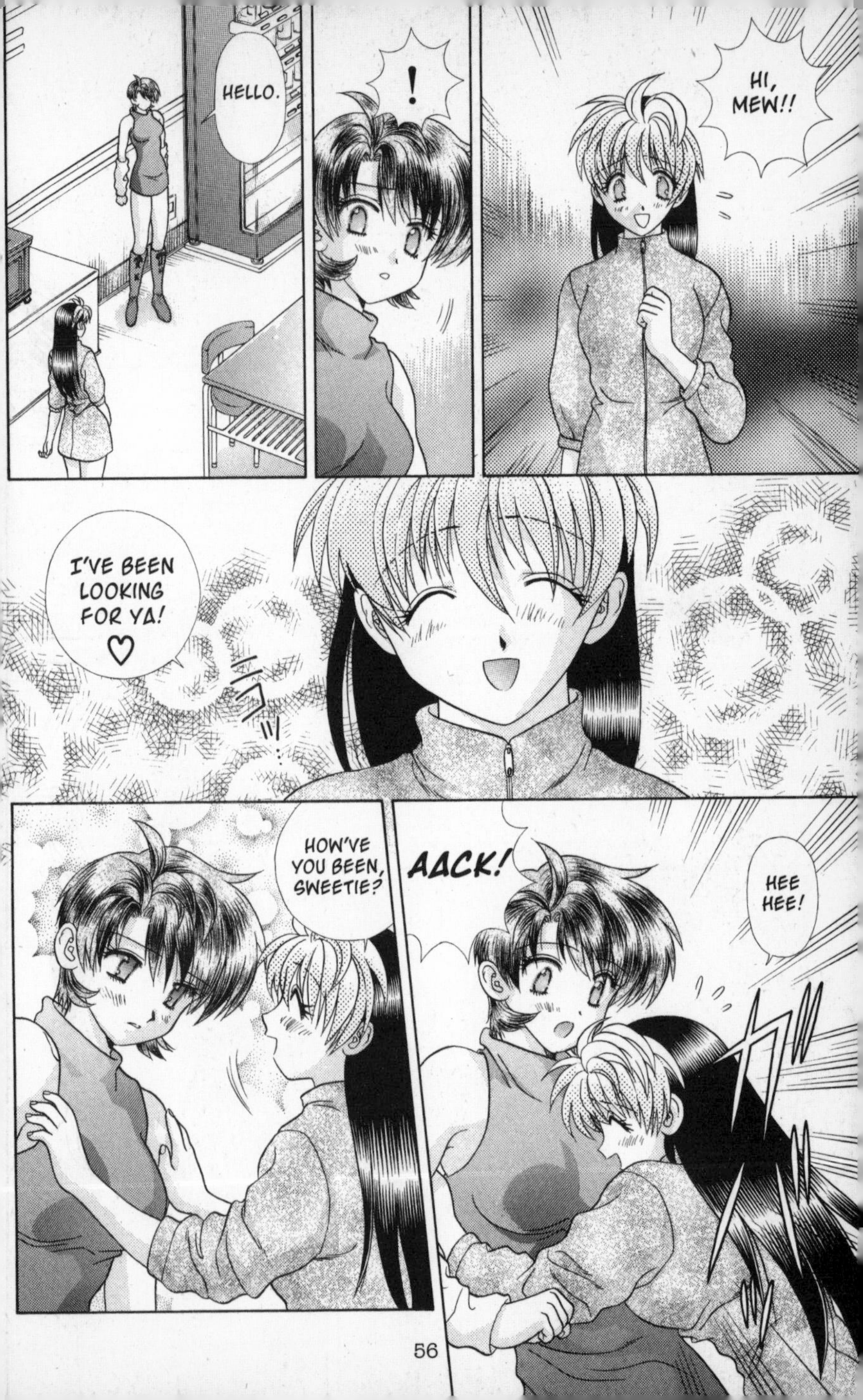
HI, MEW!!
!
HELLO.
I'VE BEEN LOOKING FOR YA! ♡
AACK!
HEE HEE!
HOW'VE YOU BEEN, SWEETIE?

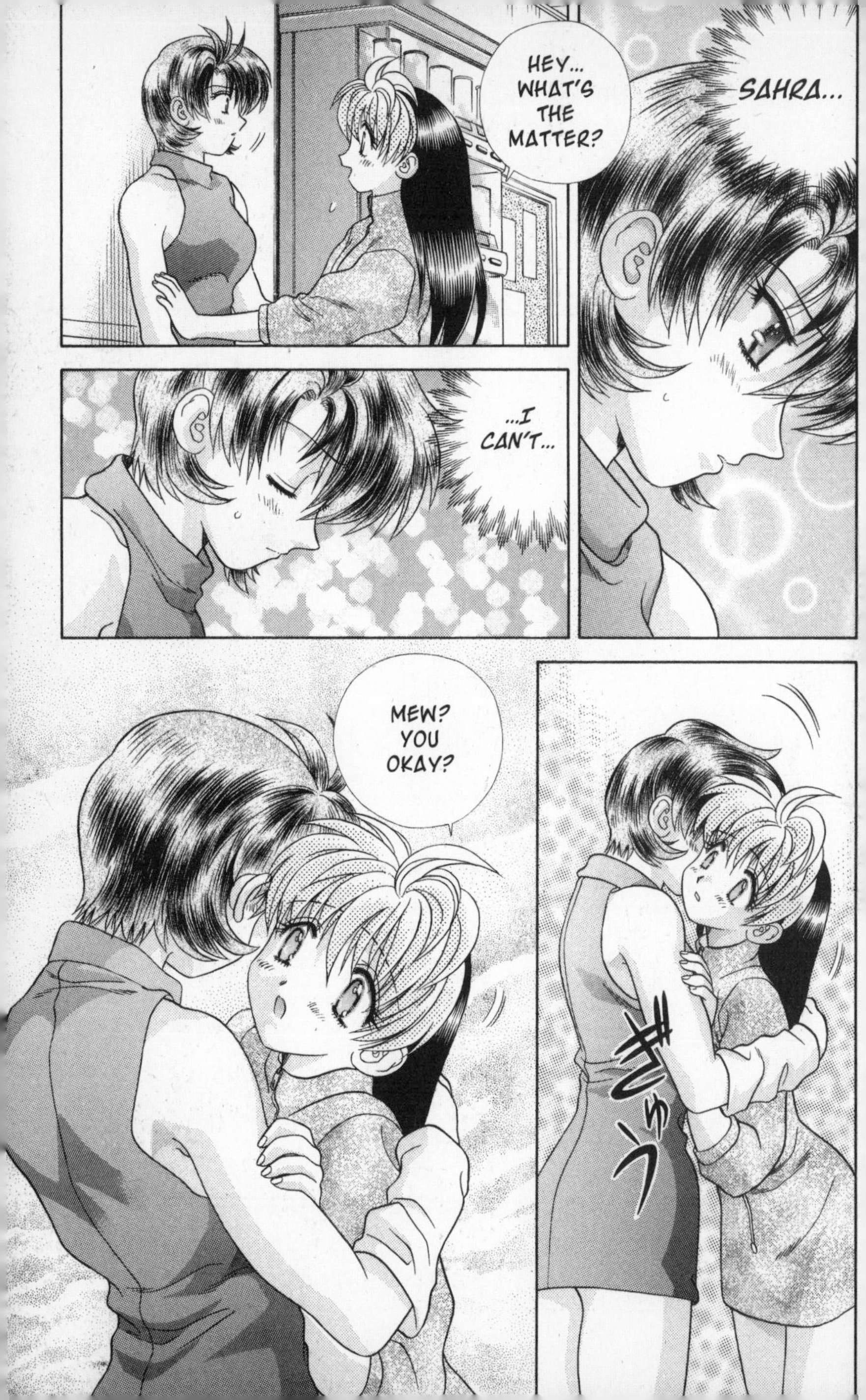
SAHRA...
HEY... WHAT'S THE MATTER?
...I CAN'T...
ぎゅう
MEW? YOU OKAY?

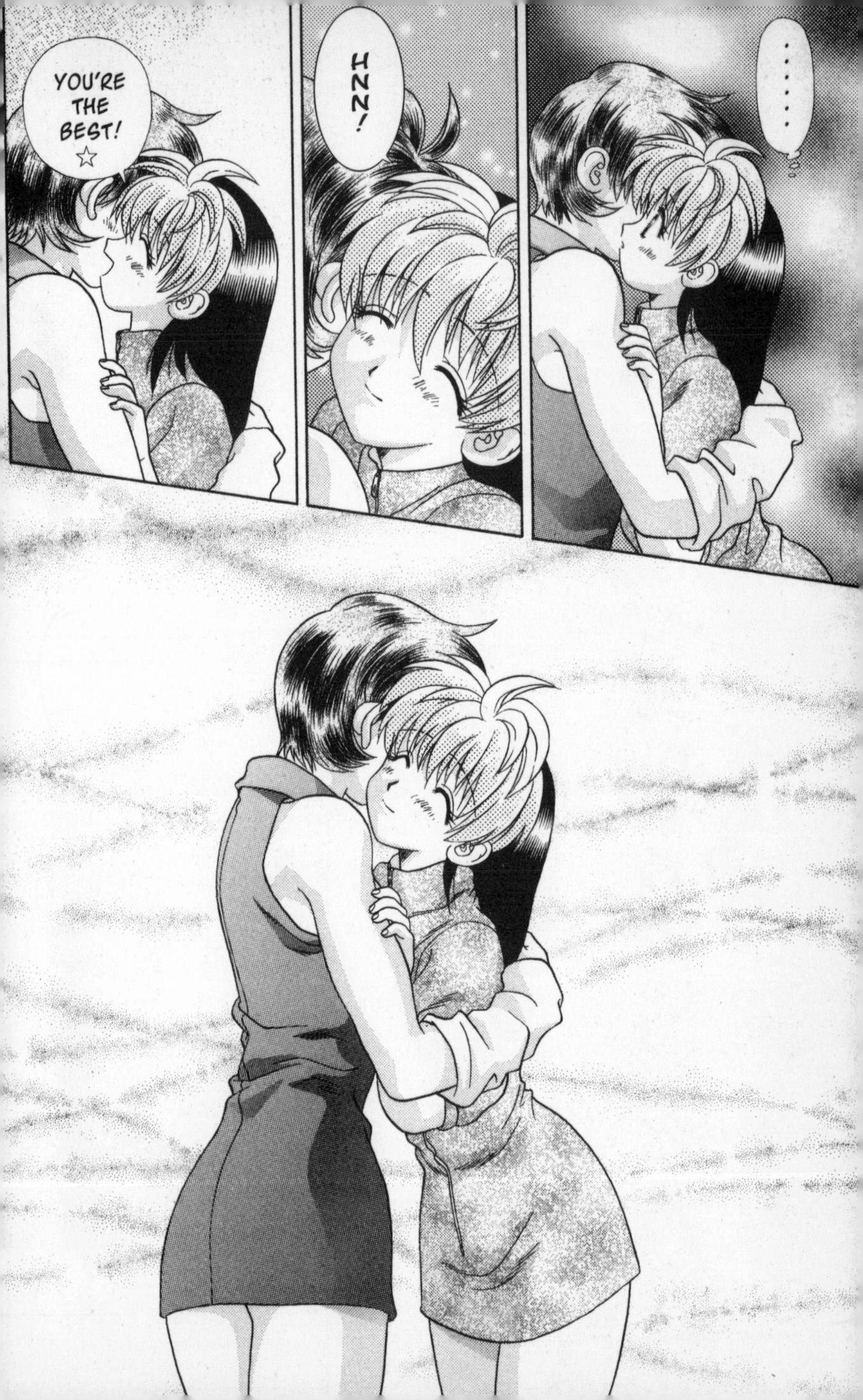
......
HNN!
YOU'RE THE BEST! ☆

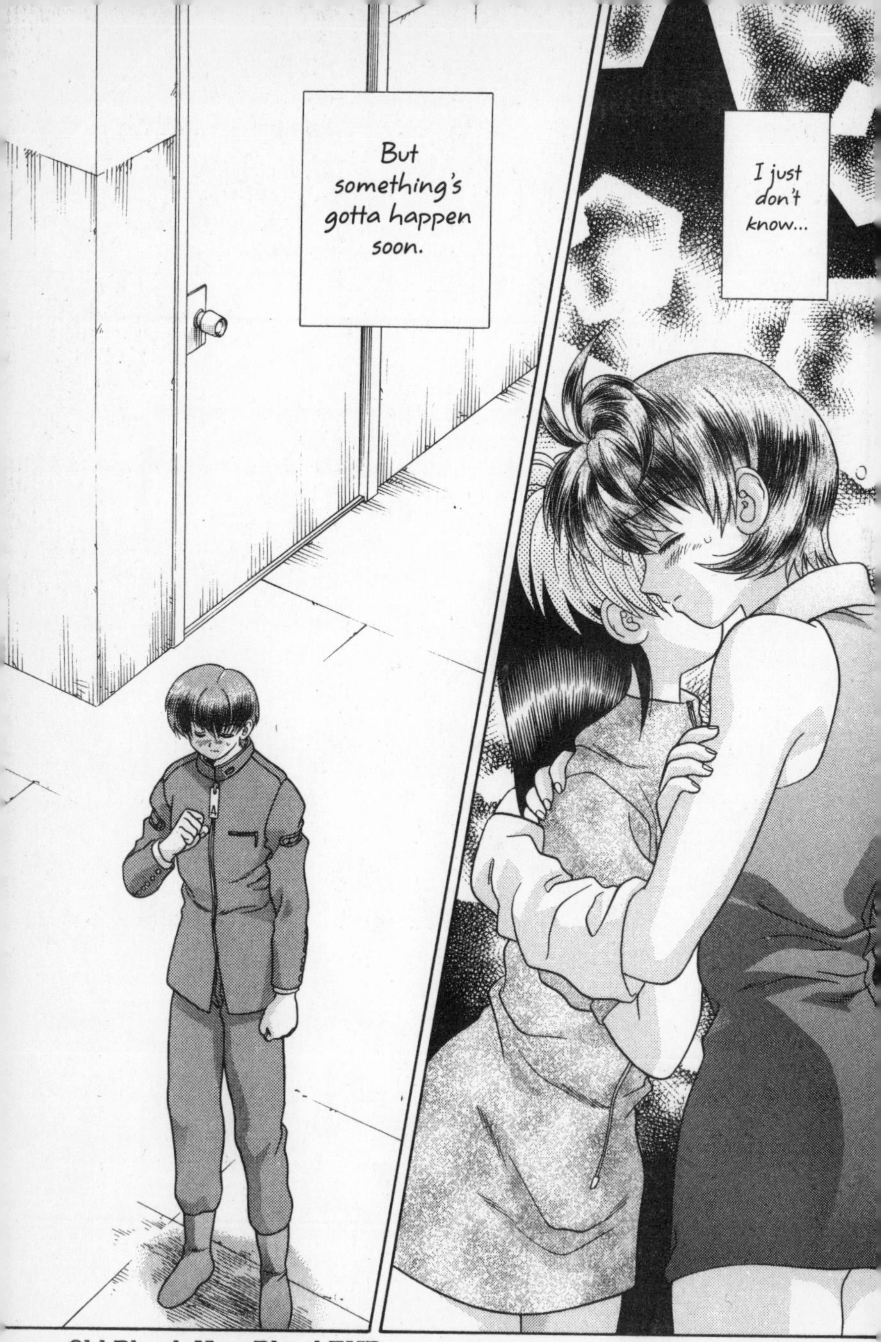
I just don't know...
But something's gotta happen soon.

Old Blood, New Blood END

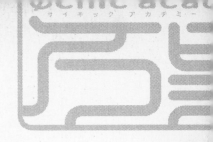

Chapter 33 Gabriella's Hunt

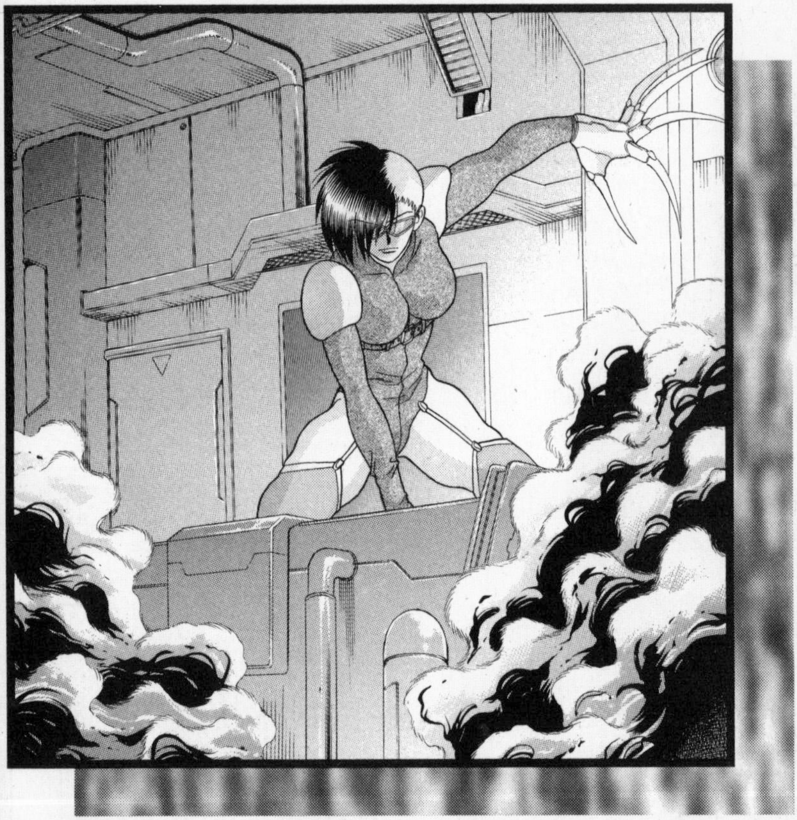

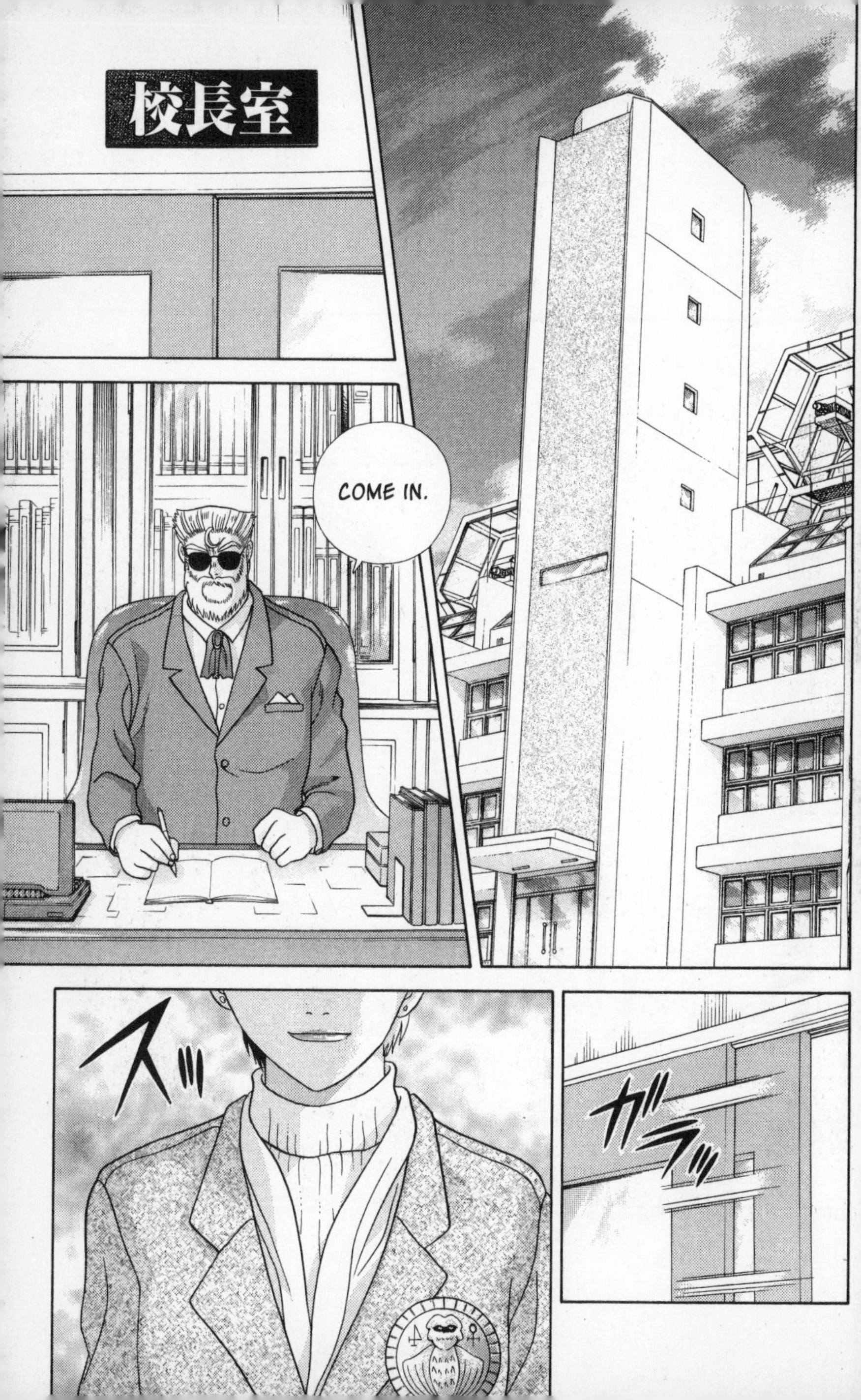
校長室
COME IN.
ガラッ
スッ

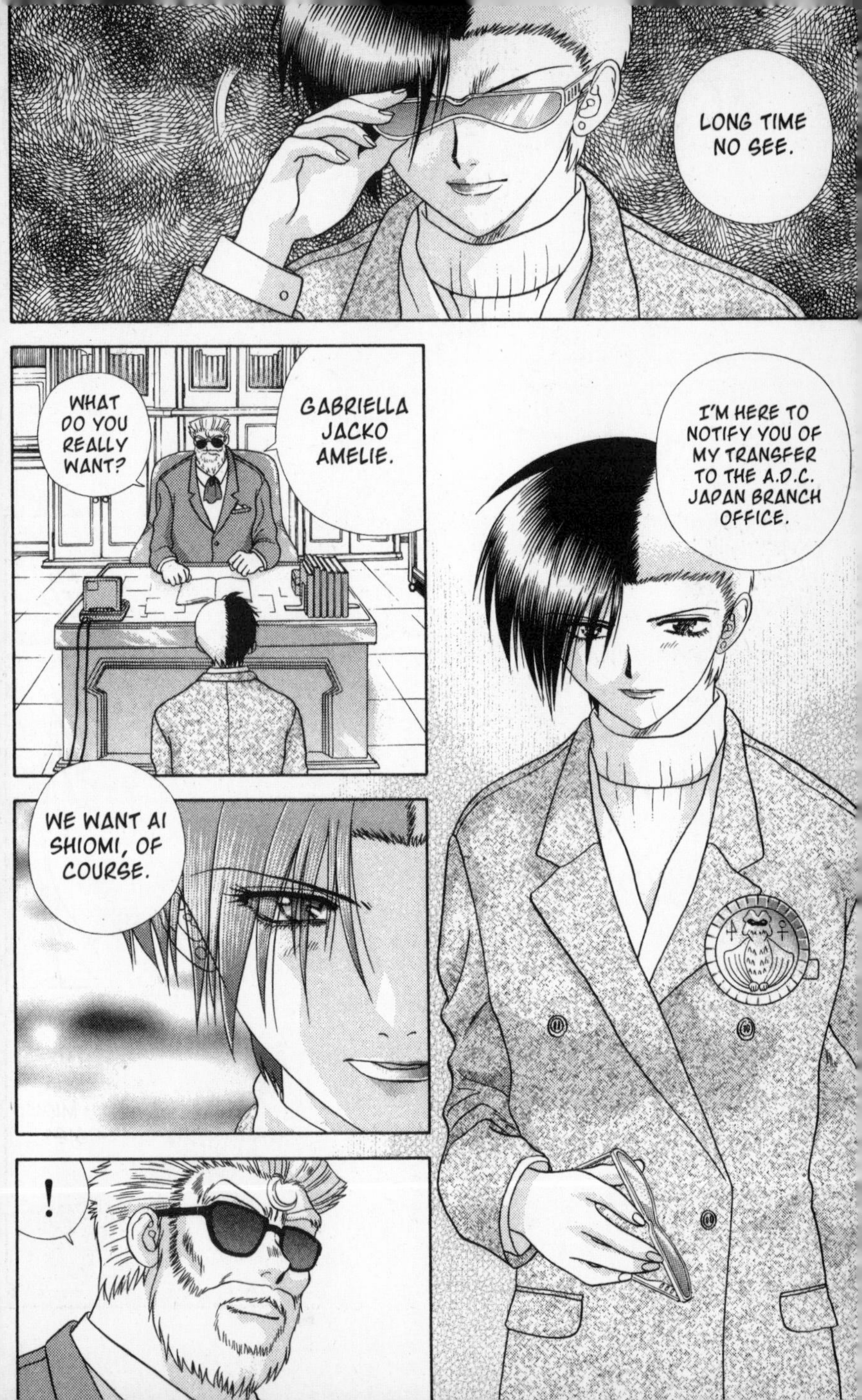
LONG TIME NO SEE.
I'M HERE TO NOTIFY YOU OF MY TRANSFER TO THE A.D.C. JAPAN BRANCH OFFICE.
GABRIELLA JACKO AMELIE.
WHAT DO YOU REALLY WANT?
WE WANT AI SHIOMI, OF COURSE.
!

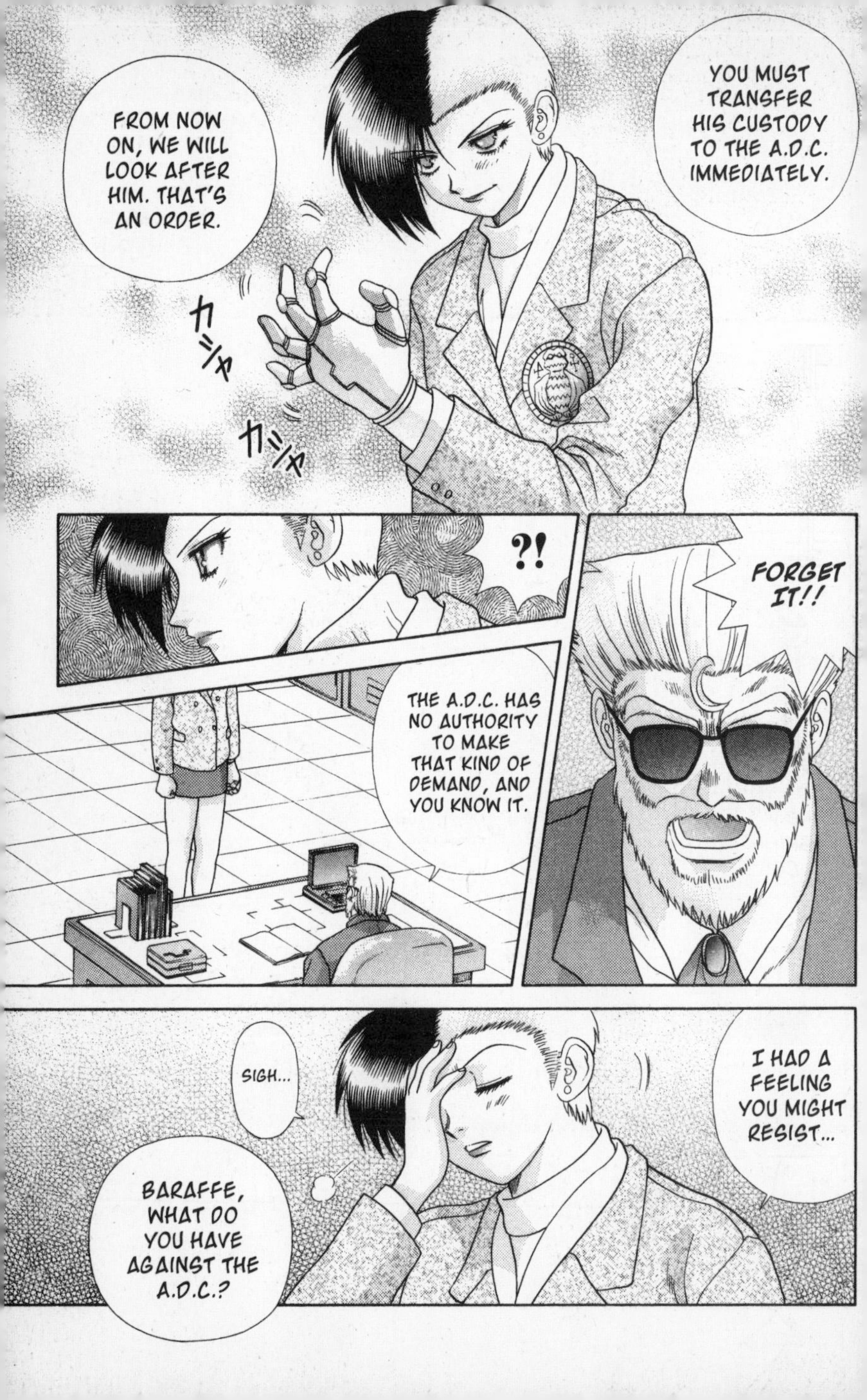
YOU MUST TRANSFER HIS CUSTODY TO THE A.D.C. IMMEDIATELY.
FROM NOW ON, WE WILL LOOK AFTER HIM. THAT'S AN ORDER.
カシャ
カシャ
FORGET IT!!
?!
THE A.D.C. HAS NO AUTHORITY TO MAKE THAT KIND OF DEMAND, AND YOU KNOW IT.
I HAD A FEELING YOU MIGHT RESIST...
SIGH...
BARAFFE, WHAT DO YOU HAVE AGAINST THE A.D.C.?

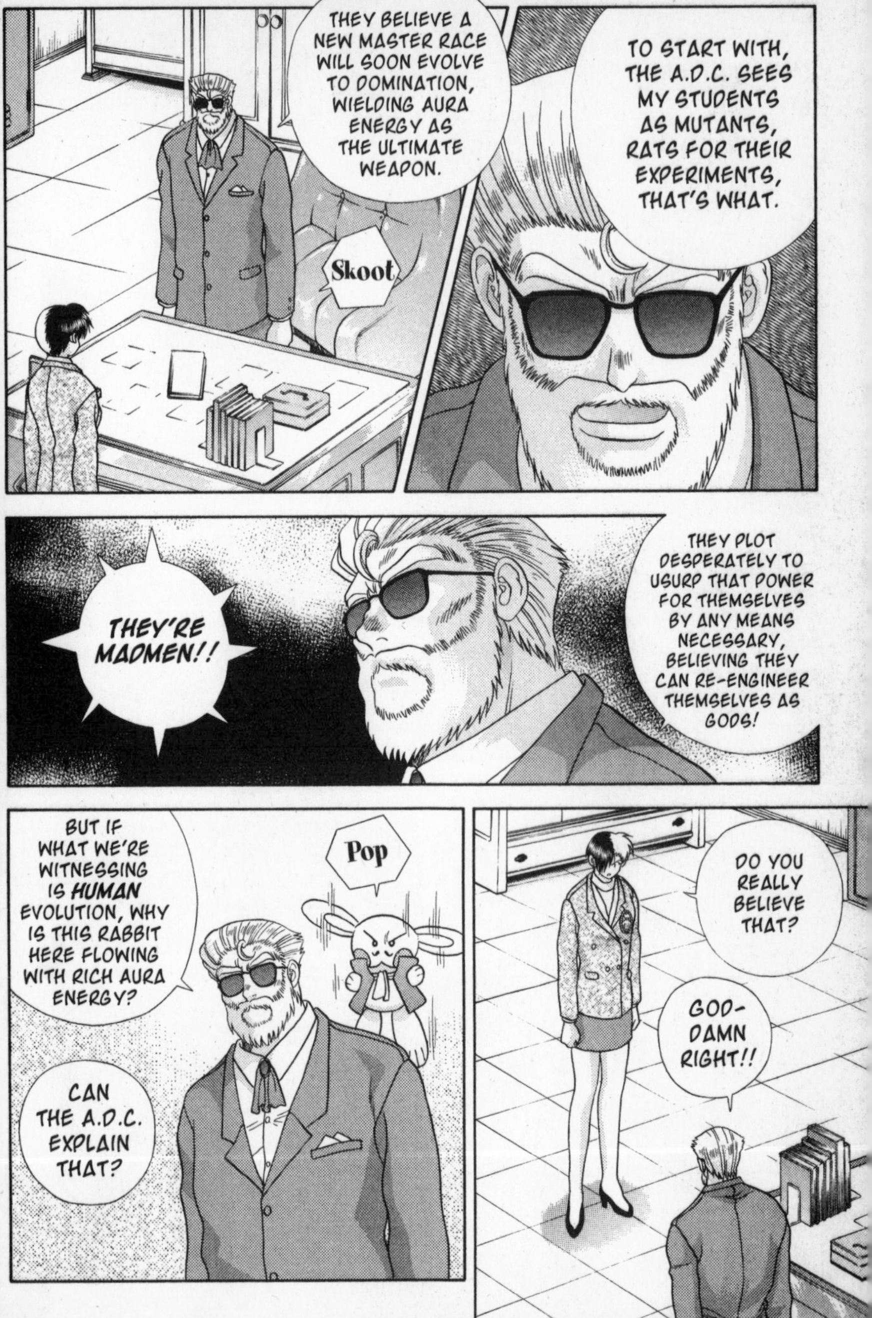
TO START WITH, THE A.D.C. SEES MY STUDENTS AS MUTANTS, RATS FOR THEIR EXPERIMENTS, THAT'S WHAT.
THEY BELIEVE A NEW MASTER RACE WILL SOON EVOLVE TO DOMINATION, WIELDING AURA ENERGY AS THE ULTIMATE WEAPON.
Skoot
THEY PLOT DESPERATELY TO USURP THAT POWER FOR THEMSELVES BY ANY MEANS NECESSARY, BELIEVING THEY CAN RE-ENGINEER THEMSELVES AS GODS!
THEY'RE MADMEN!!
DO YOU REALLY BELIEVE THAT?
GOD-DAMN RIGHT!!
Pop
BUT IF WHAT WE'RE WITNESSING IS ***HUMAN*** EVOLUTION, WHY IS THIS RABBIT HERE FLOWING WITH RICH AURA ENERGY?
CAN THE A.D.C. EXPLAIN THAT?

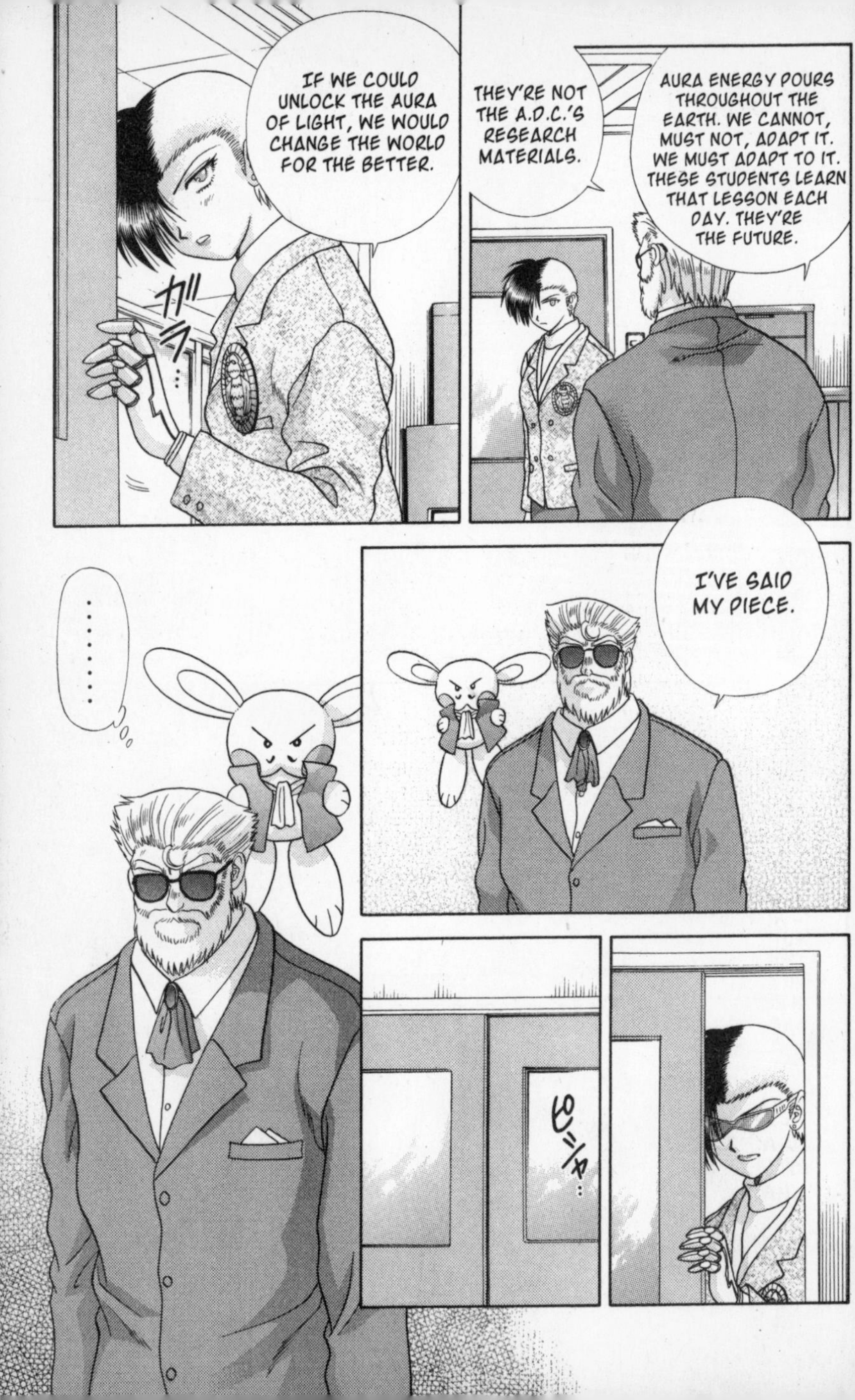
THEY'RE NOT THE A.D.C.'S RESEARCH MATERIALS.
AURA ENERGY POURS THROUGHOUT THE EARTH. WE CANNOT, MUST NOT, ADAPT IT. WE MUST ADAPT TO IT. THESE STUDENTS LEARN THAT LESSON EACH DAY. THEY'RE THE FUTURE.
IF WE COULD UNLOCK THE AURA OF LIGHT, WE WOULD CHANGE THE WORLD FOR THE BETTER.
ガラ…
I'VE SAID MY PIECE.
……
ピシャ…

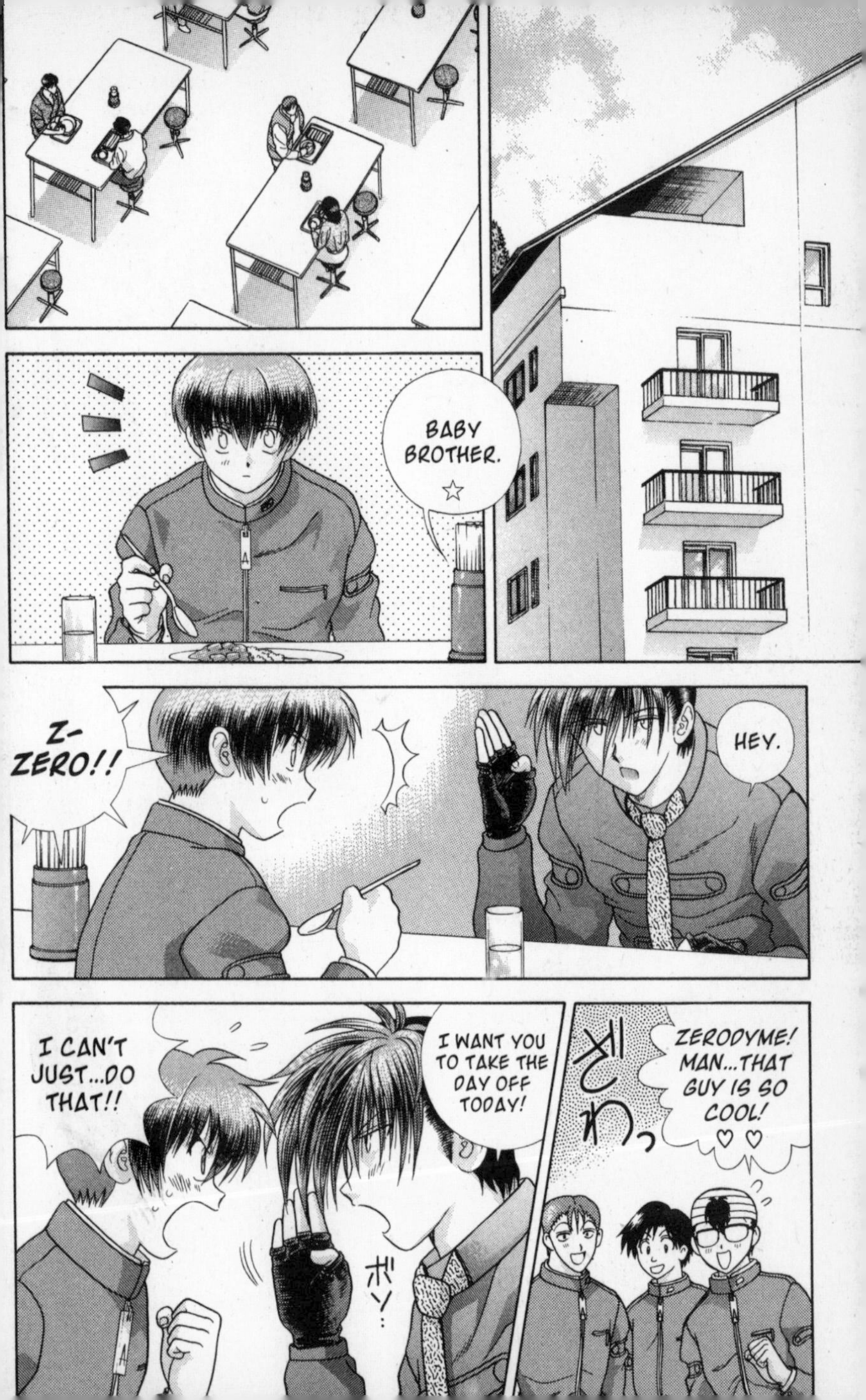
BABY BROTHER. ☆
HEY.
Z-ZERO!!
ざわっ
ZERODYME! MAN...THAT GUY IS SO COOL! ♡ ♡
I WANT YOU TO TAKE THE DAY OFF TODAY!
ボソ…
I CAN'T JUST...DO THAT!!

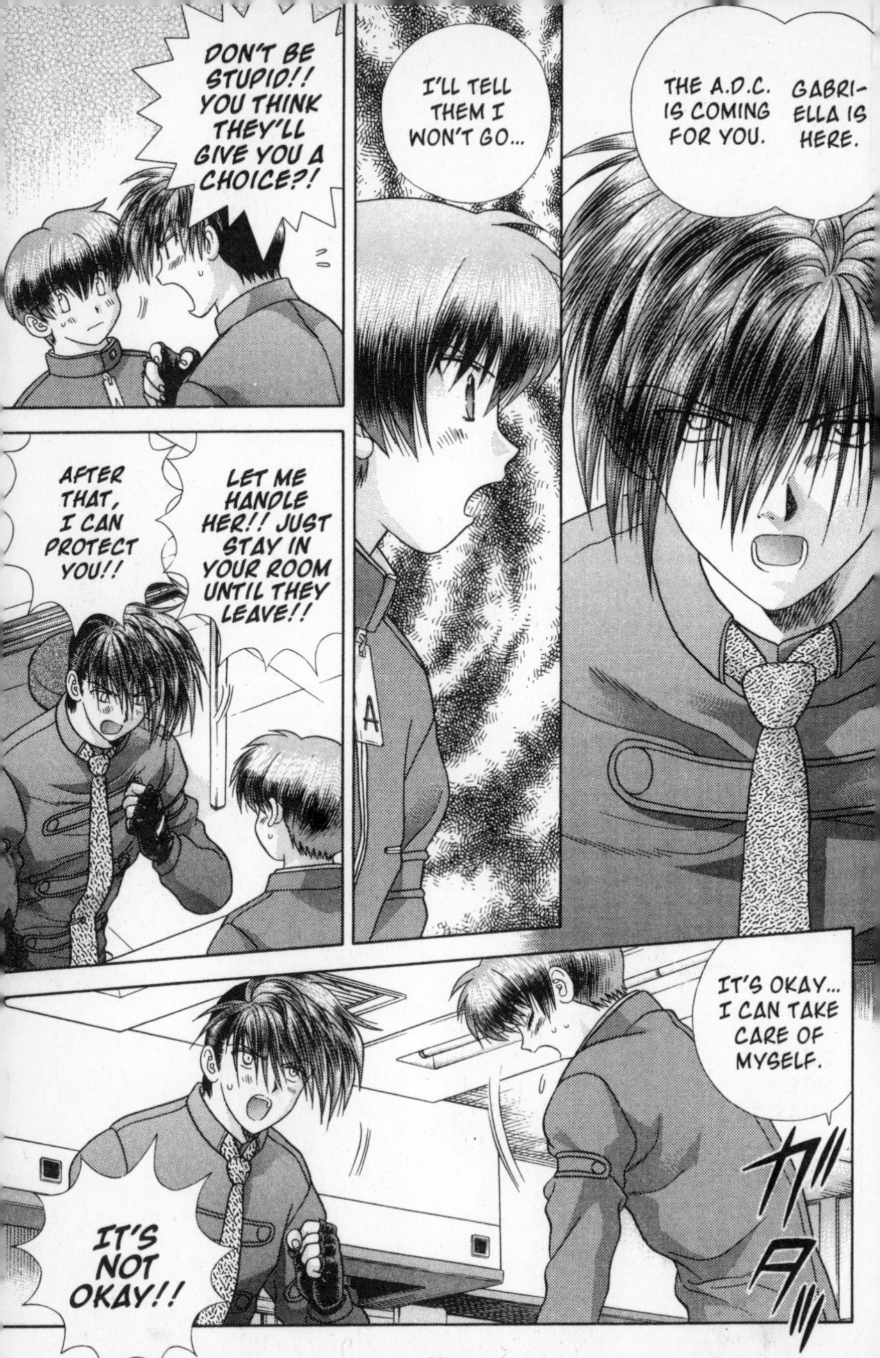
GABRI-ELLA IS HERE.
THE A.D.C. IS COMING FOR YOU.
I'LL TELL THEM I WON'T GO...
DON'T BE STUPID!! YOU THINK THEY'LL GIVE YOU A CHOICE?!
LET ME HANDLE HER!! JUST STAY IN YOUR ROOM UNTIL THEY LEAVE!!
AFTER THAT, I CAN PROTECT YOU!!
IT'S OKAY... I CAN TAKE CARE OF MYSELF.
ガタ
IT'S NOT OKAY!!

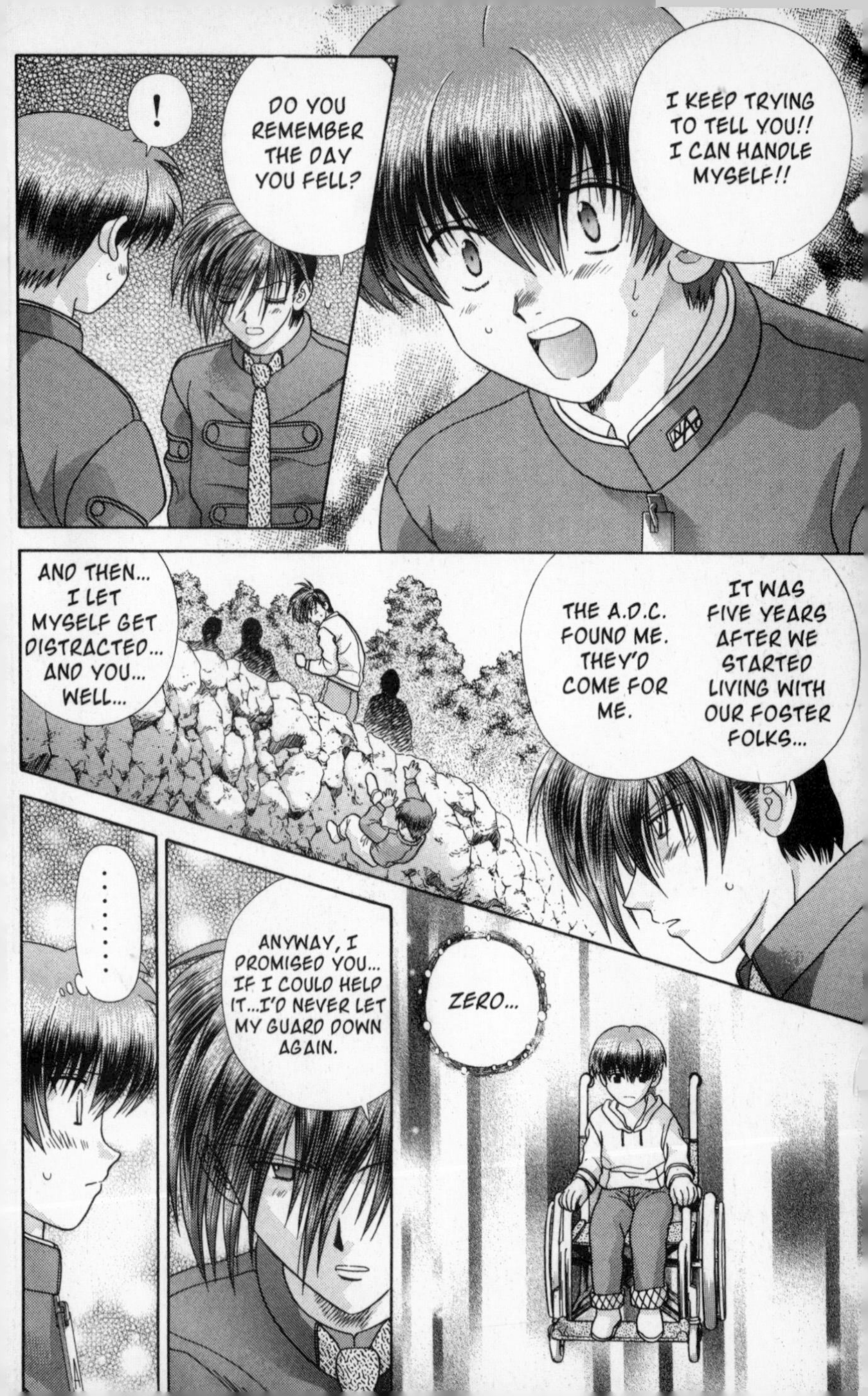
I KEEP TRYING TO TELL YOU!! I CAN HANDLE MYSELF!!
DO YOU REMEMBER THE DAY YOU FELL?
!
IT WAS FIVE YEARS AFTER WE STARTED LIVING WITH OUR FOSTER FOLKS...
THE A.D.C. FOUND ME. THEY'D COME FOR ME.
AND THEN... I LET MYSELF GET DISTRACTED... AND YOU... WELL...
ZERO...
ANYWAY, I PROMISED YOU... IF I COULD HELP IT...I'D NEVER LET MY GUARD DOWN AGAIN.
....

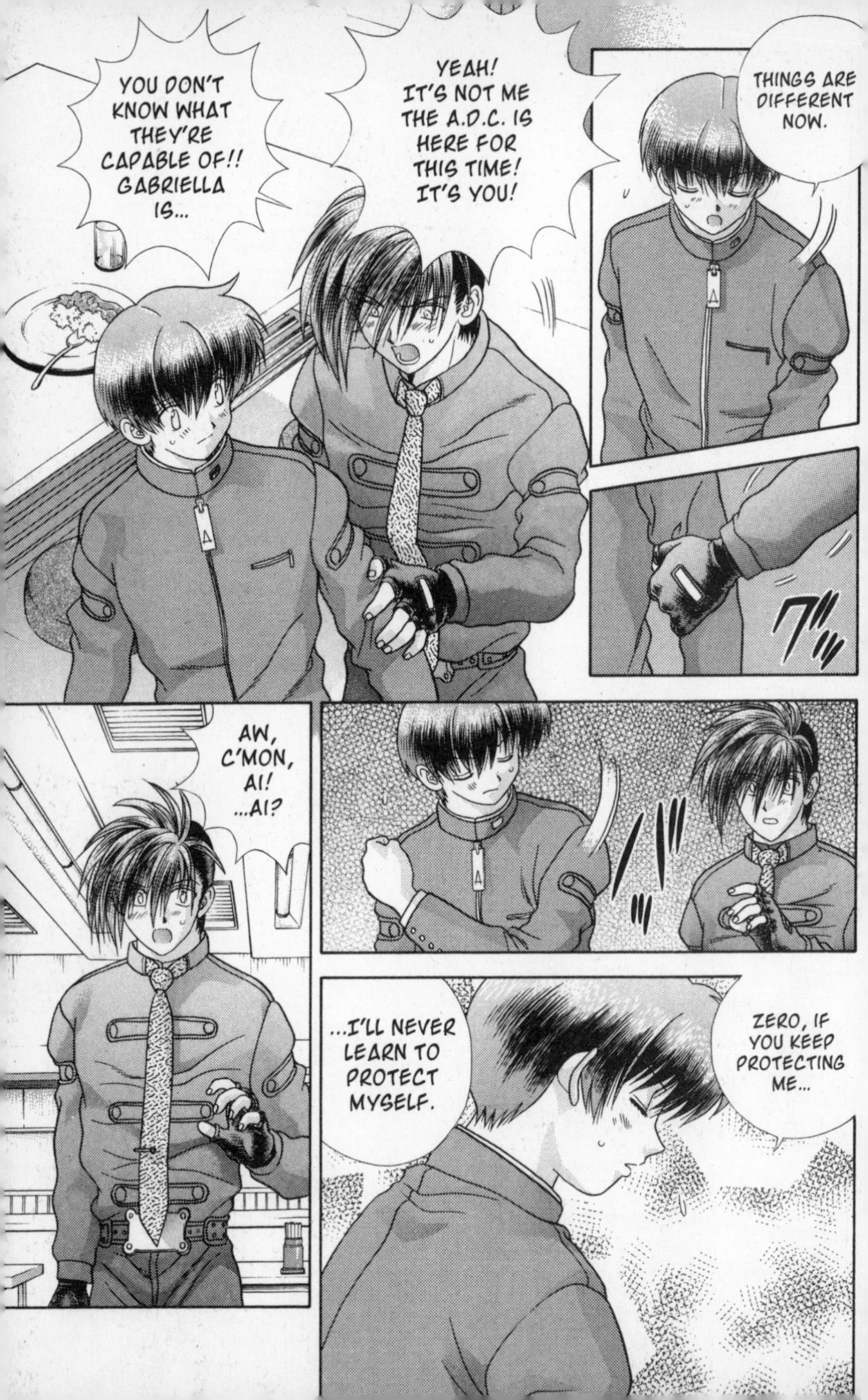
YOU DON'T KNOW WHAT THEY'RE CAPABLE OF!! GABRIELLA IS...
YEAH! IT'S NOT ME THE A.D.C. IS HERE FOR THIS TIME! IT'S YOU!
THINGS ARE DIFFERENT NOW.
AW, C'MON, AI! ...AI?
ZERO, IF YOU KEEP PROTECTING ME...
...I'LL NEVER LEARN TO PROTECT MYSELF.

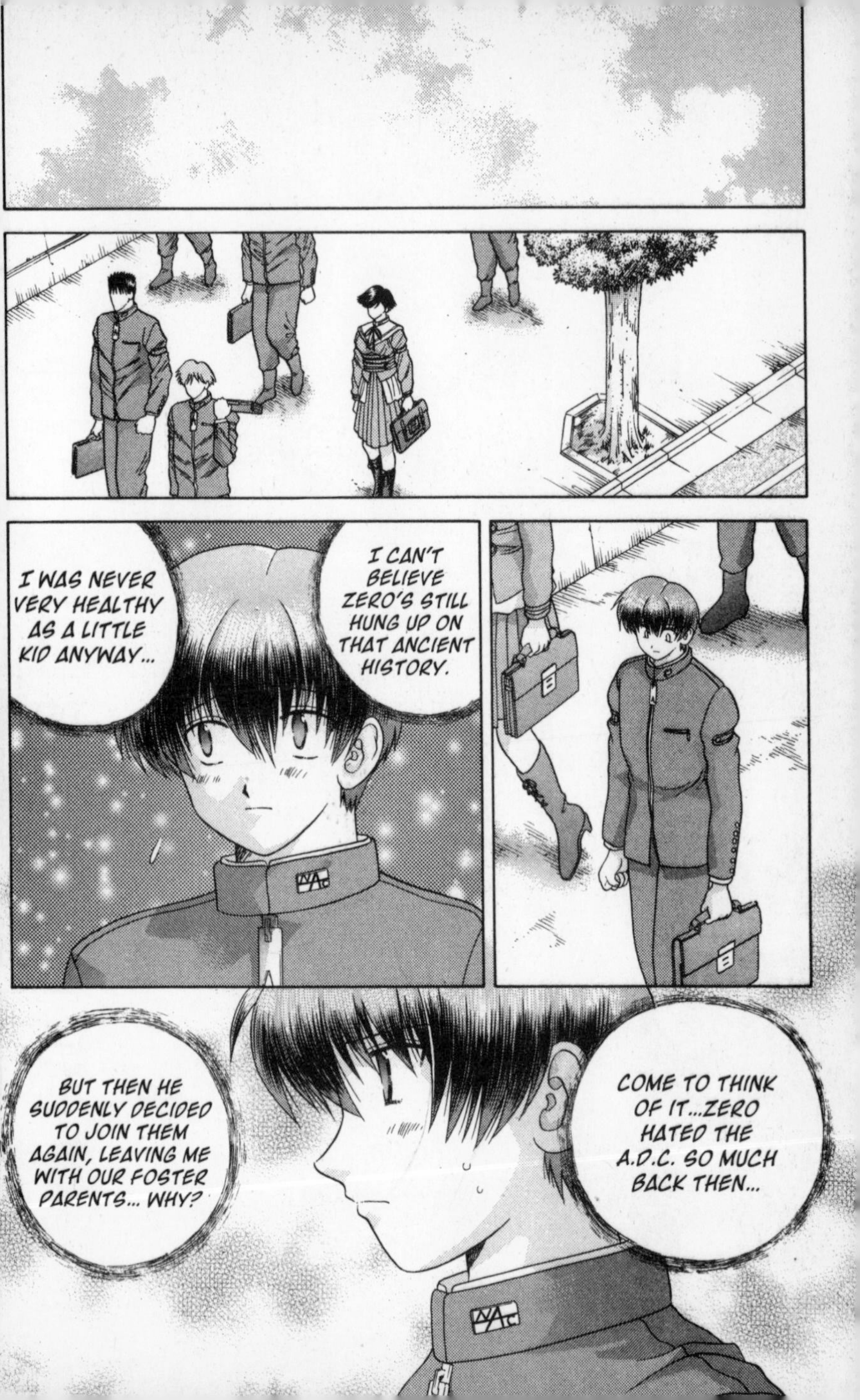
I CAN'T BELIEVE ZERO'S STILL HUNG UP ON THAT ANCIENT HISTORY.
I WAS NEVER VERY HEALTHY AS A LITTLE KID ANYWAY...
COME TO THINK OF IT...ZERO HATED THE A.D.C. SO MUCH BACK THEN...
BUT THEN HE SUDDENLY DECIDED TO JOIN THEM AGAIN, LEAVING ME WITH OUR FOSTER PARENTS... WHY?

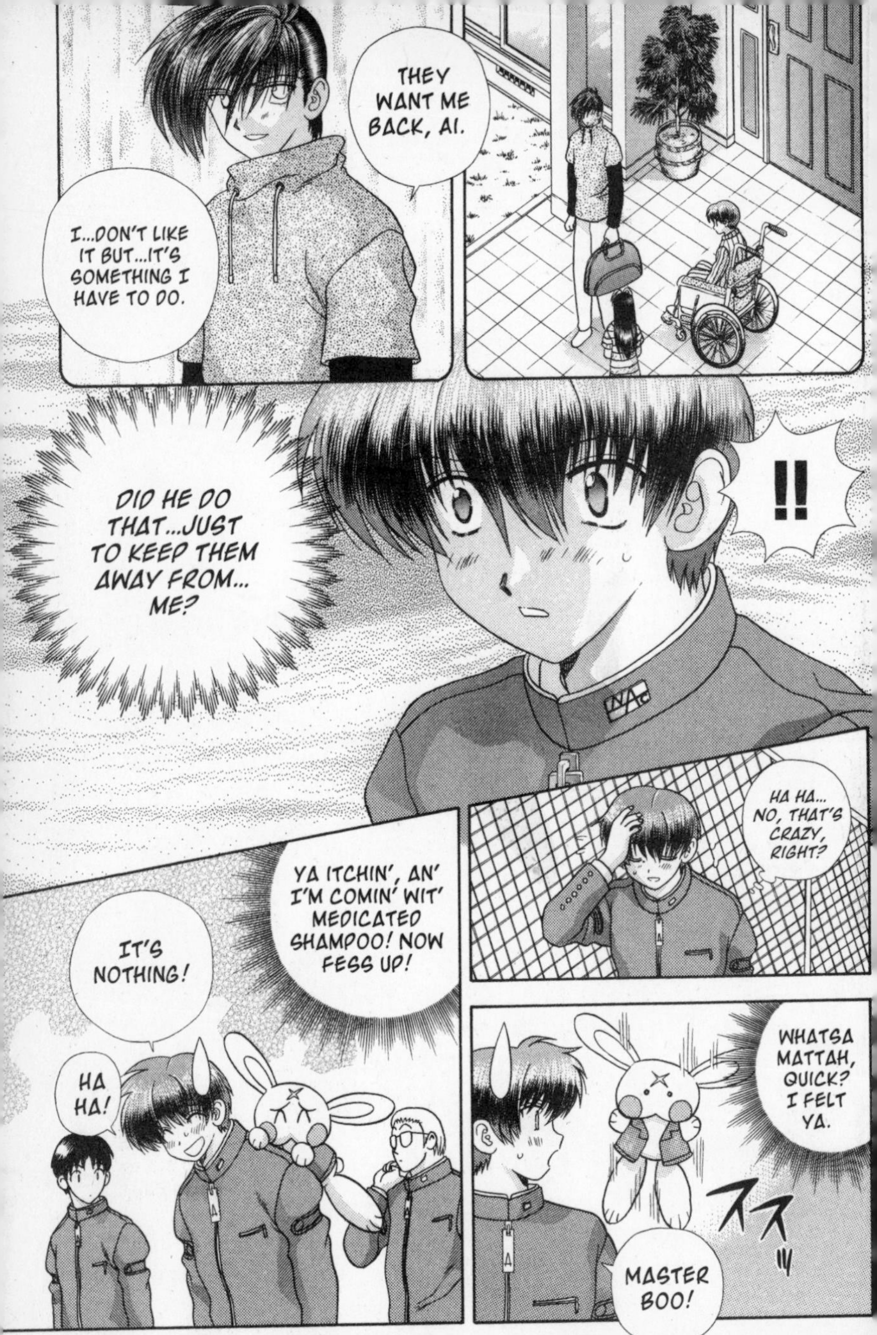
THEY WANT ME BACK, AI.
I...DON'T LIKE IT BUT...IT'S SOMETHING I HAVE TO DO.
!!
DID HE DO THAT...JUST TO KEEP THEM AWAY FROM... ME?
HA HA... NO, THAT'S CRAZY, RIGHT?
WHATSA MATTAH, QUICK? I FELT YA.
ススッ
MASTER BOO!
YA ITCHIN', AN' I'M COMIN' WIT' MEDICATED SHAMPOO! NOW FESS UP!
IT'S NOTHING!
HA HA!

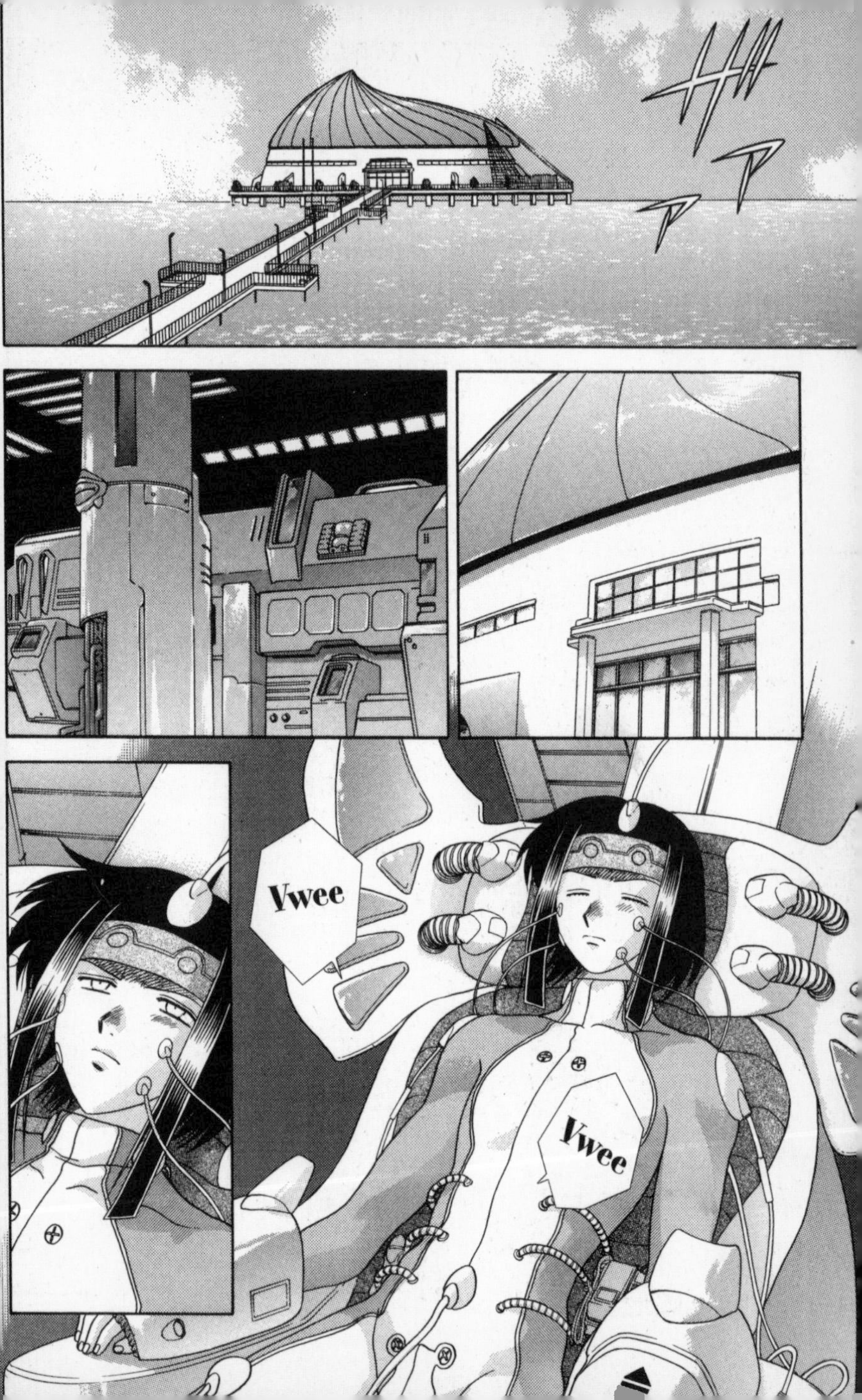
Vwee
Vwee

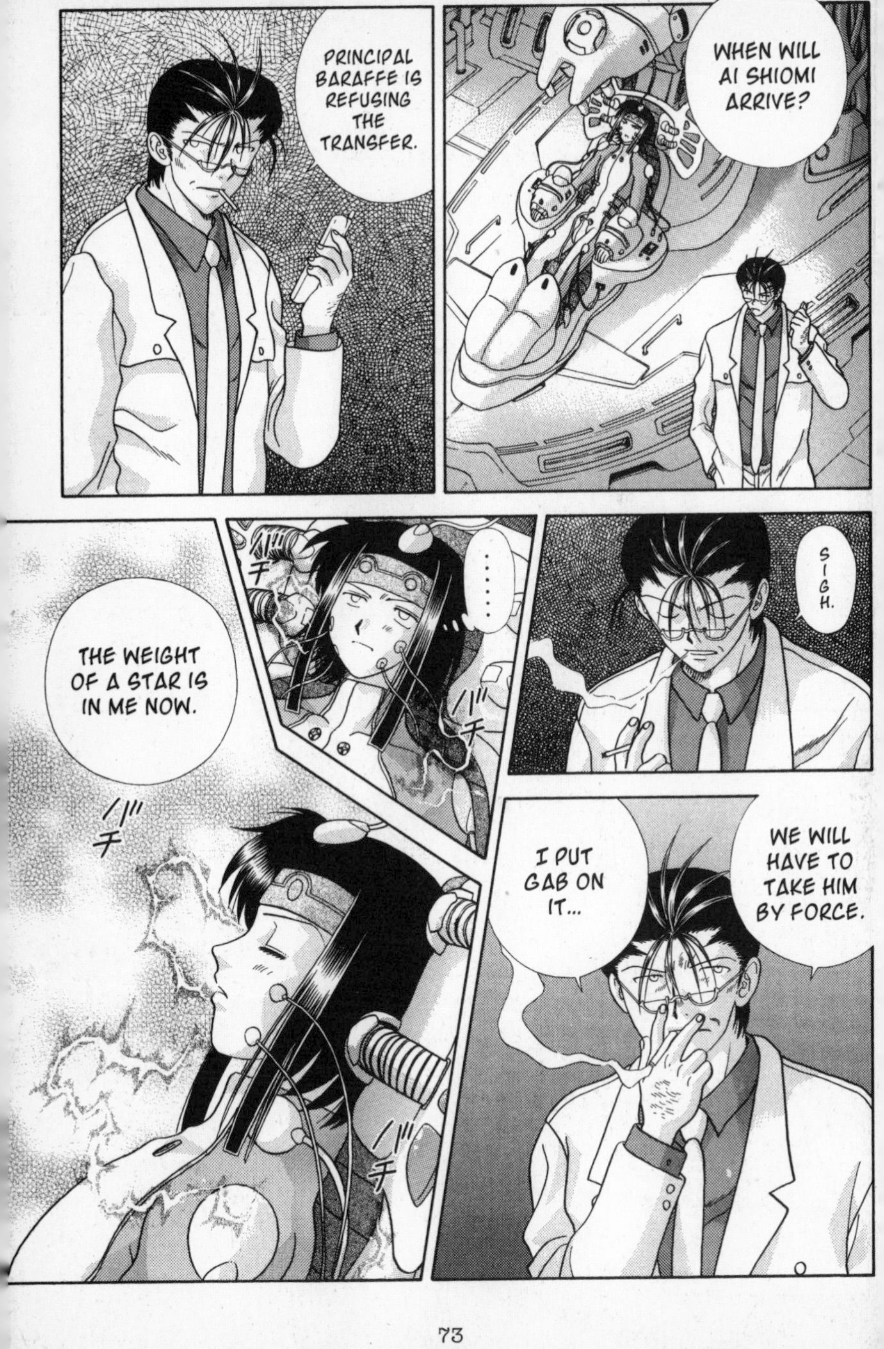
WHEN WILL AI SHIOMI ARRIVE?
PRINCIPAL BARAFFE IS REFUSING THE TRANSFER.
SIGH.
......
バチ
バチ
WE WILL HAVE TO TAKE HIM BY FORCE.
I PUT GAB ON IT...
THE WEIGHT OF A STAR IS IN ME NOW.
バチ
バチ

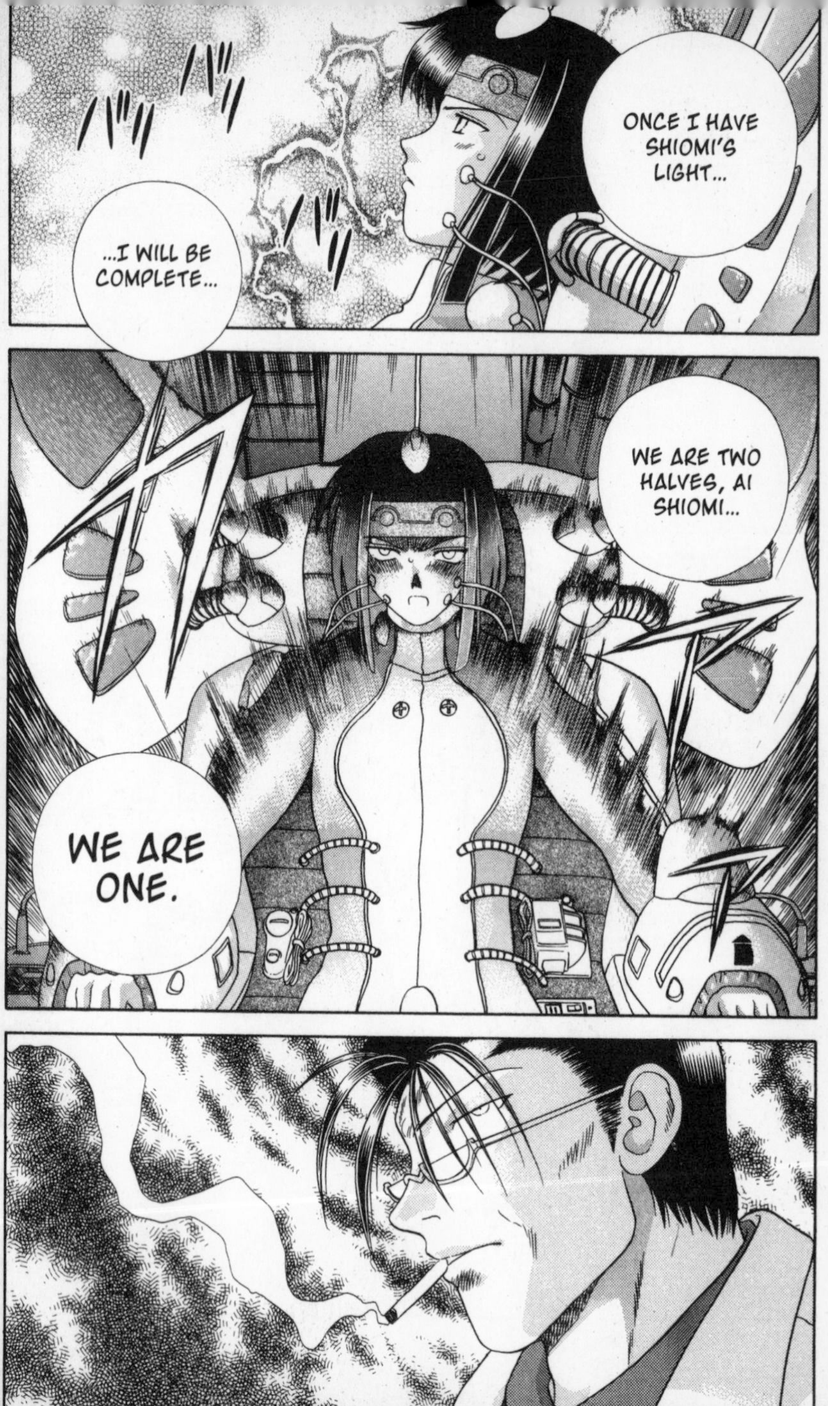
ONCE I HAVE SHIOMI'S LIGHT...
...I WILL BE COMPLETE...
WE ARE TWO HALVES, AI SHIOMI...
WE ARE ONE.

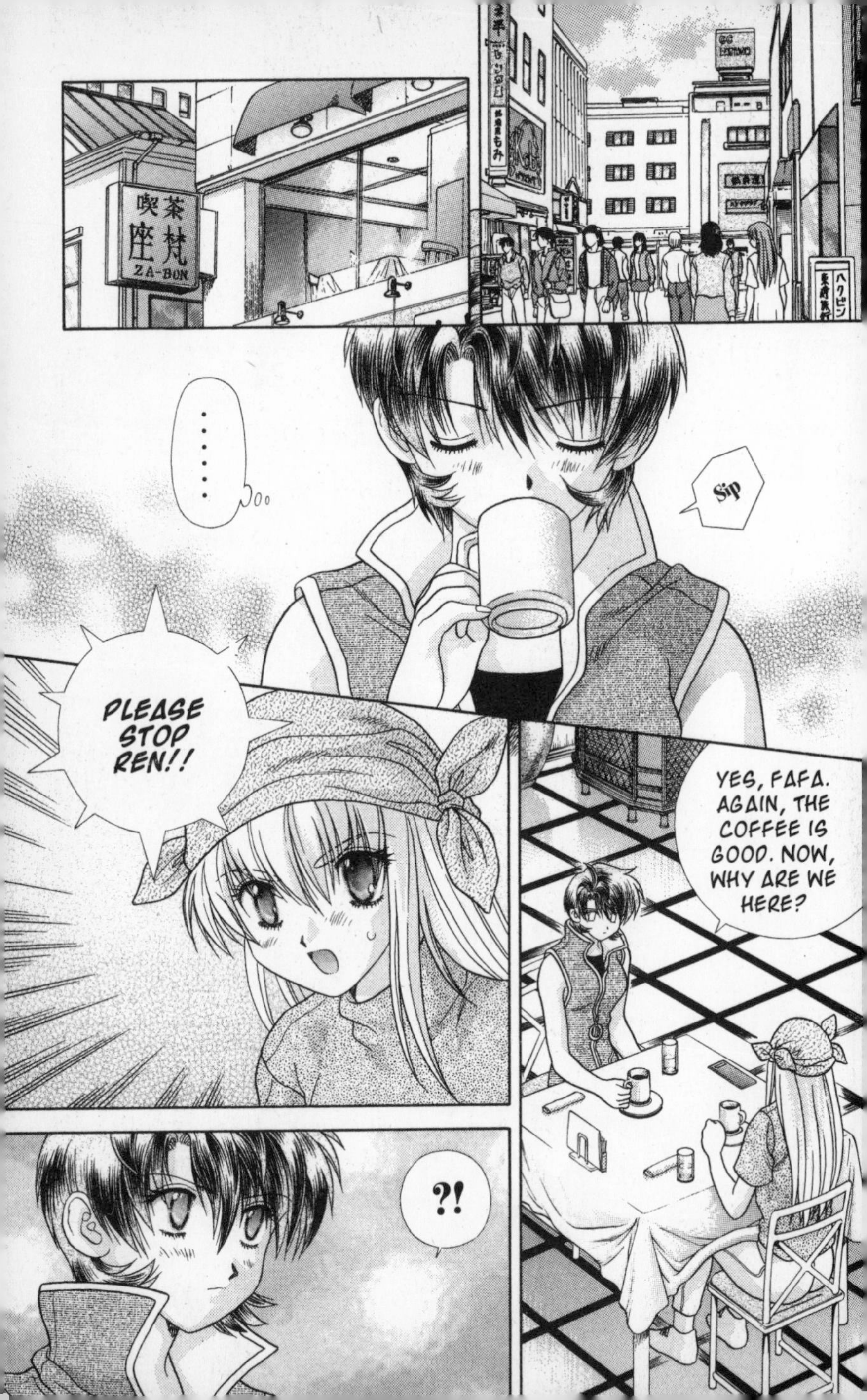
喫茶
座梵
ZA-BUN
......
Sip
YES, FAFA. AGAIN, THE COFFEE IS GOOD. NOW, WHY ARE WE HERE?
PLEASE STOP REN!!
?!

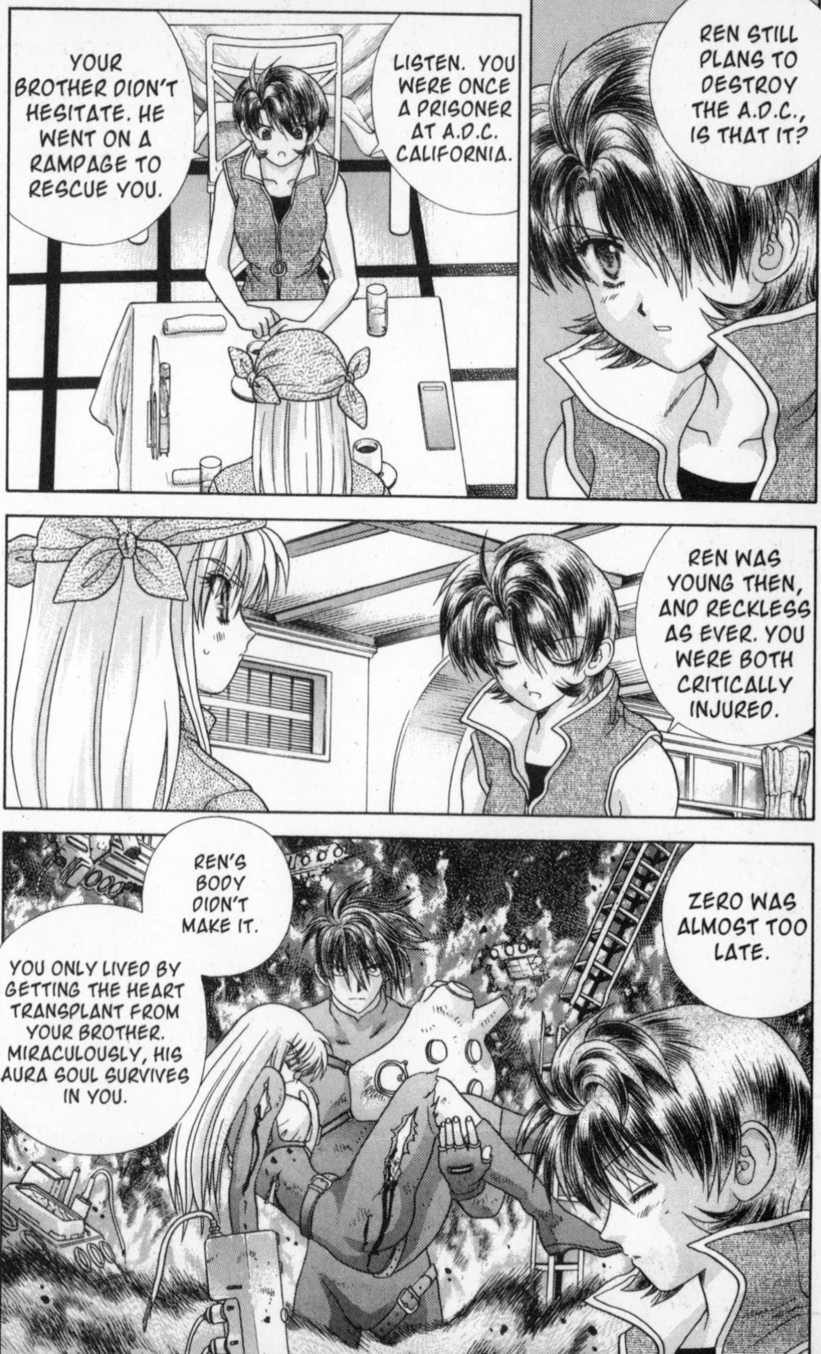
REN STILL PLANS TO DESTROY THE A.D.C., IS THAT IT?
LISTEN. YOU WERE ONCE A PRISONER AT A.D.C. CALIFORNIA.
YOUR BROTHER DIDN'T HESITATE. HE WENT ON A RAMPAGE TO RESCUE YOU.
REN WAS YOUNG THEN, AND RECKLESS AS EVER. YOU WERE BOTH CRITICALLY INJURED.
ZERO WAS ALMOST TOO LATE.
REN'S BODY DIDN'T MAKE IT.
YOU ONLY LIVED BY GETTING THE HEART TRANSPLANT FROM YOUR BROTHER. MIRACULOUSLY, HIS AURA SOUL SURVIVES IN YOU.

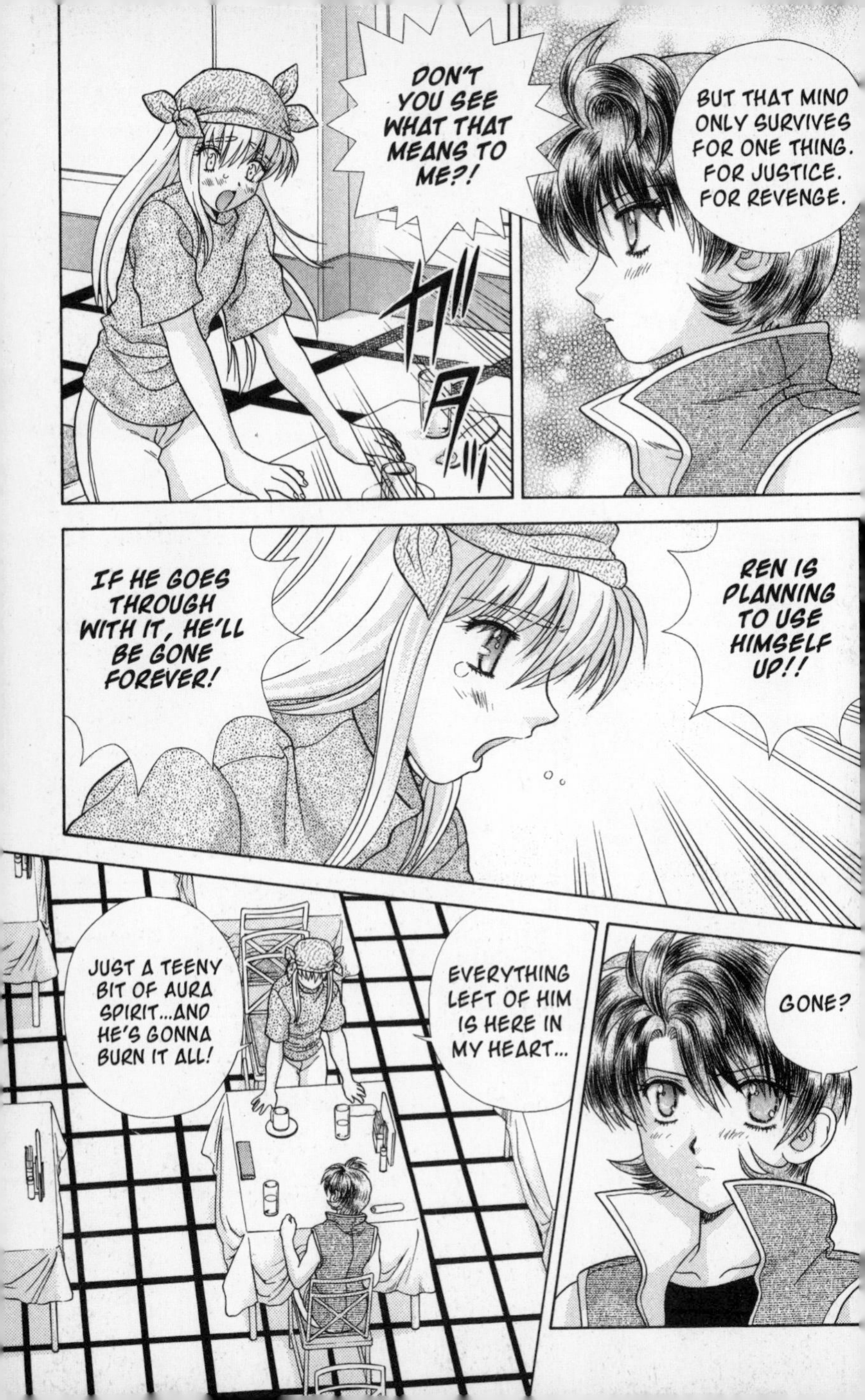
BUT THAT MIND ONLY SURVIVES FOR ONE THING. FOR JUSTICE. FOR REVENGE.
DON'T YOU SEE WHAT THAT MEANS TO ME?!
ガタ
REN IS PLANNING TO USE HIMSELF UP!!
IF HE GOES THROUGH WITH IT, HE'LL BE GONE FOREVER!
GONE?
EVERYTHING LEFT OF HIM IS HERE IN MY HEART...
JUST A TEENY BIT OF AURA SPIRIT...AND HE'S GONNA BURN IT ALL!

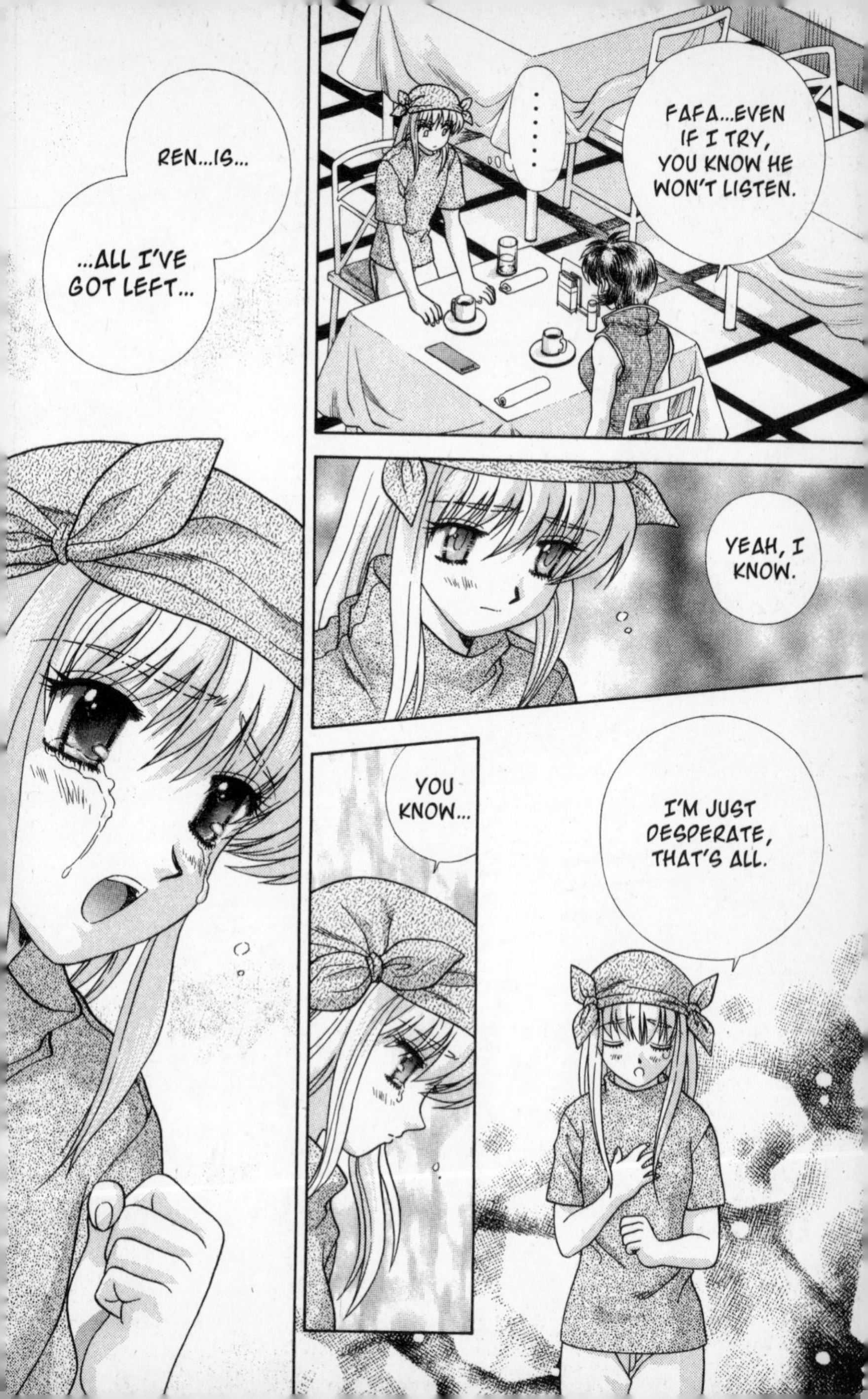
FAFA...EVEN IF I TRY, YOU KNOW HE WON'T LISTEN.
......
YEAH, I KNOW.
I'M JUST DESPERATE, THAT'S ALL.
YOU KNOW...
REN...IS...
...ALL I'VE GOT LEFT...

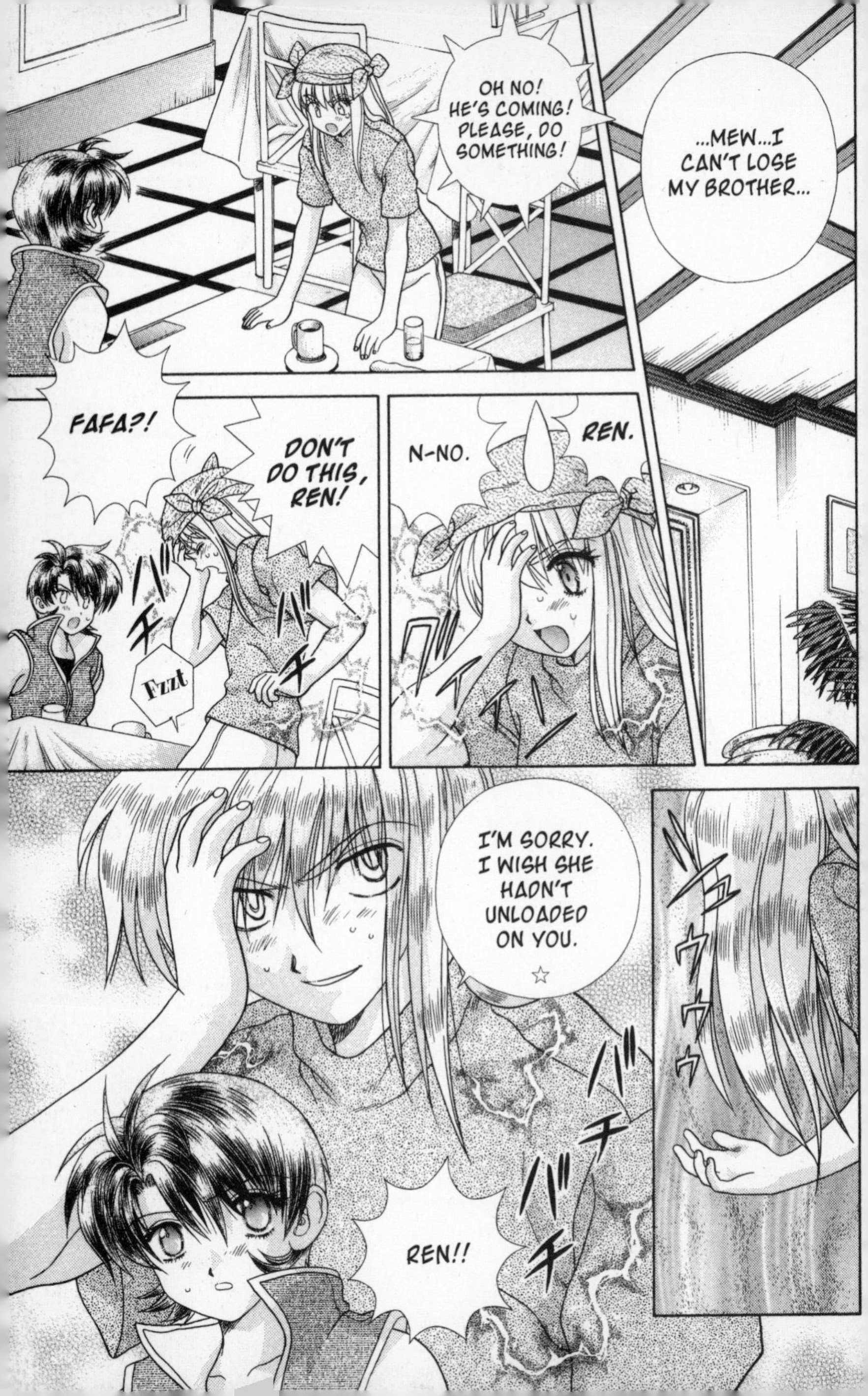
...MEW...I CAN'T LOSE MY BROTHER...
OH NO! HE'S COMING! PLEASE, DO SOMETHING!
REN.
N-NO.
DON'T DO THIS, REN!
FAFA?!
Fzzt
I'M SORRY. I WISH SHE HADN'T UNLOADED ON YOU. ☆
REN!!

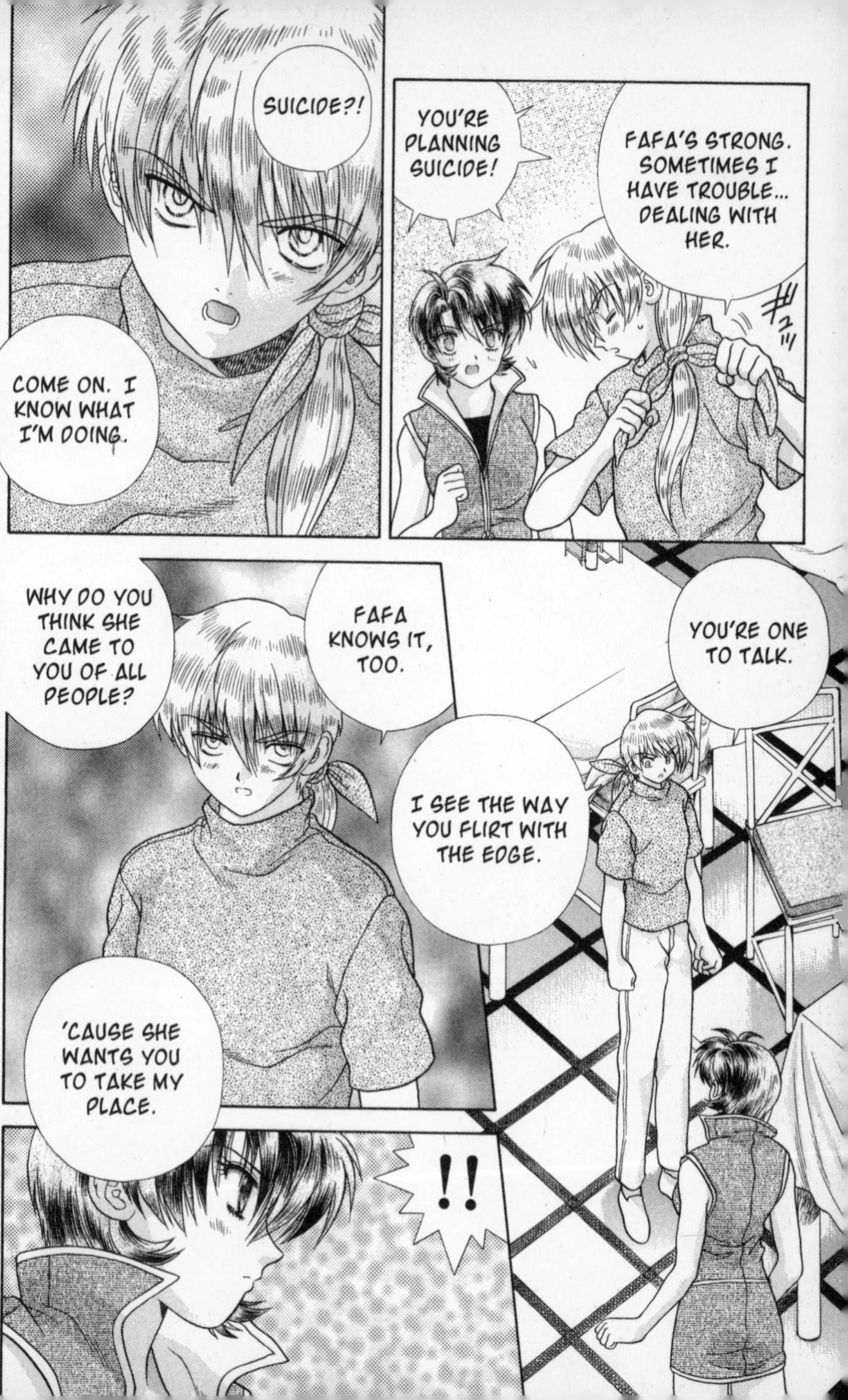
FAFA'S STRONG. SOMETIMES I HAVE TROUBLE... DEALING WITH HER.
YOU'RE PLANNING SUICIDE!
SUICIDE?!
COME ON. I KNOW WHAT I'M DOING.
YOU'RE ONE TO TALK.
I SEE THE WAY YOU FLIRT WITH THE EDGE.
FAFA KNOWS IT, TOO.
WHY DO YOU THINK SHE CAME TO YOU OF ALL PEOPLE?
'CAUSE SHE WANTS YOU TO TAKE MY PLACE.
!!

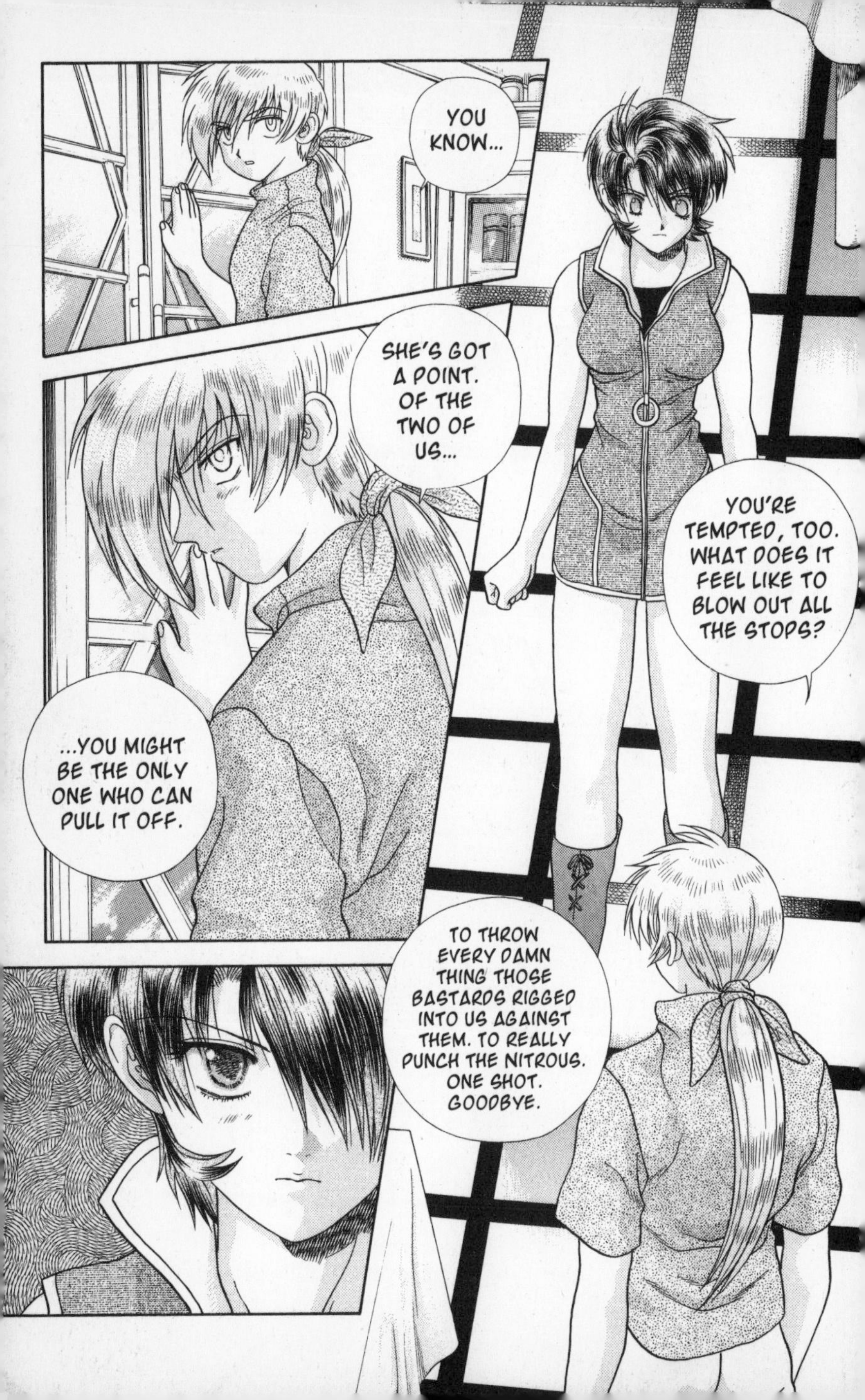
YOU'RE TEMPTED, TOO. WHAT DOES IT FEEL LIKE TO BLOW OUT ALL THE STOPS?
TO THROW EVERY DAMN THING THOSE BASTARDS RIGGED INTO US AGAINST THEM. TO REALLY PUNCH THE NITROUS. ONE SHOT. GOODBYE.
YOU KNOW...
SHE'S GOT A POINT. OF THE TWO OF US...
...YOU MIGHT BE THE ONLY ONE WHO CAN PULL IT OFF.

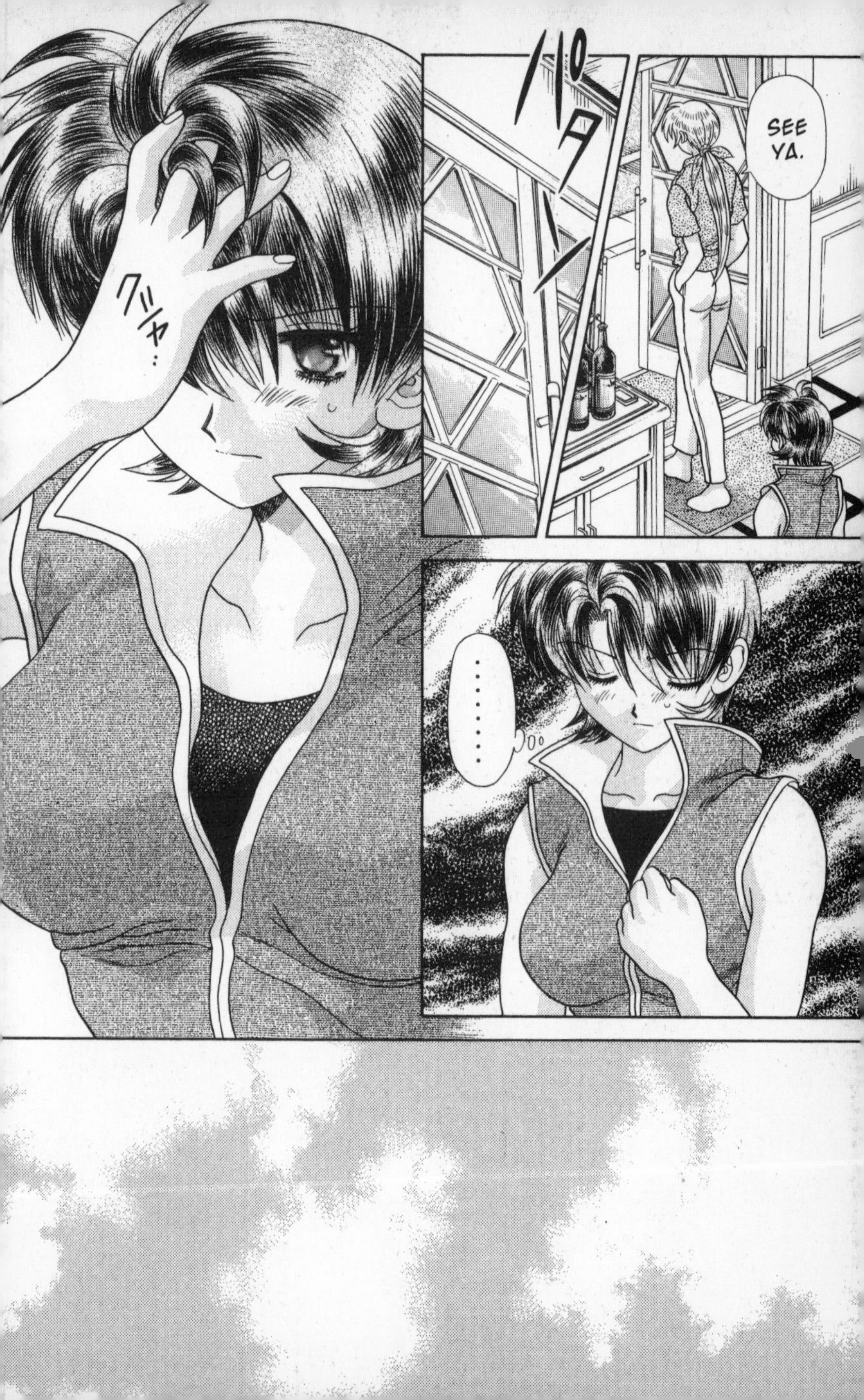
SEE YA.
パタン
....
クシャ..

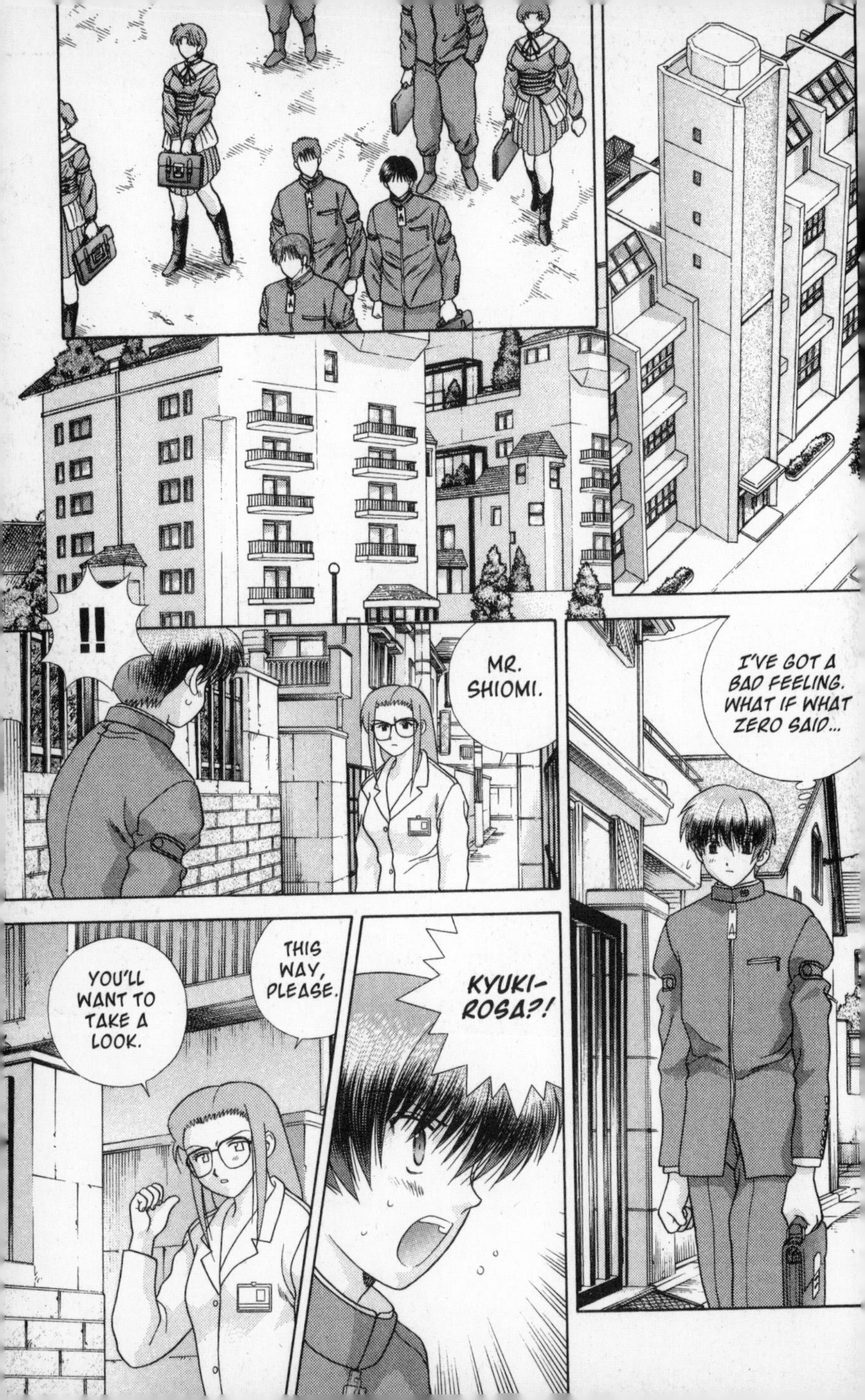
I'VE GOT A BAD FEELING. WHAT IF WHAT ZERO SAID...
MR. SHIOMI.
!!
KYUKI-ROSA?!
THIS WAY, PLEASE.
YOU'LL WANT TO TAKE A LOOK.

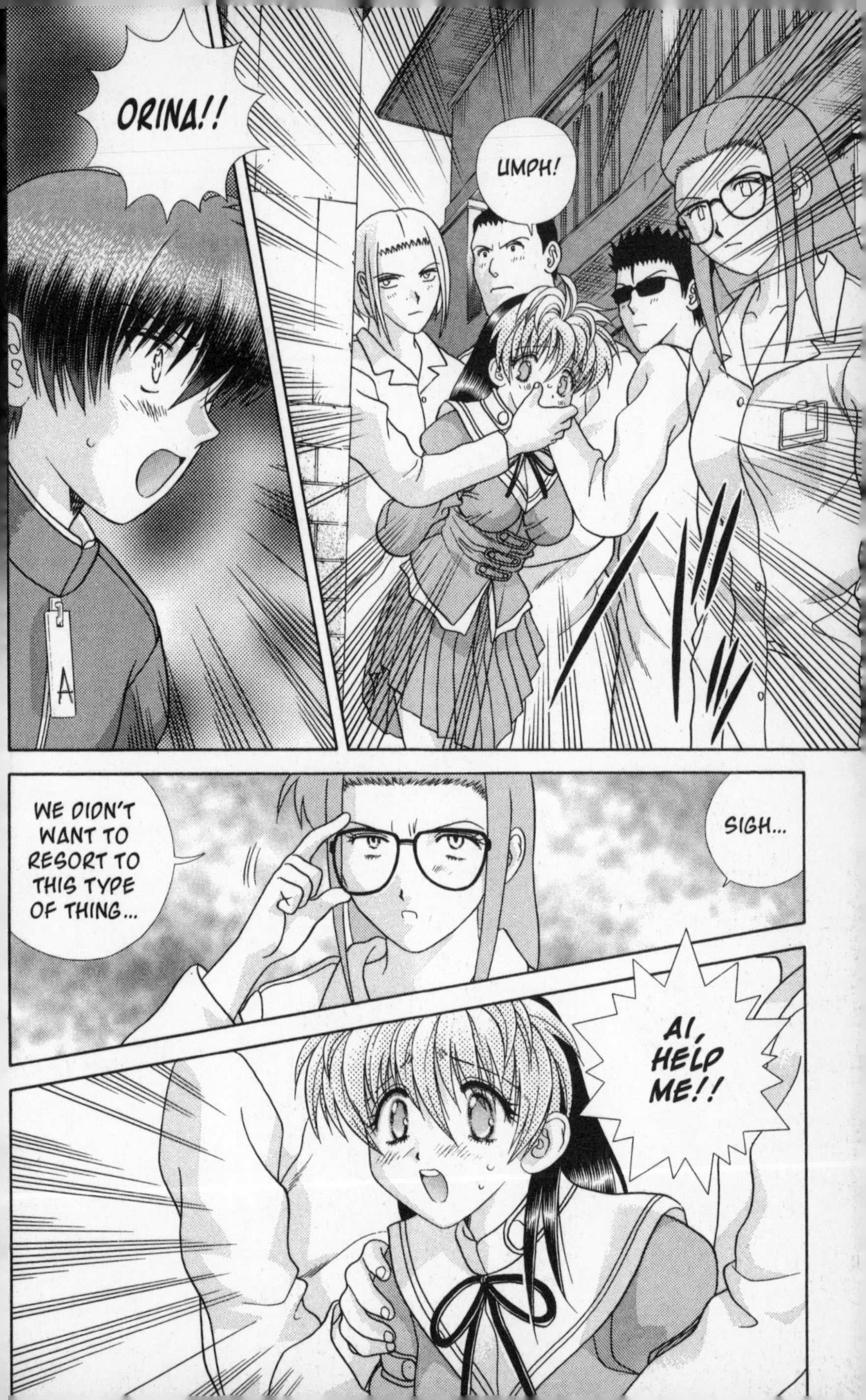
UMPH!
ORINA!!
SIGH...
WE DIDN'T WANT TO RESORT TO THIS TYPE OF THING...
AI, HELP ME!!

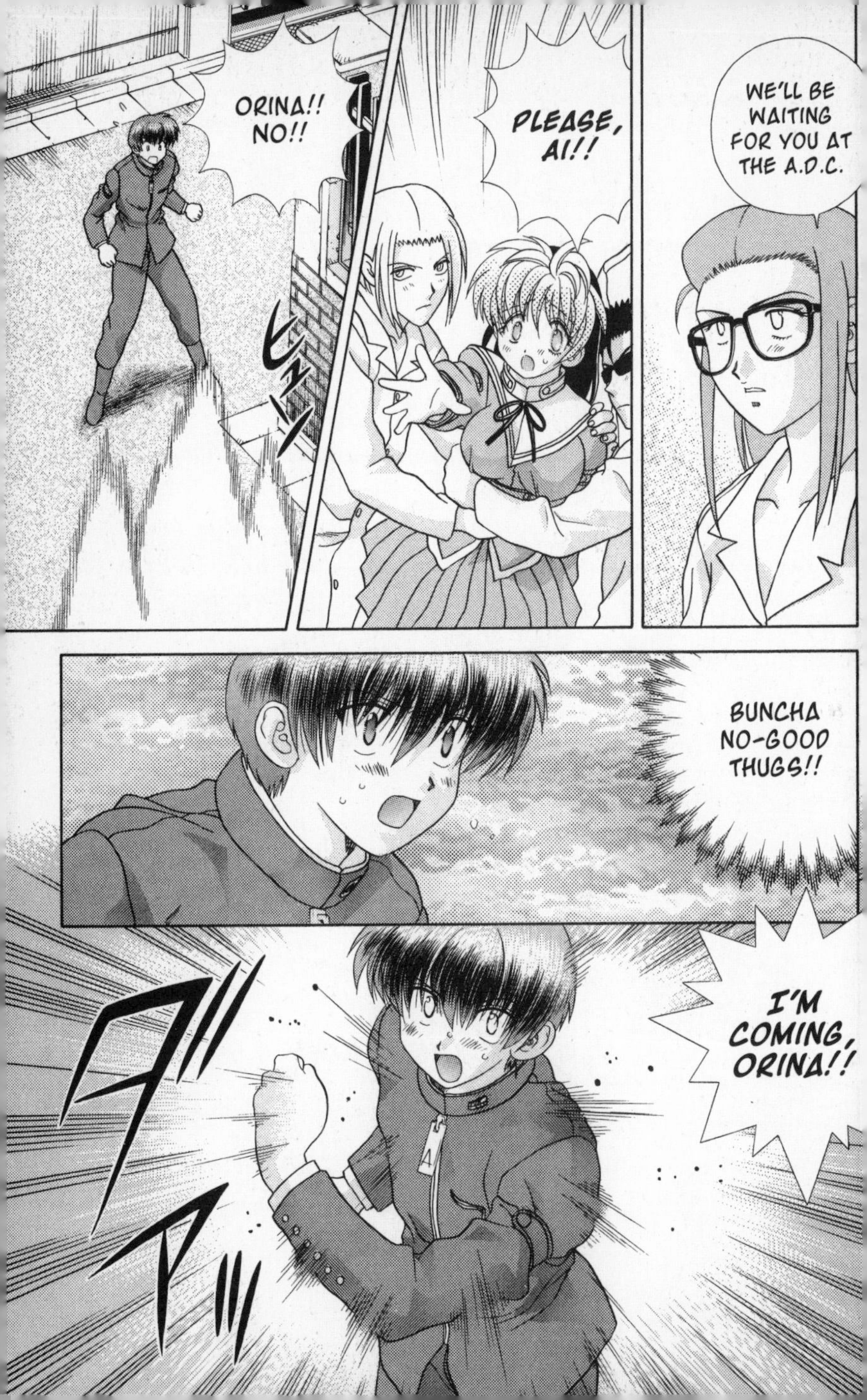
WE'LL BE WAITING FOR YOU AT THE A.D.C.
PLEASE, AI!!
ビュン
ORINA!! NO!!
BUNCHA NO-GOOD THUGS!!
I'M COMING, ORINA!!

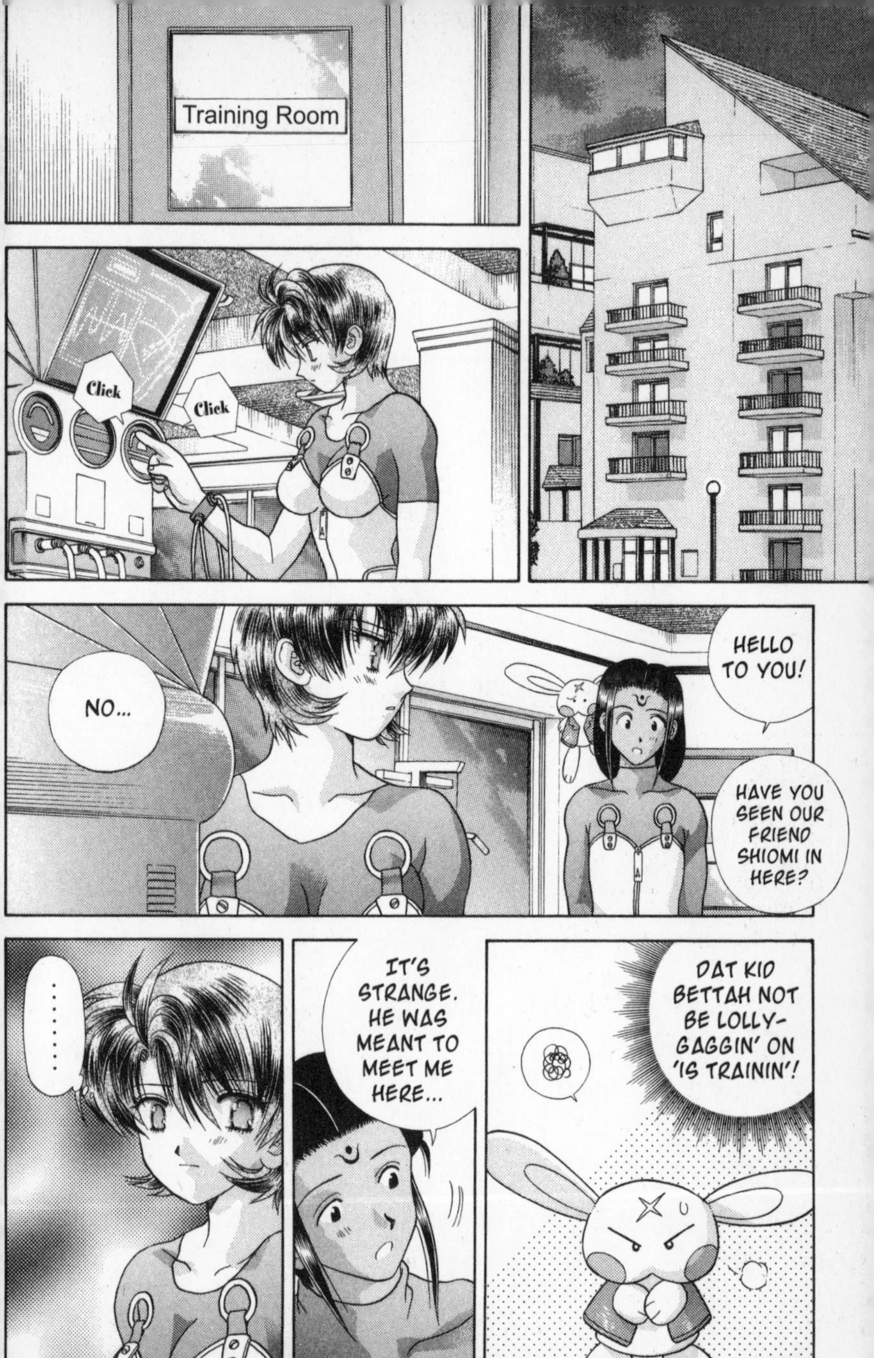
Training Room
Click
Click
HELLO TO YOU!
HAVE YOU SEEN OUR FRIEND SHIOMI IN HERE?
NO...
DAT KID BETTAH NOT BE LOLLY-GAGGIN' ON 'IS TRAININ'!
IT'S STRANGE. HE WAS MEANT TO MEET ME HERE...
......

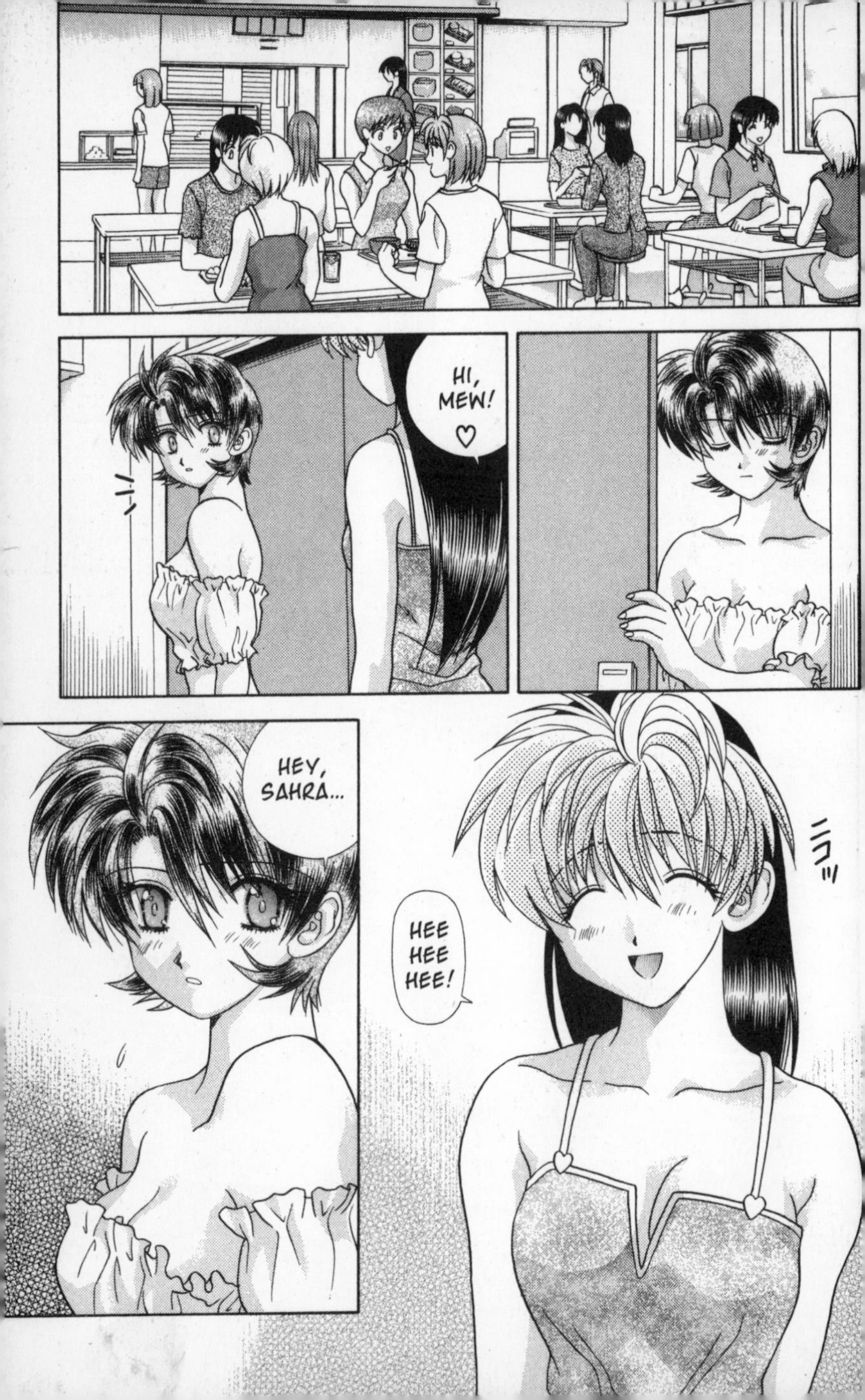
HI, MEW! ♡
ニコッ
HEE HEE HEE!
HEY, SAHRA...

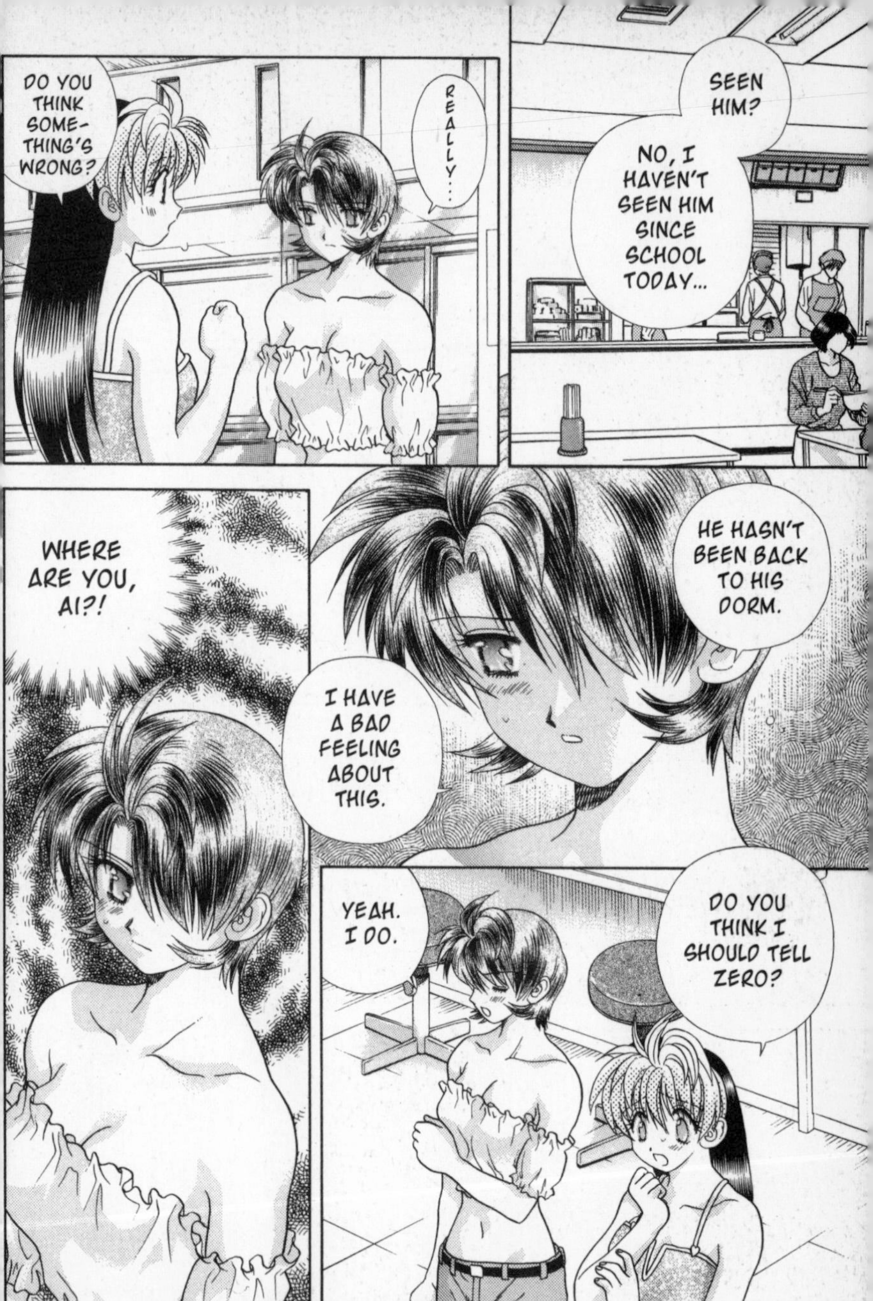
SEEN HIM?
NO, I HAVEN'T SEEN HIM SINCE SCHOOL TODAY...
REALLY...
DO YOU THINK SOME-THING'S WRONG?
HE HASN'T BEEN BACK TO HIS DORM.
I HAVE A BAD FEELING ABOUT THIS.
DO YOU THINK I SHOULD TELL ZERO?
YEAH. I DO.
WHERE ARE YOU, AI?!

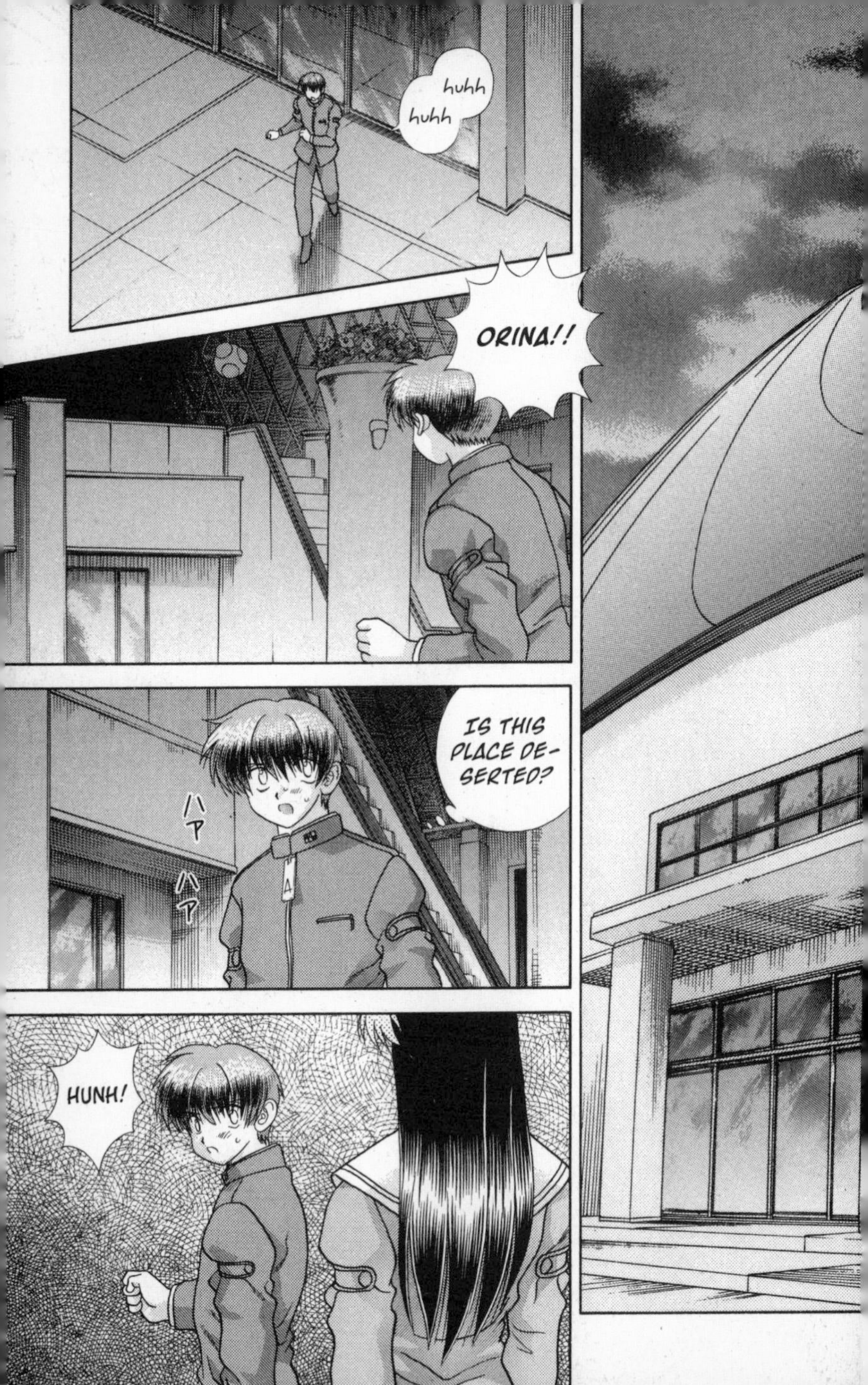
huhh huhh
ORINA!!
IS THIS PLACE DESERTED?
ハア ハア
HUNH!

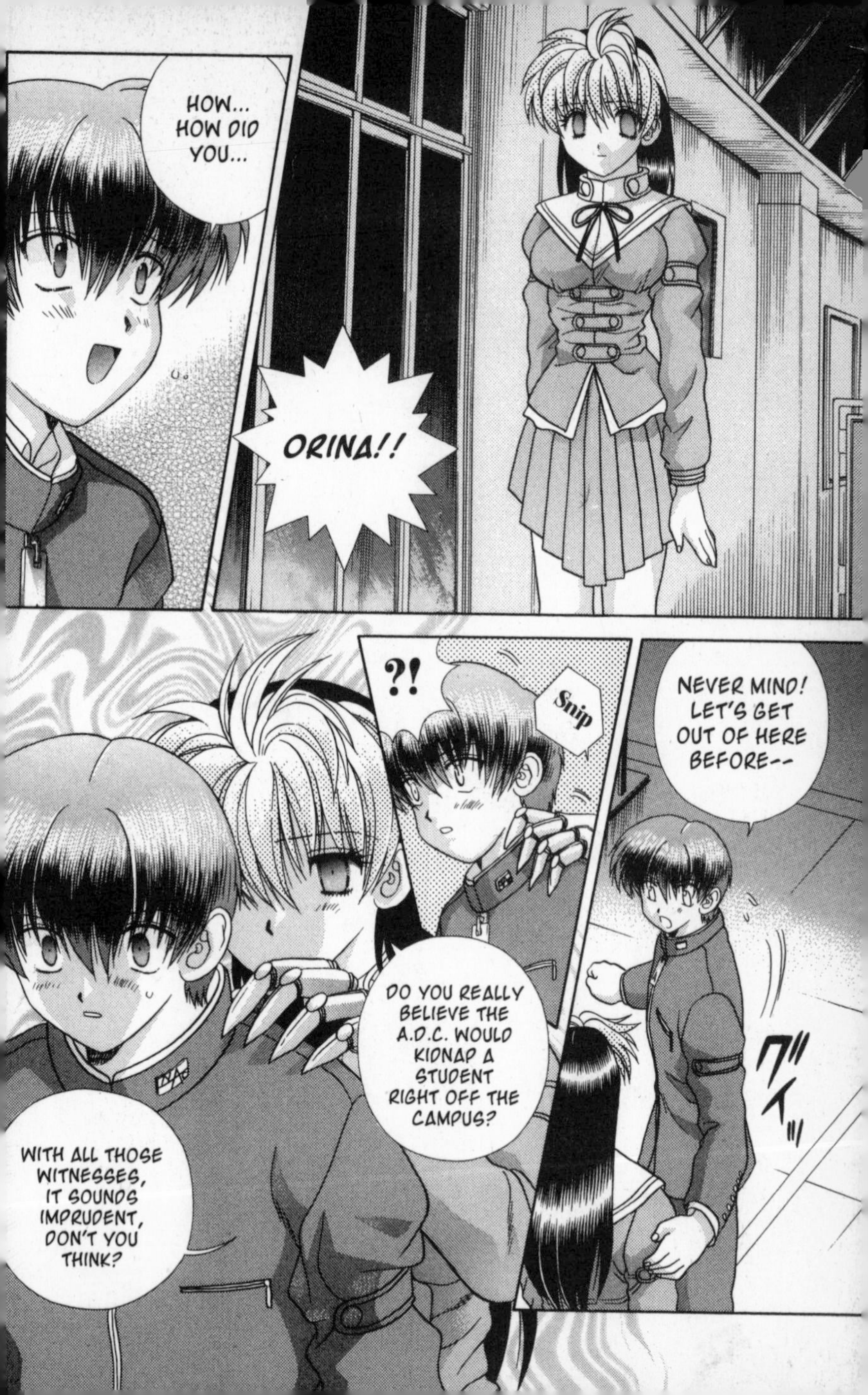
ORINA!!
HOW... HOW DID YOU...
NEVER MIND! LET'S GET OUT OF HERE BEFORE--
グイッ
?!
Snip
DO YOU REALLY BELIEVE THE A.D.C. WOULD KIDNAP A STUDENT RIGHT OFF THE CAMPUS?
WITH ALL THOSE WITNESSES, IT SOUNDS IMPRUDENT, DON'T YOU THINK?

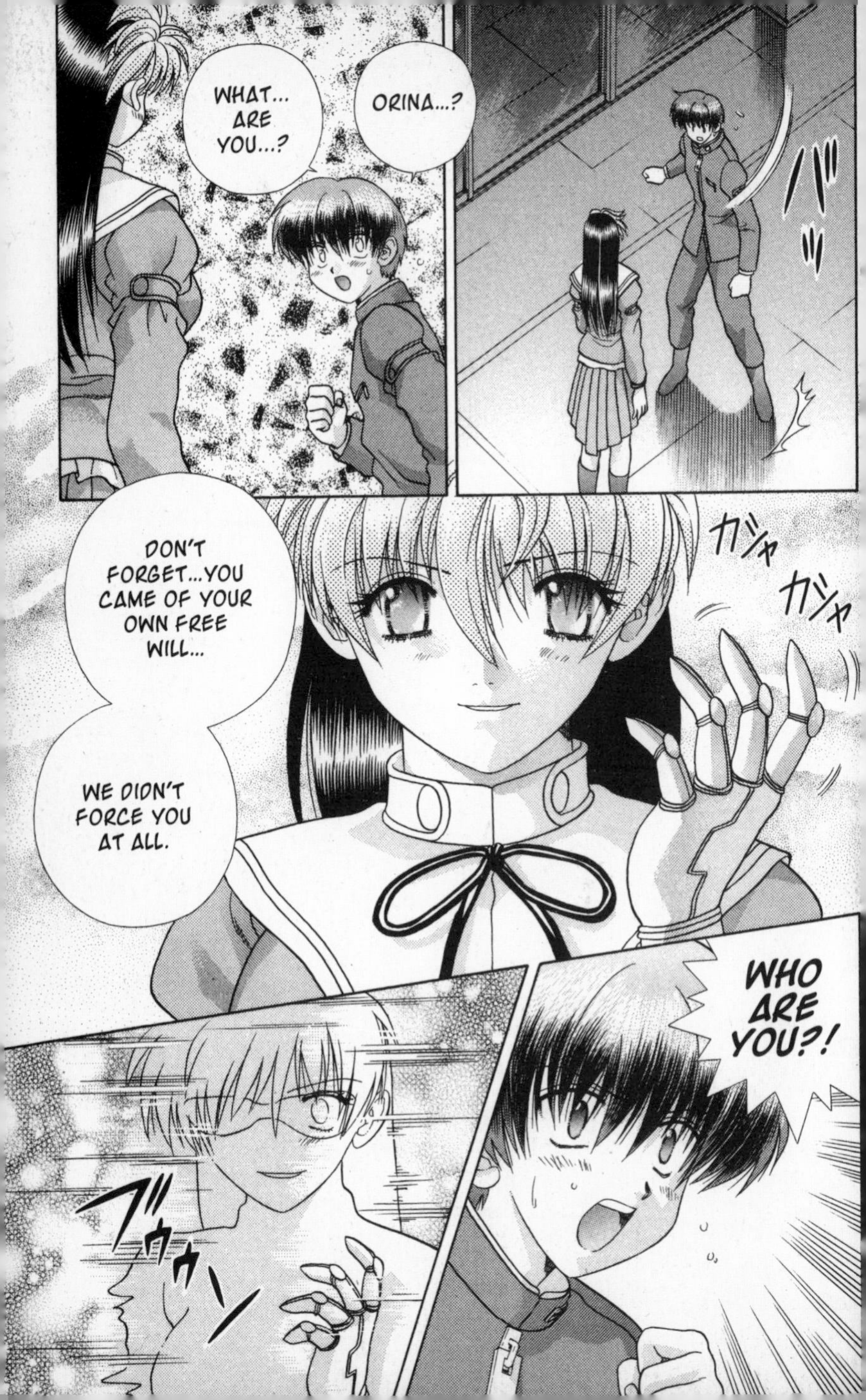
バッ
ORINA...?
WHAT... ARE YOU...?
カシャ
カシャ
DON'T FORGET...YOU CAME OF YOUR OWN FREE WILL...
WE DIDN'T FORCE YOU AT ALL.
WHO ARE YOU?!

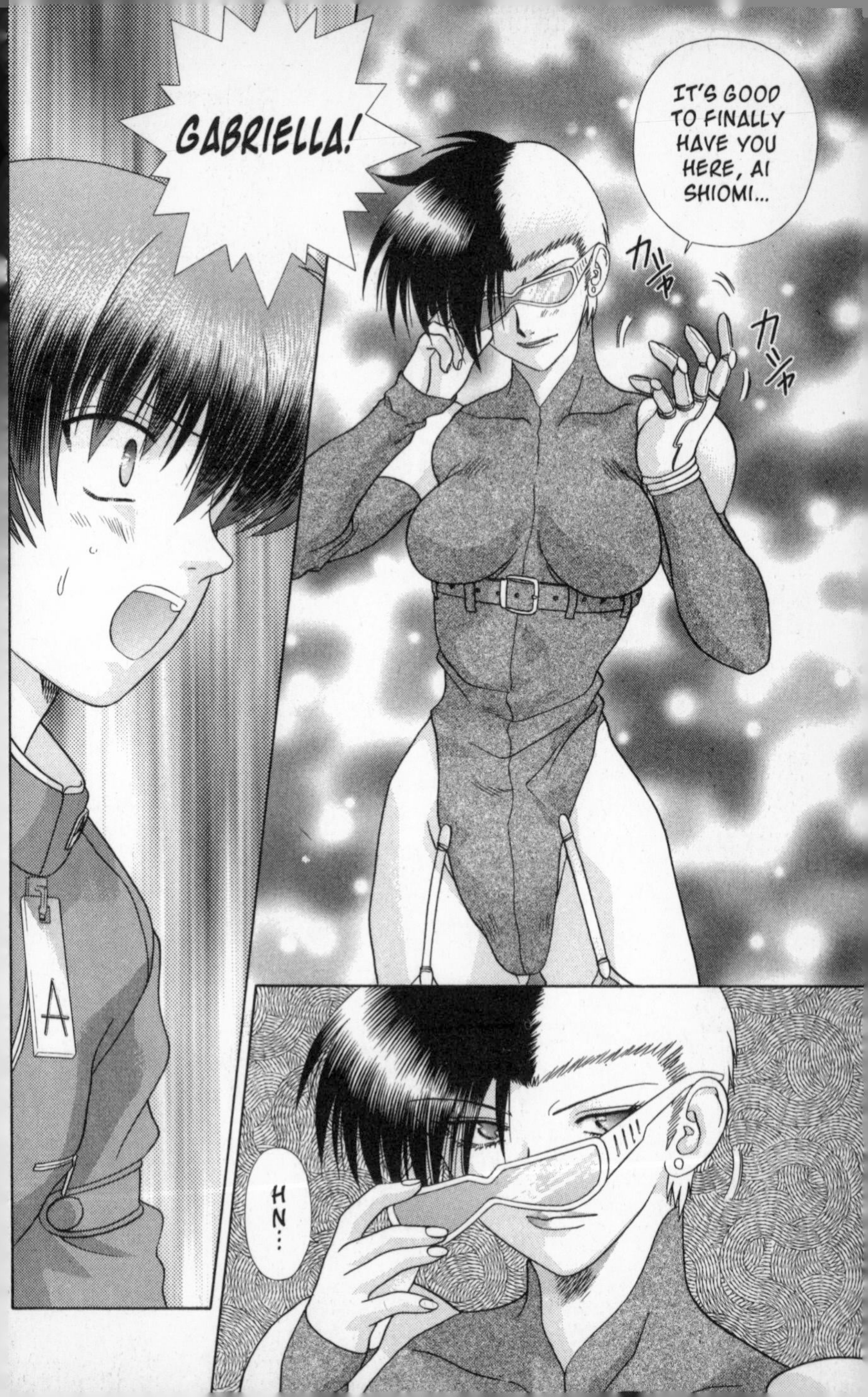
IT'S GOOD TO FINALLY HAVE YOU HERE, AI SHIOMI...
カシャ
カシャ
GABRIELLA!
HN...

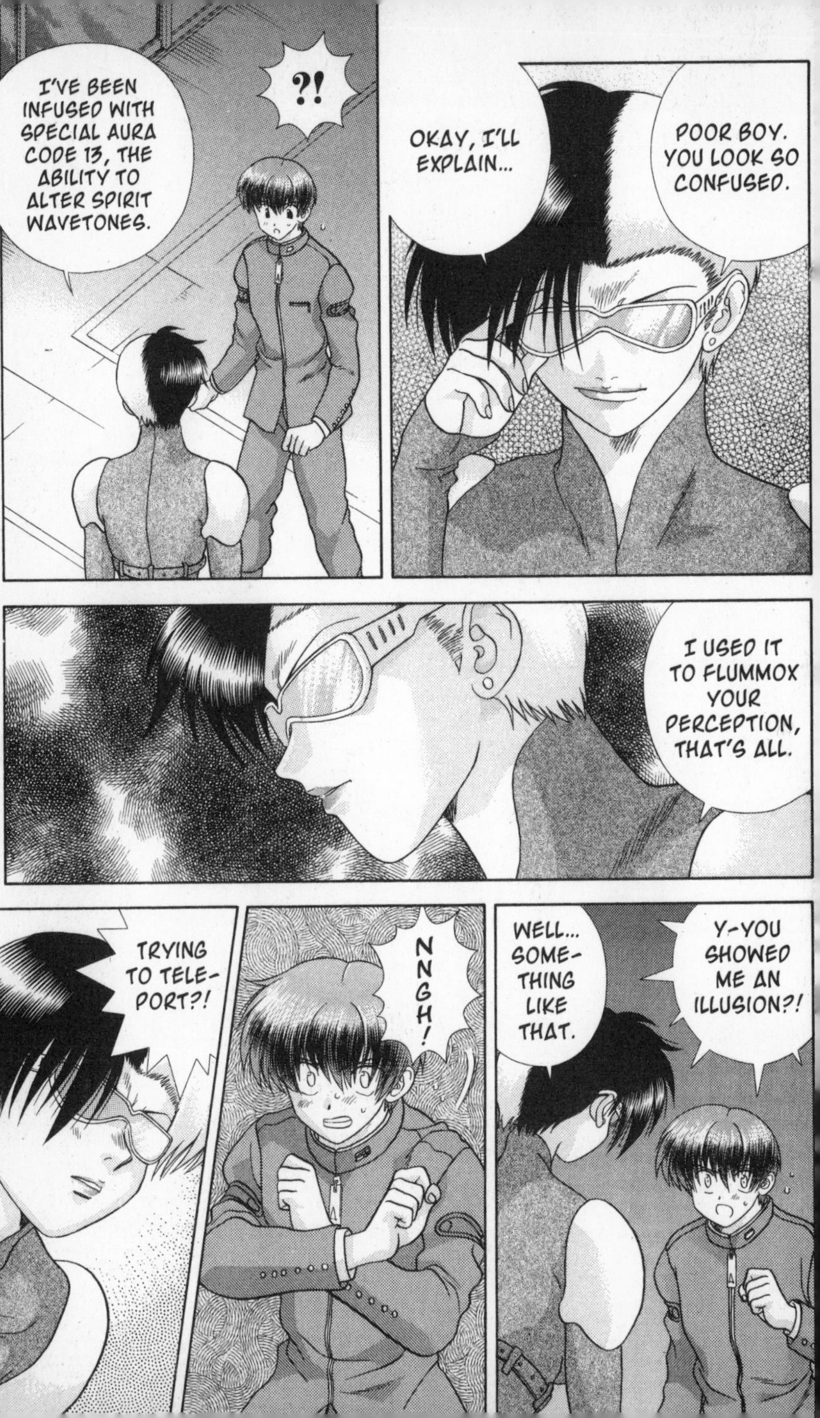
POOR BOY. YOU LOOK SO CONFUSED.
OKAY, I'LL EXPLAIN...
?!
I'VE BEEN INFUSED WITH SPECIAL AURA CODE 13, THE ABILITY TO ALTER SPIRIT WAVETONES.
I USED IT TO FLUMMOX YOUR PERCEPTION, THAT'S ALL.
Y-YOU SHOWED ME AN ILLUSION?!
WELL... SOME-THING LIKE THAT.
NNGH!
TRYING TO TELE-PORT?!

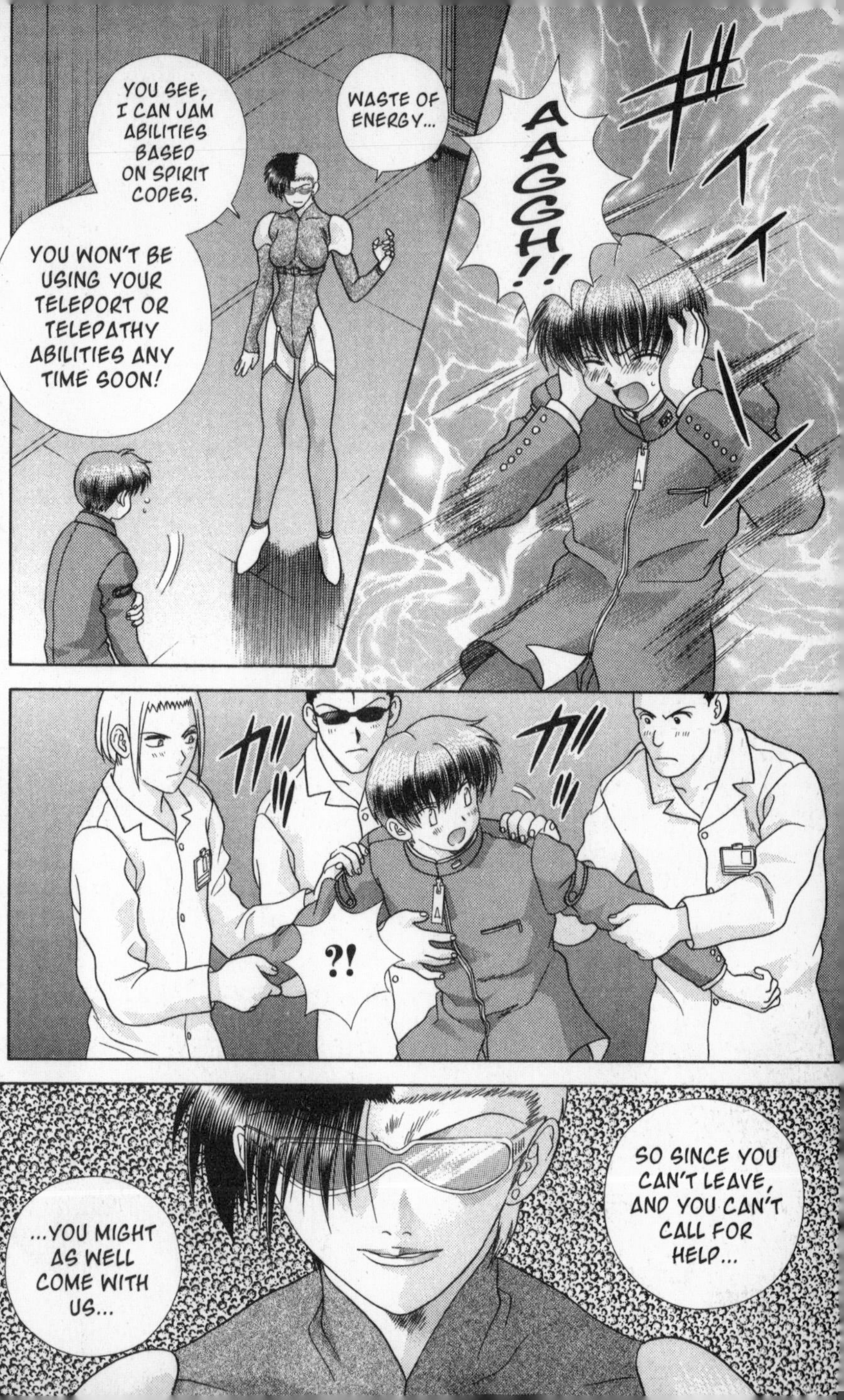
AAGGH!!
WASTE OF ENERGY...
YOU SEE, I CAN JAM ABILITIES BASED ON SPIRIT CODES.
YOU WON'T BE USING YOUR TELEPORT OR TELEPATHY ABILITIES ANY TIME SOON!
?!
SO SINCE YOU CAN'T LEAVE, AND YOU CAN'T CALL FOR HELP...
...YOU MIGHT AS WELL COME WITH US...

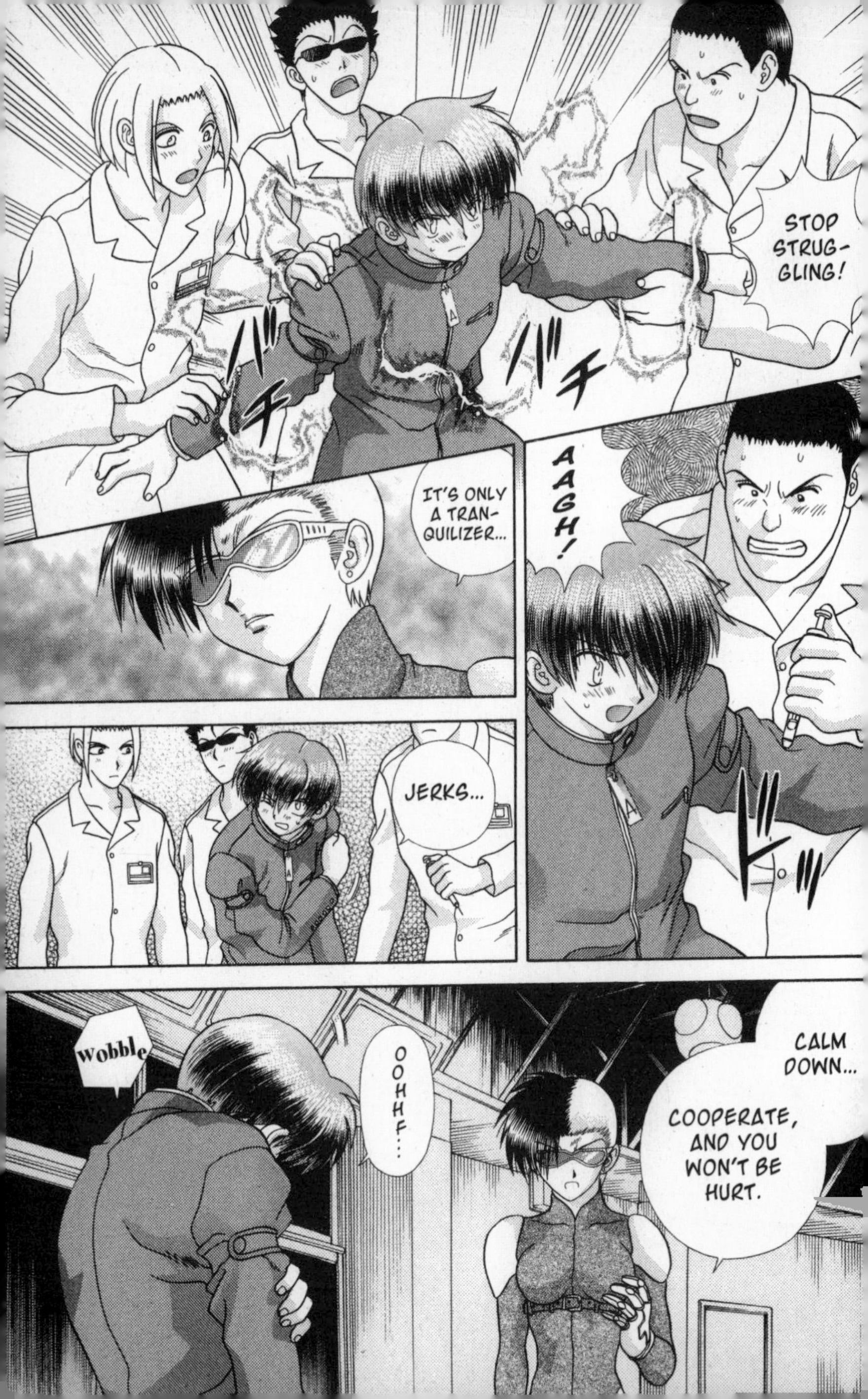
STOP STRUG-GLING!
バチ
バチ
AAGH!
ド
IT'S ONLY A TRAN-QUILIZER...
JERKS...
CALM DOWN...
COOPERATE, AND YOU WON'T BE HURT.
OOHHF...
Wobble

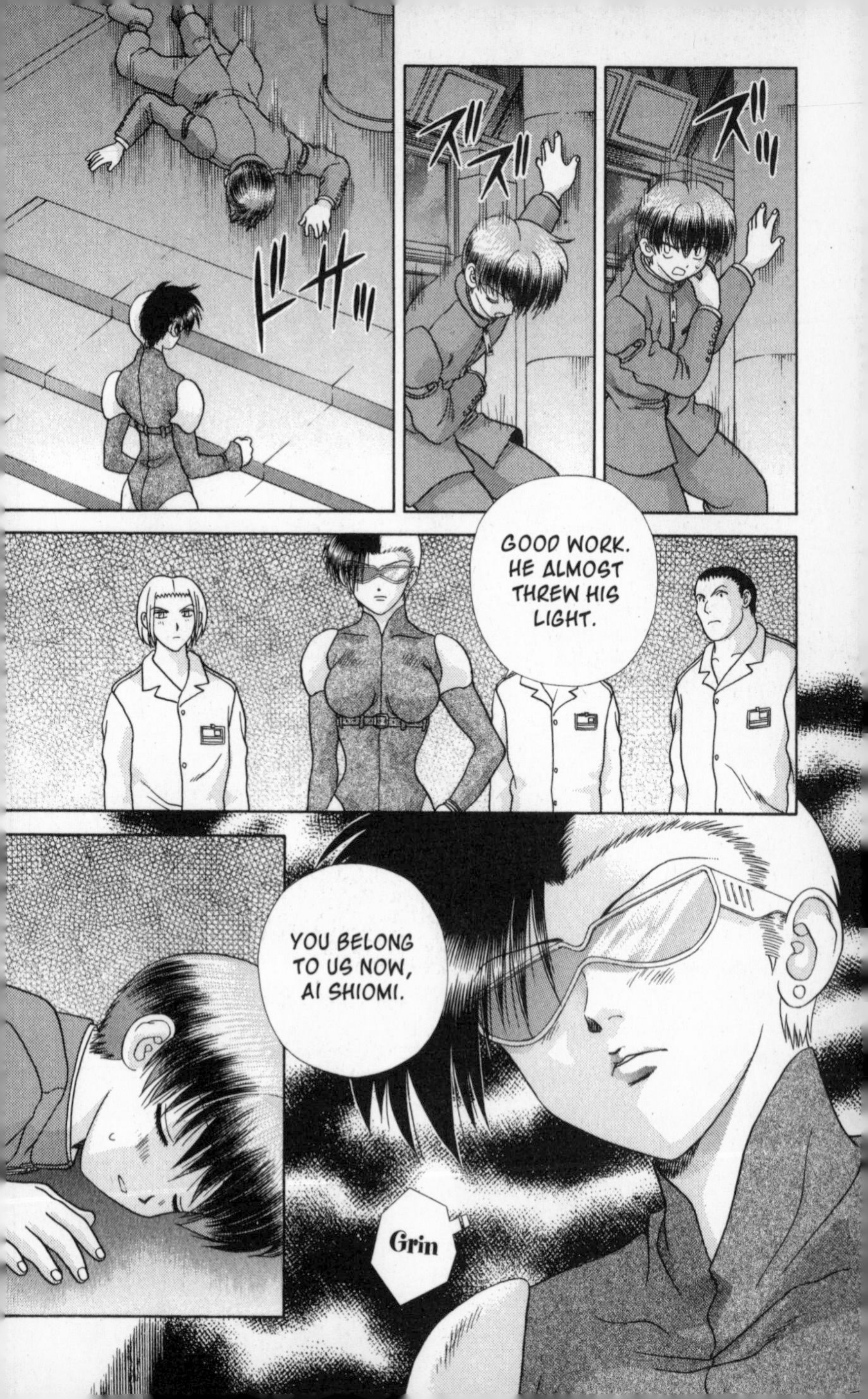
ズズ
ズズ ズズ
ドサッ
GOOD WORK. HE ALMOST THREW HIS LIGHT.
YOU BELONG TO US NOW, AI SHIOMI.
Grin

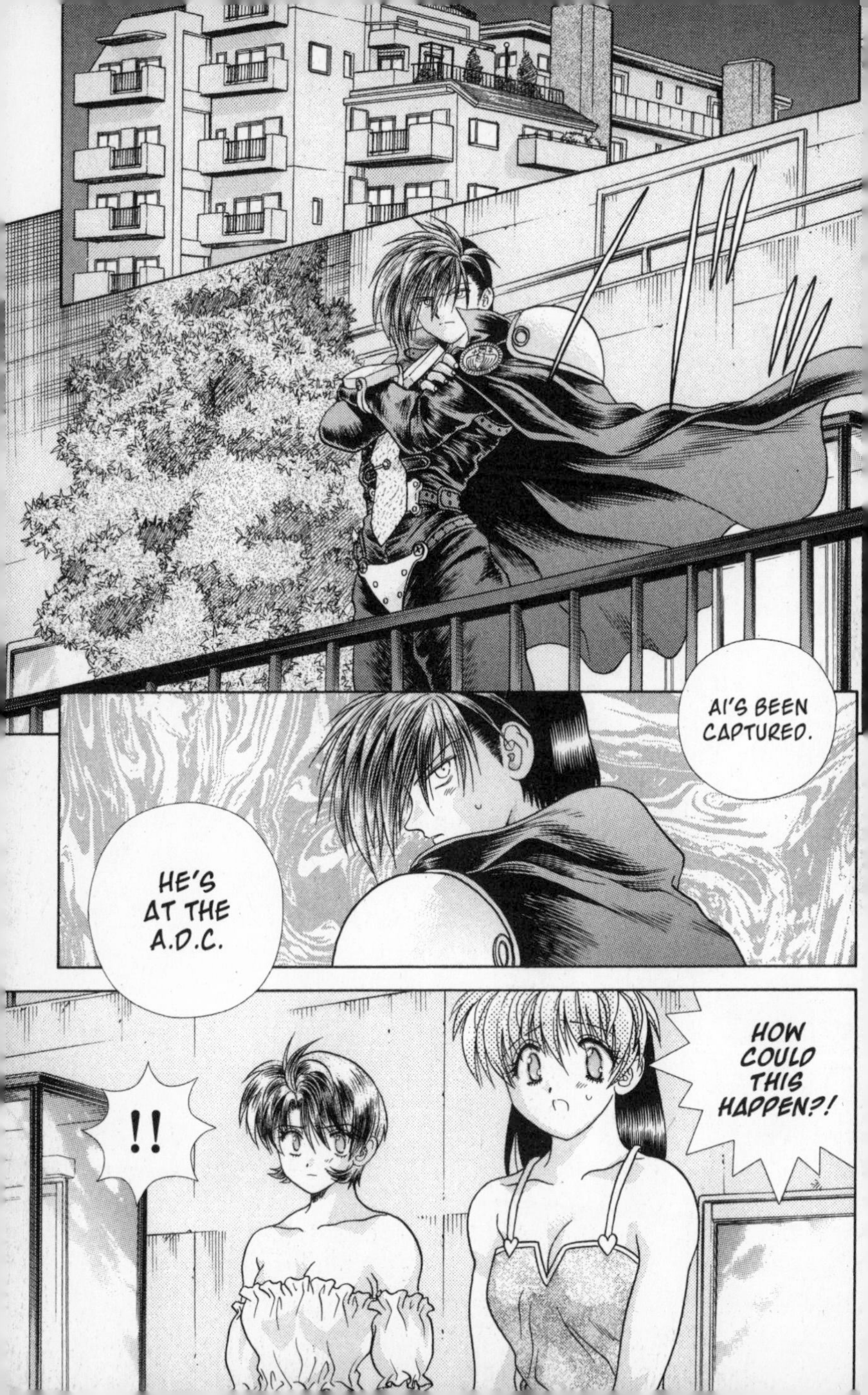
AI'S BEEN CAPTURED.
HE'S AT THE A.D.C.
HOW COULD THIS HAPPEN?!
!!

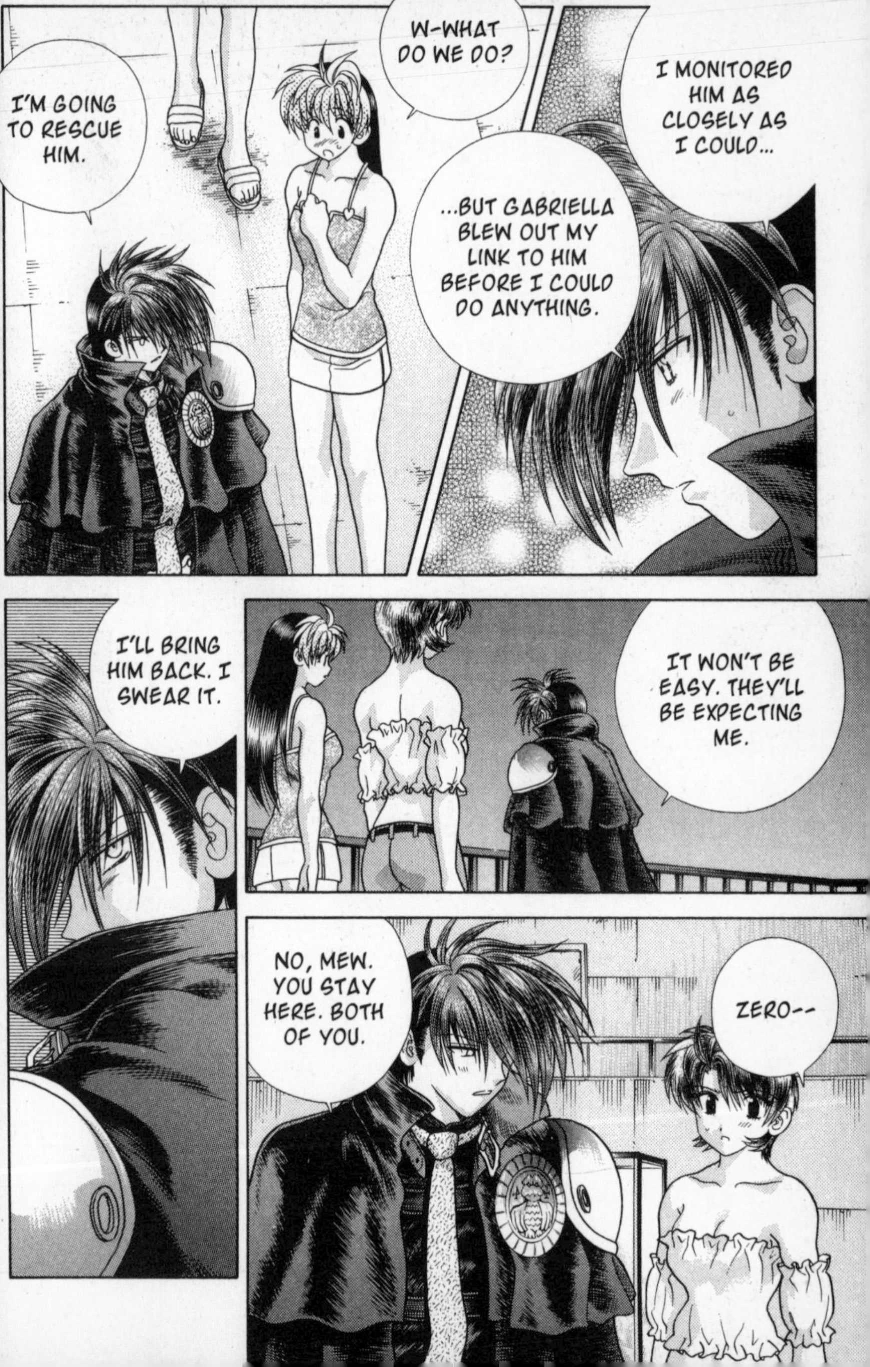
I MONITORED HIM AS CLOSELY AS I COULD...
...BUT GABRIELLA BLEW OUT MY LINK TO HIM BEFORE I COULD DO ANYTHING.
W-WHAT DO WE DO?
I'M GOING TO RESCUE HIM.
IT WON'T BE EASY. THEY'LL BE EXPECTING ME.
ZERO--
NO, MEW. YOU STAY HERE. BOTH OF YOU.
I'LL BRING HIM BACK. I SWEAR IT.

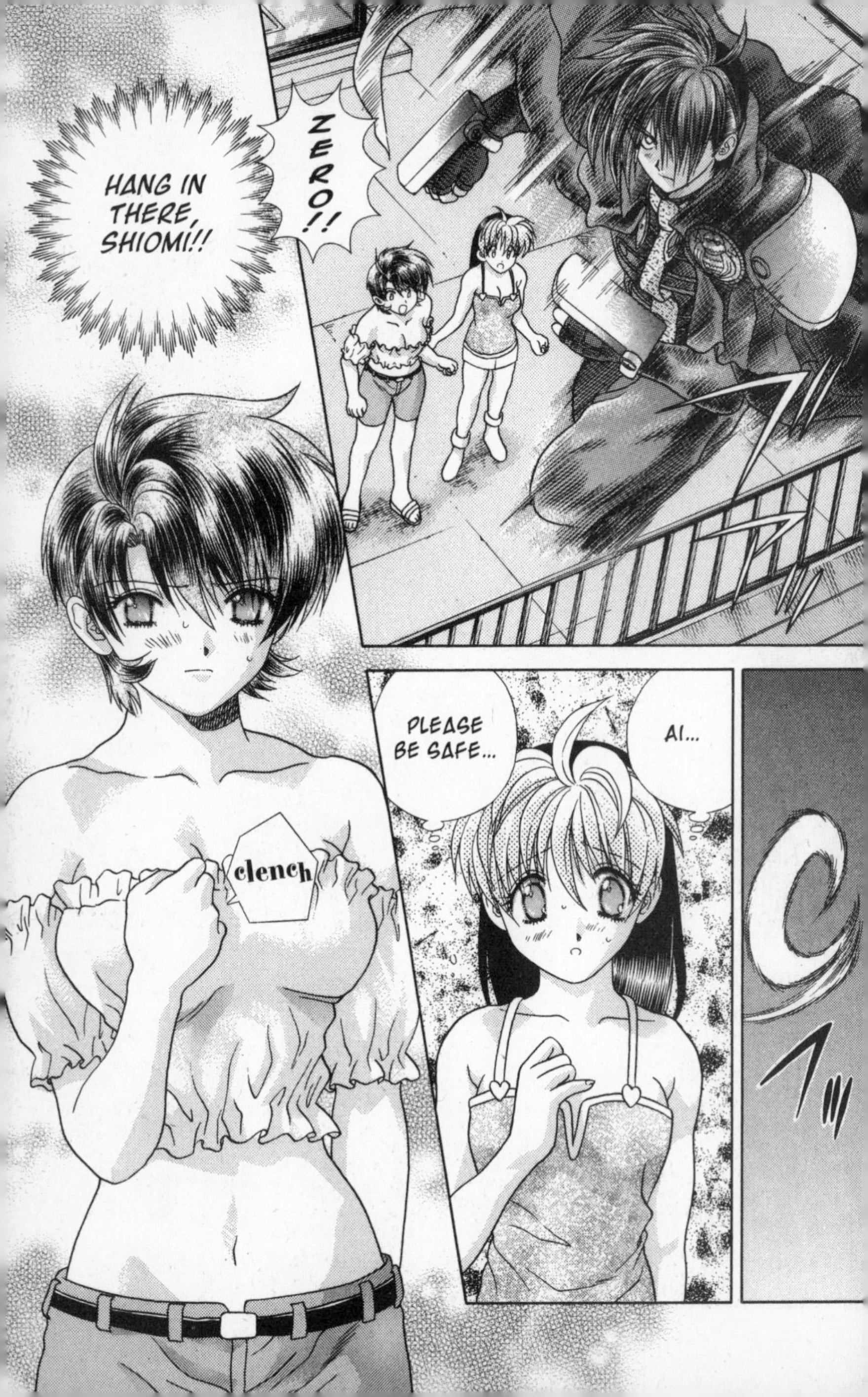
ZERO!!
AI...
PLEASE BE SAFE...
HANG IN THERE, SHIOMI!!
clench

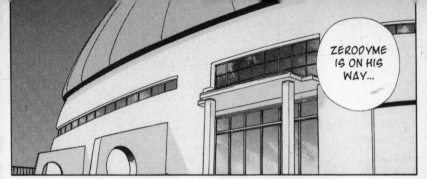

ZERODYME IS ON HIS WAY...

YES, SIR.

IT'S UP TO YOU, GAB...

GOOD...

I'LL STOP HIM.

I KNOW HIM. I KNOW HIS WEAKNESS...

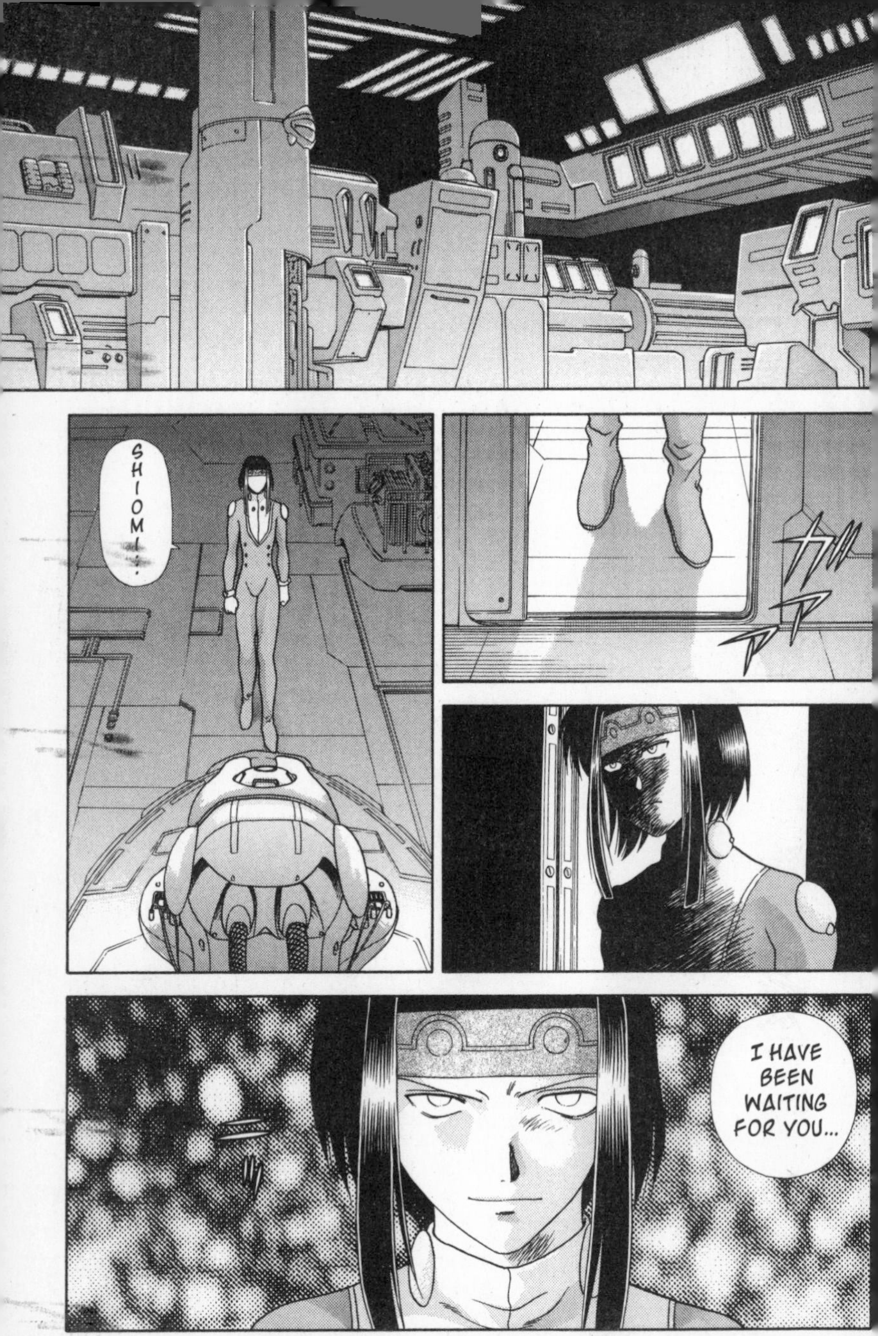
SHIOMI...
I HAVE BEEN WAITING FOR YOU...

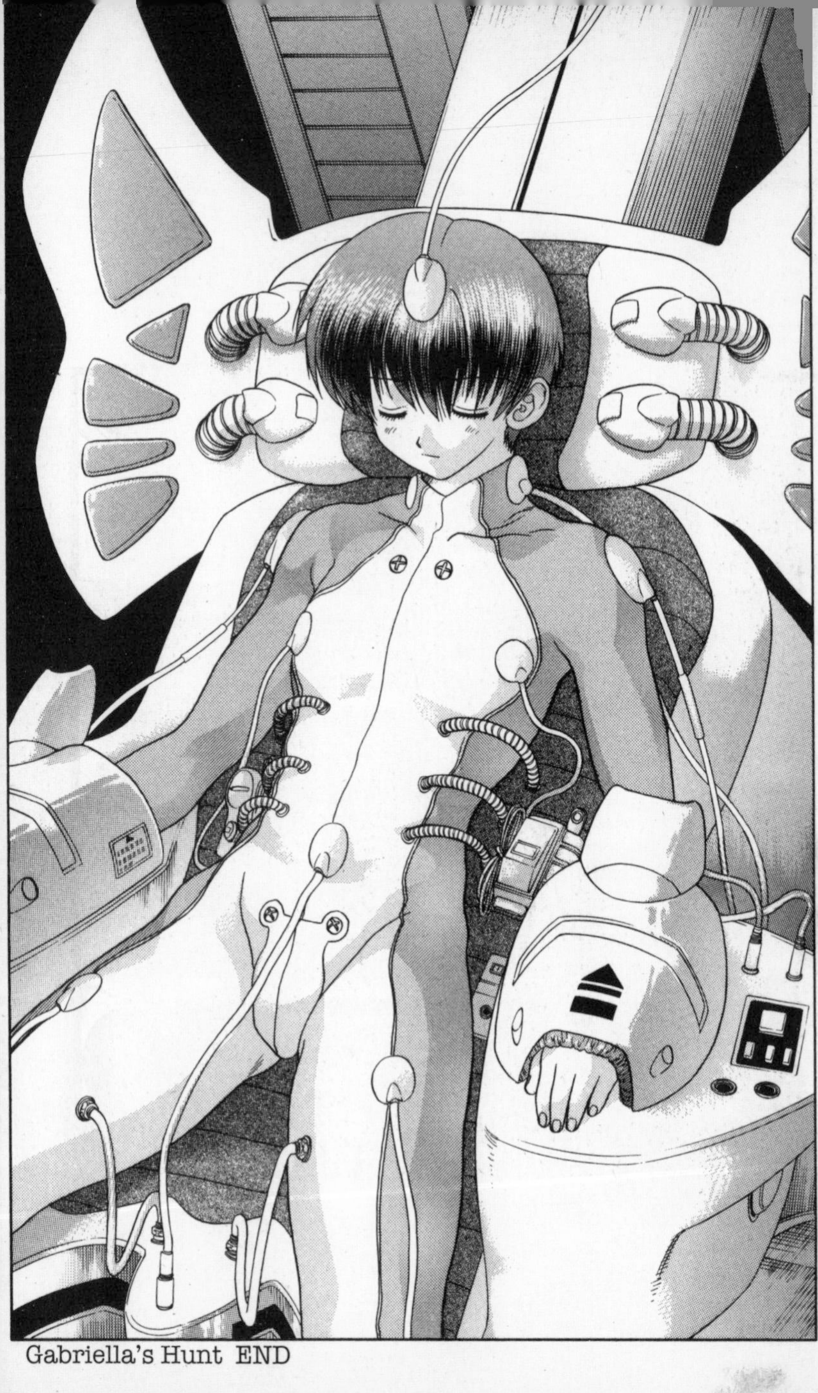

Gabriella's Hunt END

academy

Chapter 34 Inside the Trap

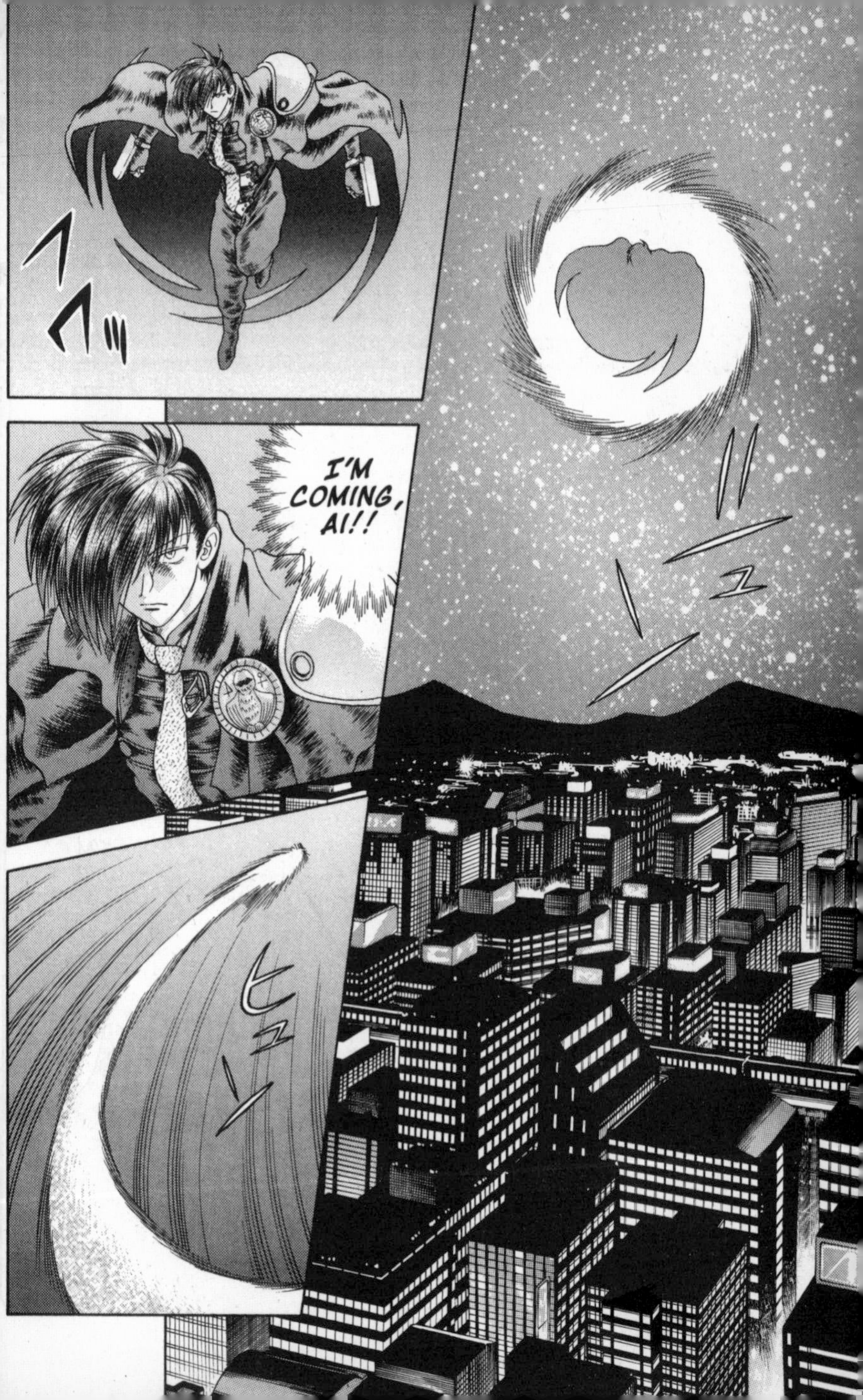
I'M COMING, AI!!

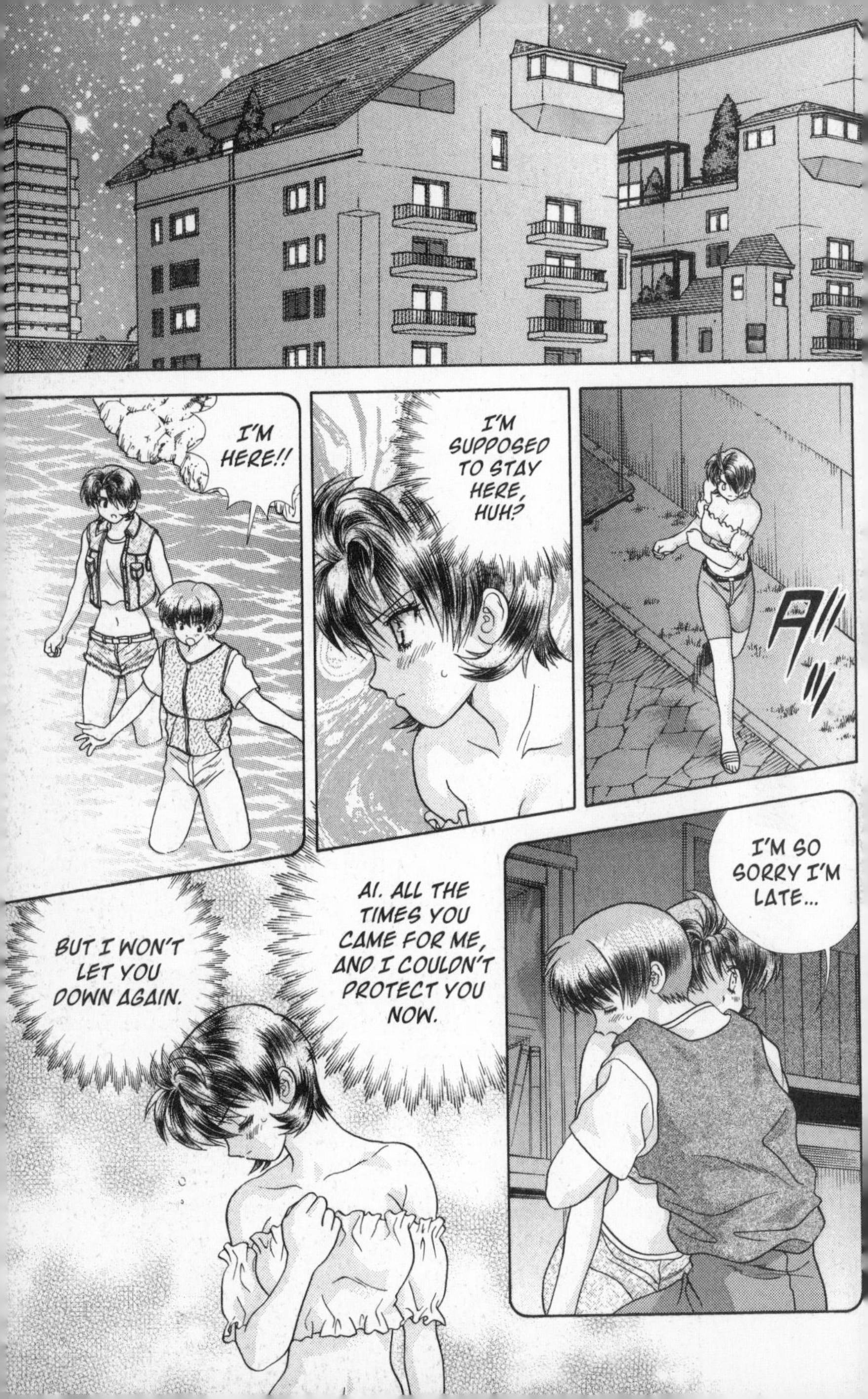
I'M SUPPOSED TO STAY HERE, HUH?
I'M HERE!!
I'M SO SORRY I'M LATE...
AI. ALL THE TIMES YOU CAME FOR ME, AND I COULDN'T PROTECT YOU NOW.
BUT I WON'T LET YOU DOWN AGAIN.

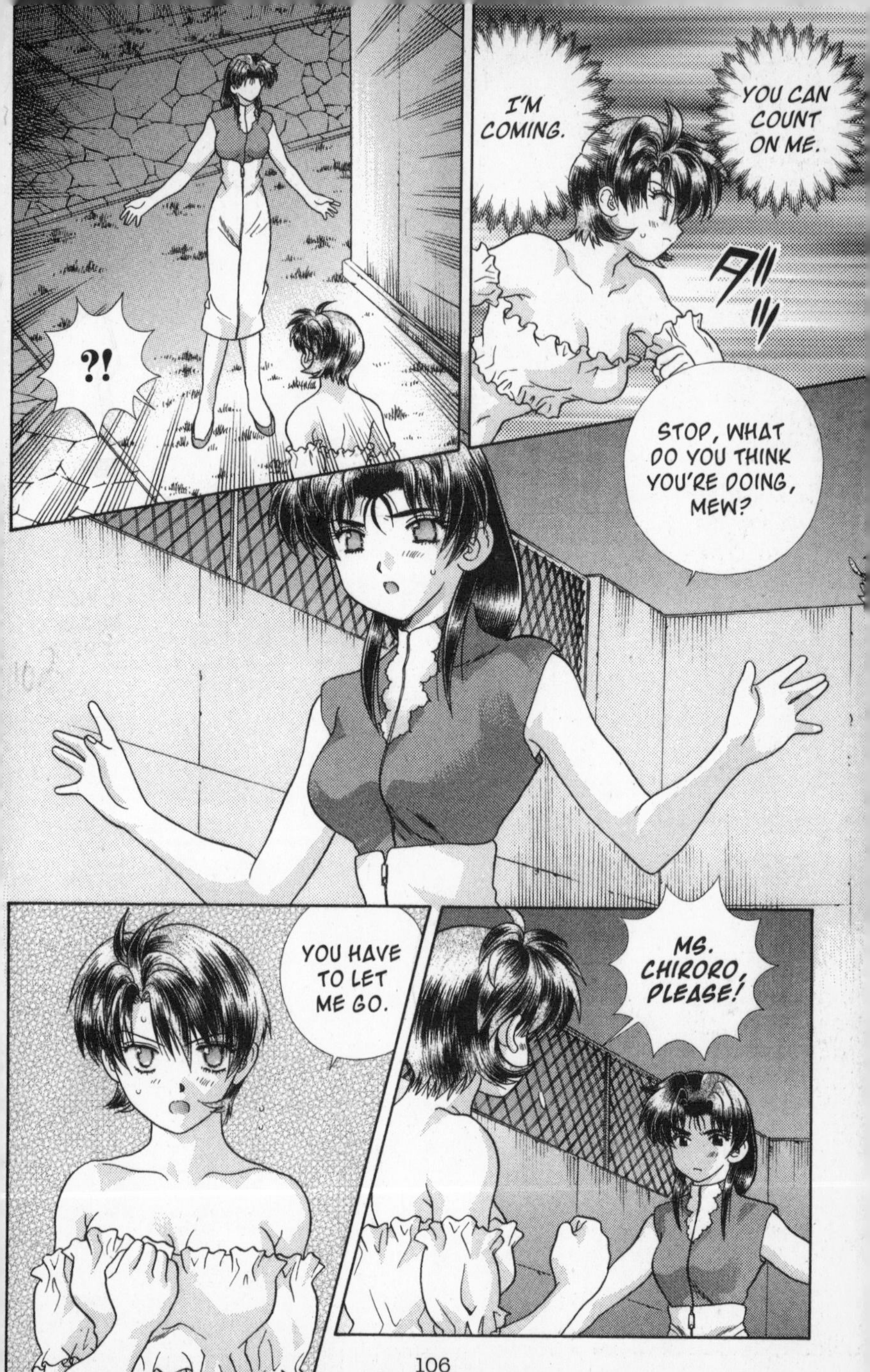
YOU CAN COUNT ON ME.
I'M COMING.
?!
STOP, WHAT DO YOU THINK YOU'RE DOING, MEW?
MS. CHIRORO, PLEASE!
YOU HAVE TO LET ME GO.

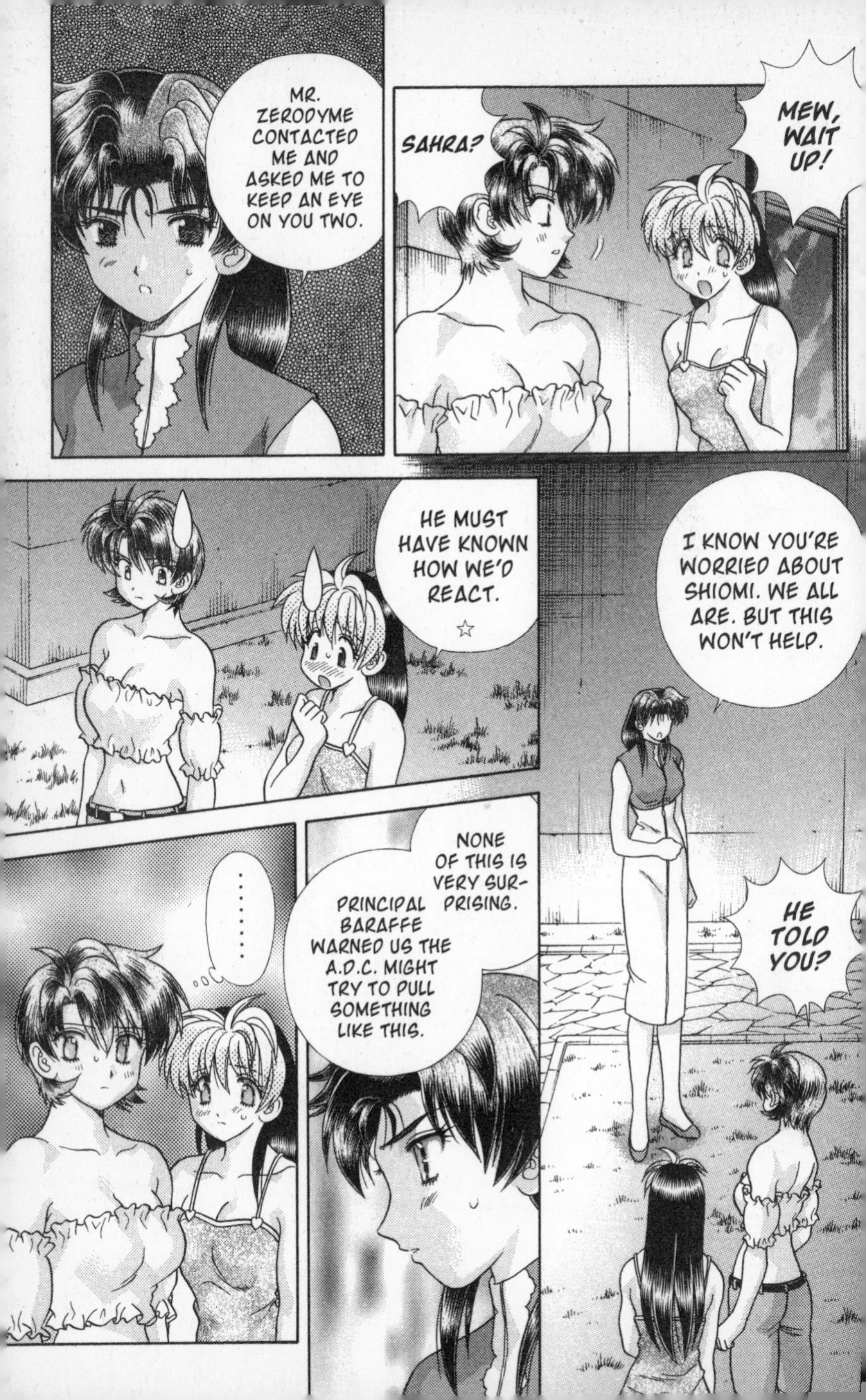
MEW, WAIT UP!
SAHRA?
MR. ZERODYME CONTACTED ME AND ASKED ME TO KEEP AN EYE ON YOU TWO.
I KNOW YOU'RE WORRIED ABOUT SHIOMI. WE ALL ARE. BUT THIS WON'T HELP.
HE TOLD YOU?
HE MUST HAVE KNOWN HOW WE'D REACT. ☆
NONE OF THIS IS VERY SUR-PRISING.
PRINCIPAL BARAFFE WARNED US THE A.D.C. MIGHT TRY TO PULL SOMETHING LIKE THIS.
....

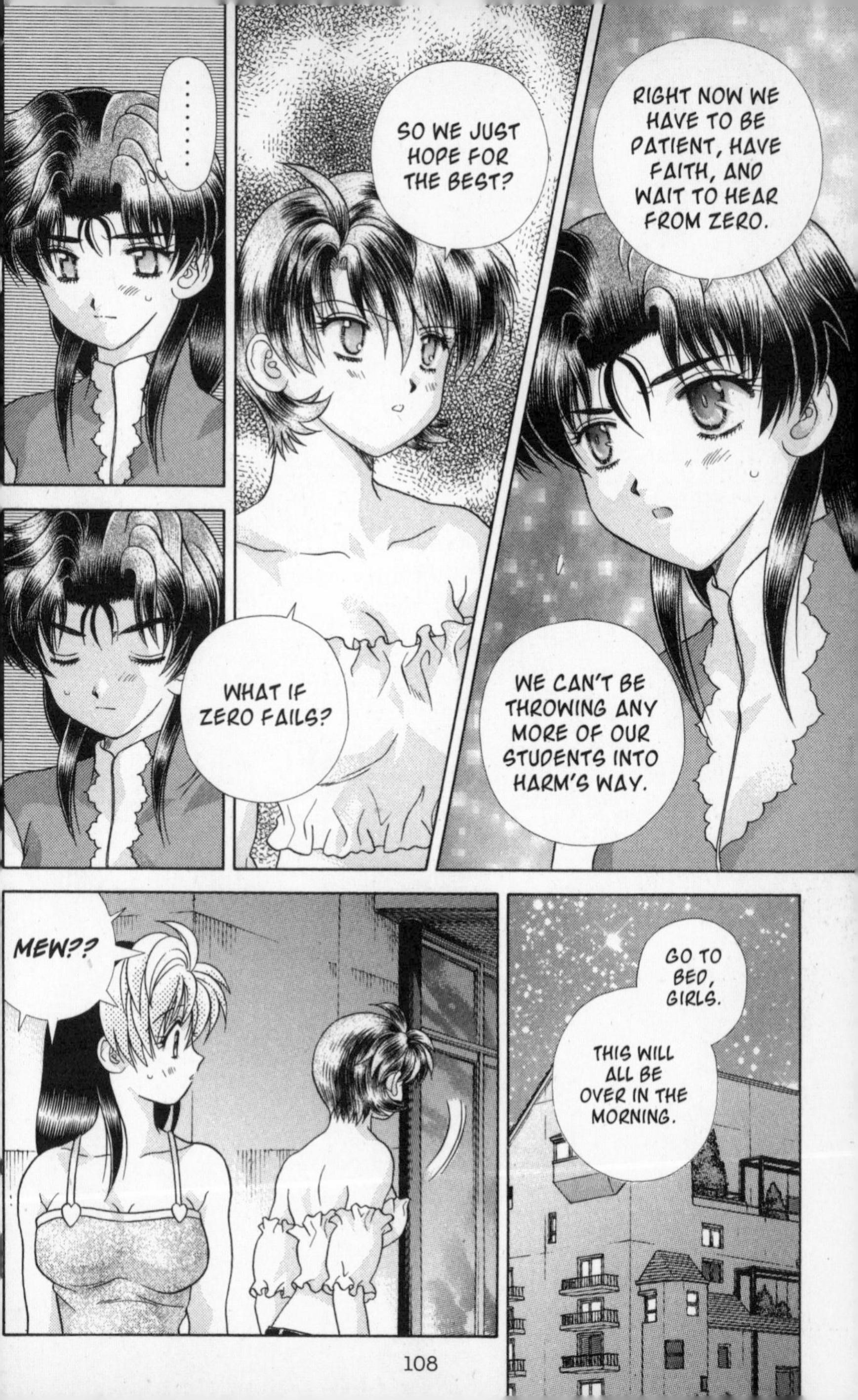
RIGHT NOW WE HAVE TO BE PATIENT, HAVE FAITH, AND WAIT TO HEAR FROM ZERO.
WE CAN'T BE THROWING ANY MORE OF OUR STUDENTS INTO HARM'S WAY.
SO WE JUST HOPE FOR THE BEST?
......
WHAT IF ZERO FAILS?
GO TO BED, GIRLS.
THIS WILL ALL BE OVER IN THE MORNING.
MEW??

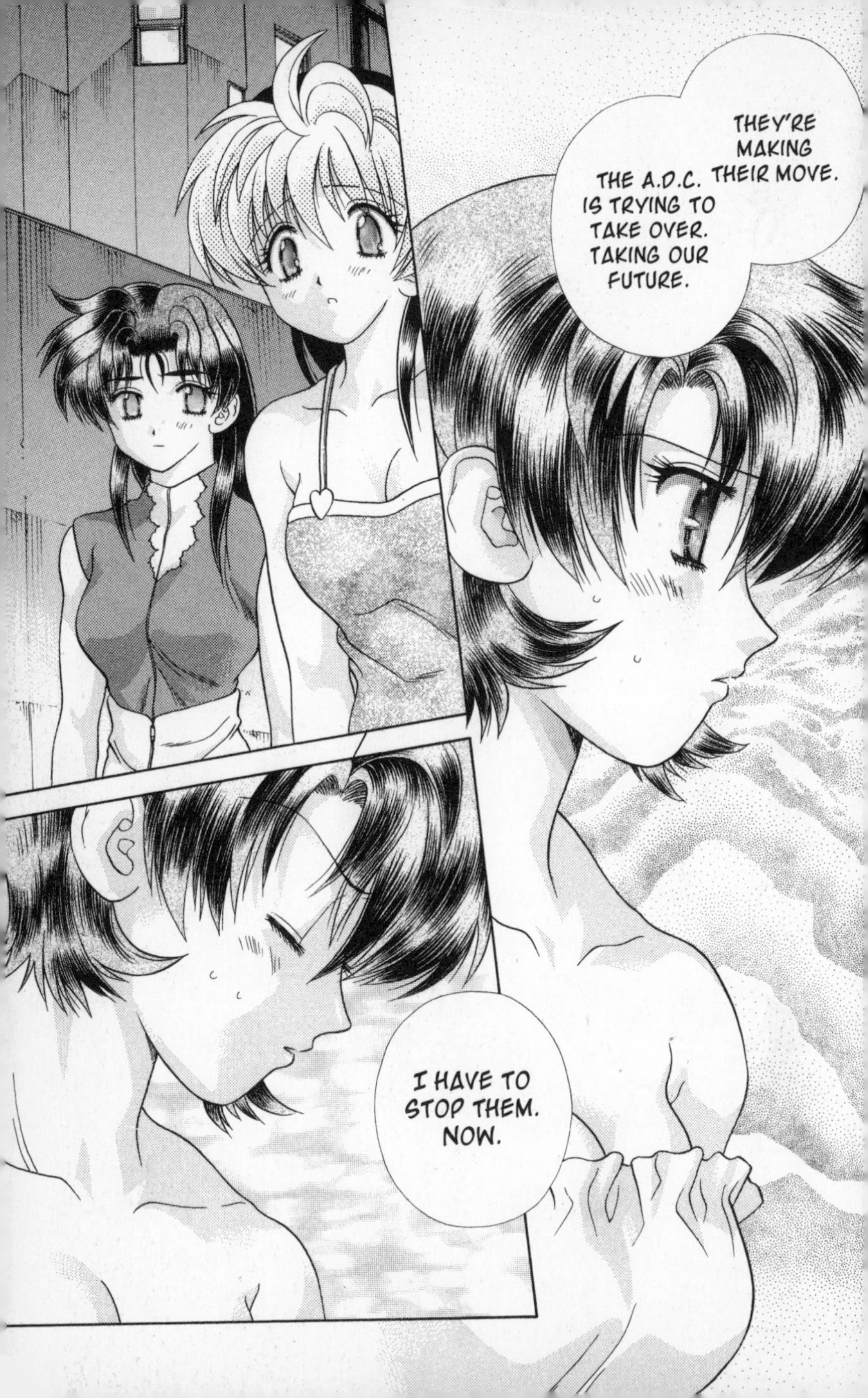
THEY'RE MAKING THEIR MOVE.
THE A.D.C. IS TRYING TO TAKE OVER. TAKING OUR FUTURE.
I HAVE TO STOP THEM. NOW.

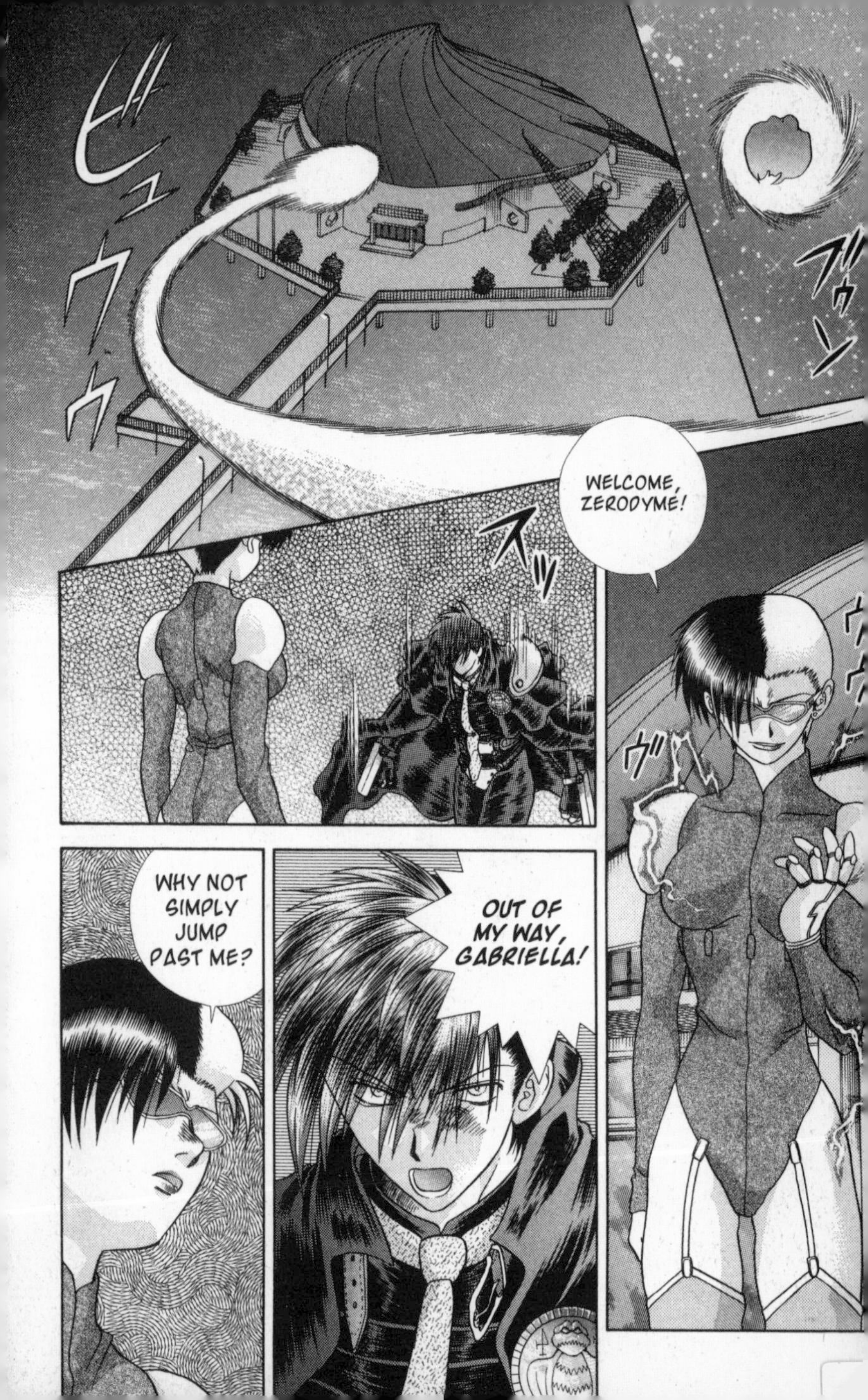

ブゥン
ビュウウゥ
WELCOME, ZERODYMÉ!
ヴ
スッ
OUT OF MY WAY, GABRIELLA!
WHY NOT SIMPLY JUMP PAST ME?

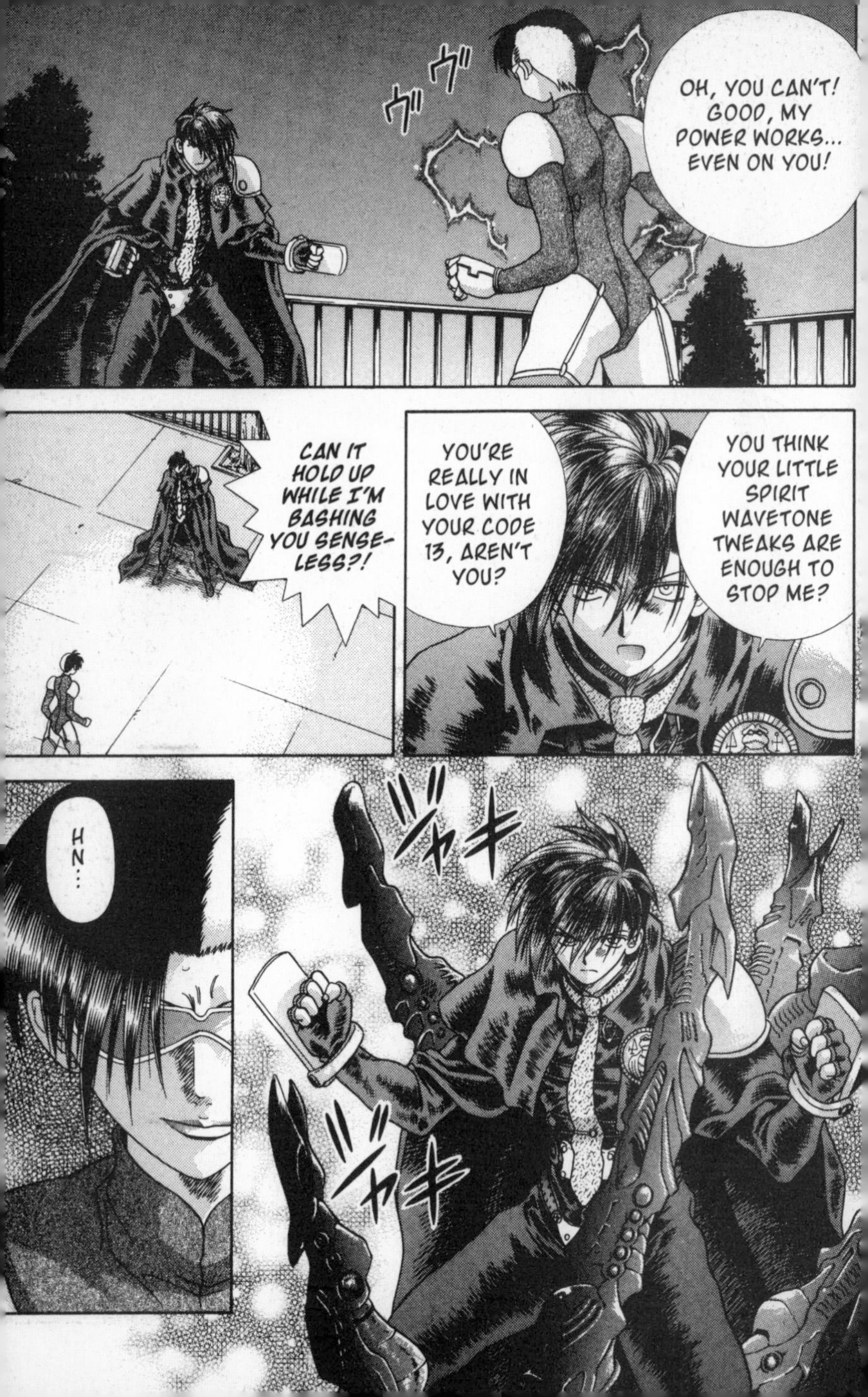
ヴヴヴ
OH, YOU CAN'T! GOOD, MY POWER WORKS... EVEN ON YOU!
YOU THINK YOUR LITTLE SPIRIT WAVETONE TWEAKS ARE ENOUGH TO STOP ME?
YOU'RE REALLY IN LOVE WITH YOUR CODE 13, AREN'T YOU?
CAN IT HOLD UP WHILE I'M BASHING YOU SENSE-LESS?!
ジャキ
ジャキ
HN...

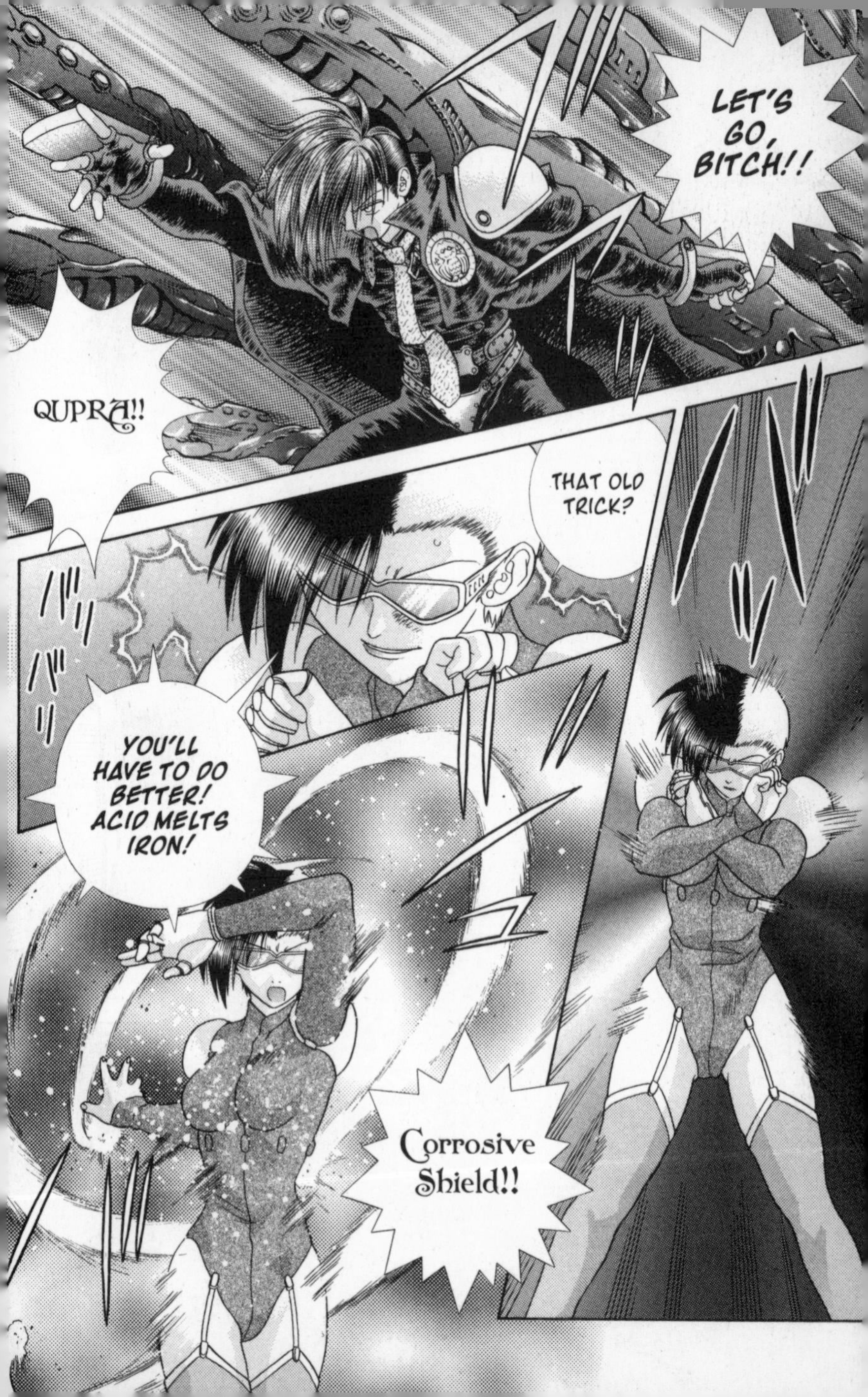
LET'S GO, BITCH!!
QUPRA!!
THAT OLD TRICK?
YOU'LL HAVE TO DO BETTER! ACID MELTS IRON!
Corrosive Shield!!

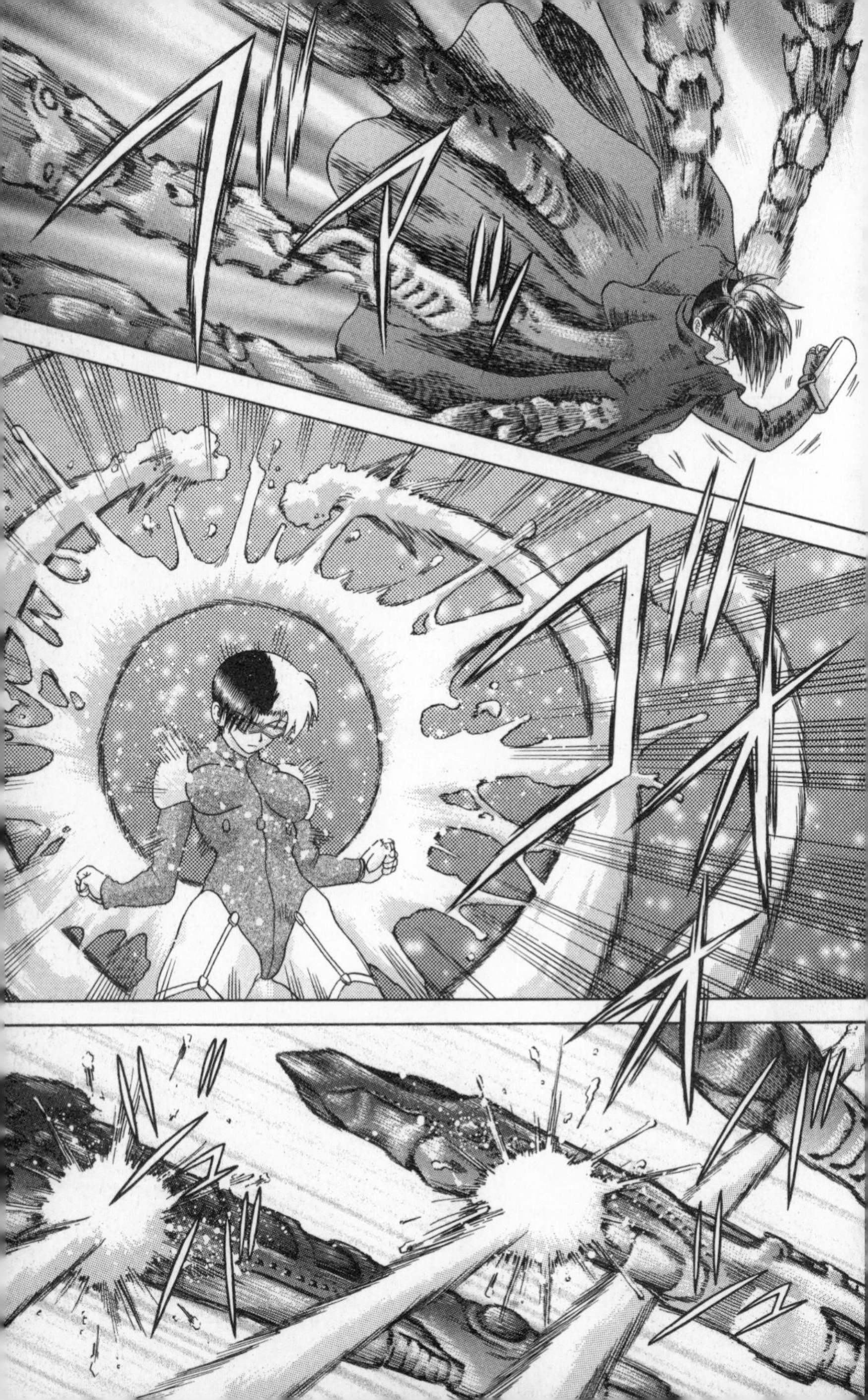

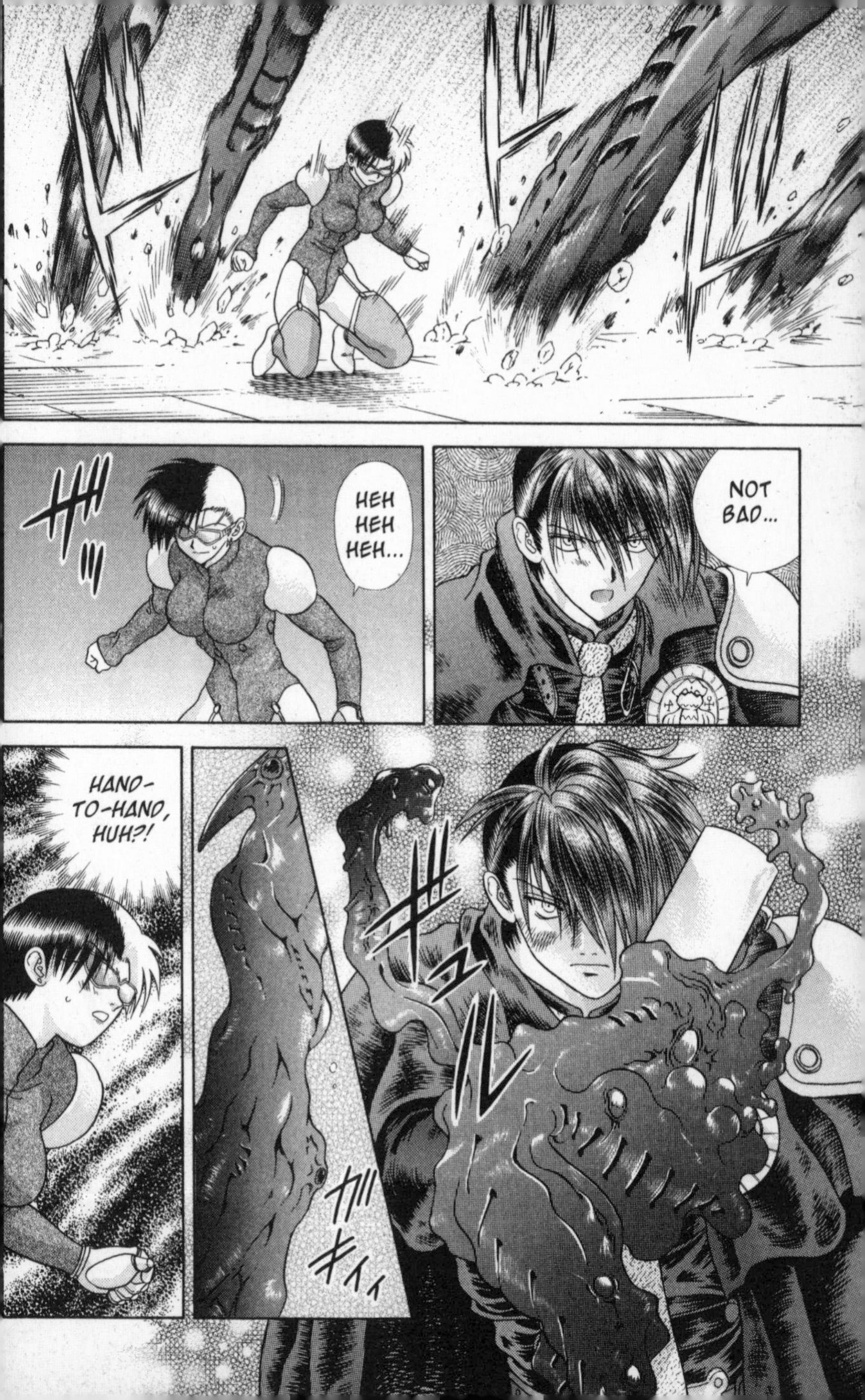
NOT BAD...
HEH HEH HEH...
HAND-TO-HAND, HUH?!

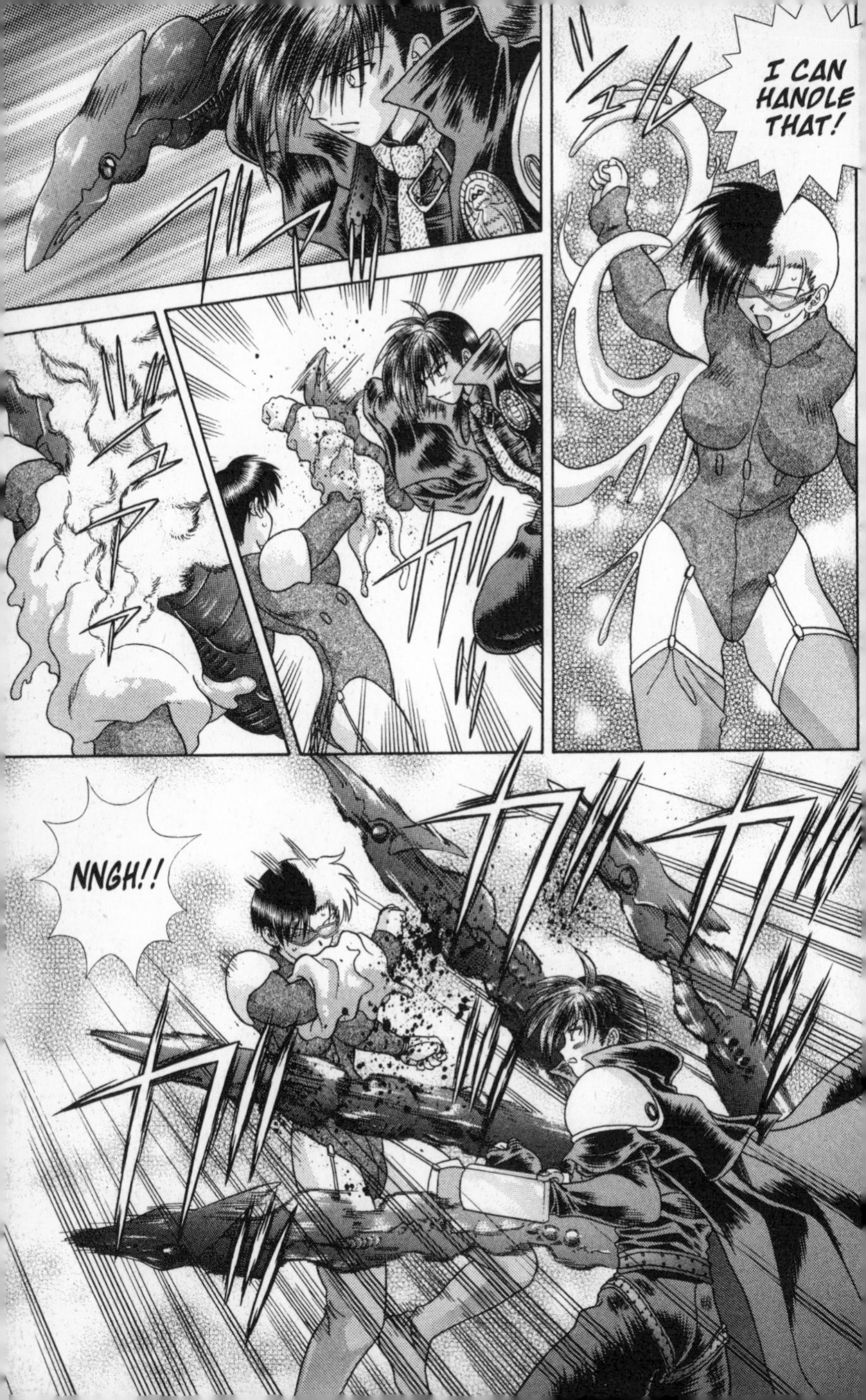
I CAN HANDLE THAT!
NNGH!!

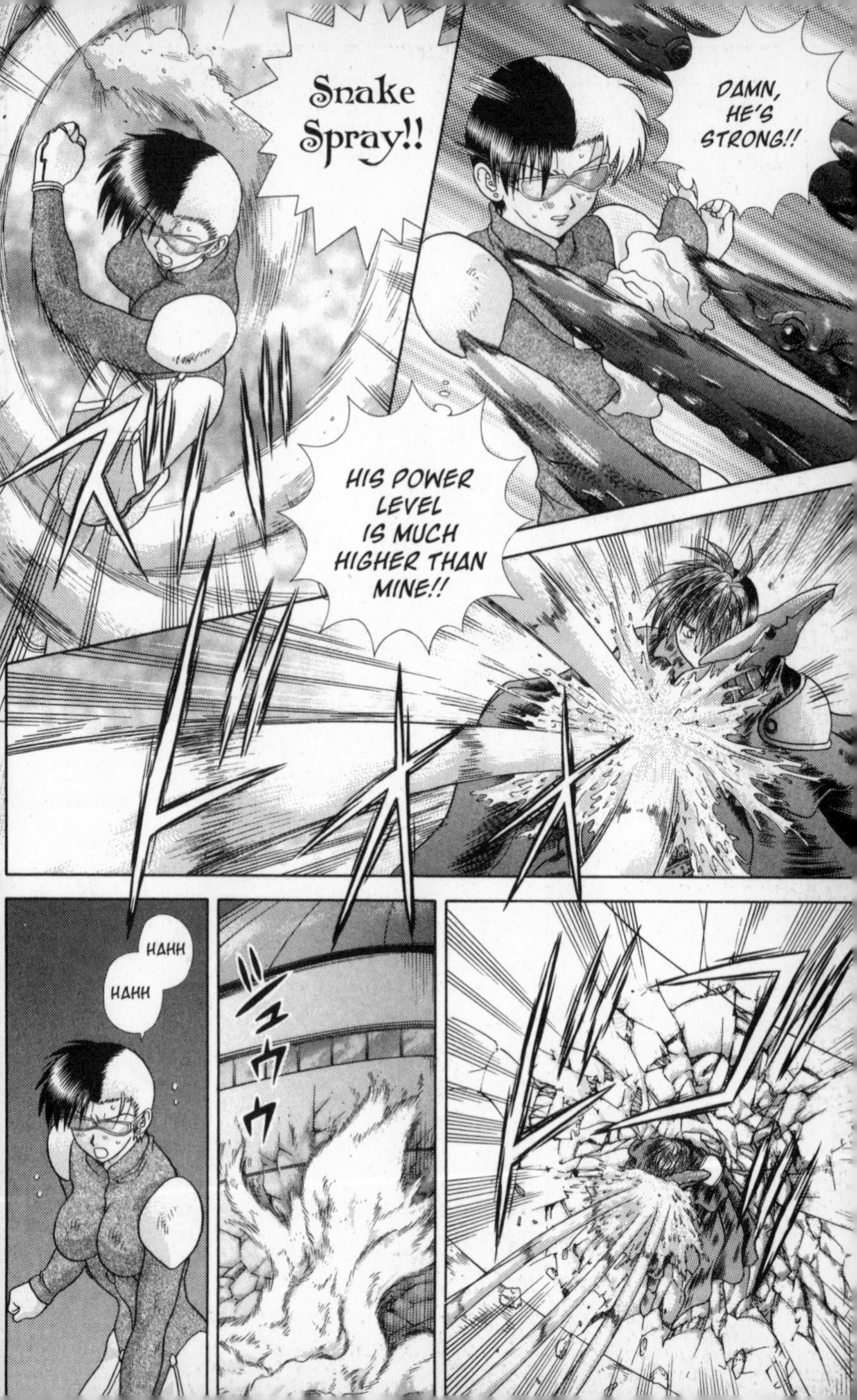
DAMN, HE'S STRONG!!
Snake Spray!!
HIS POWER LEVEL IS MUCH HIGHER THAN MINE!!
HAHH
HAHH

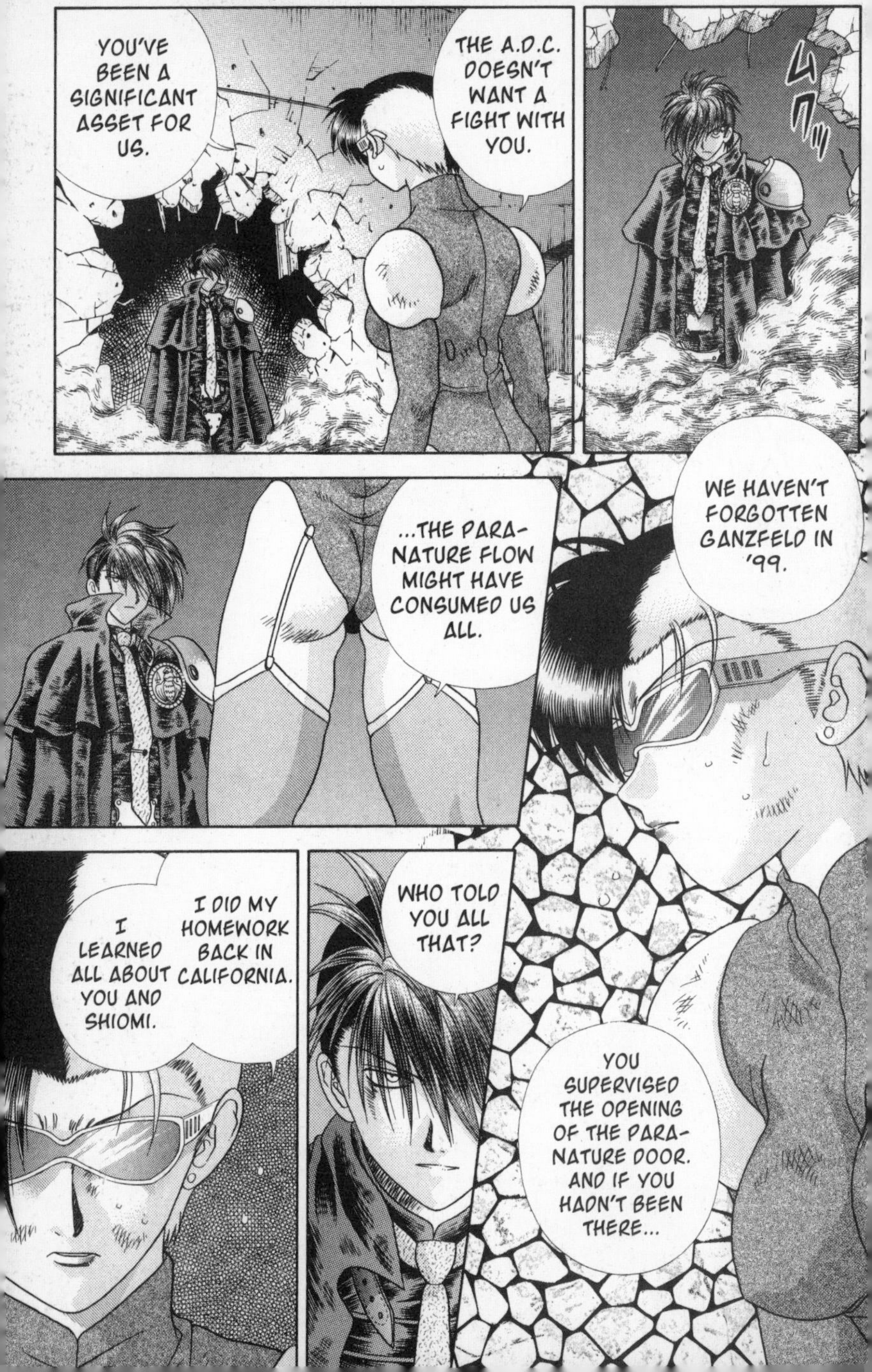
ムクッ
THE A.D.C. DOESN'T WANT A FIGHT WITH YOU.
YOU'VE BEEN A SIGNIFICANT ASSET FOR US.
WE HAVEN'T FORGOTTEN GANZFELD IN '99.
YOU SUPERVISED THE OPENING OF THE PARA-NATURE DOOR. AND IF YOU HADN'T BEEN THERE...
...THE PARA-NATURE FLOW MIGHT HAVE CONSUMED US ALL.
WHO TOLD YOU ALL THAT?
I DID MY HOMEWORK BACK IN CALIFORNIA.
I LEARNED ALL ABOUT YOU AND SHIOMI.

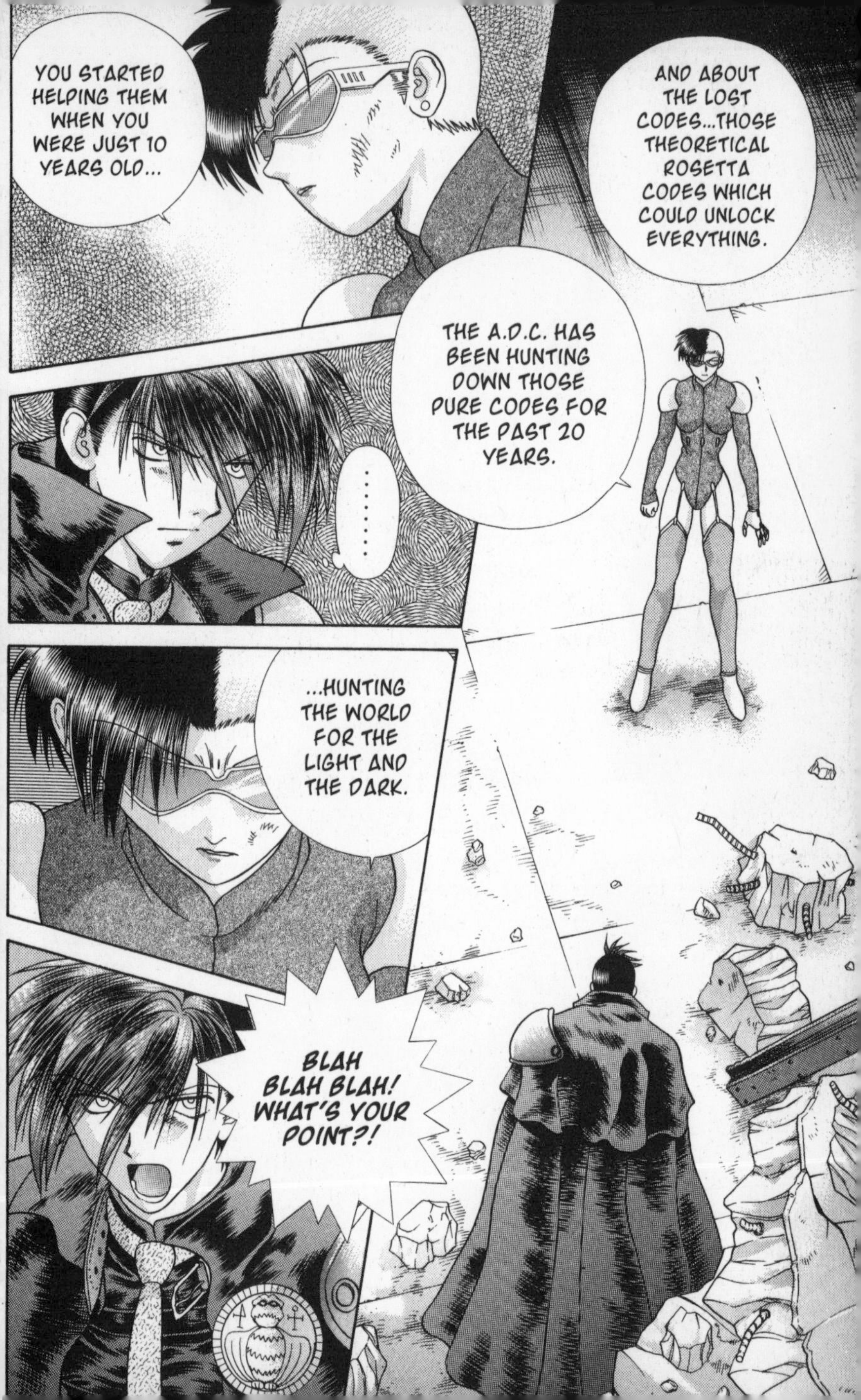
AND ABOUT THE LOST CODES...THOSE THEORETICAL ROSETTA CODES WHICH COULD UNLOCK EVERYTHING.
THE A.D.C. HAS BEEN HUNTING DOWN THOSE PURE CODES FOR THE PAST 20 YEARS.
YOU STARTED HELPING THEM WHEN YOU WERE JUST 10 YEARS OLD...
......
...HUNTING THE WORLD FOR THE LIGHT AND THE DARK.
BLAH BLAH BLAH! WHAT'S YOUR POINT?!

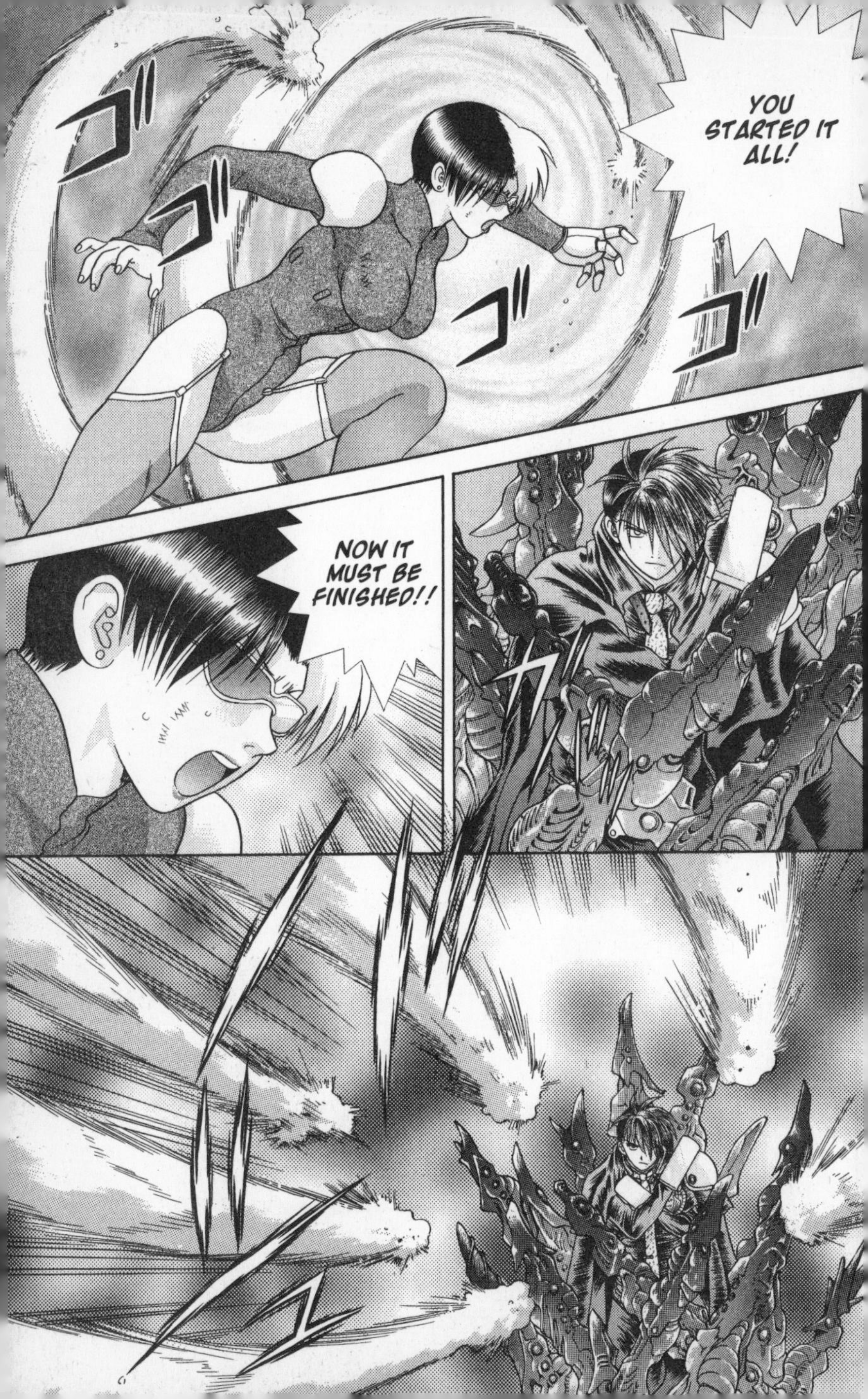
YOU STARTED IT ALL!
ゴ
ゴ
ゴ
ゴ
NOW IT MUST BE FINISHED!!

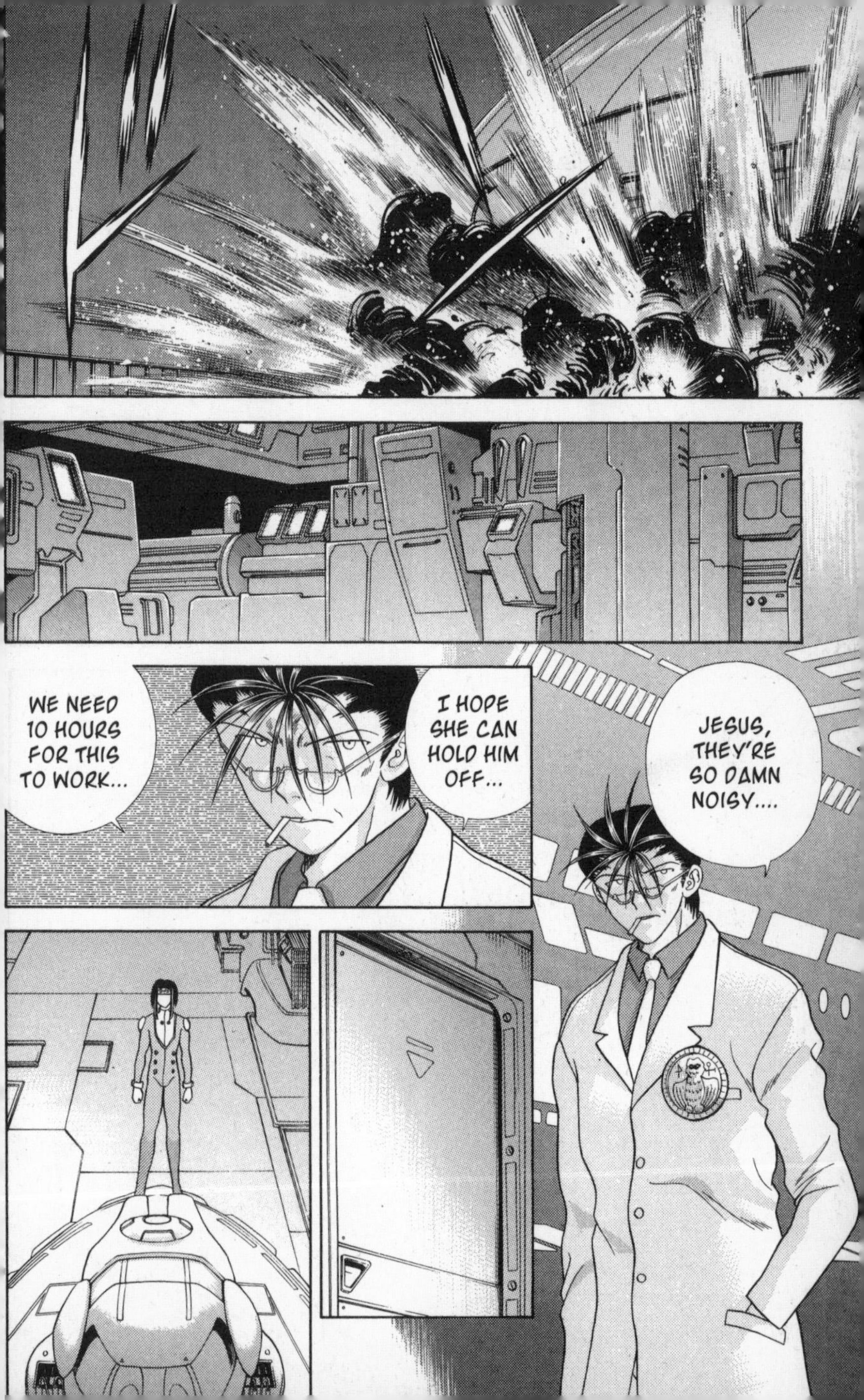
JESUS, THEY'RE SO DAMN NOISY....
I HOPE SHE CAN HOLD HIM OFF...
WE NEED 10 HOURS FOR THIS TO WORK...

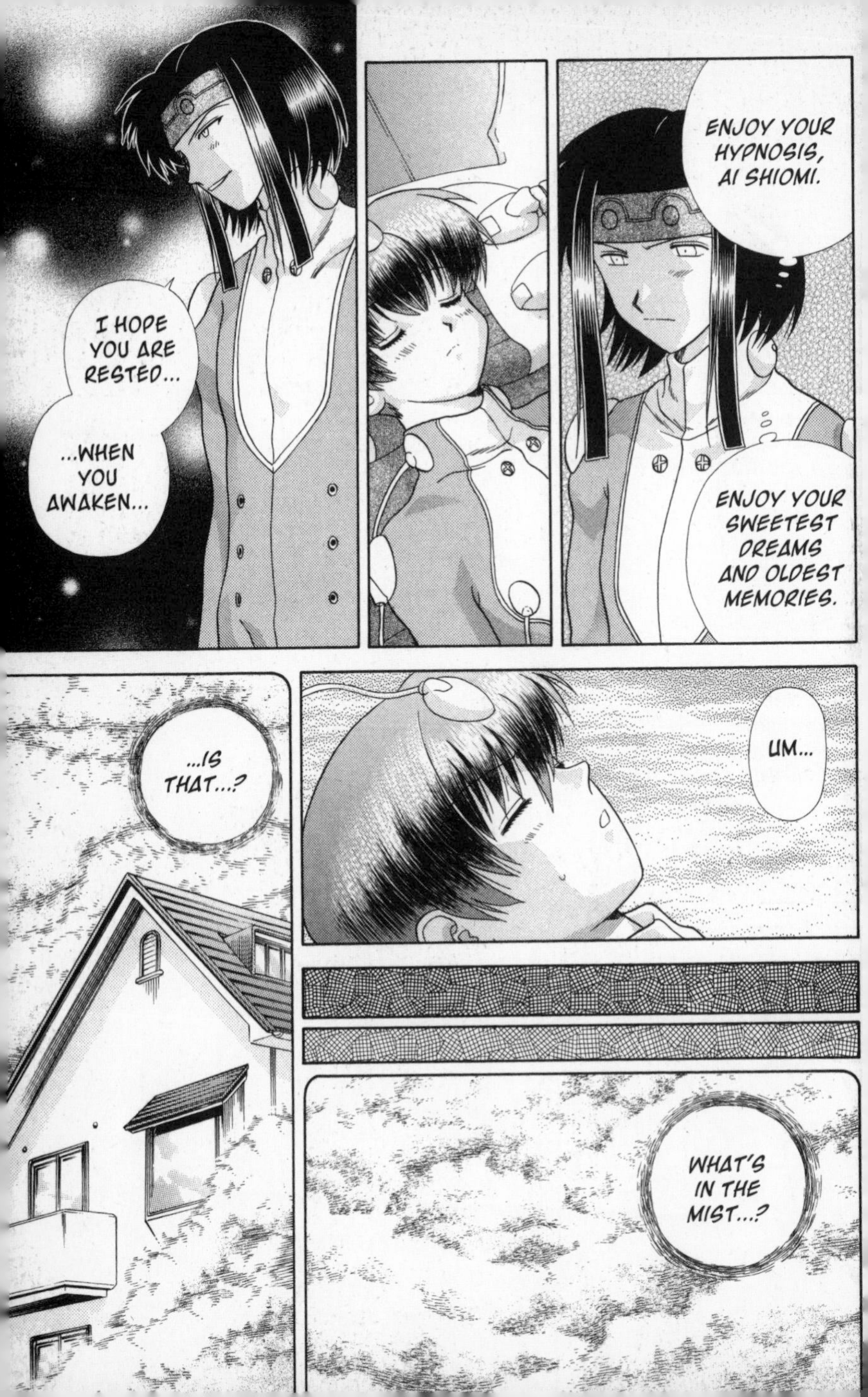
ENJOY YOUR HYPNOSIS, AI SHIOMI.
ENJOY YOUR SWEETEST DREAMS AND OLDEST MEMORIES.
I HOPE YOU ARE RESTED...
...WHEN YOU AWAKEN...
UM...
WHAT'S IN THE MIST...?
...IS THAT...?

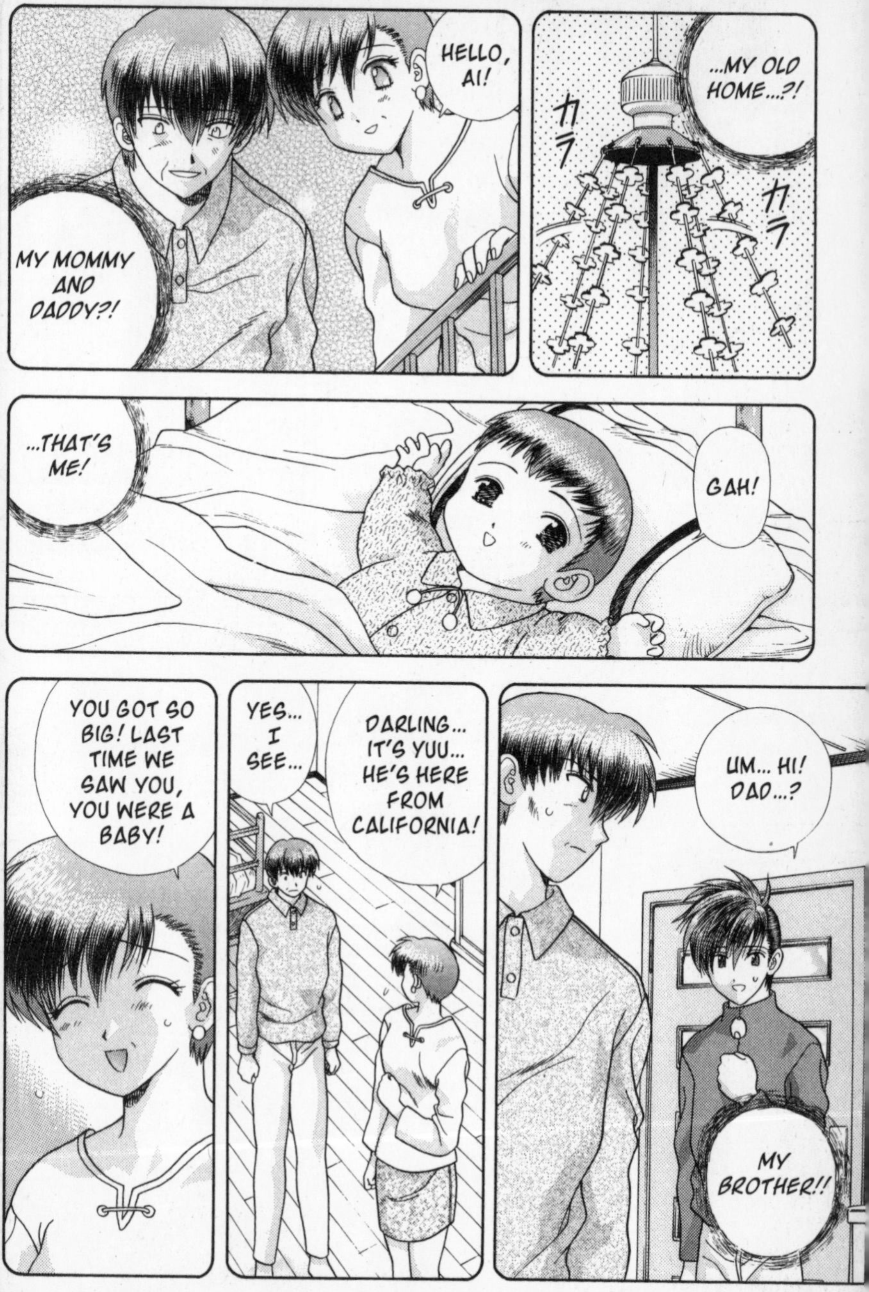
...MY OLD HOME...?!
カラ
カラ
HELLO, AI!
MY MOMMY AND DADDY?!
GAH!
...THAT'S ME!
UM... HI! DAD...?
MY BROTHER!!
DARLING... IT'S YUU... HE'S HERE FROM CALIFORNIA!
YES... I SEE...
YOU GOT SO BIG! LAST TIME WE SAW YOU, YOU WERE A BABY!

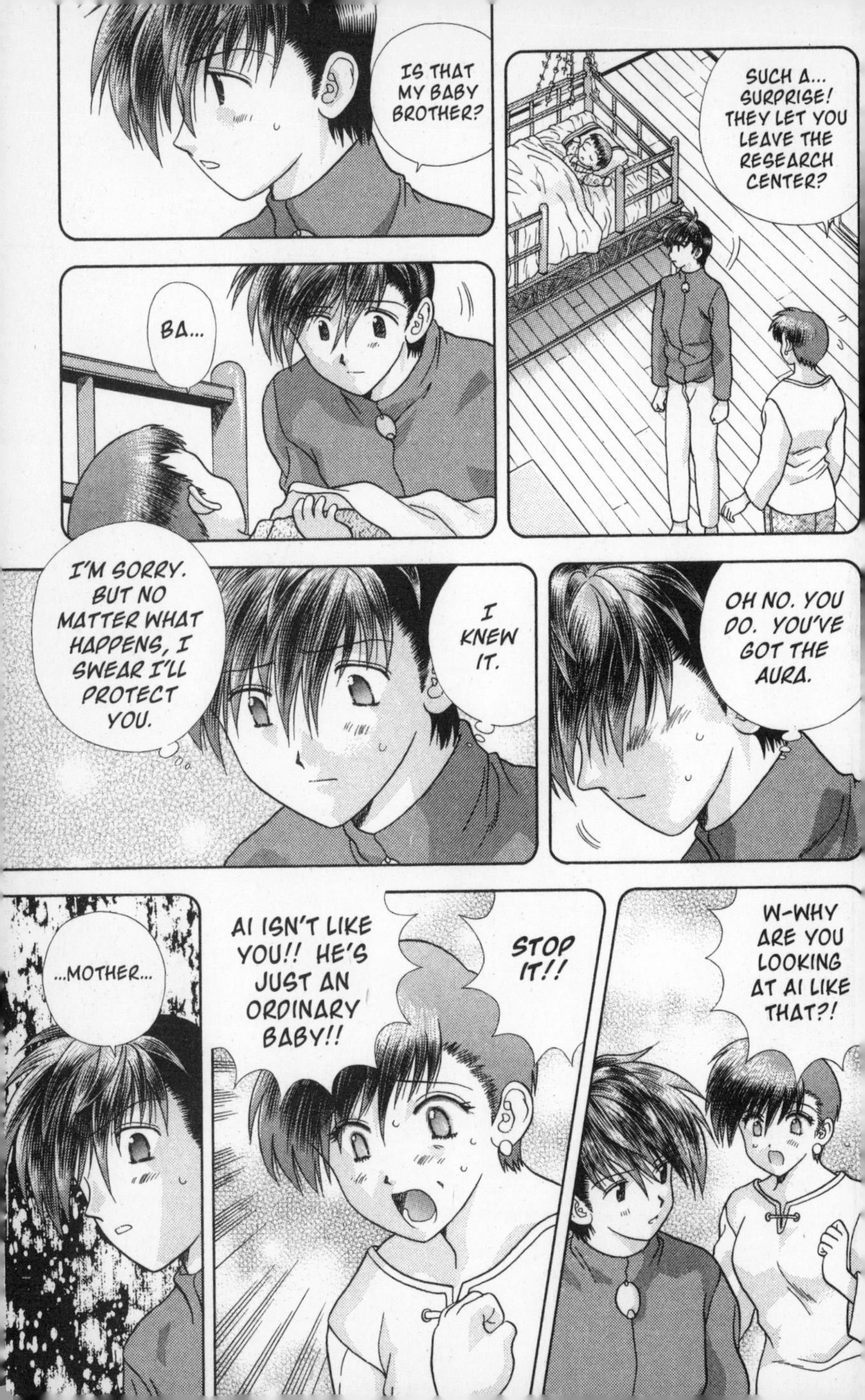
SUCH A... SURPRISE! THEY LET YOU LEAVE THE RESEARCH CENTER?
IS THAT MY BABY BROTHER?
BA...
OH NO. YOU DO. YOU'VE GOT THE AURA.
I KNEW IT.
I'M SORRY. BUT NO MATTER WHAT HAPPENS, I SWEAR I'LL PROTECT YOU.
W-WHY ARE YOU LOOKING AT AI LIKE THAT?!
STOP IT!!
AI ISN'T LIKE YOU!! HE'S JUST AN ORDINARY BABY!!
...MOTHER...

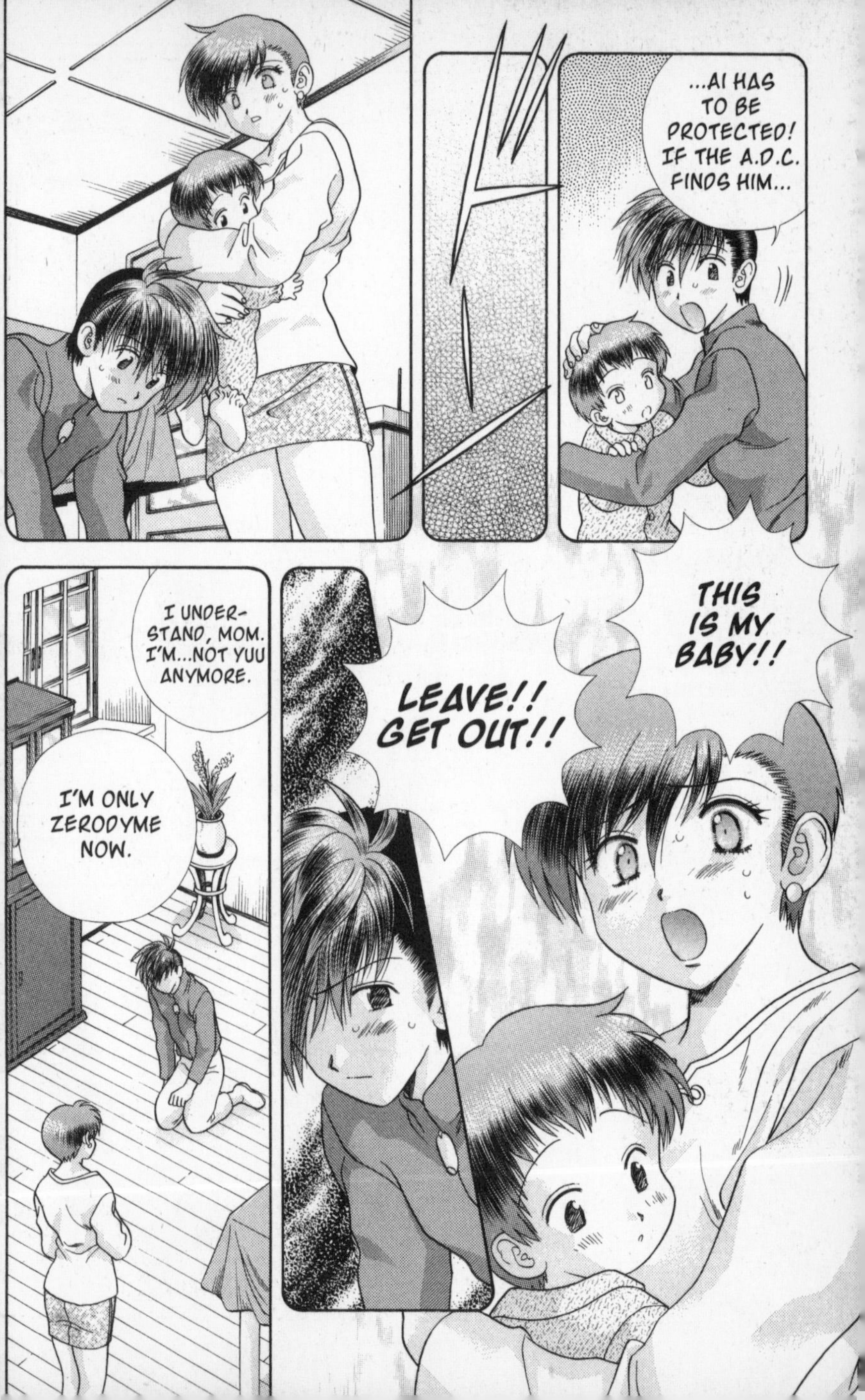
...AI HAS TO BE PROTECTED! IF THE A.D.C. FINDS HIM...
THIS IS MY BABY!!
LEAVE!! GET OUT!!
I UNDER-STAND, MOM. I'M...NOT YUU ANYMORE.
I'M ONLY ZERODYME NOW.

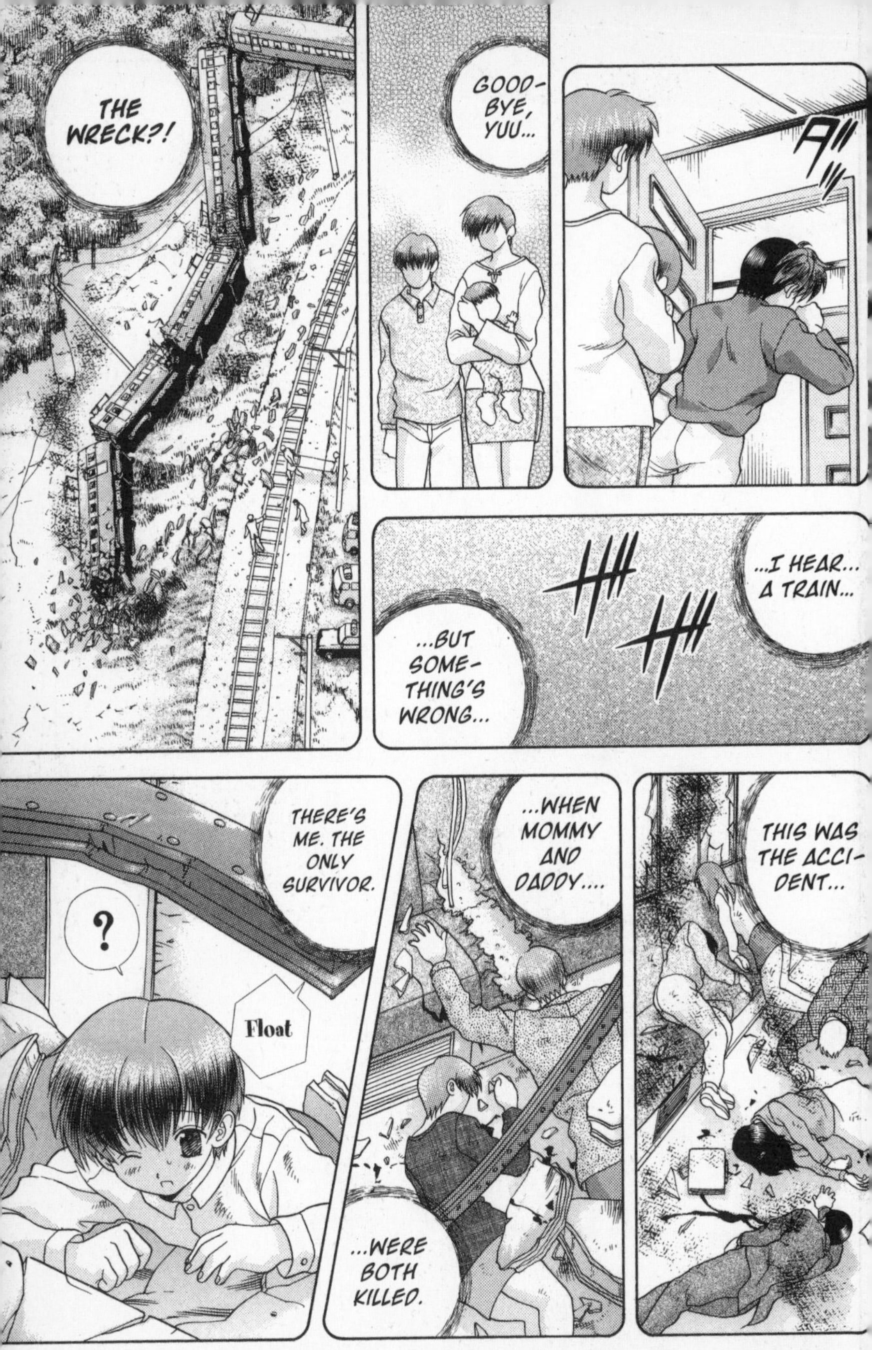
A!!
GOOD-BYE, YUU...
...I HEAR... A TRAIN...
...BUT SOME-THING'S WRONG...
THE WRECK?!
THIS WAS THE ACCI-DENT...
...WHEN MOMMY AND DADDY....
...WERE BOTH KILLED.
THERE'S ME. THE ONLY SURVIVOR.
?
Float

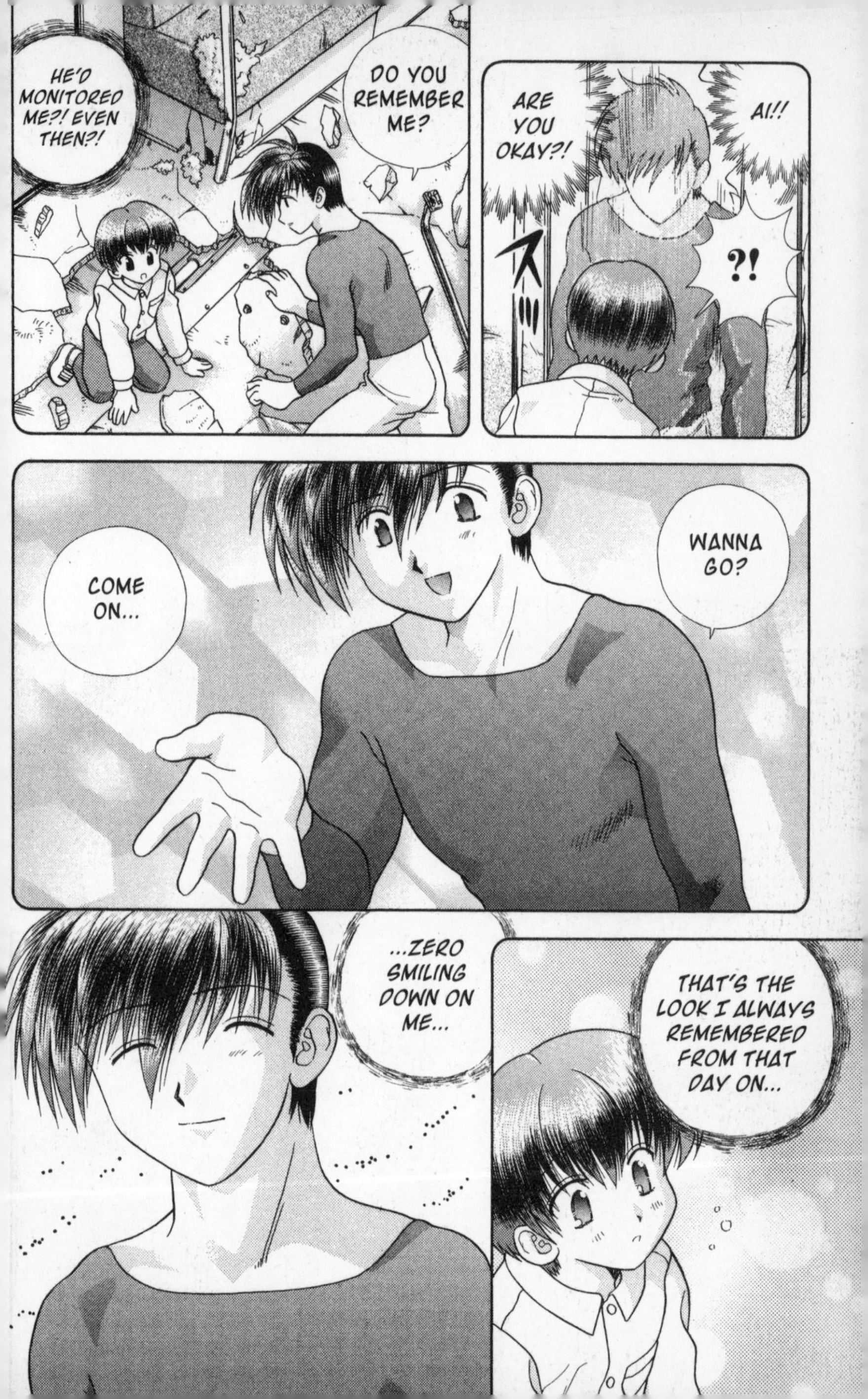
AI!!
?!
ARE YOU OKAY?!
ス
DO YOU REMEMBER ME?
HE'D MONITORED ME?! EVEN THEN?!
WANNA GO?
COME ON...
...ZERO SMILING DOWN ON ME...
THAT'S THE LOOK I ALWAYS REMEMBERED FROM THAT DAY ON...

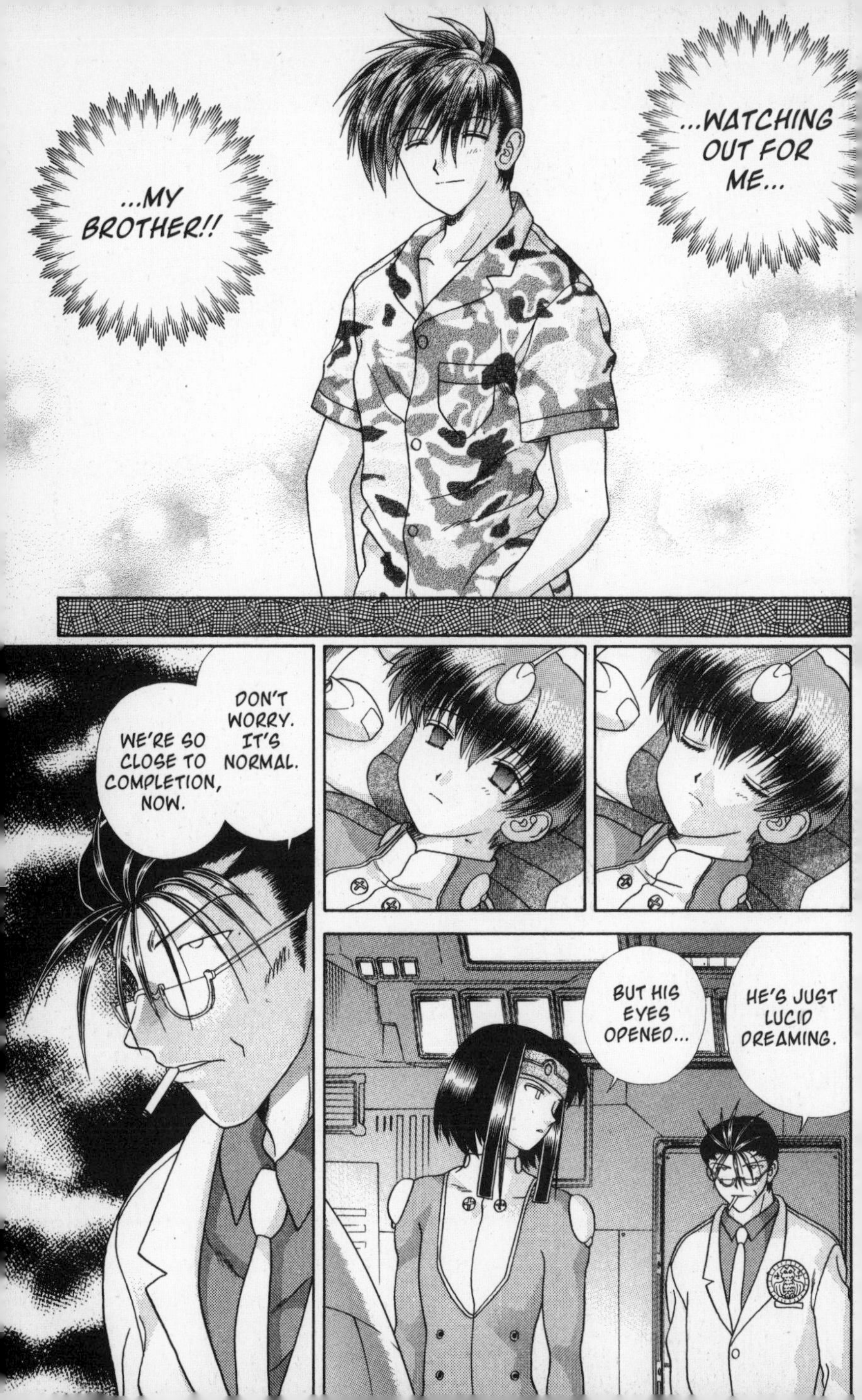
...WATCHING OUT FOR ME...
...MY BROTHER!!
HE'S JUST LUCID DREAMING.
BUT HIS EYES OPENED...
DON'T WORRY. IT'S NORMAL.
WE'RE SO CLOSE TO COMPLETION, NOW.

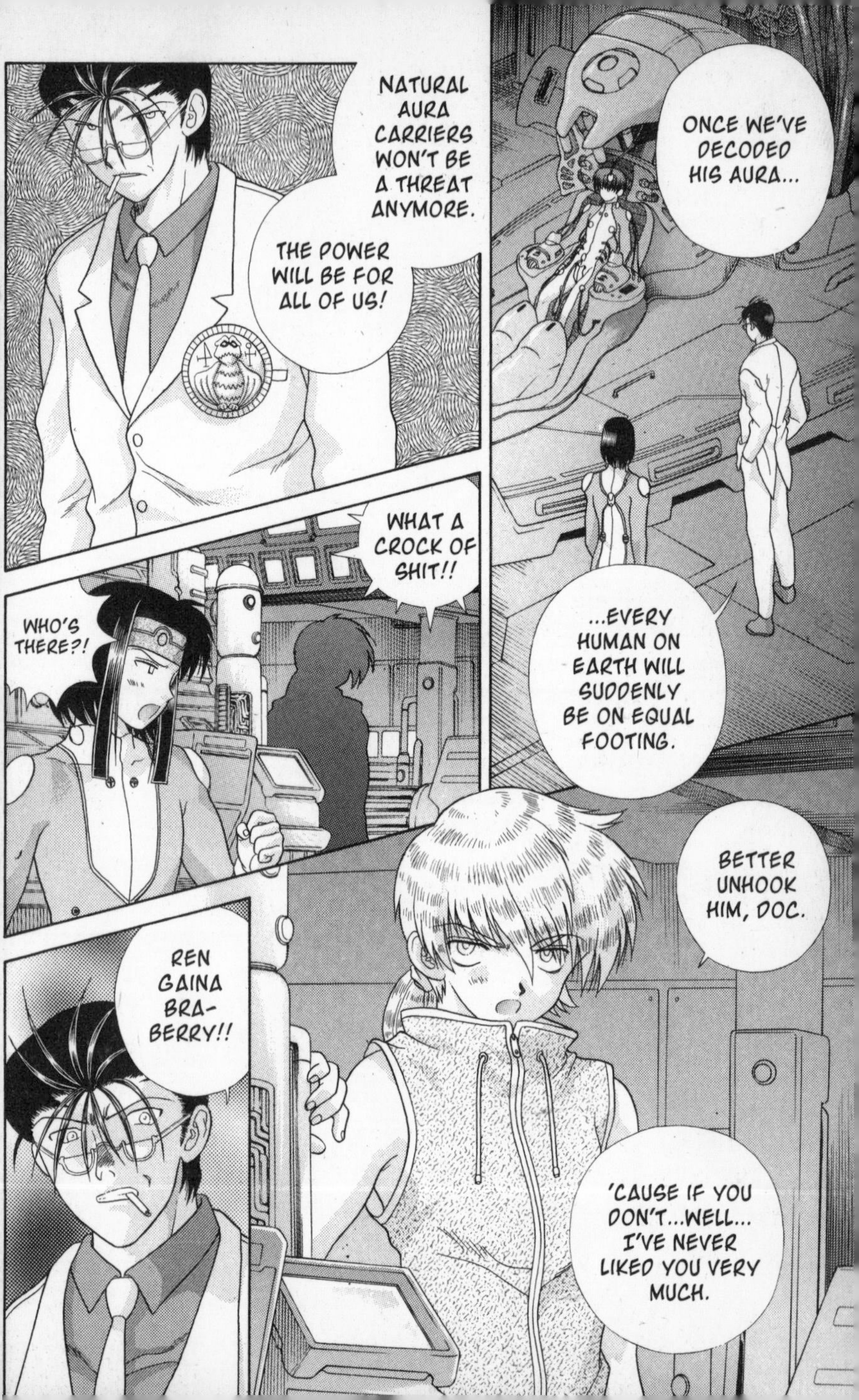

ONCE WE'VE DECODED HIS AURA...
...EVERY HUMAN ON EARTH WILL SUDDENLY BE ON EQUAL FOOTING.
NATURAL AURA CARRIERS WON'T BE A THREAT ANYMORE.
THE POWER WILL BE FOR ALL OF US!
WHAT A CROCK OF SHIT!!
WHO'S THERE?!
BETTER UNHOOK HIM, DOC.
'CAUSE IF YOU DON'T...WELL... I'VE NEVER LIKED YOU VERY MUCH.
REN GAINA BRA-BERRY!!

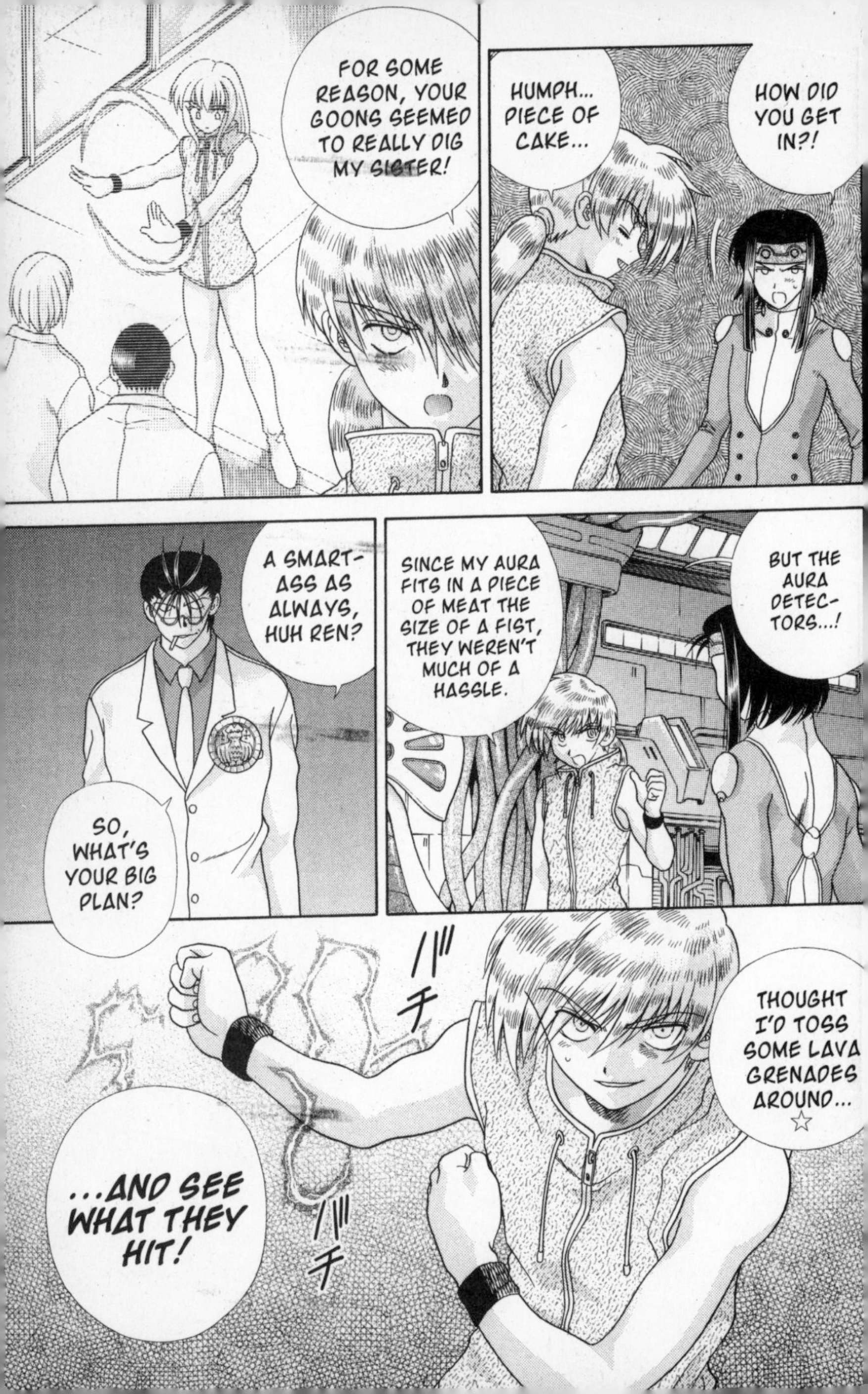
HOW DID YOU GET IN?!
HUMPH... PIECE OF CAKE...
FOR SOME REASON, YOUR GOONS SEEMED TO REALLY DIG MY SISTER!
BUT THE AURA DETECTORS...!
SINCE MY AURA FITS IN A PIECE OF MEAT THE SIZE OF A FIST, THEY WEREN'T MUCH OF A HASSLE.
A SMART-ASS AS ALWAYS, HUH REN?
SO, WHAT'S YOUR BIG PLAN?
バチ
THOUGHT I'D TOSS SOME LAVA GRENADES AROUND... ☆
バチ
...AND SEE WHAT THEY HIT!

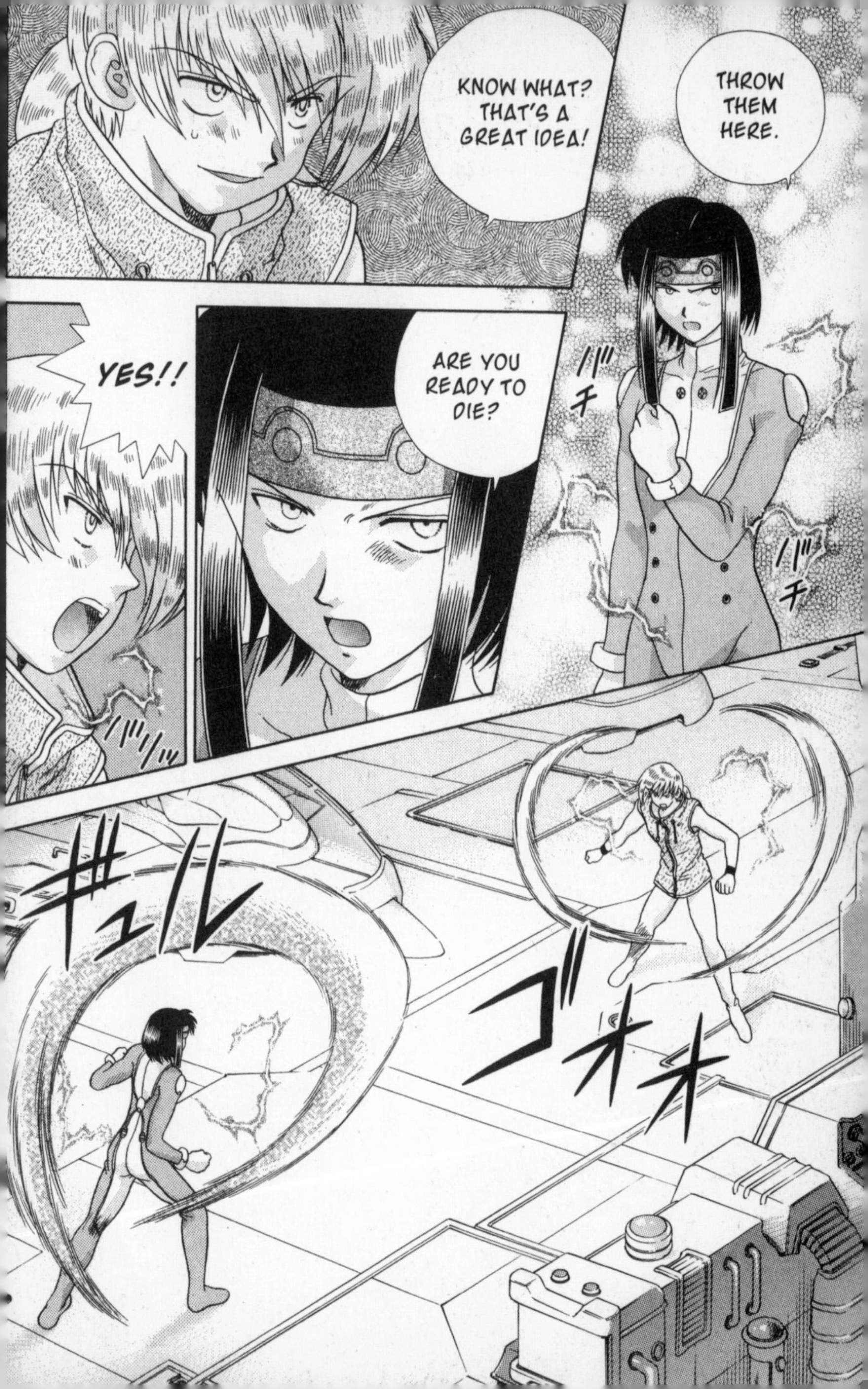
THROW THEM HERE.
バチ
バチ
KNOW WHAT? THAT'S A GREAT IDEA!
ARE YOU READY TO DIE?
YES!!
バリッ
ギュル
ゴオオ

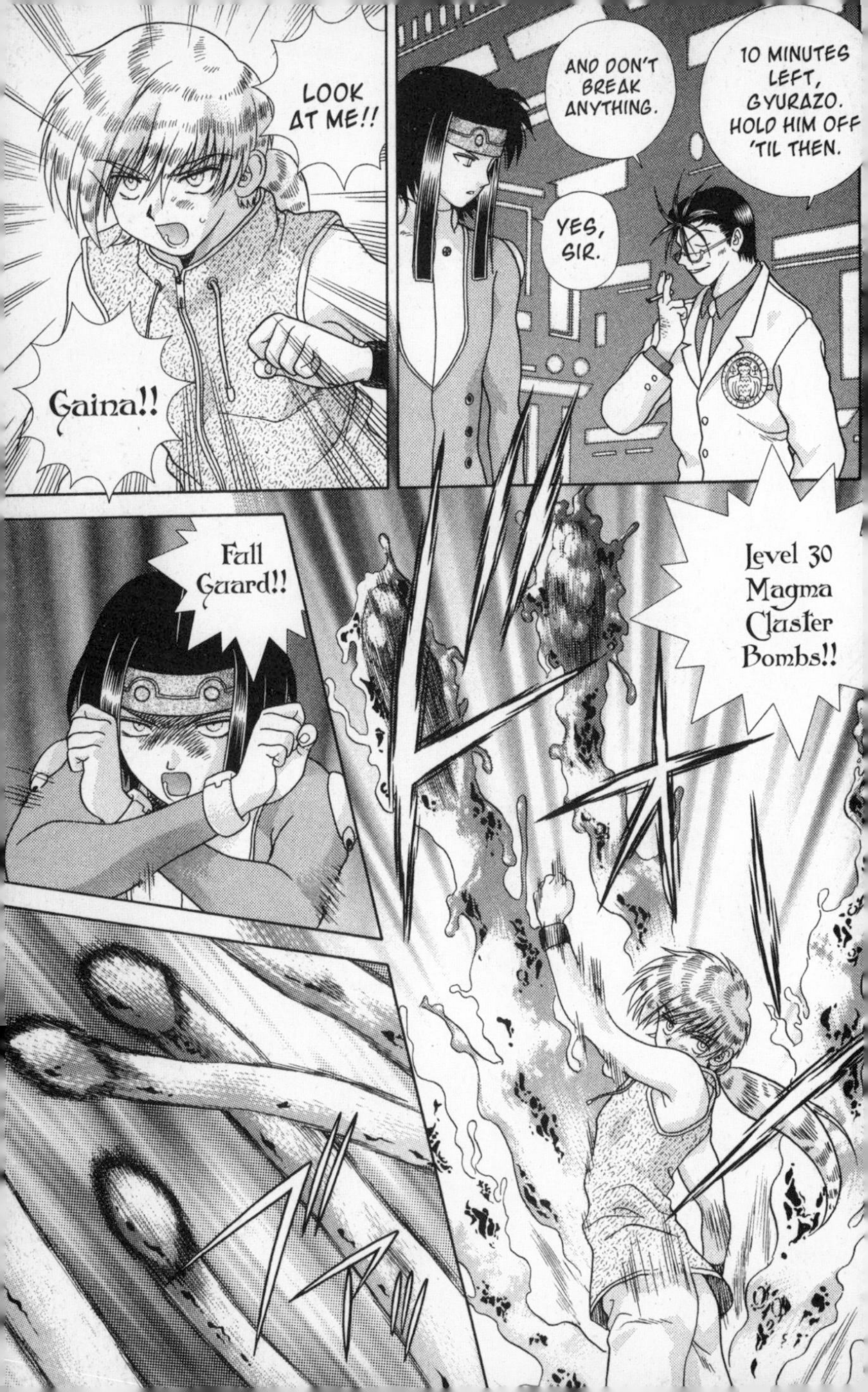
10 MINUTES LEFT, GYURAZO. HOLD HIM OFF 'TIL THEN.
AND DON'T BREAK ANYTHING.
YES, SIR.
LOOK AT ME!!
Gaina!!
Level 30 Magma Cluster Bombs!!
Full Guard!!

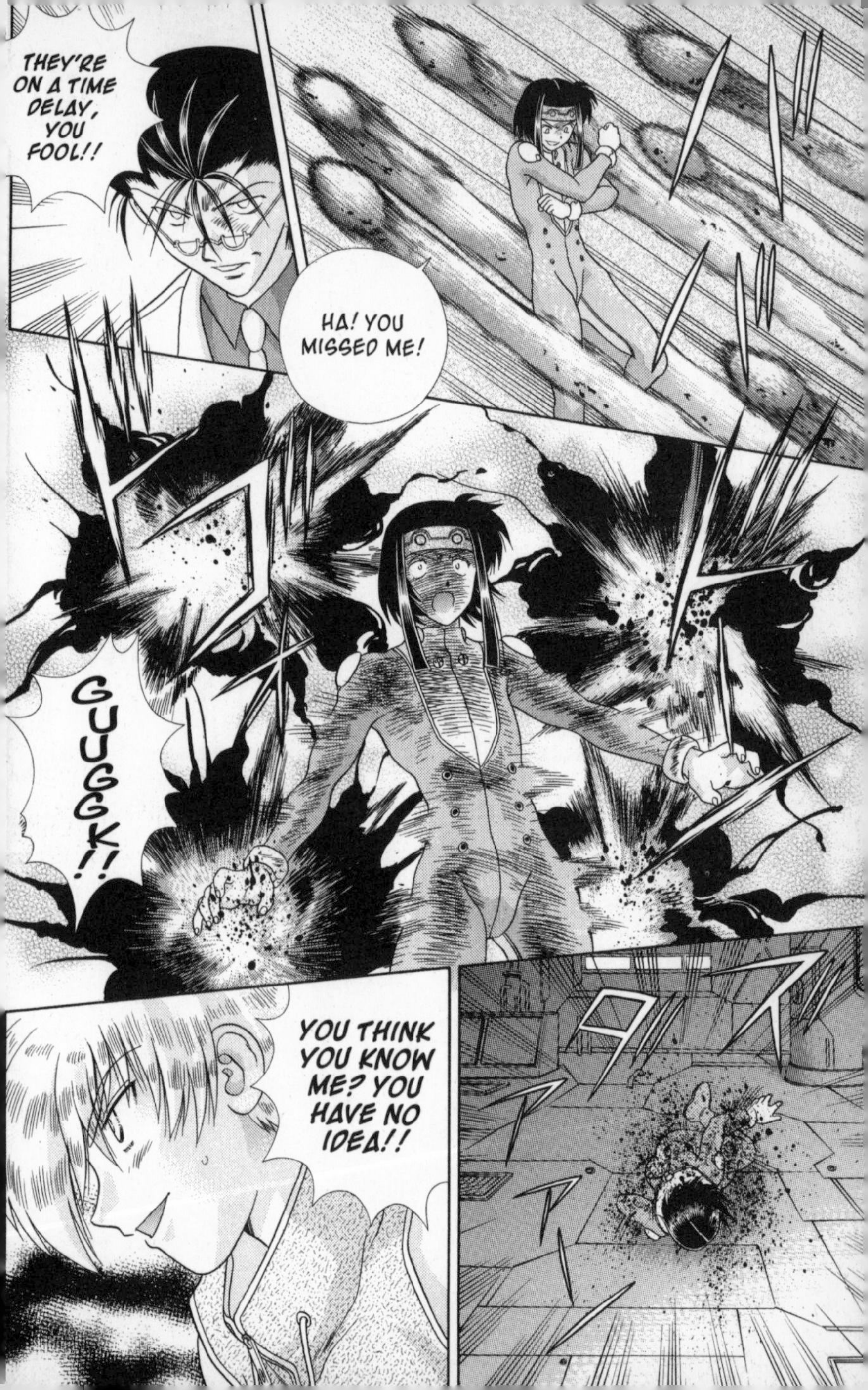
HA! YOU MISSED ME!
THEY'RE ON A TIME DELAY, YOU FOOL!!
GUUGGK!!
YOU THINK YOU KNOW ME? YOU HAVE NO IDEA!!

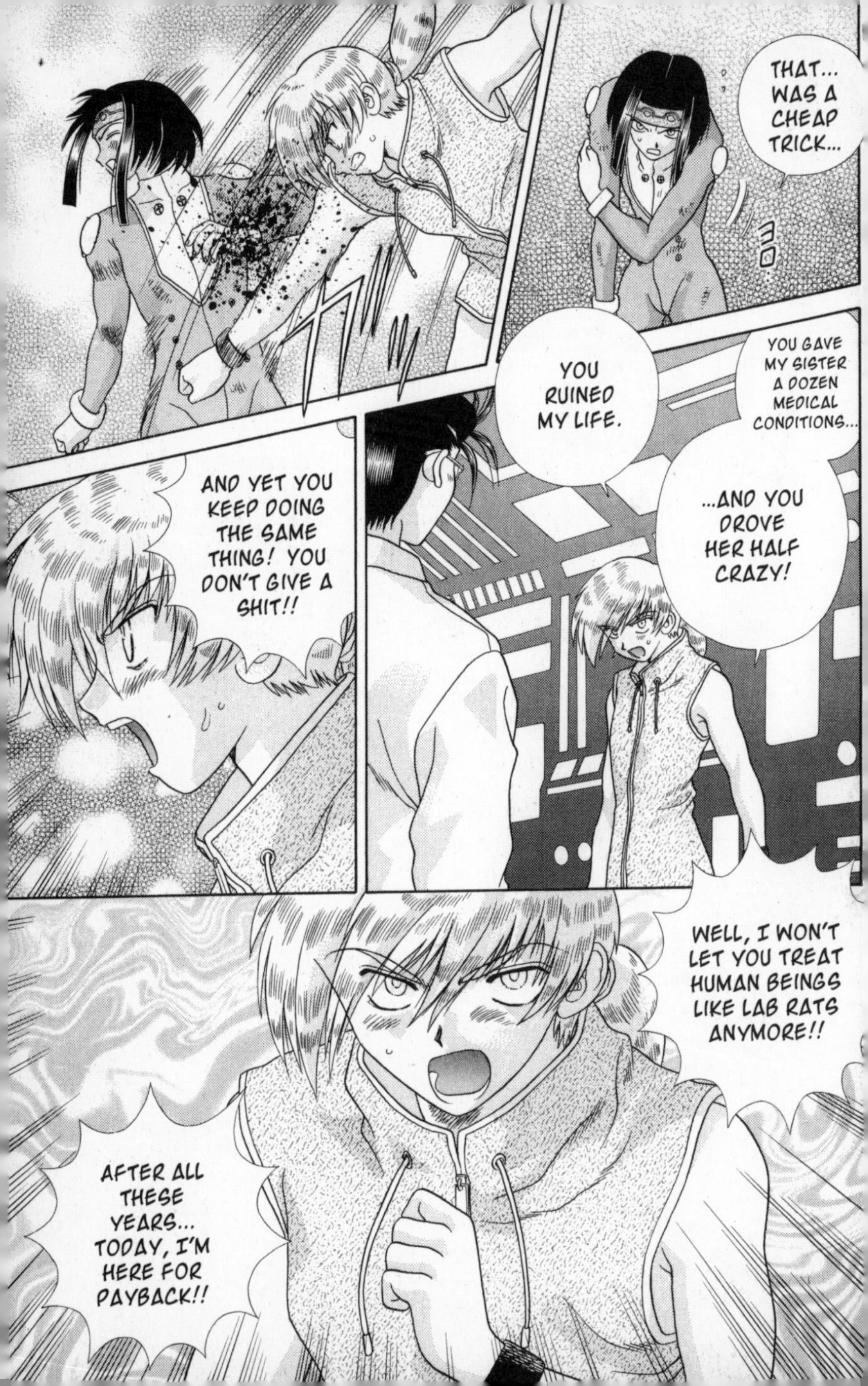
THAT... WAS A CHEAP TRICK...
YOU GAVE MY SISTER A DOZEN MEDICAL CONDITIONS...
...AND YOU DROVE HER HALF CRAZY!
YOU RUINED MY LIFE.
AND YET YOU KEEP DOING THE SAME THING! YOU DON'T GIVE A SHIT!!
WELL, I WON'T LET YOU TREAT HUMAN BEINGS LIKE LAB RATS ANYMORE!!
AFTER ALL THESE YEARS... TODAY, I'M HERE FOR PAYBACK!!

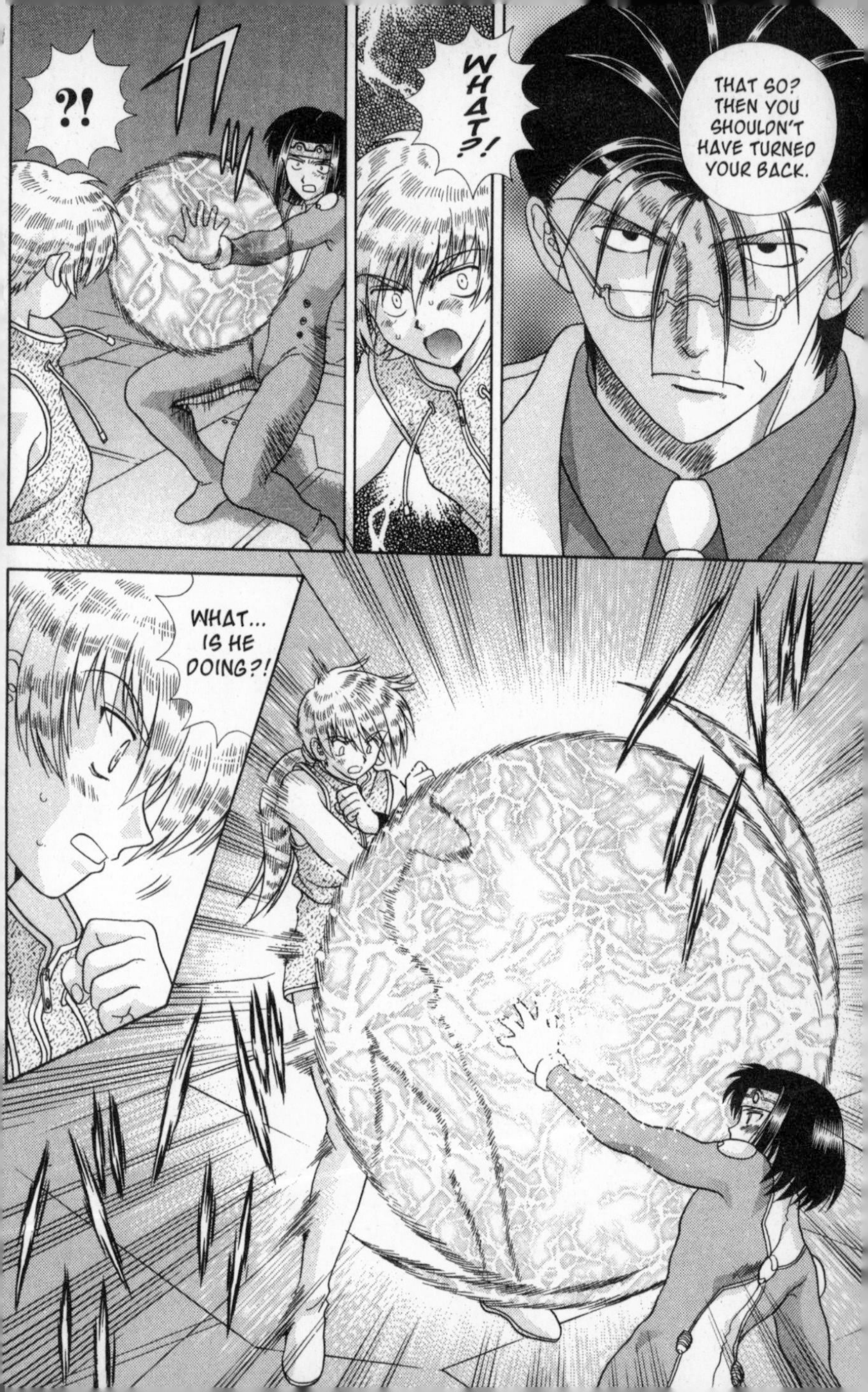
THAT SO? THEN YOU SHOULDN'T HAVE TURNED YOUR BACK.
WHAT?!
?!
WHAT... IS HE DOING?!

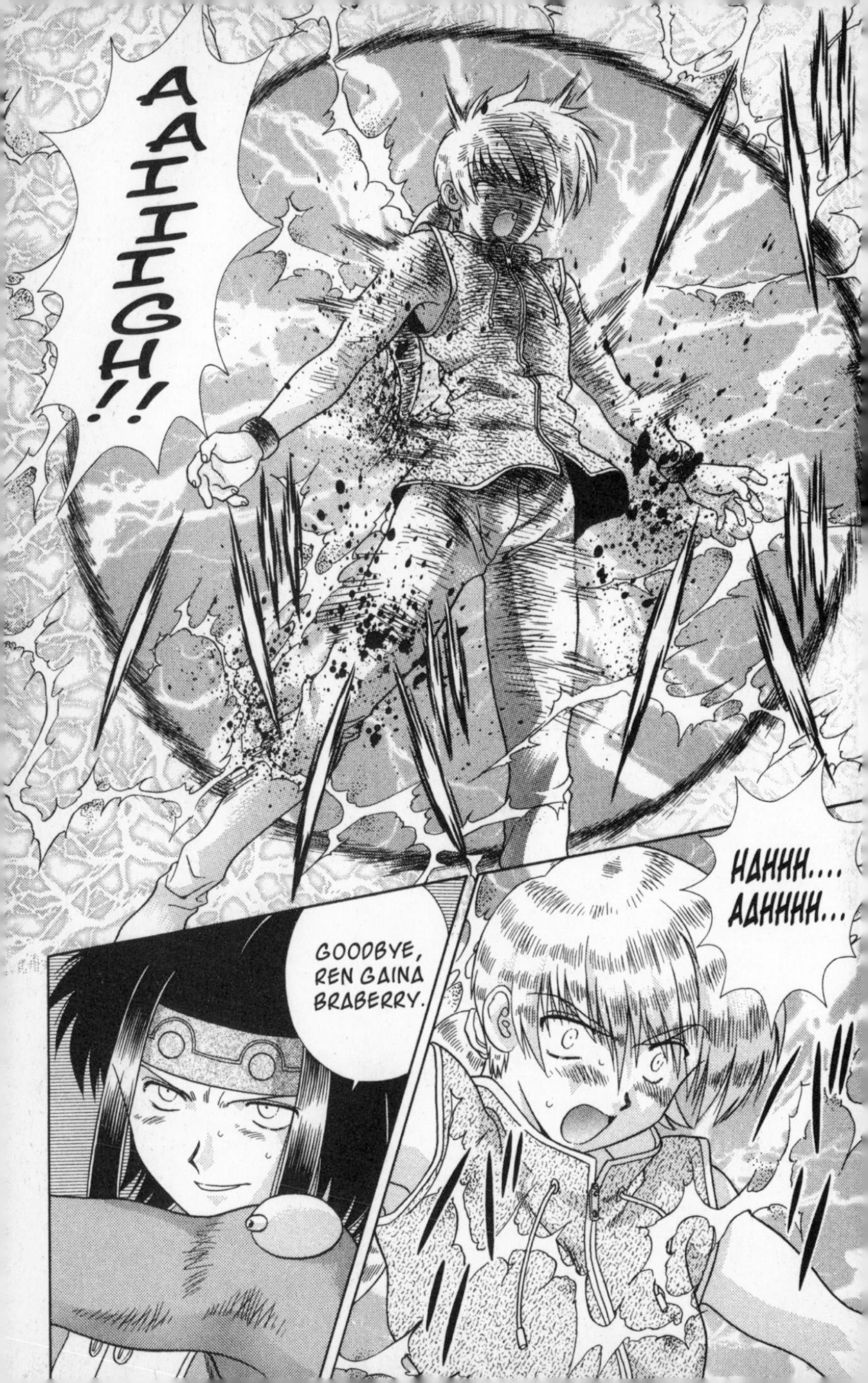
AAIIIIGH!!
HAHHH....
AAHHHH...
GOODBYE, REN GAINA BRABERRY.

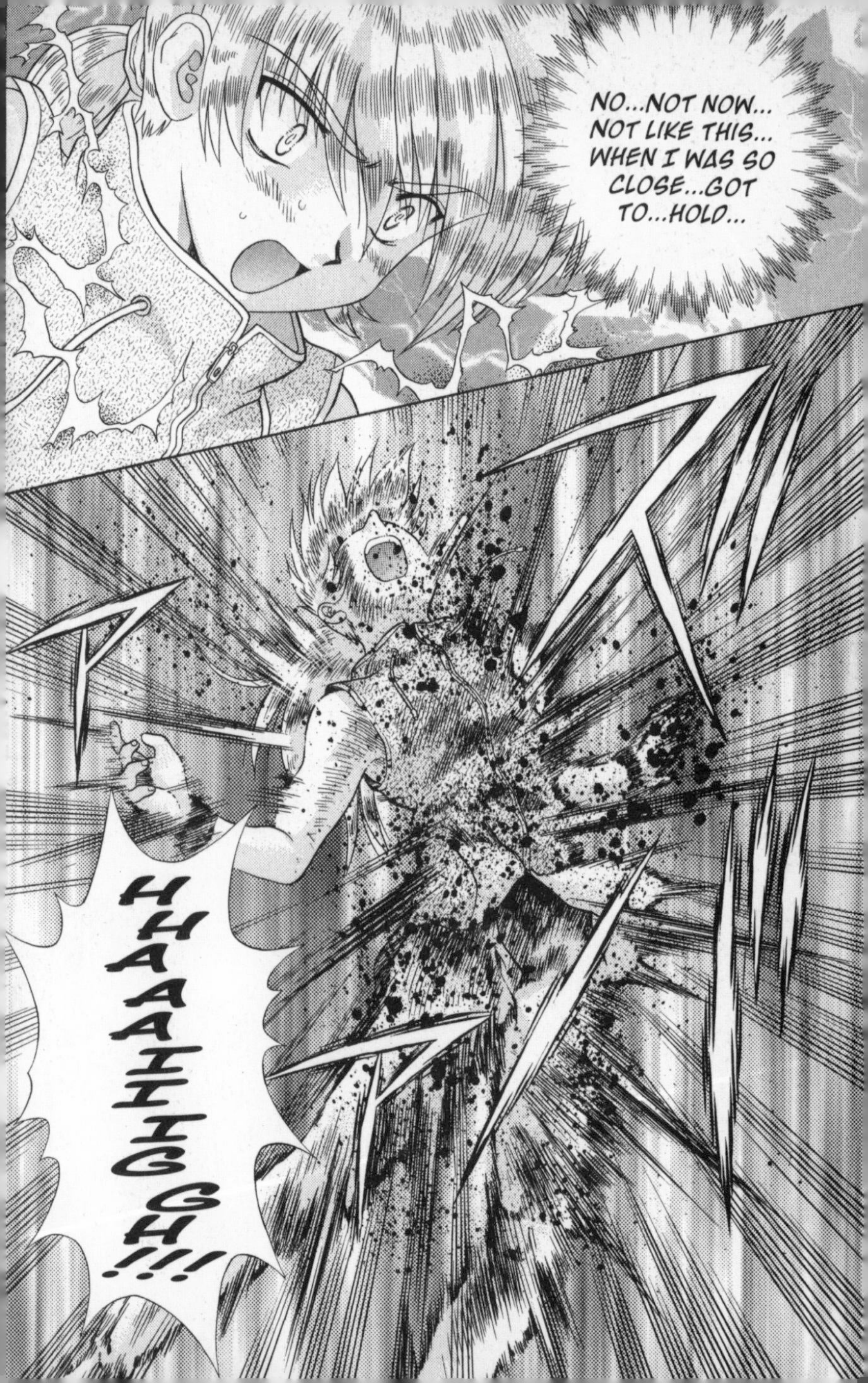
NO...NOT NOW... NOT LIKE THIS... WHEN I WAS SO CLOSE...GOT TO...HOLD...
HHAAAIIIGGH!!!

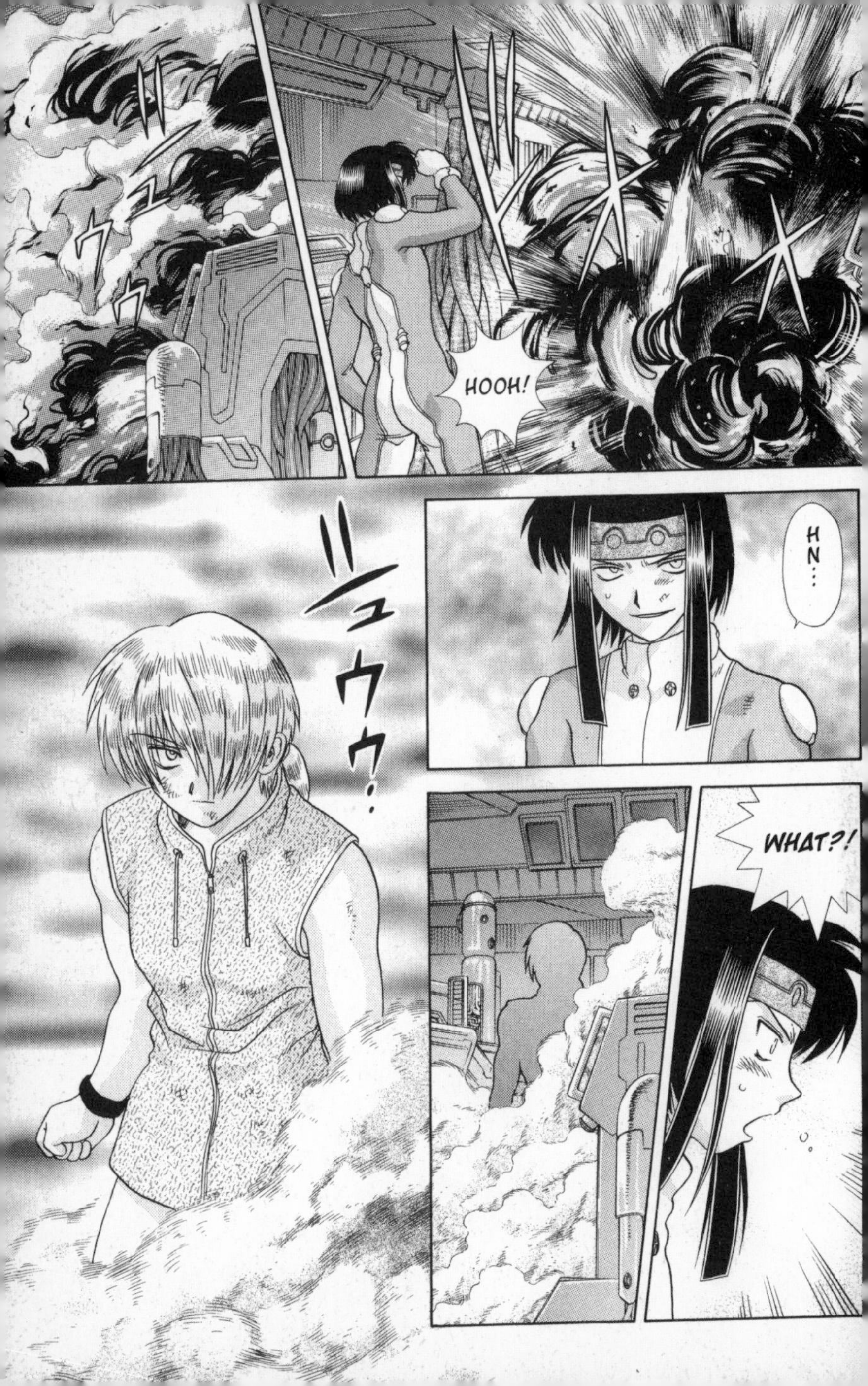
HOOH!
HN...
WHAT?!
シュウウ!

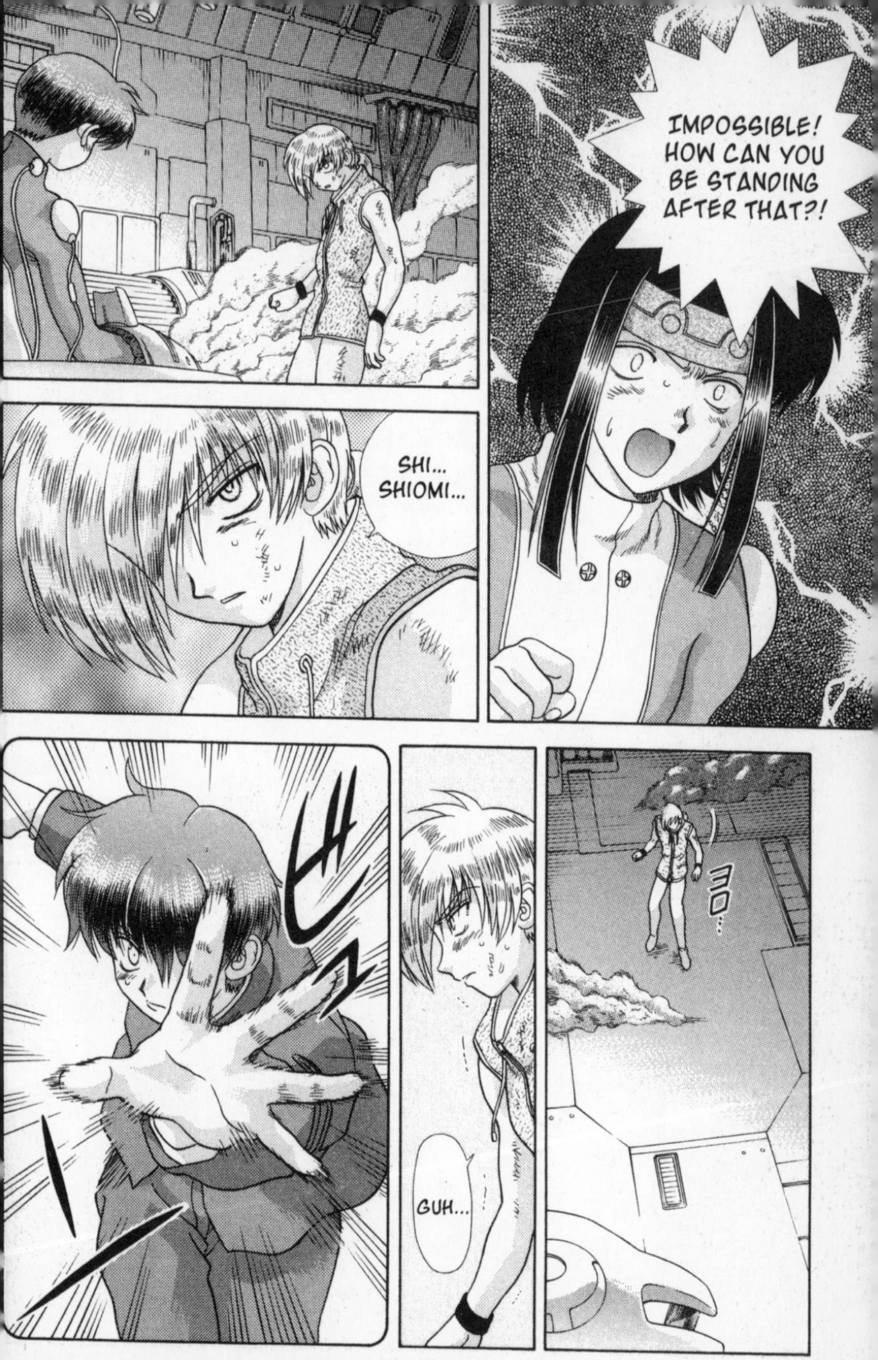
IMPOSSIBLE! HOW CAN YOU BE STANDING AFTER THAT?!
SHI... SHIOMI...
ヨロ…
GUH...

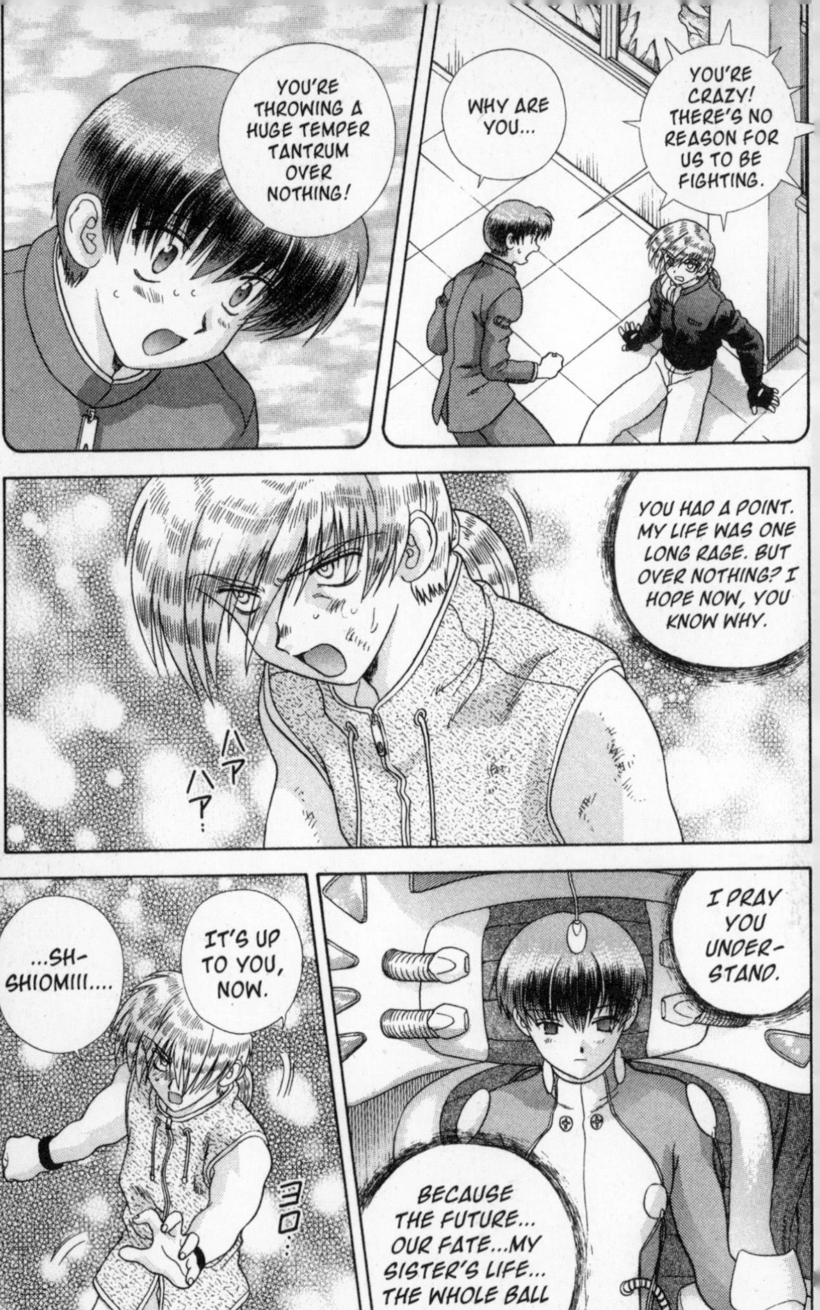
YOU'RE CRAZY! THERE'S NO REASON FOR US TO BE FIGHTING.
WHY ARE YOU...
YOU'RE THROWING A HUGE TEMPER TANTRUM OVER NOTHING!
YOU HAD A POINT. MY LIFE WAS ONE LONG RAGE. BUT OVER NOTHING? I HOPE NOW, YOU KNOW WHY.
ハァ ハァ…
I PRAY YOU UNDER-STAND.
BECAUSE THE FUTURE... OUR FATE...MY SISTER'S LIFE... THE WHOLE BALL OF WAX...
IT'S UP TO YOU, NOW.
...SH-SHIOMIII....
ヨロ…

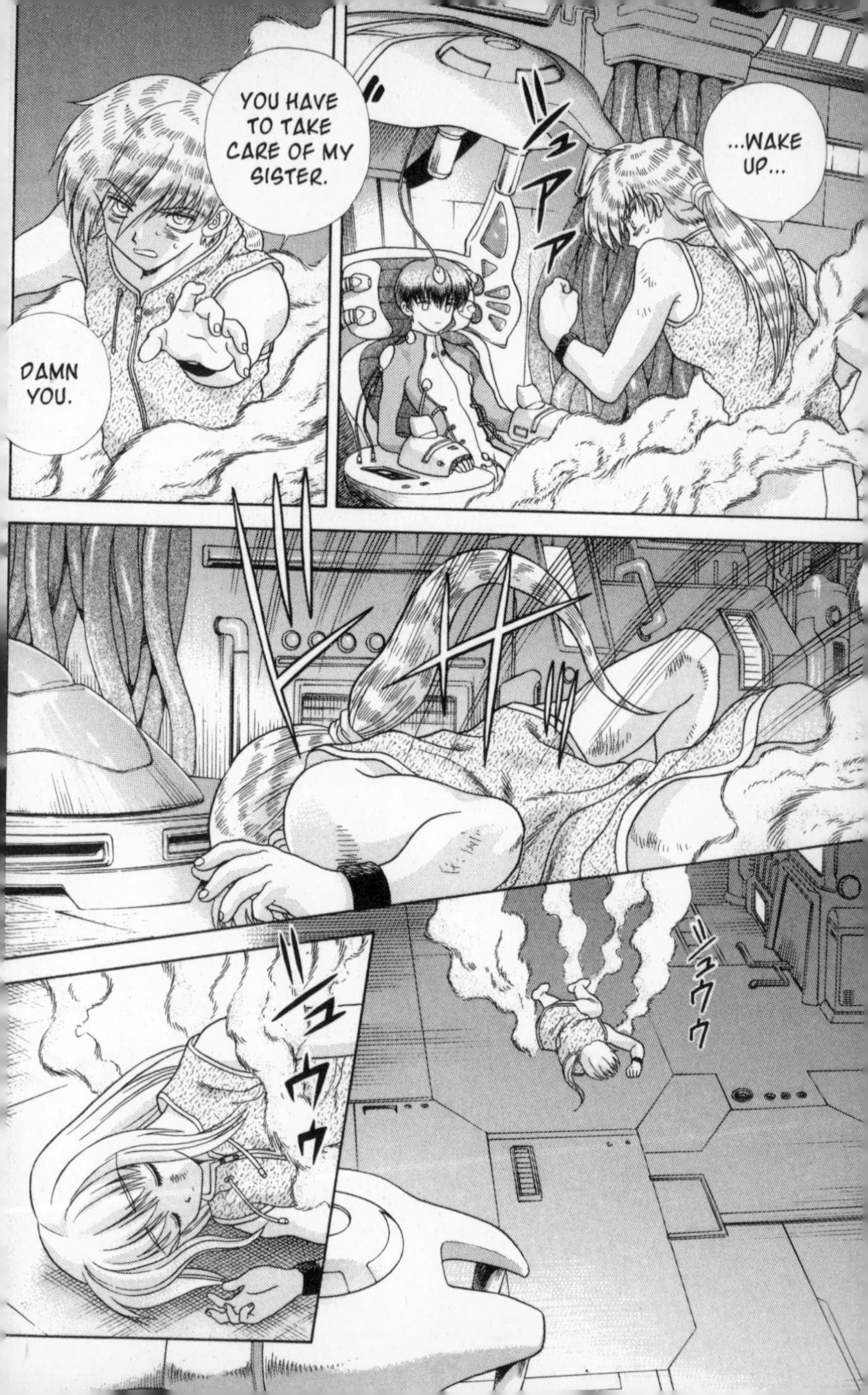
ジュアアア
...WAKE UP...
YOU HAVE TO TAKE CARE OF MY SISTER.
DAMN YOU.
ジュウウ
ジュウウ

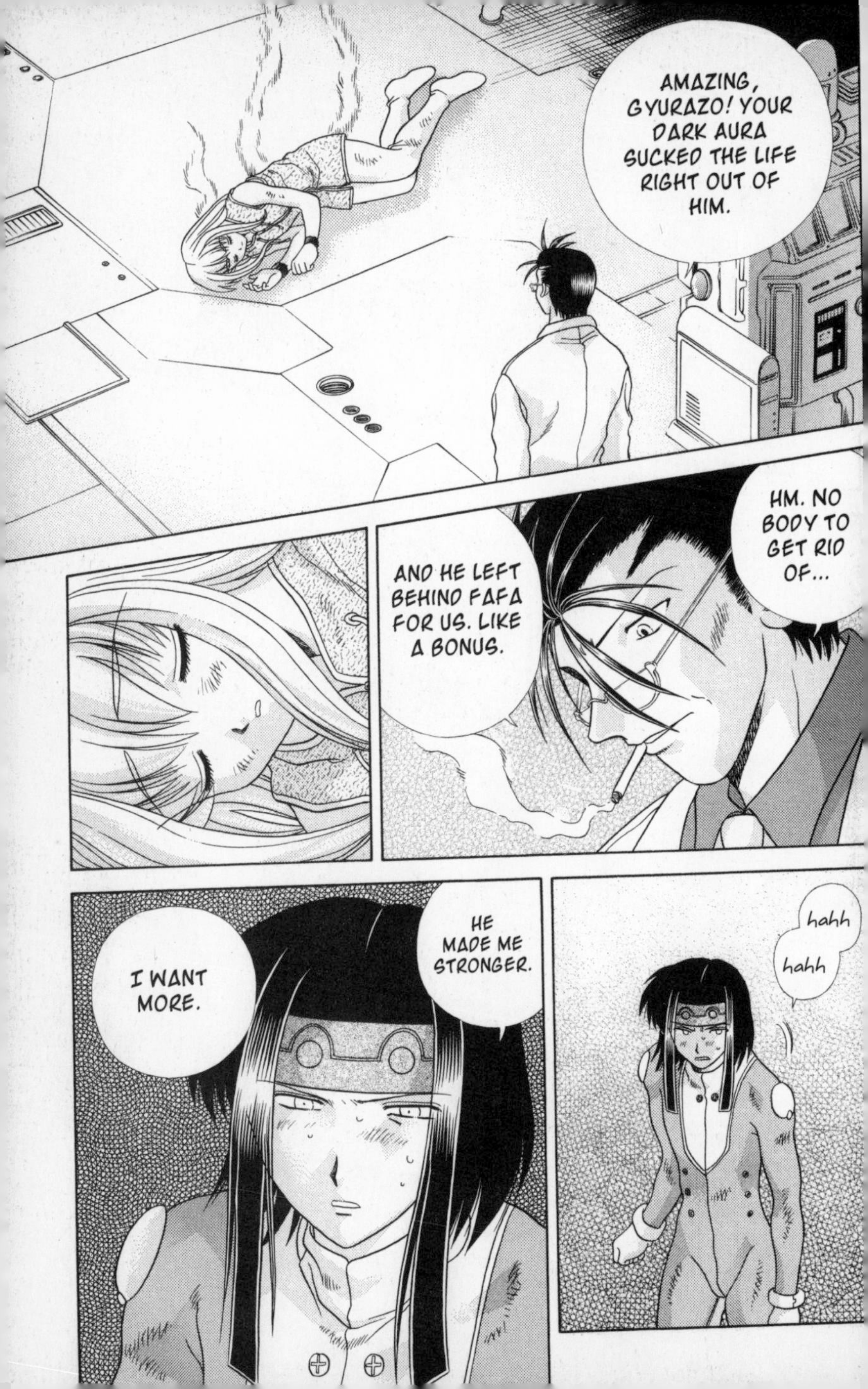
AMAZING, GYURAZO! YOUR DARK AURA SUCKED THE LIFE RIGHT OUT OF HIM.
HM. NO BODY TO GET RID OF...
AND HE LEFT BEHIND FAFA FOR US. LIKE A BONUS.
hahh
hahh
HE MADE ME STRONGER.
I WANT MORE.

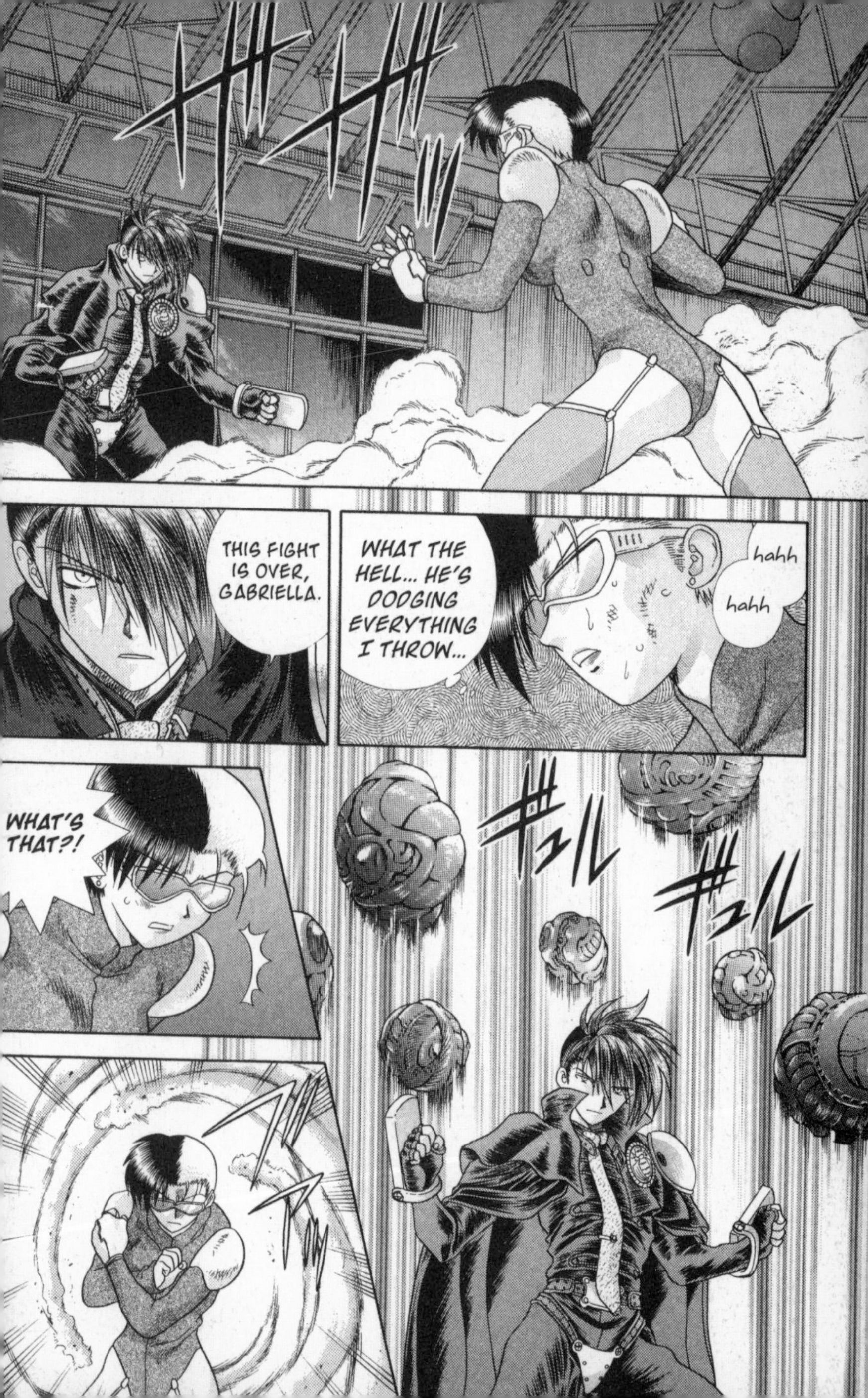
WHAT THE HELL... HE'S DODGING EVERYTHING I THROW...
hahh
hahh
THIS FIGHT IS OVER, GABRIELLA.
ギュル
ギュル
WHAT'S THAT?!

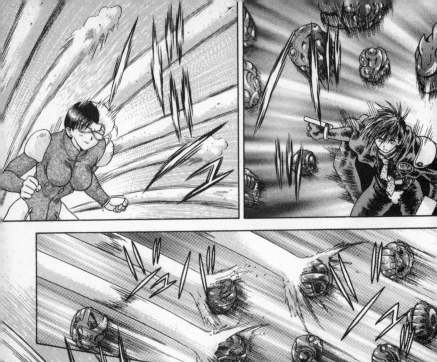

CAN'T...
KEEP
UP...

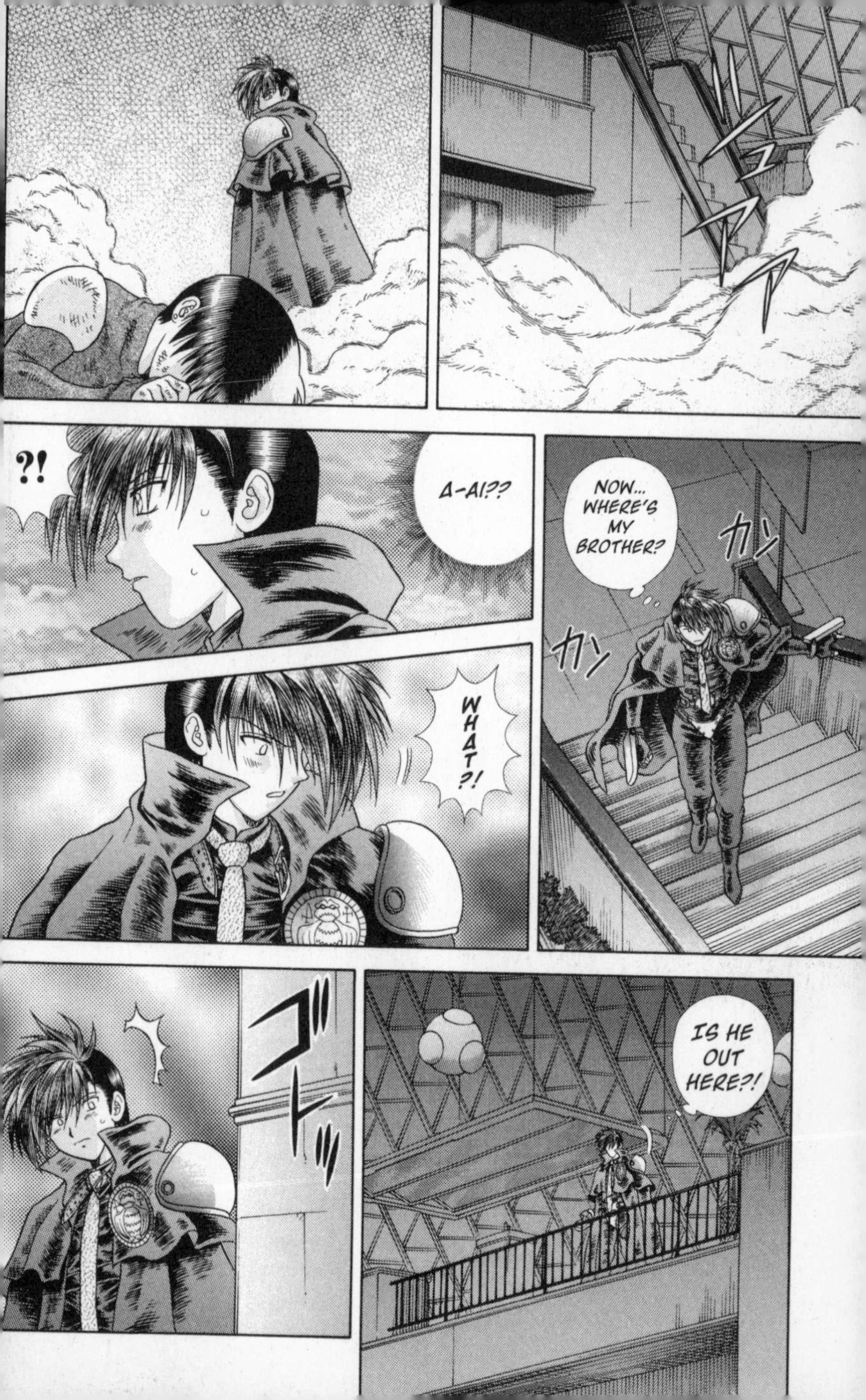
NOW... WHERE'S MY BROTHER?
カン
カン
A-AI!??
?!
WHAT?!
IS HE OUT HERE?!
ゴトッ

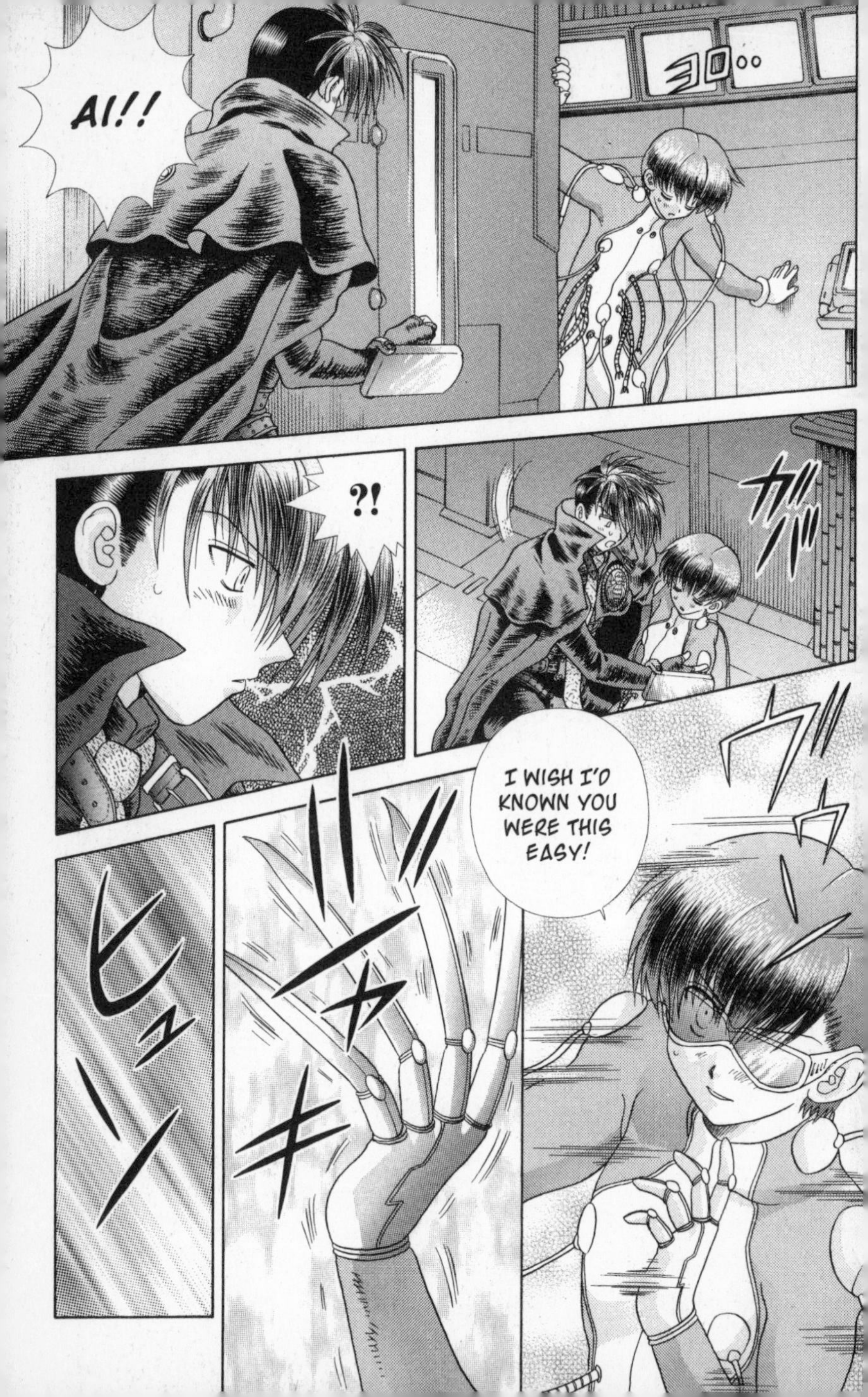
AI!!
?!
I WISH I'D KNOWN YOU WERE THIS EASY!

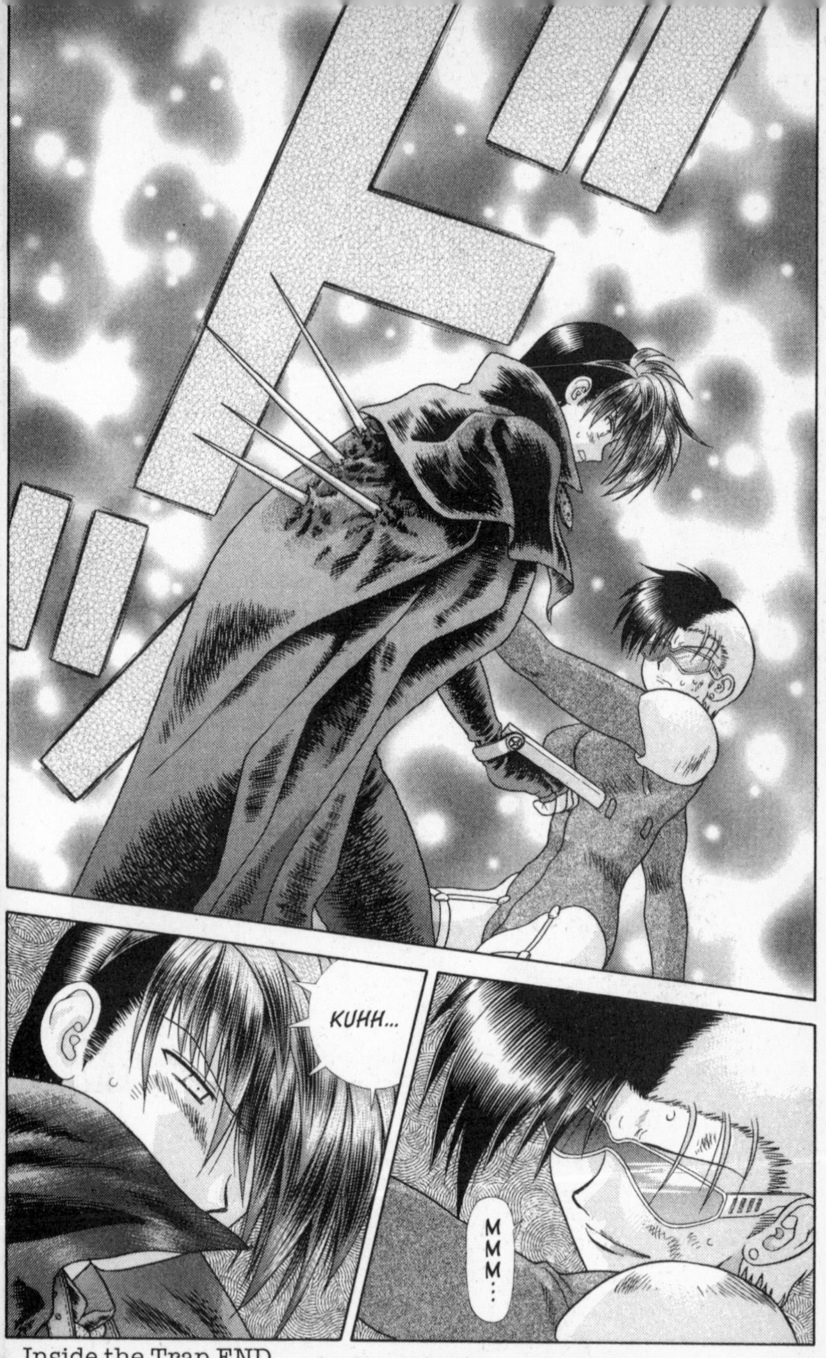
MMM...
KUHH...

Inside the Trap END

Chapter 35 Siege and Sacrifice

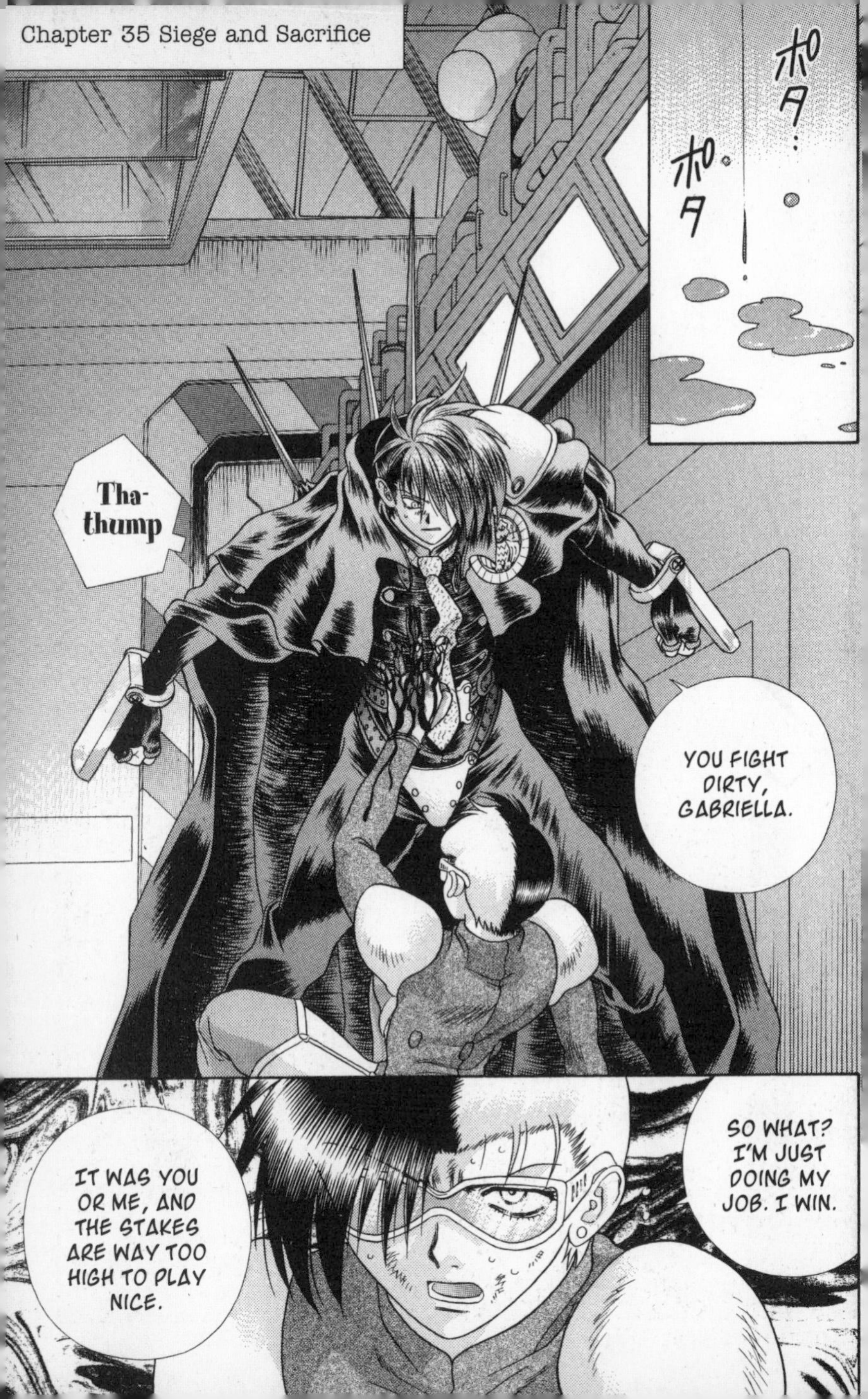
ポタ…
ポタ
Tha-thump
YOU FIGHT DIRTY, GABRIELLA.
SO WHAT? I'M JUST DOING MY JOB. I WIN.
IT WAS YOU OR ME, AND THE STAKES ARE WAY TOO HIGH TO PLAY NICE.

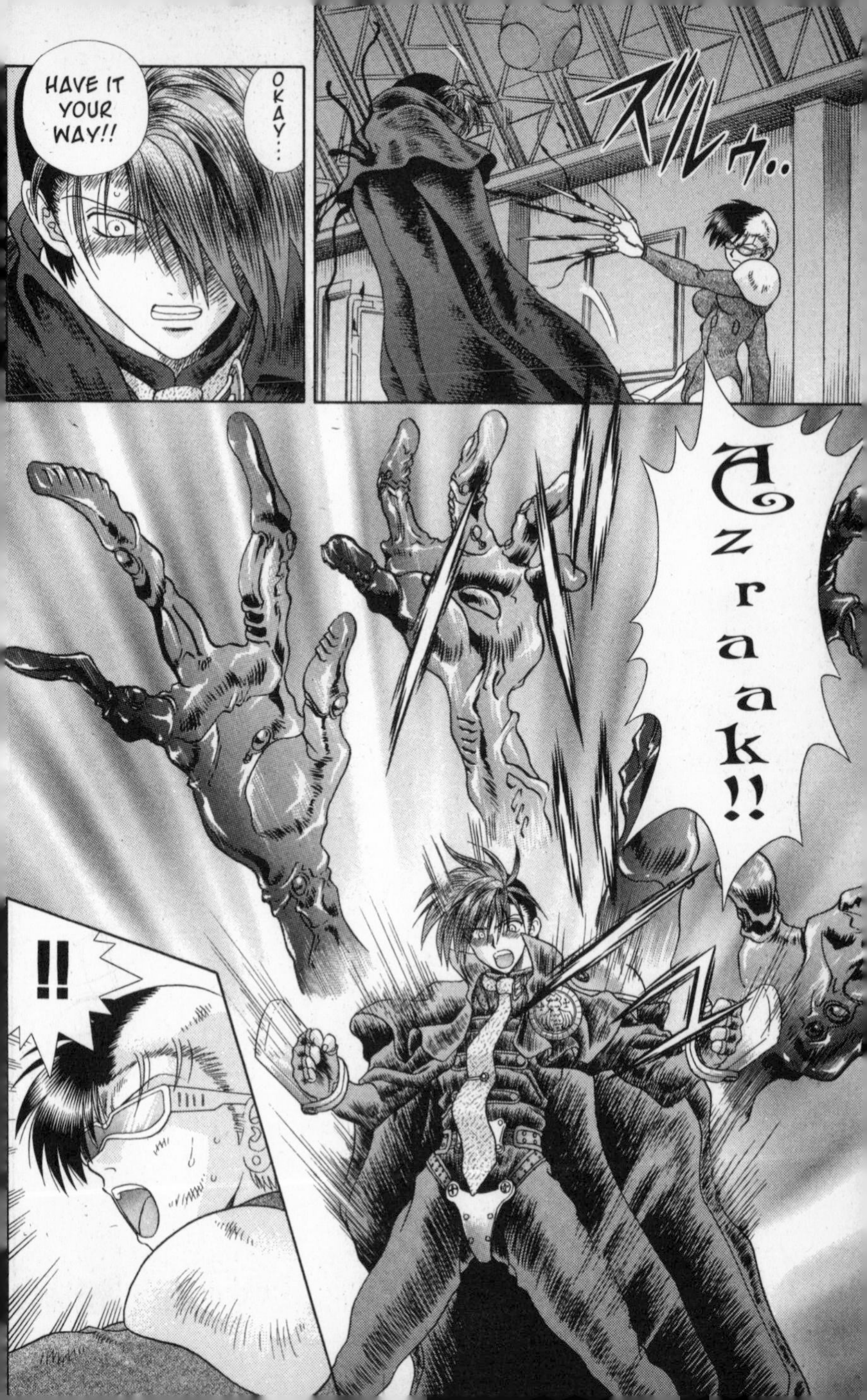
ズルゥ..
OKAY...
HAVE IT YOUR WAY!!
Azraak!!
!!

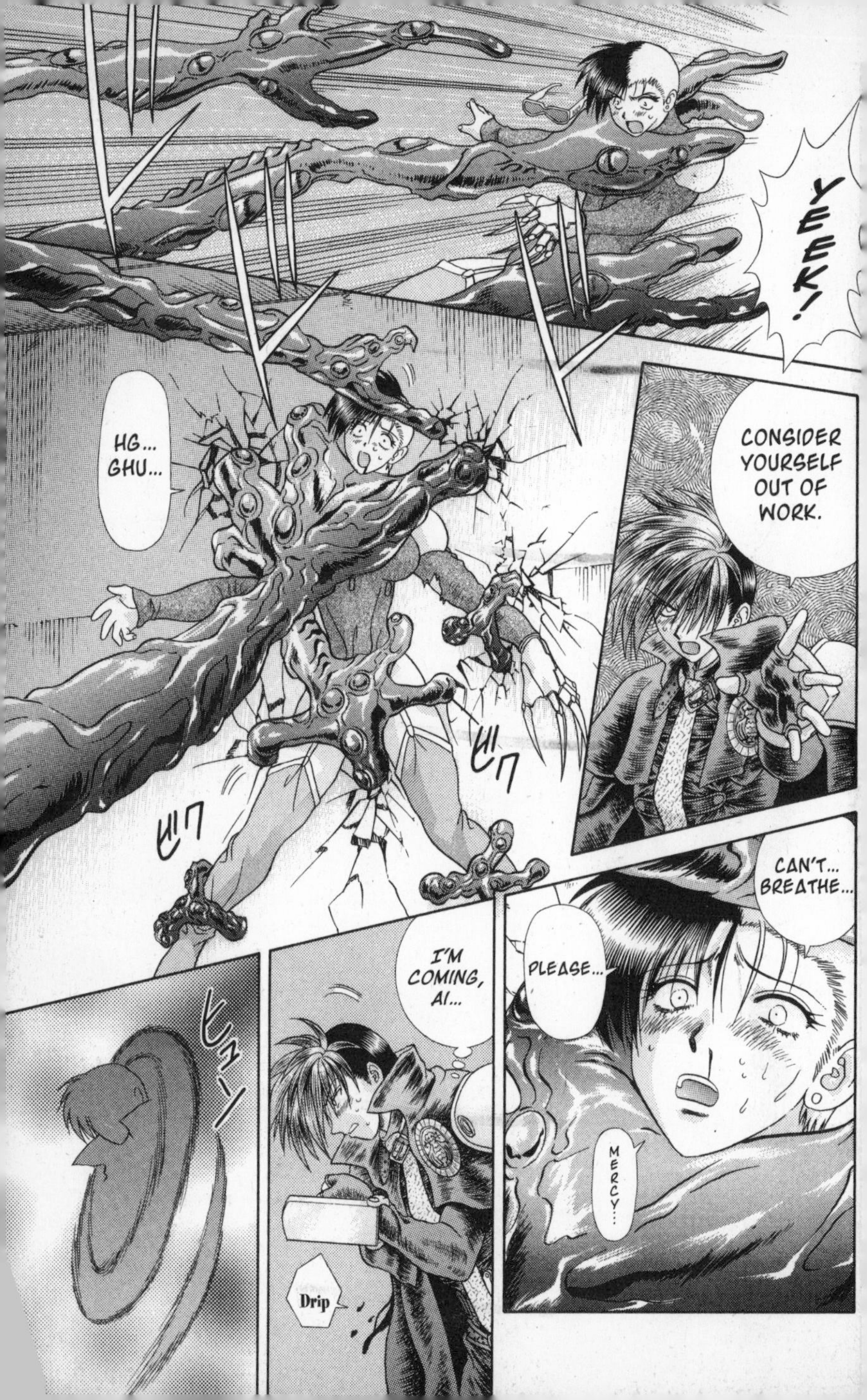
YEEK!
CONSIDER YOURSELF OUT OF WORK.
HG... GHU...
CAN'T... BREATHE...
PLEASE...
MERCY...
I'M COMING, AI...
Drip

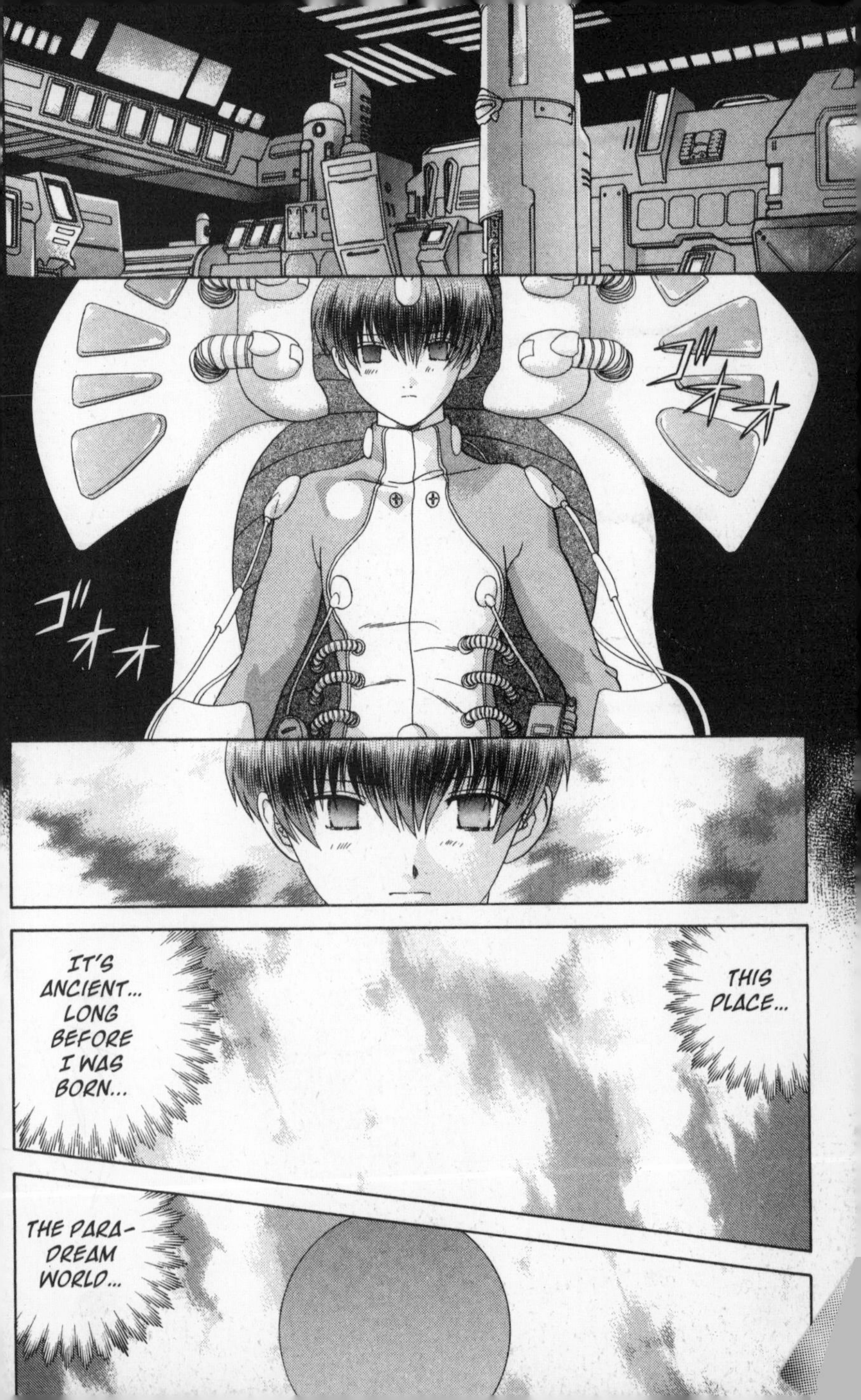
ゴオオ
ゴオオ
THIS PLACE...
IT'S ANCIENT... LONG BEFORE I WAS BORN...
THE PARA-DREAM WORLD...

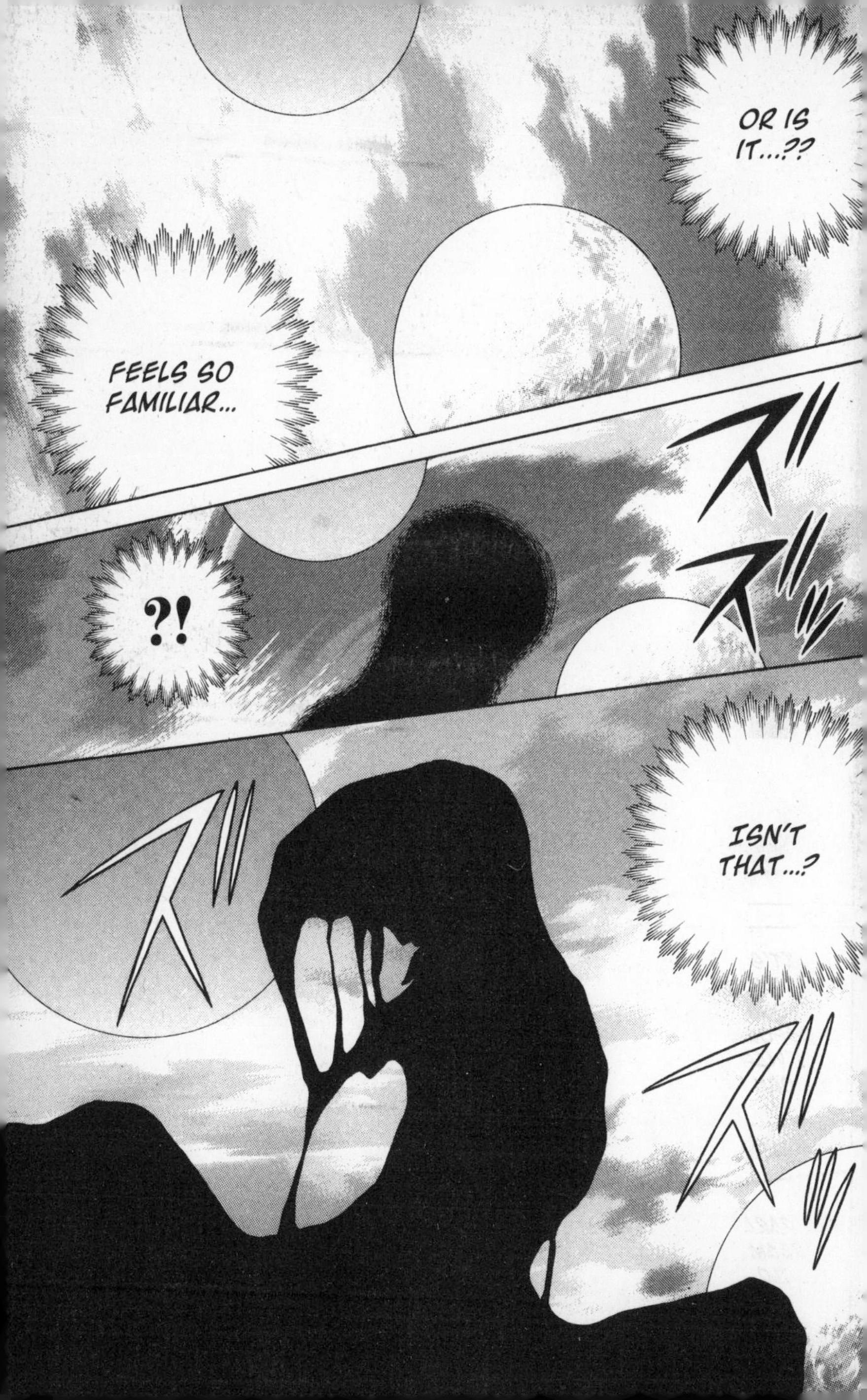
OR IS IT...??
FEELS SO FAMILIAR...
?!
ISN'T THAT...?

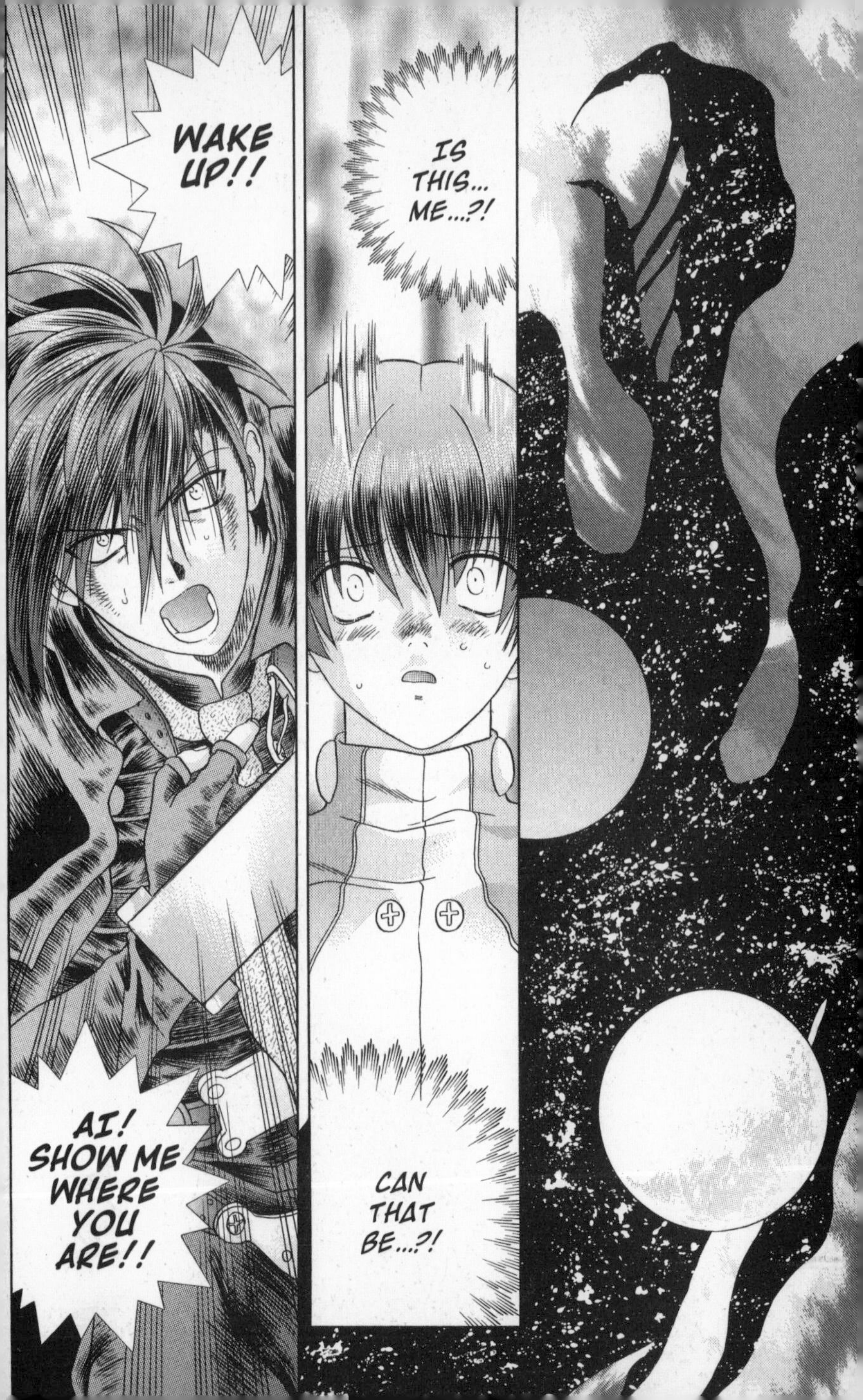
IS THIS... ME...?!
CAN THAT BE...?!
WAKE UP!!
AI! SHOW ME WHERE YOU ARE!!

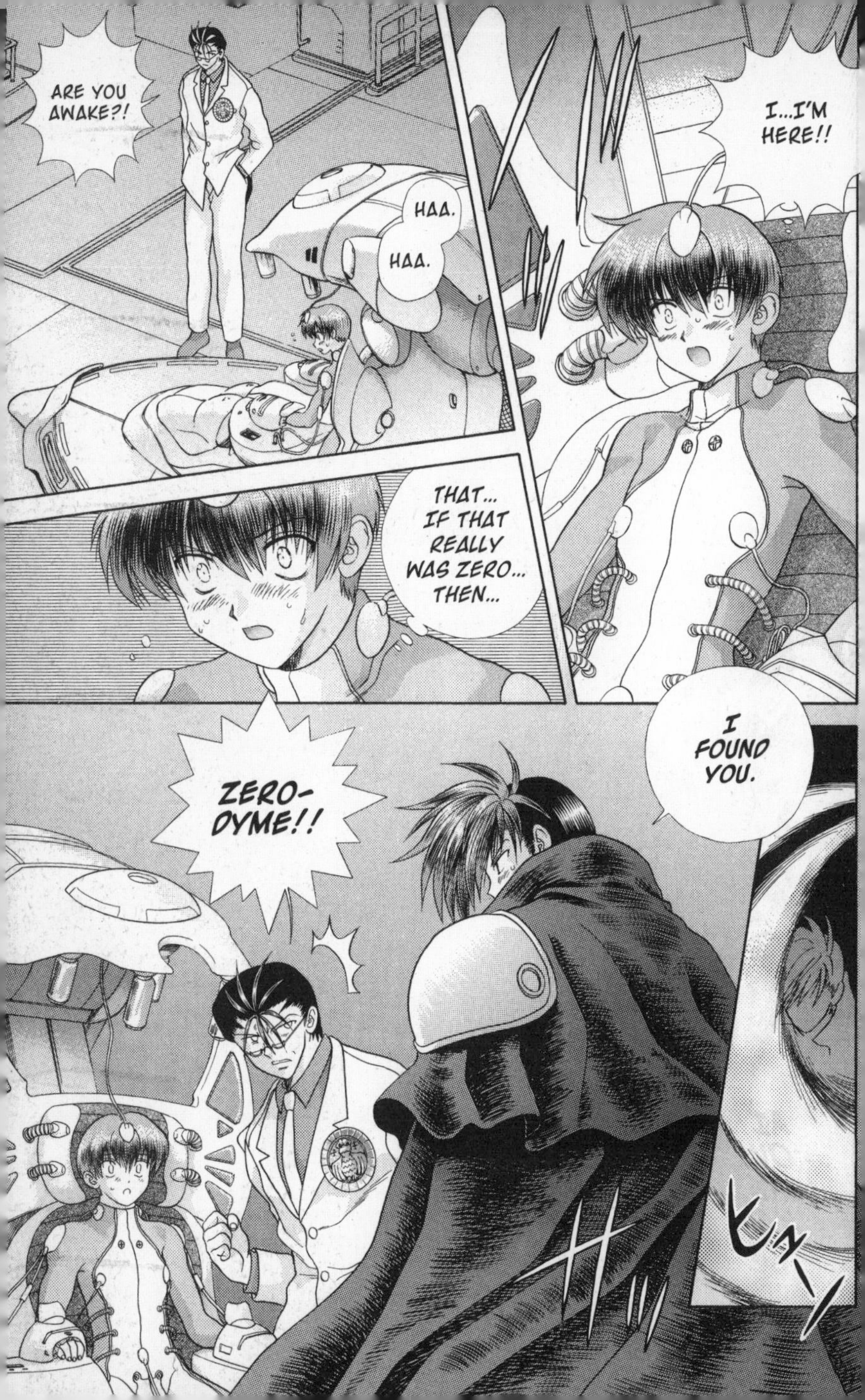

I...I'M HERE!!
ARE YOU AWAKE?!
HAA.
HAA.
THAT... IF THAT REALLY WAS ZERO... THEN...
I FOUND YOU.
ZERO-DYME!!

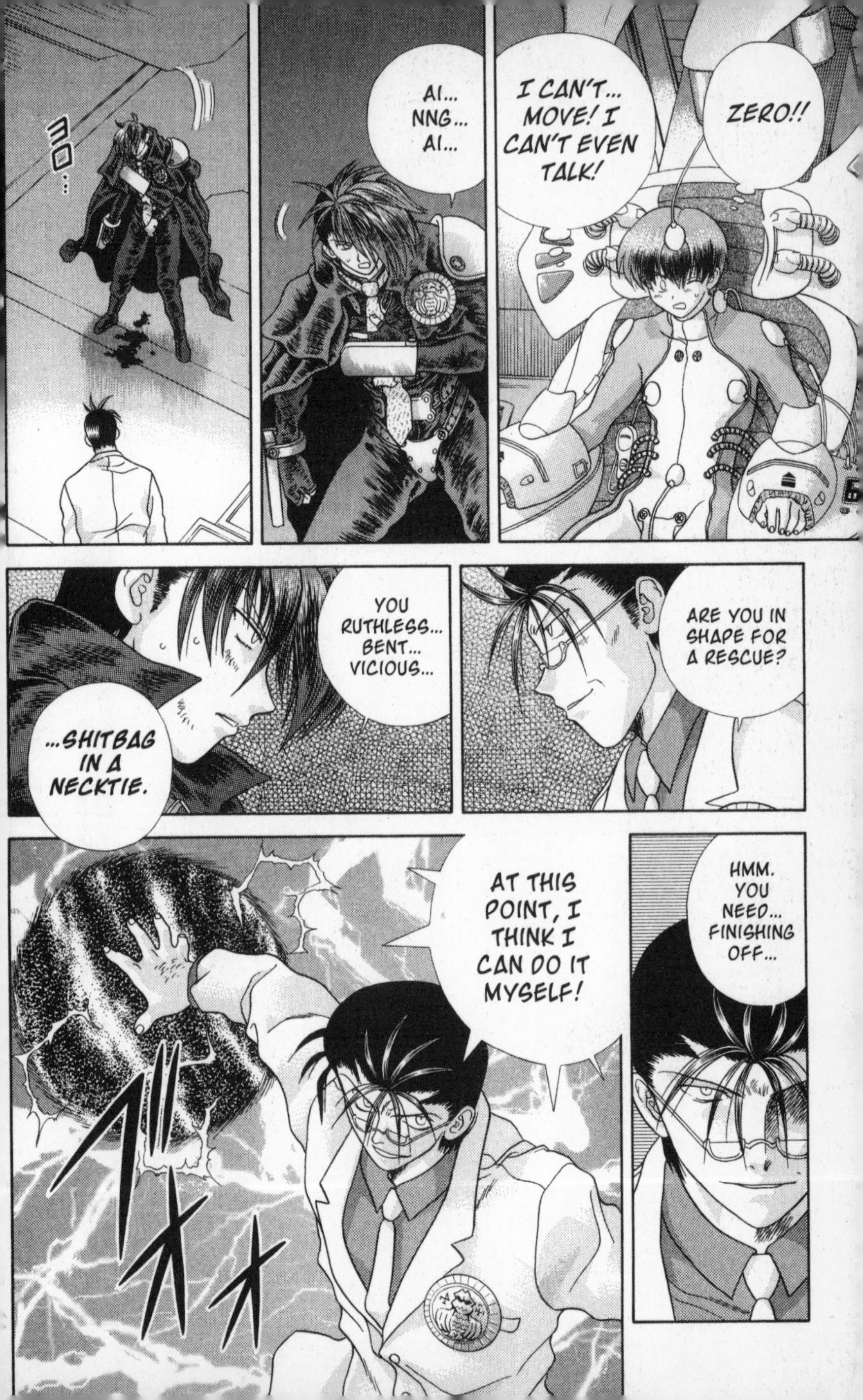
ZERO!!
I CAN'T... MOVE! I CAN'T EVEN TALK!
AI... NNG... AI...
ヨロ...
ARE YOU IN SHAPE FOR A RESCUE?
YOU RUTHLESS... BENT... VICIOUS...
...SHITBAG IN A NECKTIE.
HMM. YOU NEED... FINISHING OFF...
AT THIS POINT, I THINK I CAN DO IT MYSELF!

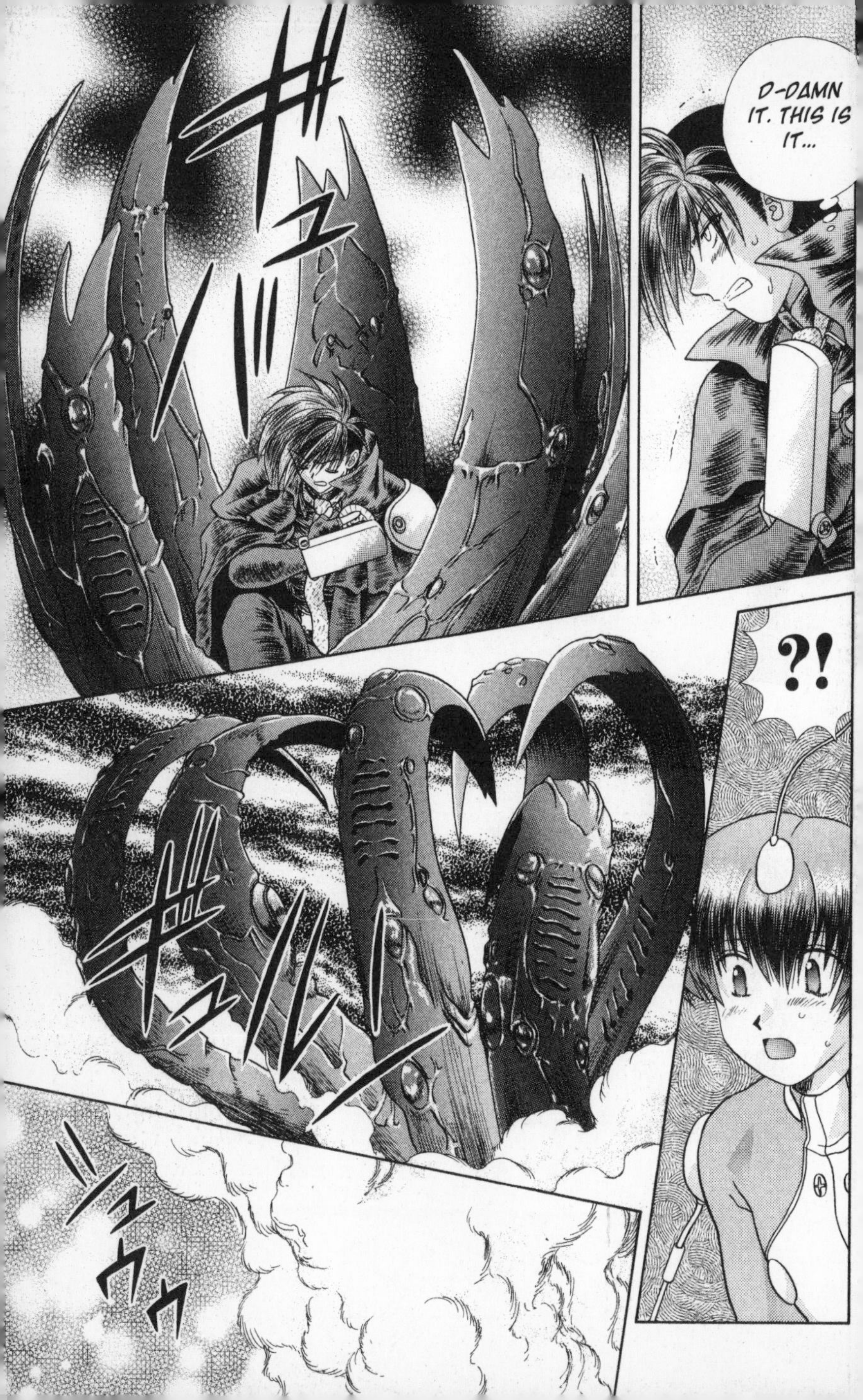
D-DAMN IT. THIS IS IT...
?!

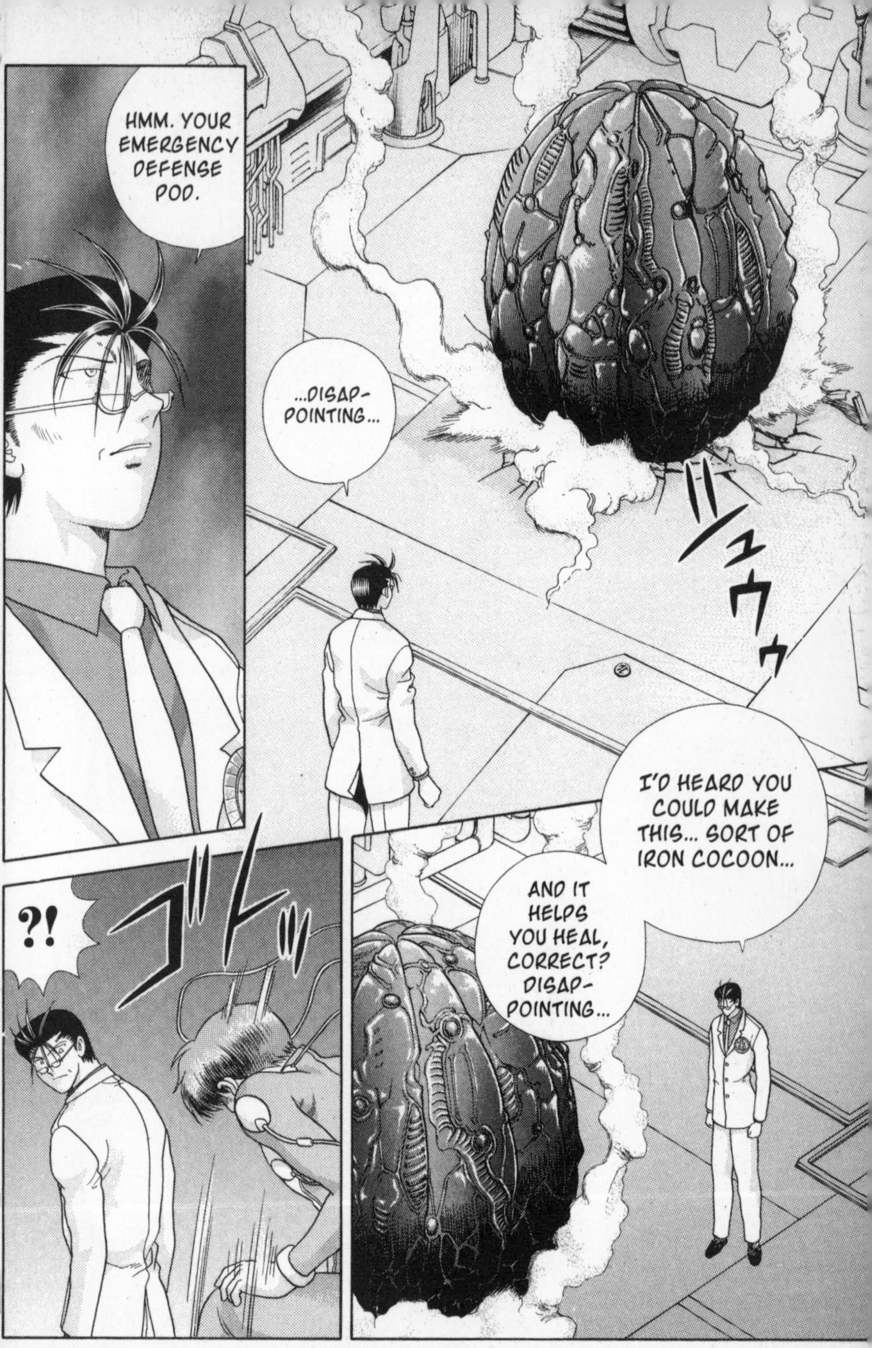
...DISAP-POINTING...
シュウゥ
HMM. YOUR EMERGENCY DEFENSE POD.
I'D HEARD YOU COULD MAKE THIS... SORT OF IRON COCOON...
AND IT HELPS YOU HEAL, CORRECT? DISAP-POINTING...
ゴトッ
?!

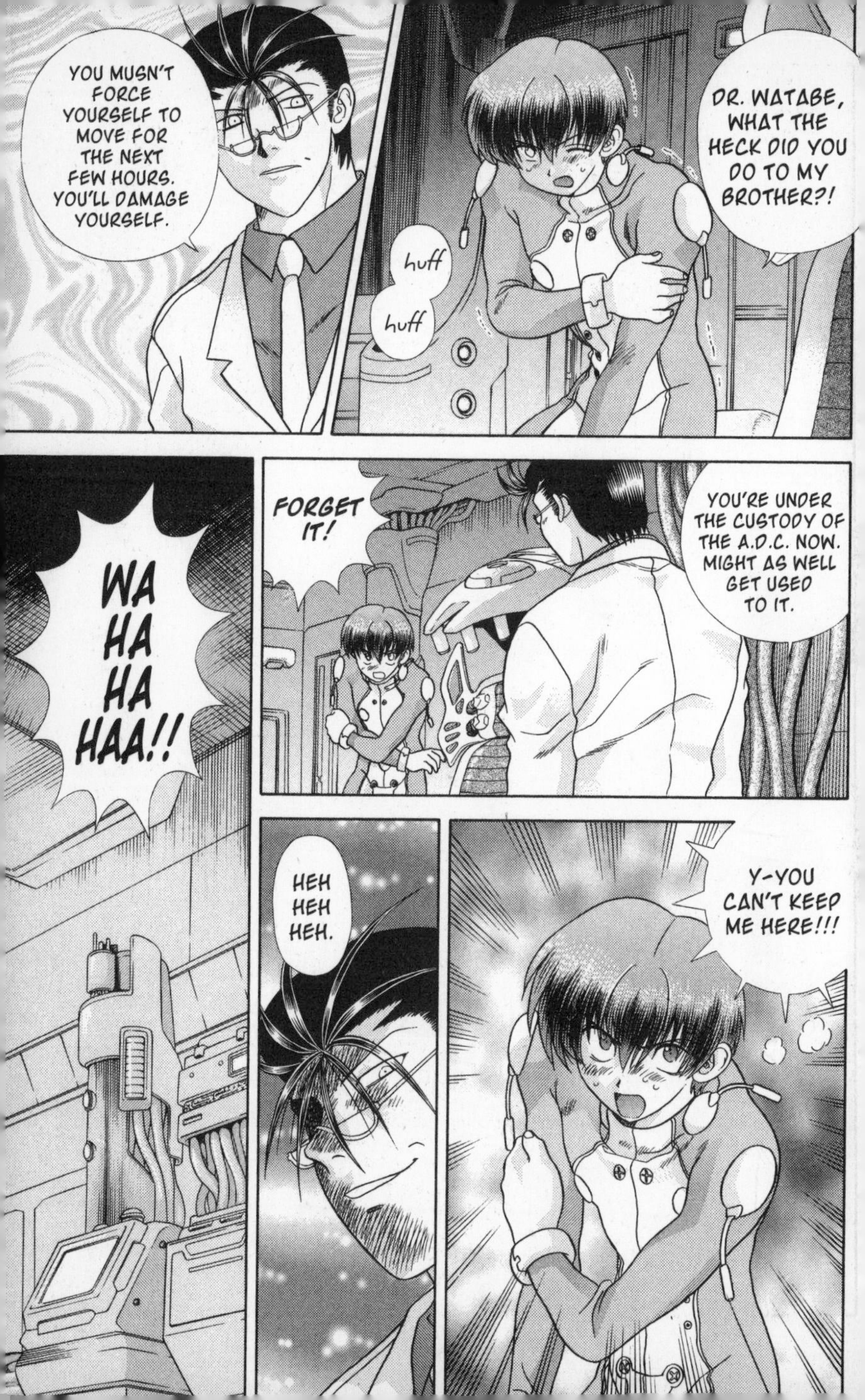

DR. WATABE, WHAT THE HECK DID YOU DO TO MY BROTHER?!
huff
huff
YOU MUSN'T FORCE YOURSELF TO MOVE FOR THE NEXT FEW HOURS. YOU'LL DAMAGE YOURSELF.
YOU'RE UNDER THE CUSTODY OF THE A.D.C. NOW. MIGHT AS WELL GET USED TO IT.
FORGET IT!
Y-YOU CAN'T KEEP ME HERE!!!
HEH HEH HEH.
WA HA HA HAA!!

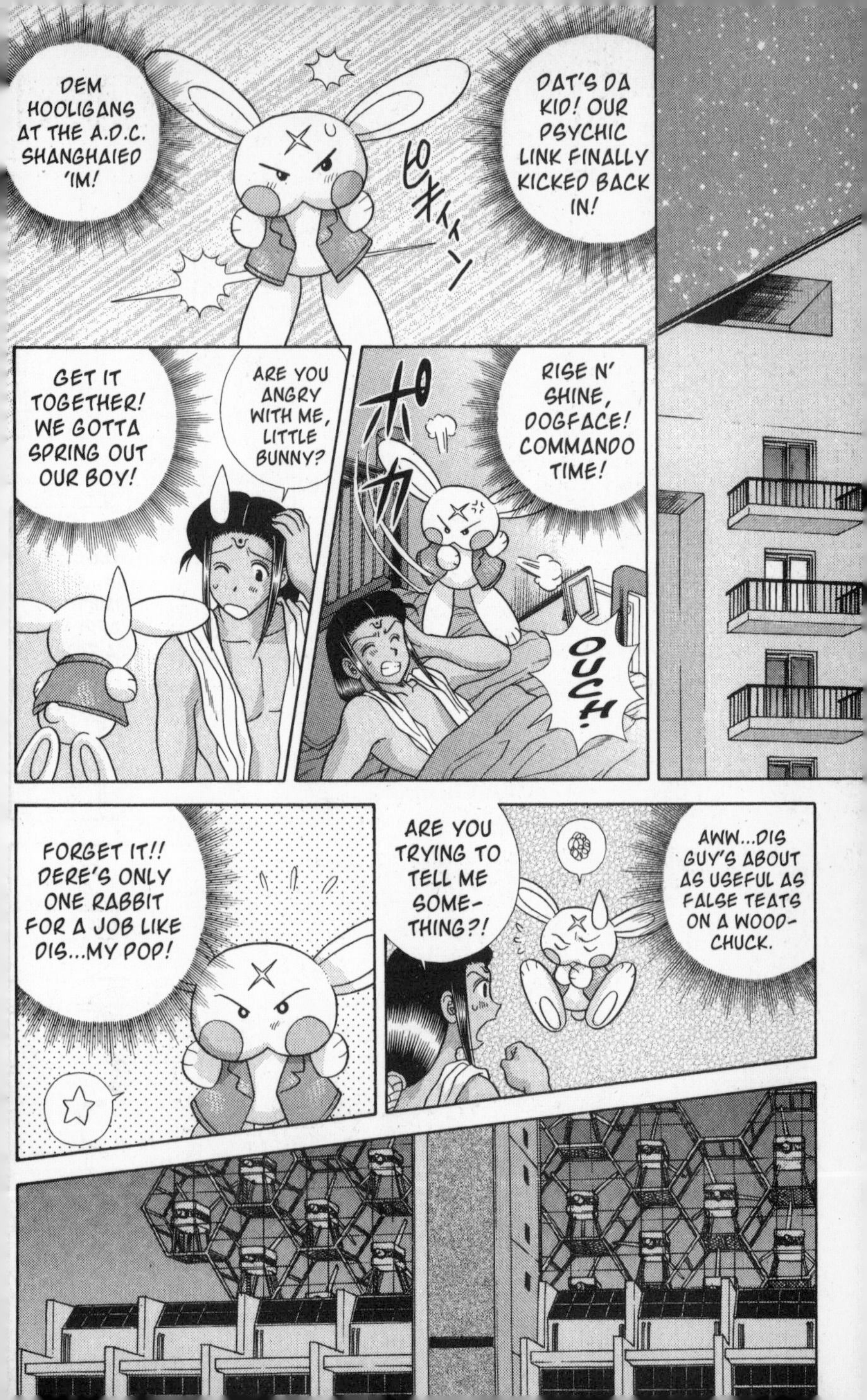
DAT'S DA KID! OUR PSYCHIC LINK FINALLY KICKED BACK IN!
ピキィィーン
DEM HOOLIGANS AT THE A.D.C. SHANGHAIED 'IM!
ポカ
RISE N' SHINE, DOGFACE! COMMANDO TIME!
OUCH!
ARE YOU ANGRY WITH ME, LITTLE BUNNY?
GET IT TOGETHER! WE GOTTA SPRING OUT OUR BOY!
AWW...DIS GUY'S ABOUT AS USEFUL AS FALSE TEATS ON A WOOD-CHUCK.
ARE YOU TRYING TO TELL ME SOME-THING?!
FORGET IT!! DERE'S ONLY ONE RABBIT FOR A JOB LIKE DIS...MY POP!

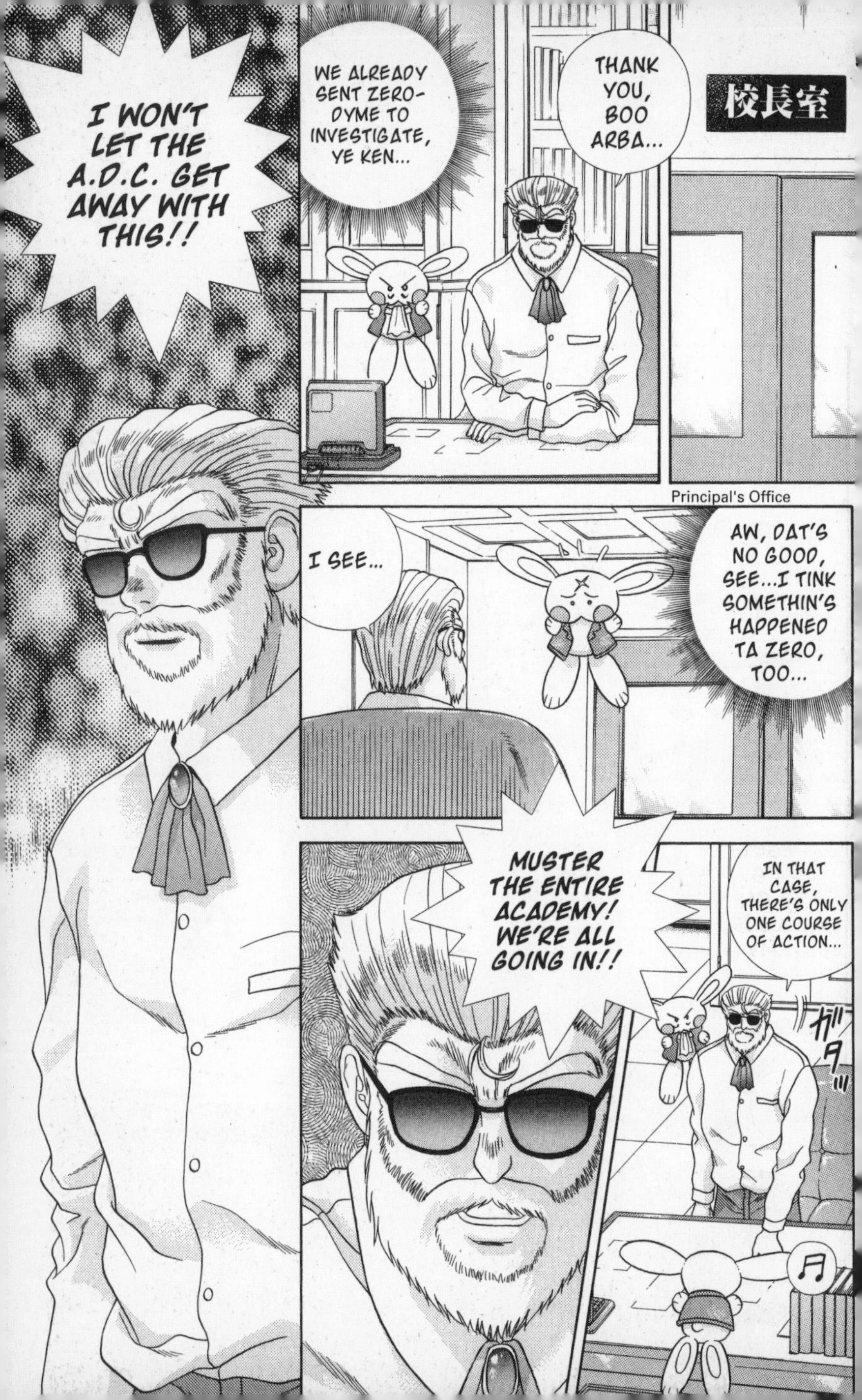

校長室
Principal's Office
THANK YOU, BOO ARBA...
WE ALREADY SENT ZERO-DYME TO INVESTIGATE, YE KEN...
AW, DAT'S NO GOOD, SEE...I TINK SOMETHIN'S HAPPENED TA ZERO, TOO...
I SEE...
IN THAT CASE, THERE'S ONLY ONE COURSE OF ACTION...
ガタッ
MUSTER THE ENTIRE ACADEMY! WE'RE ALL GOING IN!!
I WON'T LET THE A.D.C. GET AWAY WITH THIS!!

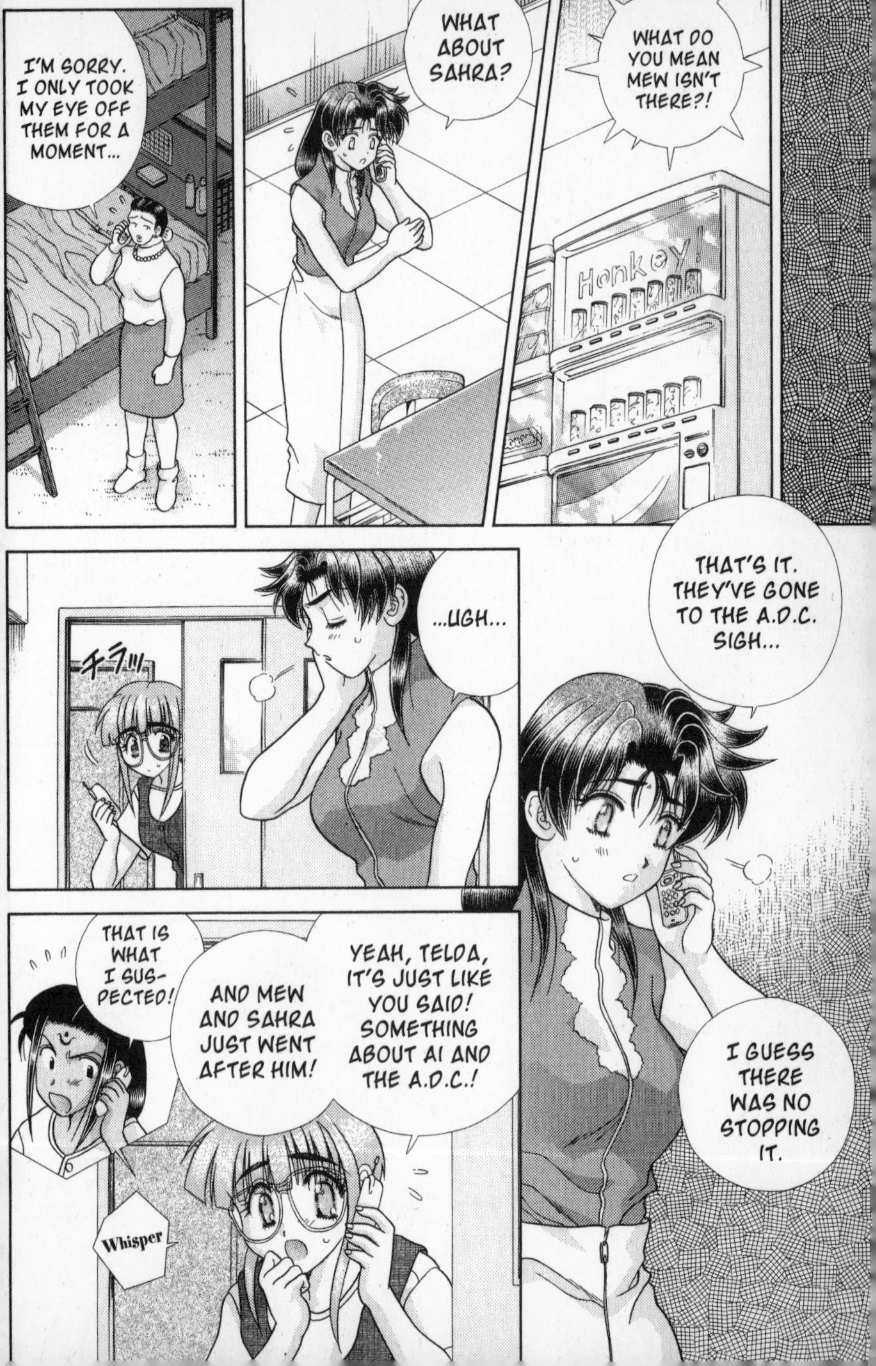
WHAT DO YOU MEAN MEW ISN'T THERE?!
WHAT ABOUT SAHRA?
Honkey!
I'M SORRY. I ONLY TOOK MY EYE OFF THEM FOR A MOMENT...
THAT'S IT. THEY'VE GONE TO THE A.D.C. SIGH...
I GUESS THERE WAS NO STOPPING IT.
...UGH...
チラッ
YEAH, TELDA, IT'S JUST LIKE YOU SAID! SOMETHING ABOUT AI AND THE A.D.C.!
AND MEW AND SAHRA JUST WENT AFTER HIM!
THAT IS WHAT I SUSPECTED!
Whisper

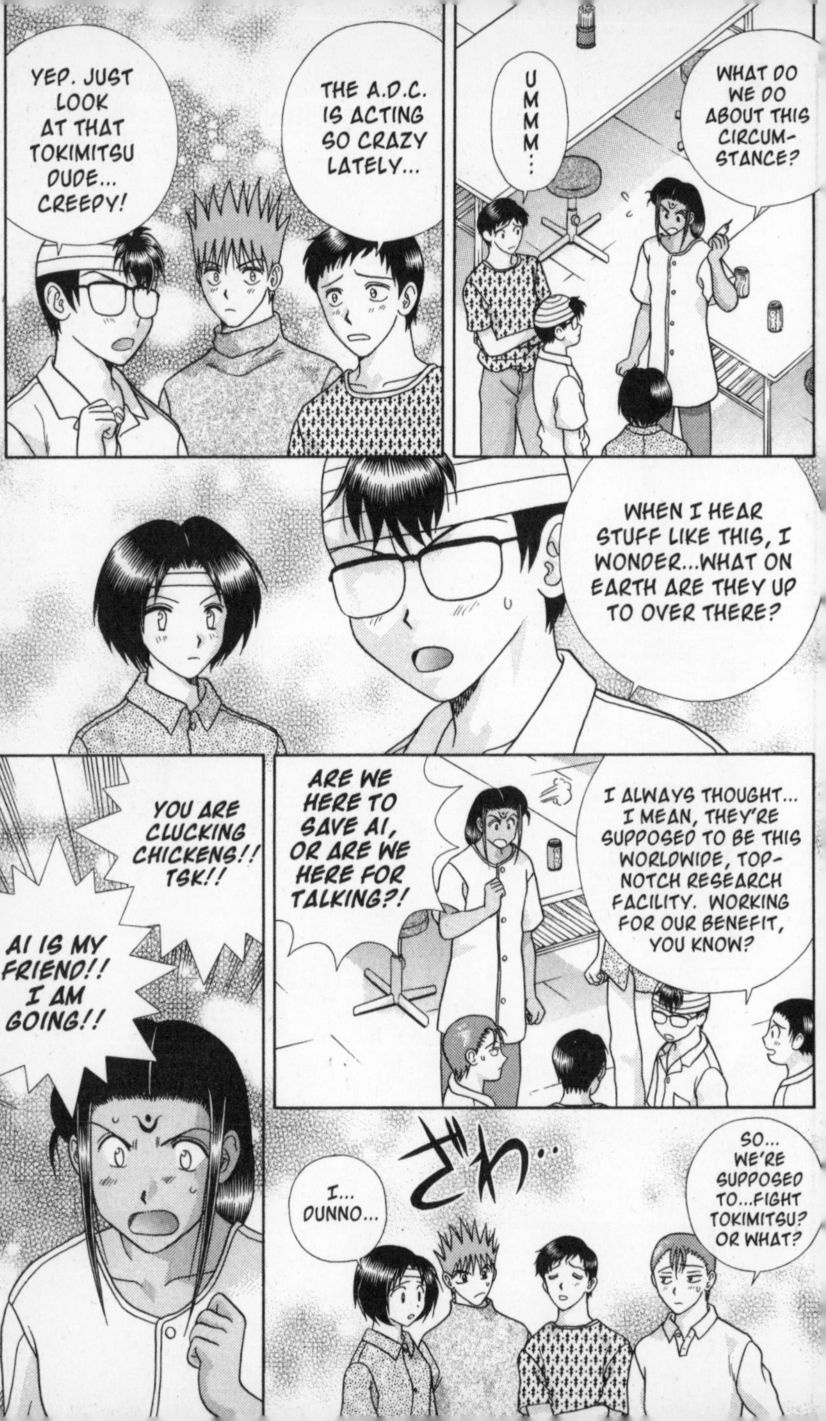
WHAT DO WE DO ABOUT THIS CIRCUM-STANCE?
UMMM...
THE A.D.C. IS ACTING SO CRAZY LATELY...
YEP. JUST LOOK AT THAT TOKIMITSU DUDE... CREEPY!
WHEN I HEAR STUFF LIKE THIS, I WONDER...WHAT ON EARTH ARE THEY UP TO OVER THERE?
I ALWAYS THOUGHT... I MEAN, THEY'RE SUPPOSED TO BE THIS WORLDWIDE, TOP-NOTCH RESEARCH FACILITY. WORKING FOR OUR BENEFIT, YOU KNOW?
ARE WE HERE TO SAVE AI, OR ARE WE HERE FOR TALKING?!
SO... WE'RE SUPPOSED TO...FIGHT TOKIMITSU? OR WHAT?
ざわ..
I... DUNNO...
YOU ARE CLUCKING CHICKENS!! TSK!!
AI IS MY FRIEND!! I AM GOING!!

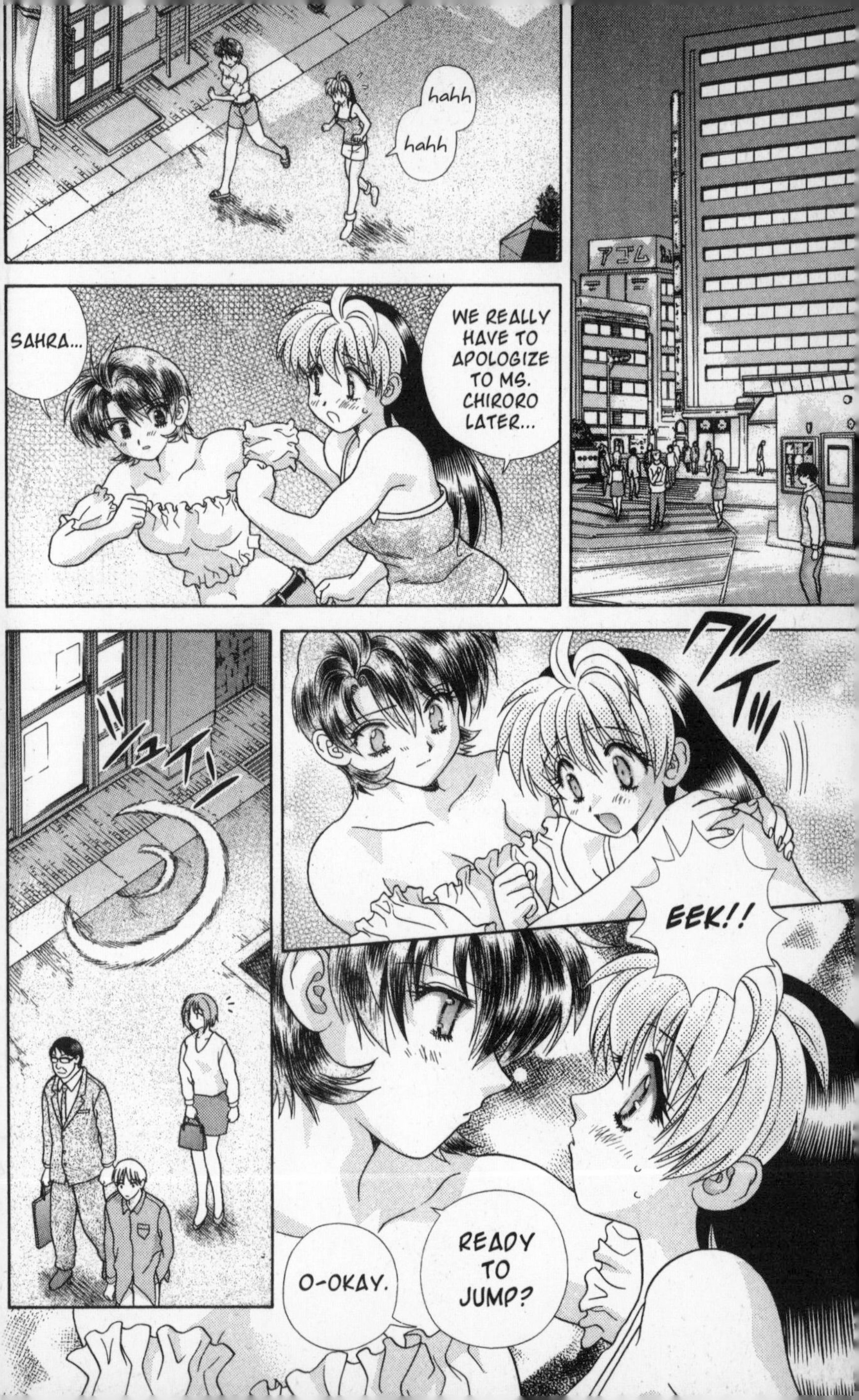
hahh
hahh
WE REALLY HAVE TO APOLOGIZE TO MS. CHIRORO LATER...
SAHRA...
EEK!!
READY TO JUMP?
O-OKAY.

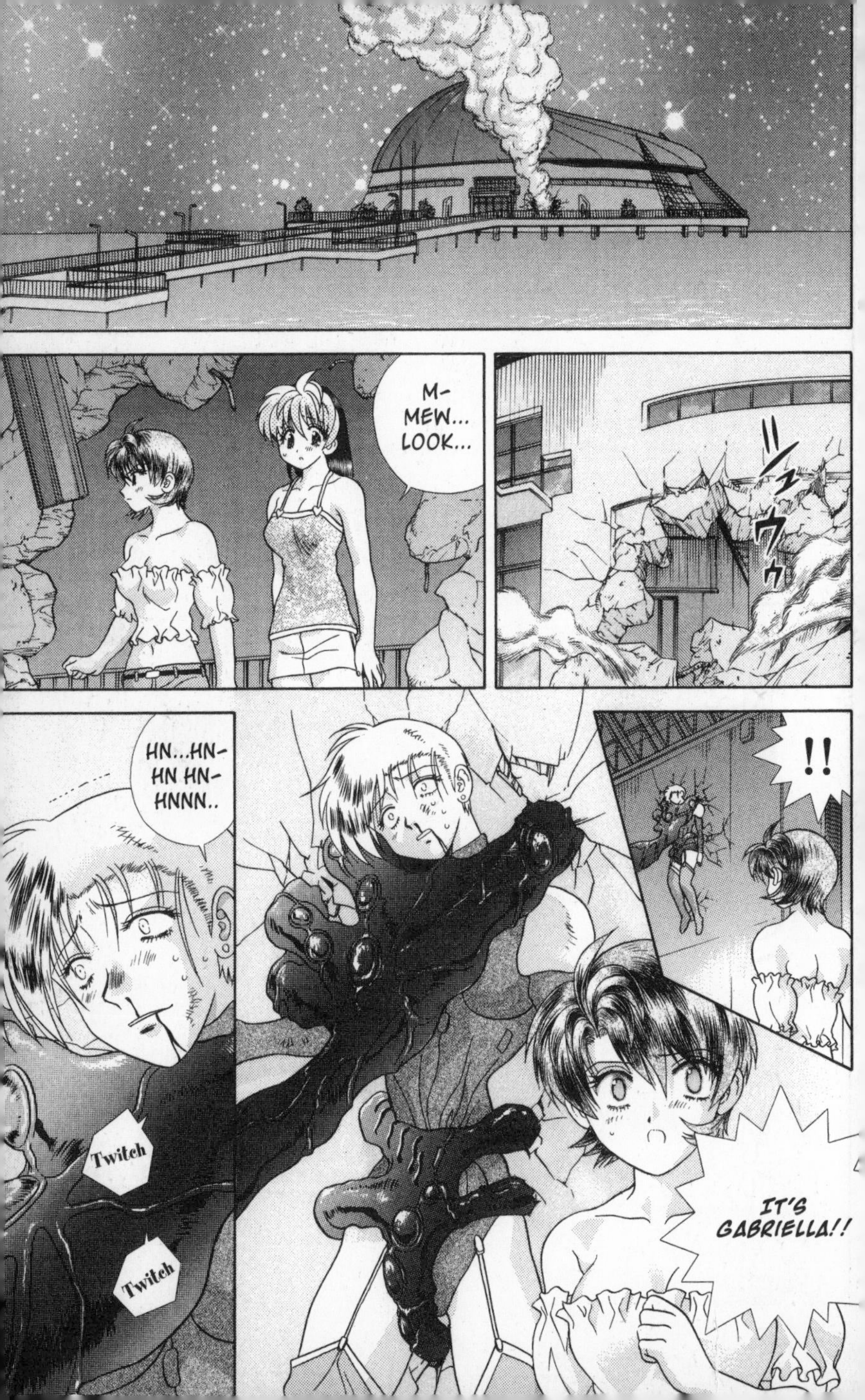
M-MEW... LOOK...
!!
IT'S GABRIELLA!!
HN...HN-HN HN-HNNN..
Twitch
Twitch

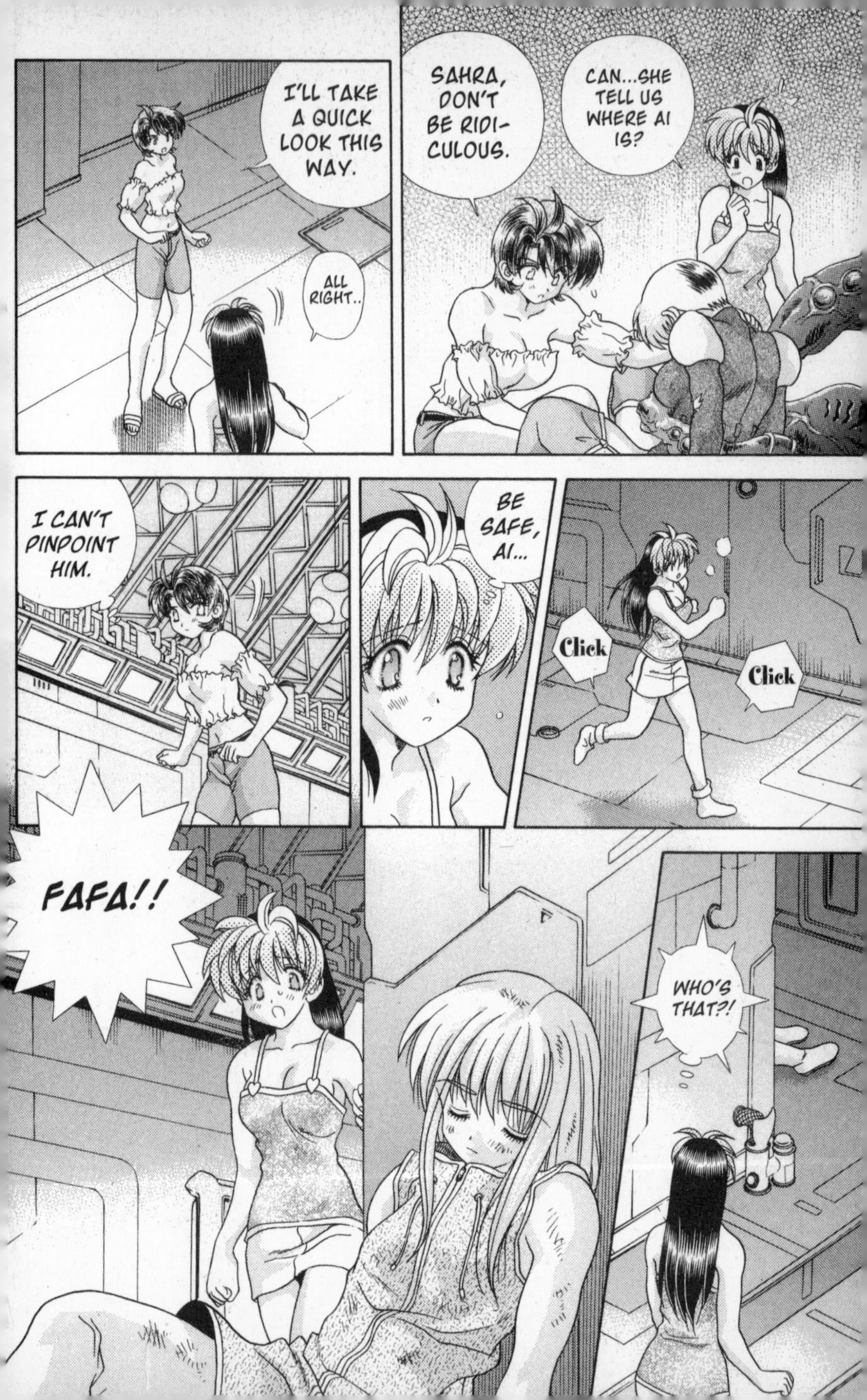
CAN...SHE TELL US WHERE AI IS?
SAHRA, DON'T BE RIDI-CULOUS.
I'LL TAKE A QUICK LOOK THIS WAY.
ALL RIGHT..
Click
Click
BE SAFE, AI...
I CAN'T PINPOINT HIM.
FAFA!!
WHO'S THAT?!

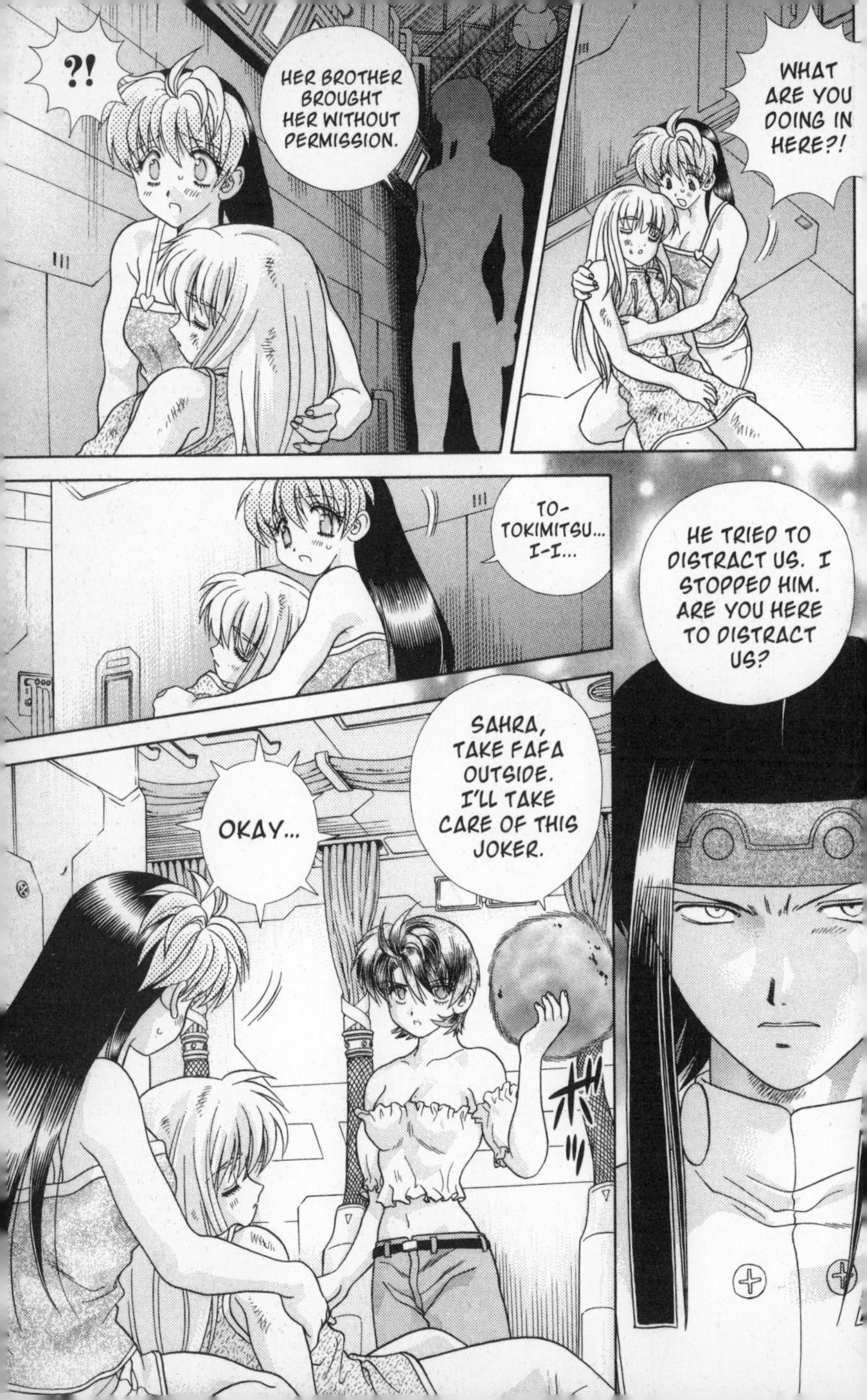
WHAT ARE YOU DOING IN HERE?!
HER BROTHER BROUGHT HER WITHOUT PERMISSION.
?!
HE TRIED TO DISTRACT US. I STOPPED HIM. ARE YOU HERE TO DISTRACT US?
TO-TOKIMITSU... I-I...
SAHRA, TAKE FAFA OUTSIDE. I'LL TAKE CARE OF THIS JOKER.
OKAY...

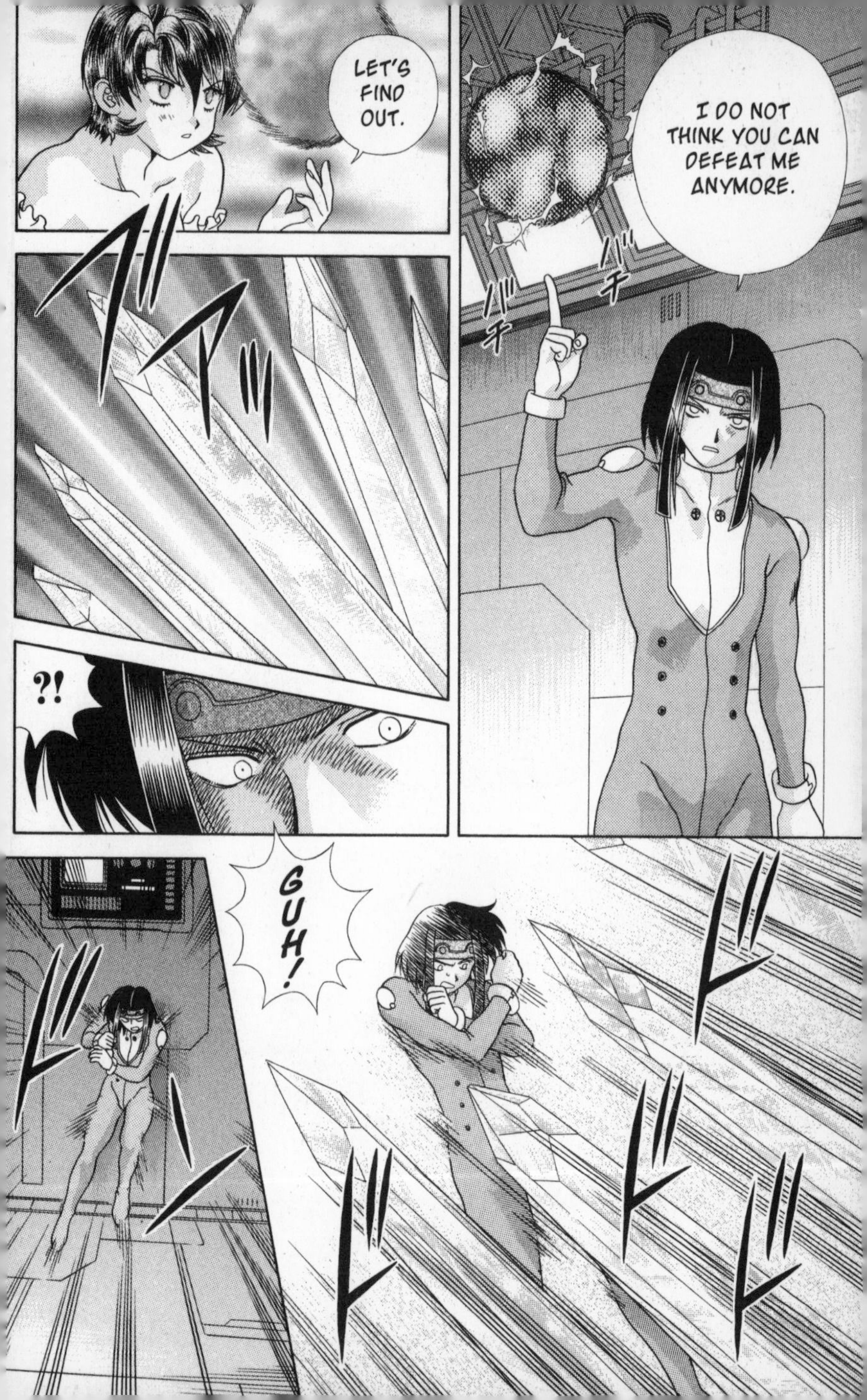
I DO NOT THINK YOU CAN DEFEAT ME ANYMORE.
LET'S FIND OUT.
?!
GUH!

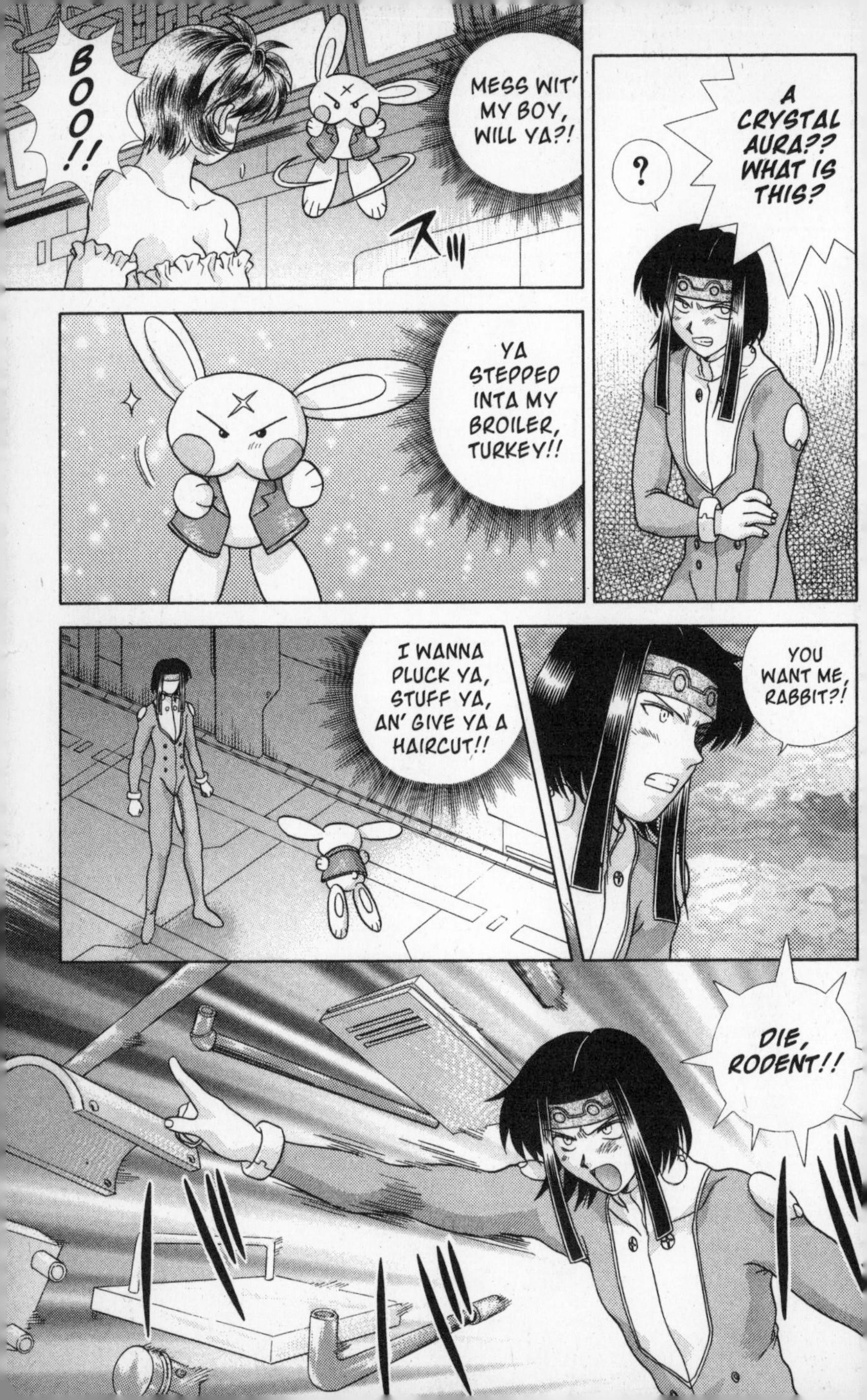
?
A CRYSTAL AURA?? WHAT IS THIS?
MESS WIT' MY BOY, WILL YA?!
ス
BOO!!
YA STEPPED INTA MY BROILER, TURKEY!!
YOU WANT ME, RABBIT?!
I WANNA PLUCK YA, STUFF YA, AN' GIVE YA A HAIRCUT!!
DIE, RODENT!!

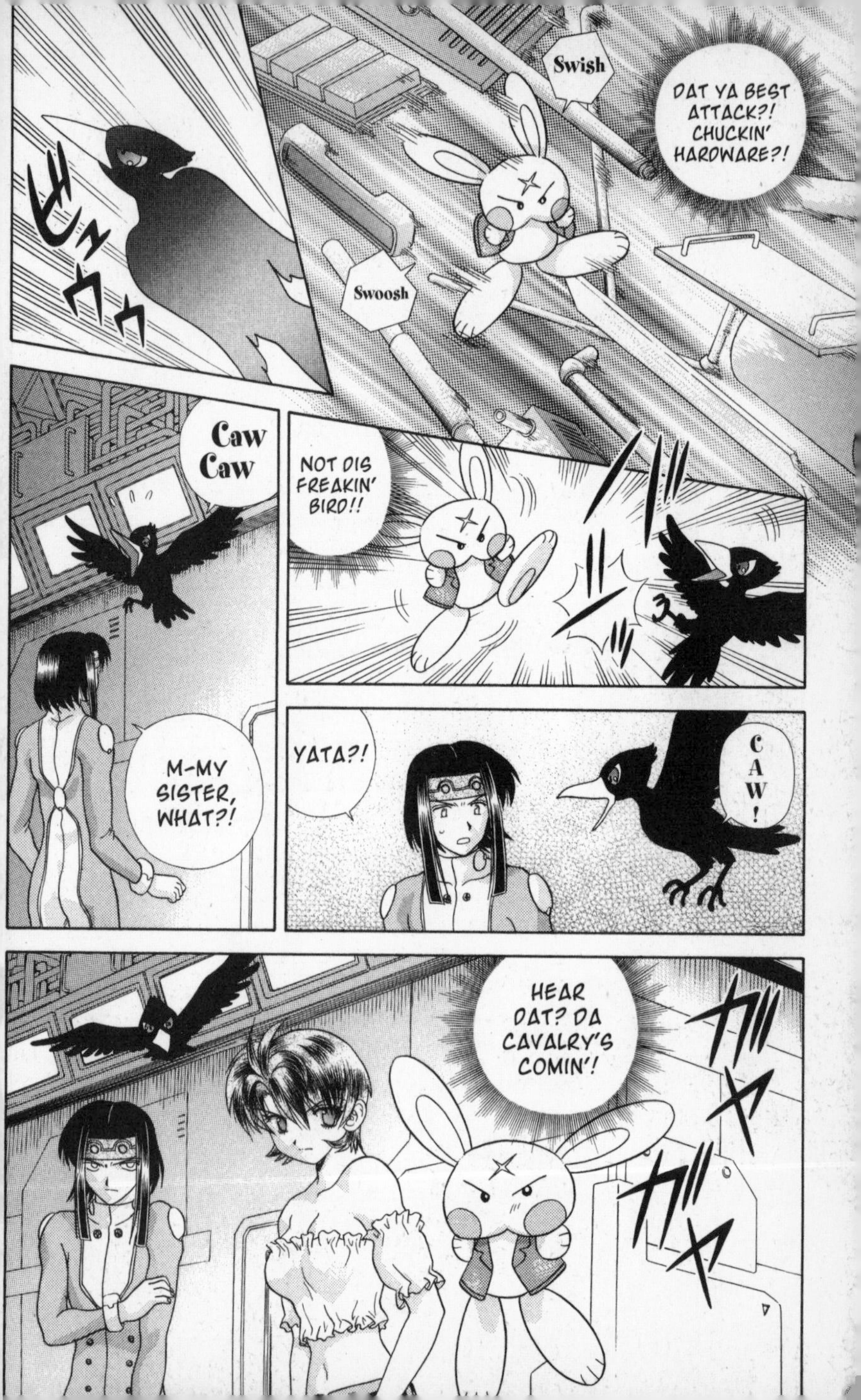
DAT YA BEST ATTACK?! CHUCKIN' HARDWARE?!
Swish
Swoosh
NOT DIS FREAKIN' BIRD!!
CAW!
YATA?!
Caw Caw
M-MY SISTER, WHAT?!
HEAR DAT? DA CAVALRY'S COMIN'!

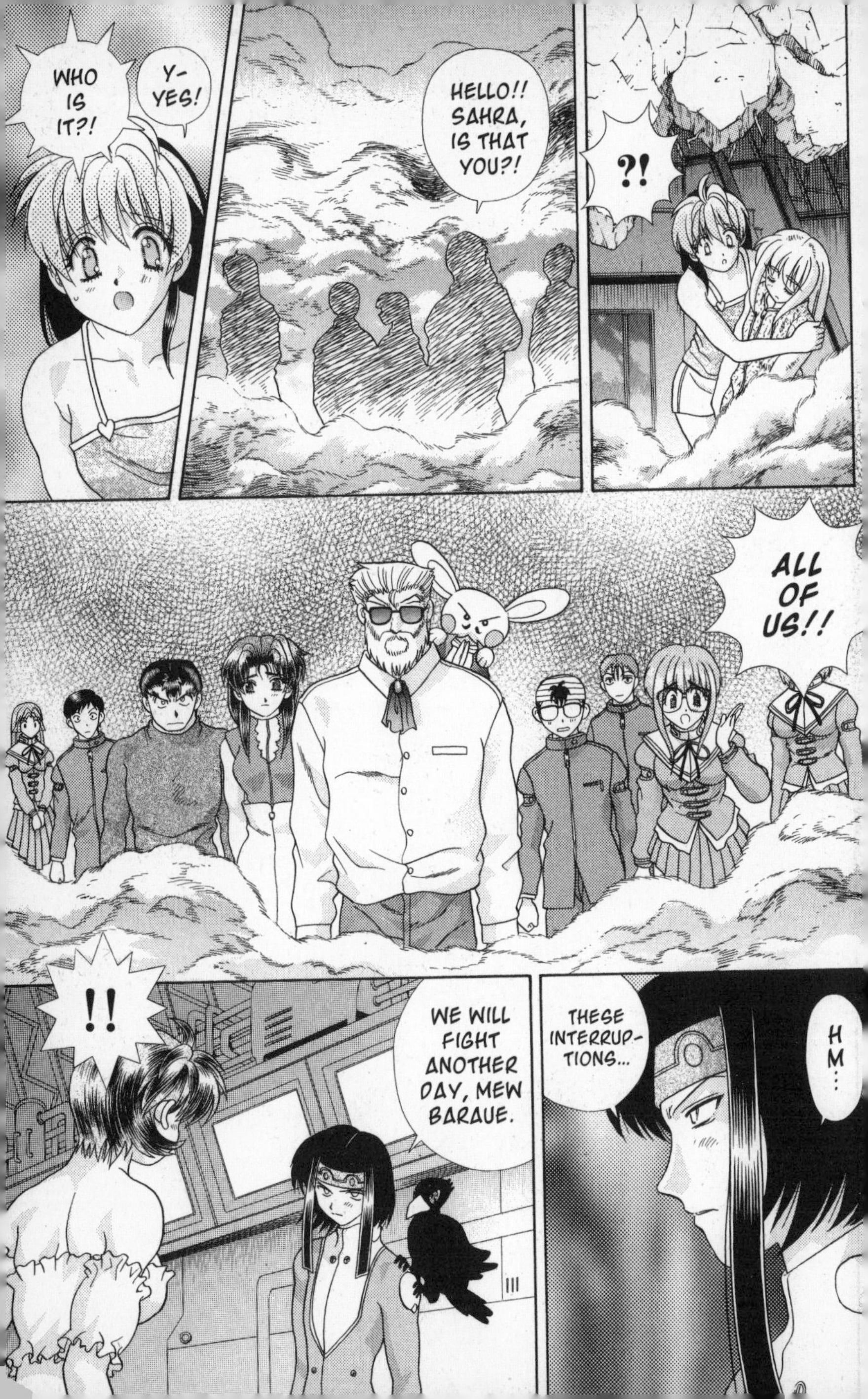
?!
HELLO!! SAHRA, IS THAT YOU?!
Y-YES!
WHO IS IT?!
ALL OF US!!
HM...
THESE INTERRUP-TIONS...
WE WILL FIGHT ANOTHER DAY, MEW BARAUE.
!!

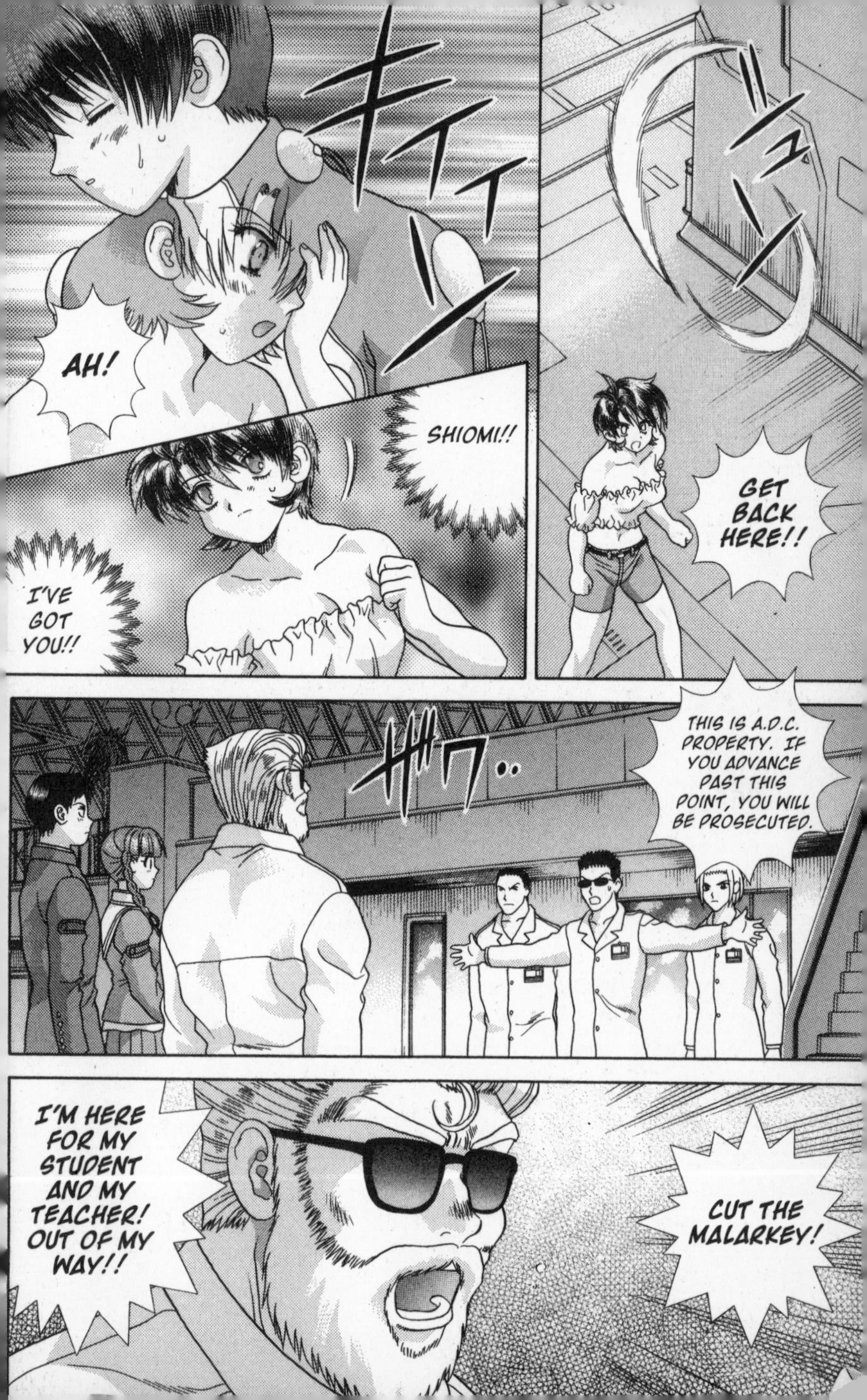
GET BACK HERE!!
AH!
SHIOMI!!
I'VE GOT YOU!!
THIS IS A.D.C. PROPERTY. IF YOU ADVANCE PAST THIS POINT, YOU WILL BE PROSECUTED.
CUT THE MALARKEY!
I'M HERE FOR MY STUDENT AND MY TEACHER! OUT OF MY WAY!!

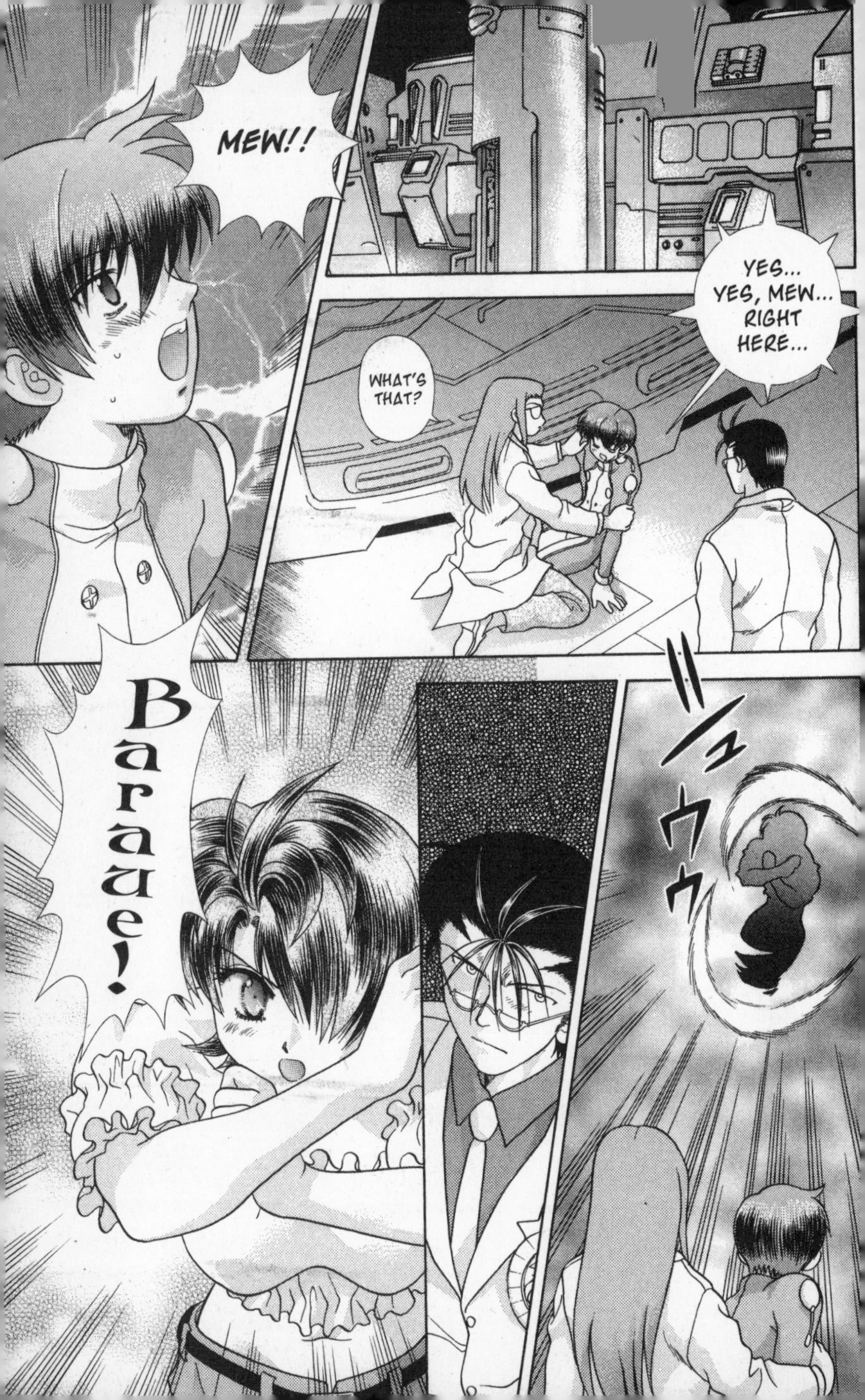
YES... YES, MEW... RIGHT HERE...
WHAT'S THAT?
MEW!!
シュウウ
Baraue!

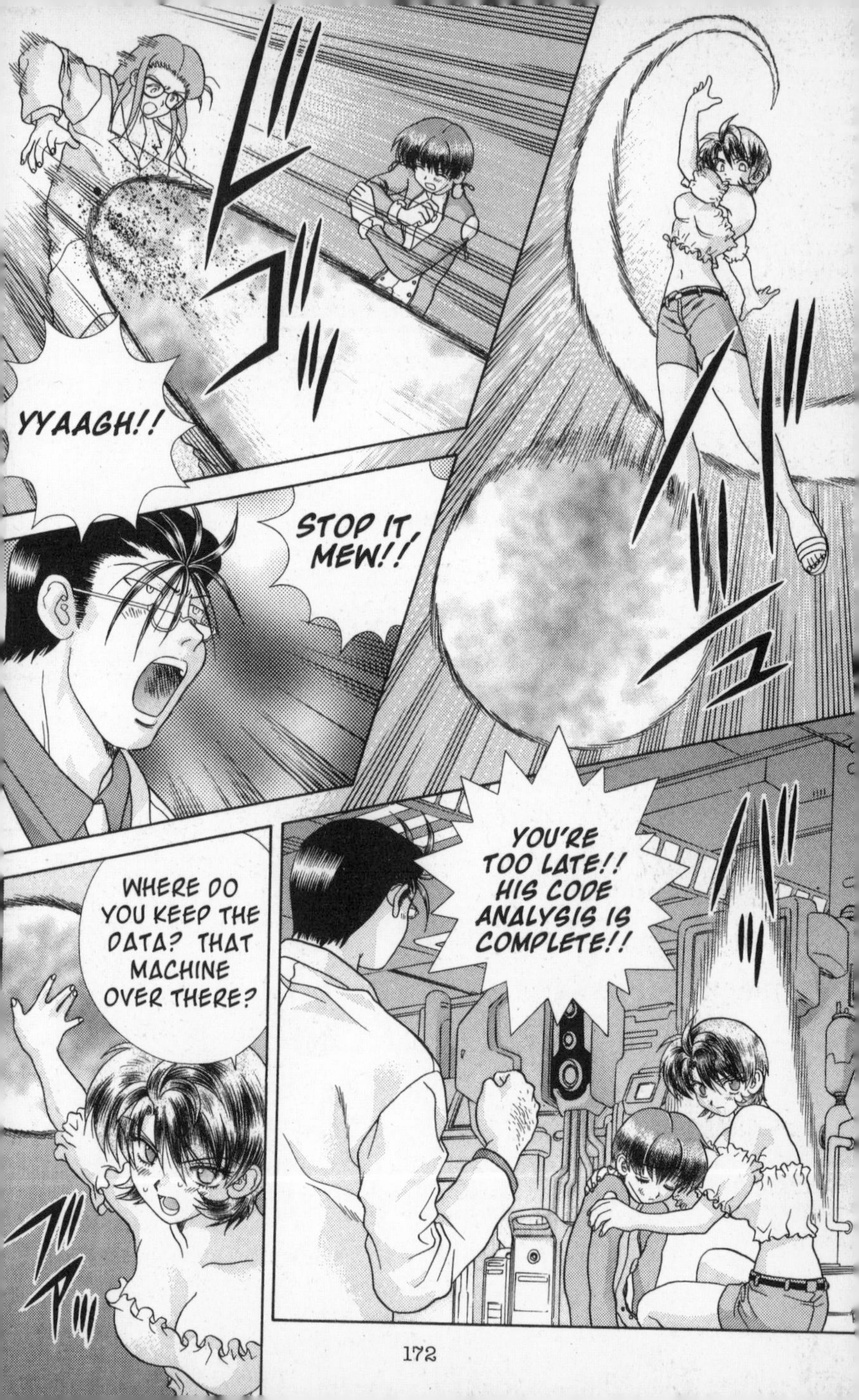
YYAAGH!!
STOP IT MEW!!
YOU'RE TOO LATE!! HIS CODE ANALYSIS IS COMPLETE!!
WHERE DO YOU KEEP THE DATA? THAT MACHINE OVER THERE?

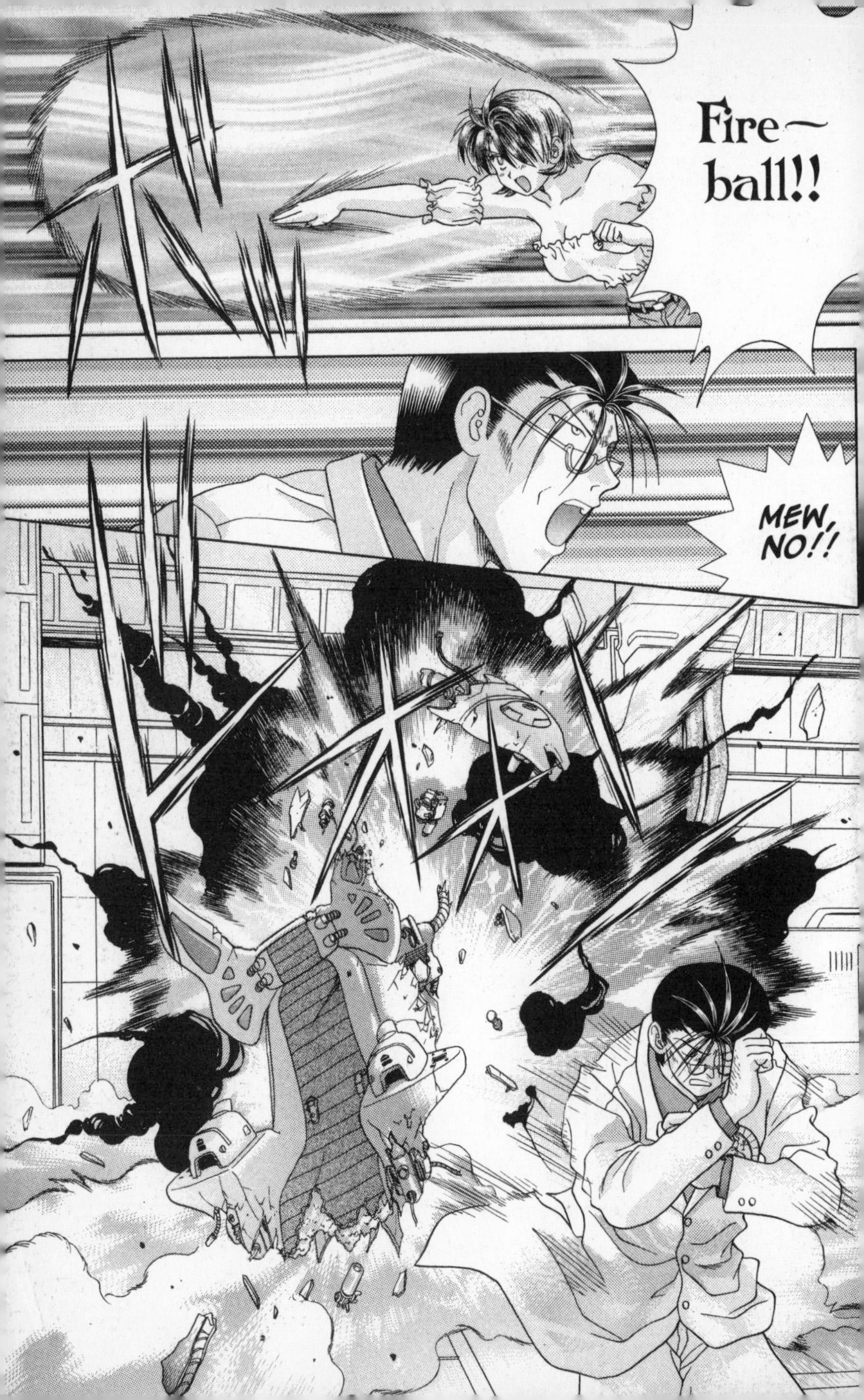
Fire-ball!!
MEW, NO!!

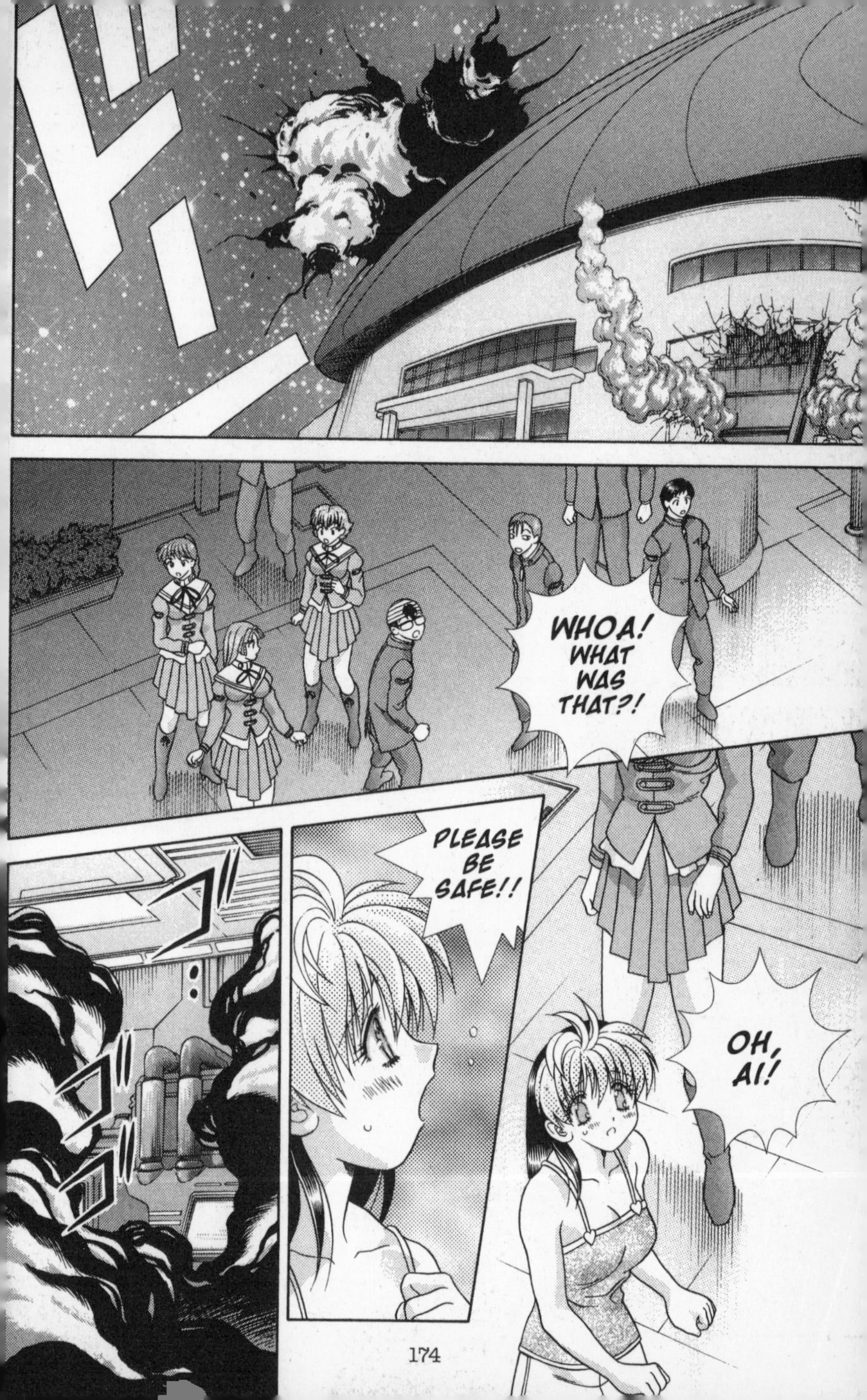
WHOA! WHAT WAS THAT?!
OH, AI!
PLEASE BE SAFE!!

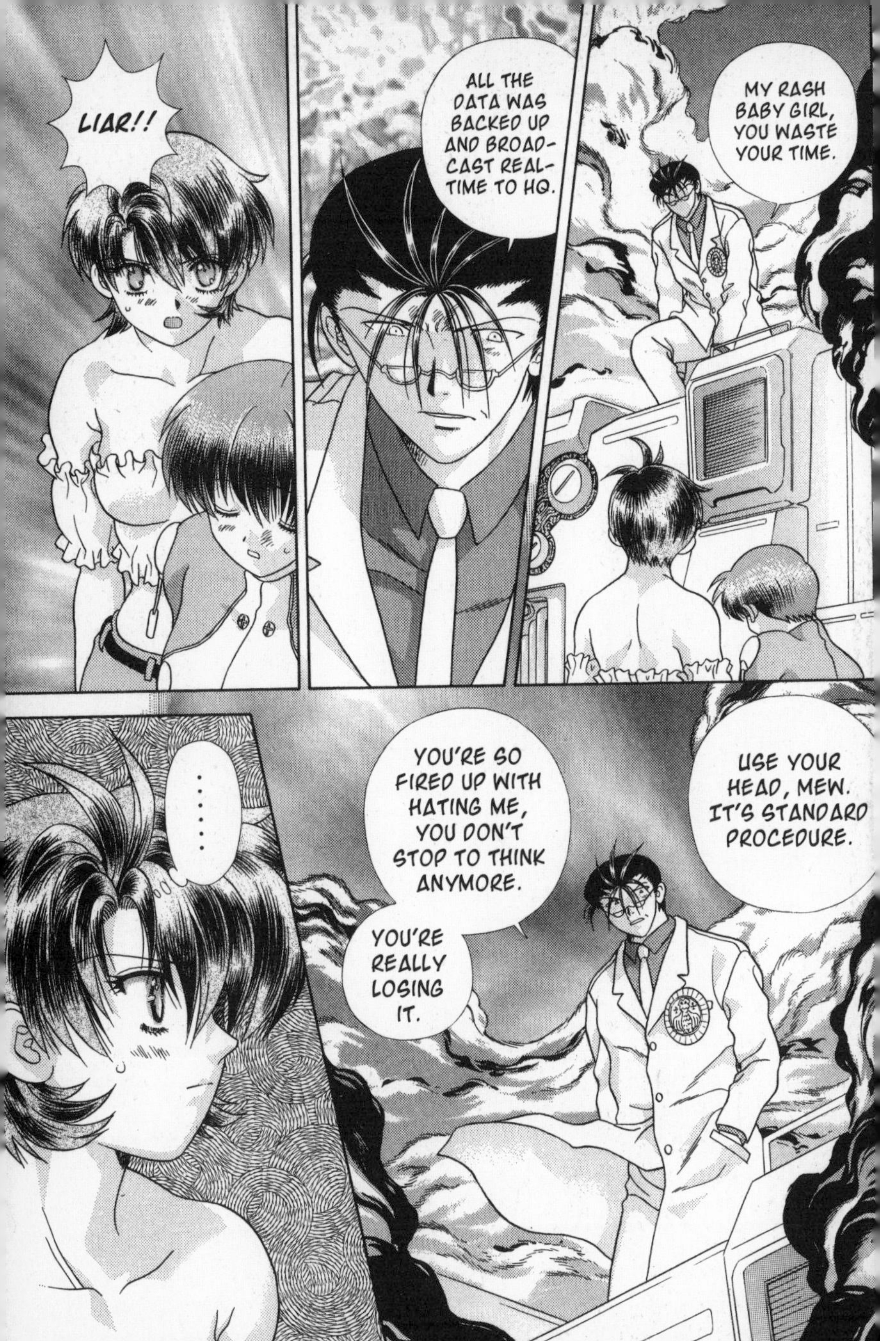
MY RASH BABY GIRL, YOU WASTE YOUR TIME.
ALL THE DATA WAS BACKED UP AND BROAD-CAST REAL-TIME TO HQ.
LIAR!!
USE YOUR HEAD, MEW. IT'S STANDARD PROCEDURE.
YOU'RE SO FIRED UP WITH HATING ME, YOU DON'T STOP TO THINK ANYMORE.
YOU'RE REALLY LOSING IT.
......

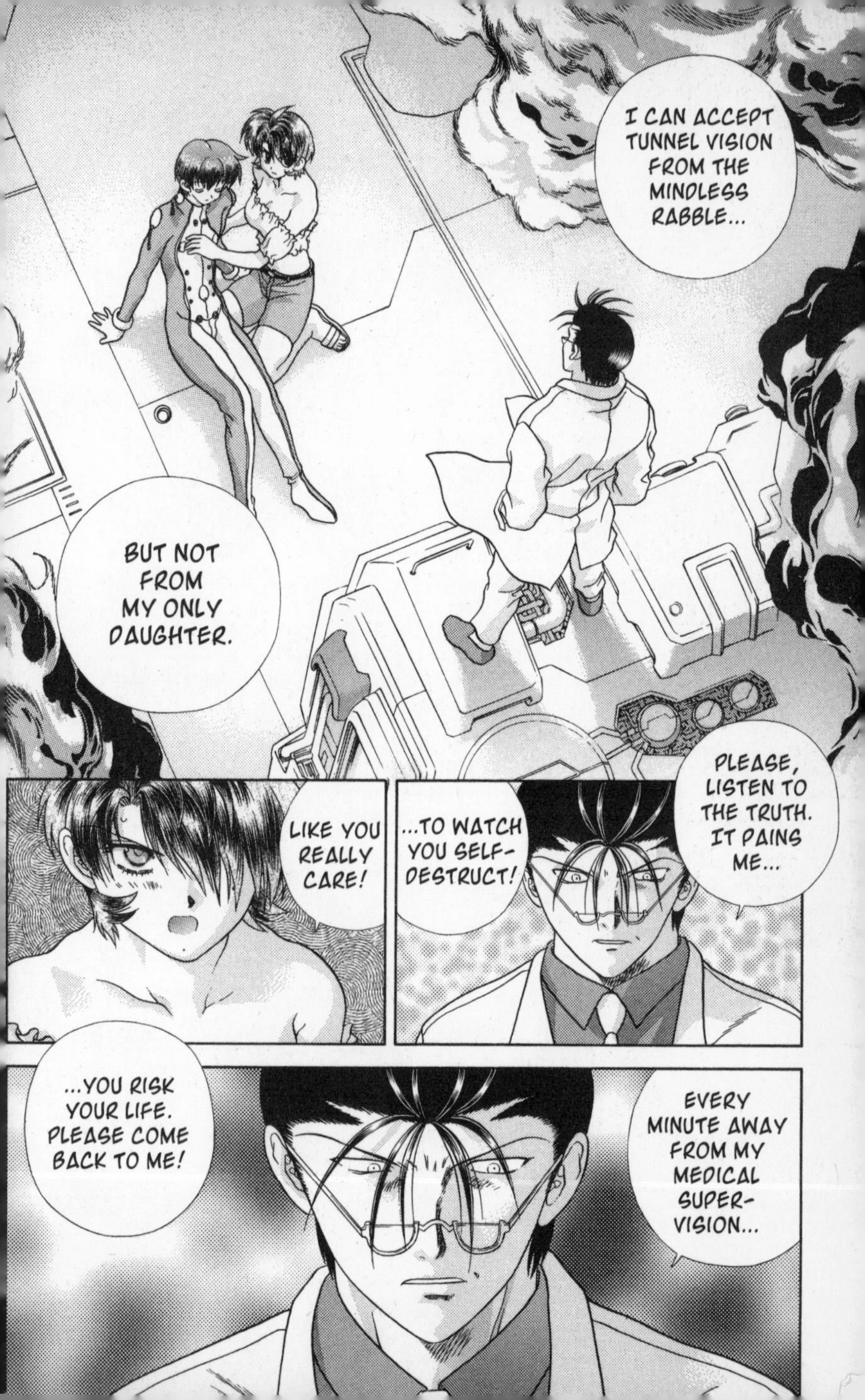
I CAN ACCEPT TUNNEL VISION FROM THE MINDLESS RABBLE...
BUT NOT FROM MY ONLY DAUGHTER.
PLEASE, LISTEN TO THE TRUTH. IT PAINS ME...
...TO WATCH YOU SELF-DESTRUCT!
LIKE YOU REALLY CARE!
EVERY MINUTE AWAY FROM MY MEDICAL SUPER-VISION...
...YOU RISK YOUR LIFE. PLEASE COME BACK TO ME!

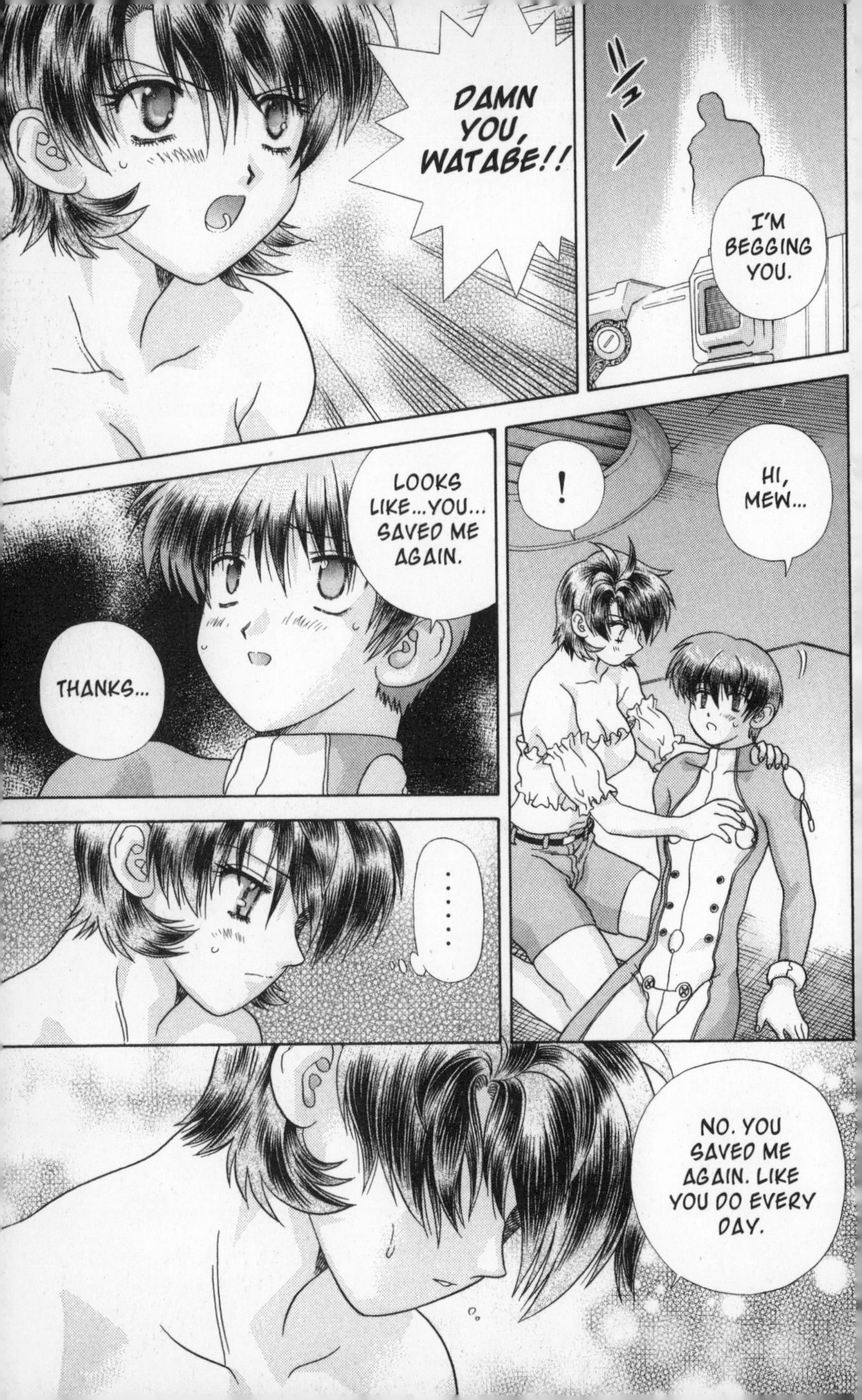
I'M BEGGING YOU.
DAMN YOU, WATABE!!
HI, MEW...
!
LOOKS LIKE...YOU... SAVED ME AGAIN.
THANKS...
......
NO. YOU SAVED ME AGAIN. LIKE YOU DO EVERY DAY.

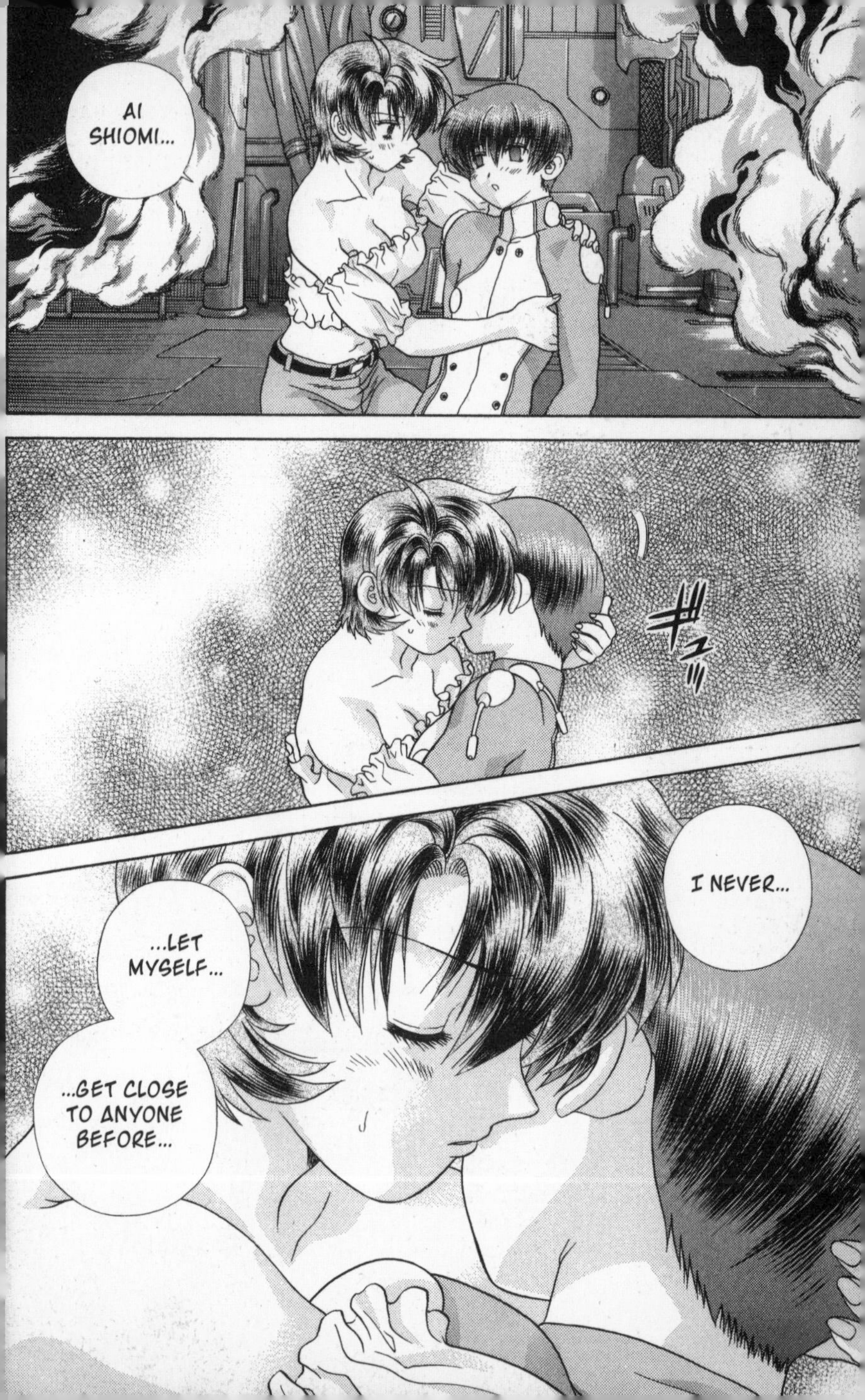
AI SHIOMI...
I NEVER...
...LET MYSELF...
...GET CLOSE TO ANYONE BEFORE...

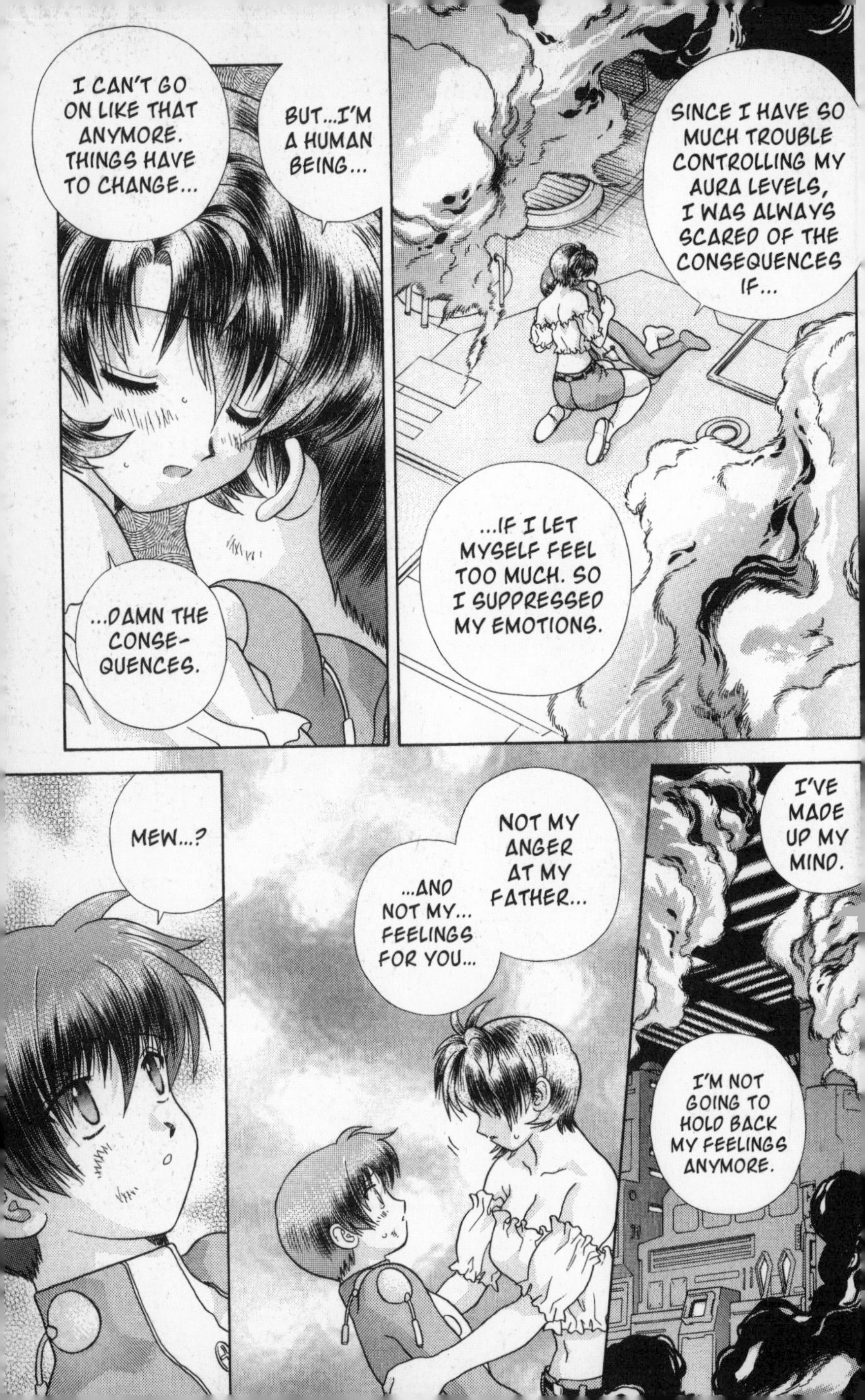
SINCE I HAVE SO MUCH TROUBLE CONTROLLING MY AURA LEVELS, I WAS ALWAYS SCARED OF THE CONSEQUENCES IF...
...IF I LET MYSELF FEEL TOO MUCH. SO I SUPPRESSED MY EMOTIONS.
BUT...I'M A HUMAN BEING...
I CAN'T GO ON LIKE THAT ANYMORE. THINGS HAVE TO CHANGE...
...DAMN THE CONSE-QUENCES.
I'VE MADE UP MY MIND.
I'M NOT GOING TO HOLD BACK MY FEELINGS ANYMORE.
NOT MY ANGER AT MY FATHER...
...AND NOT MY... FEELINGS FOR YOU...
MEW...?

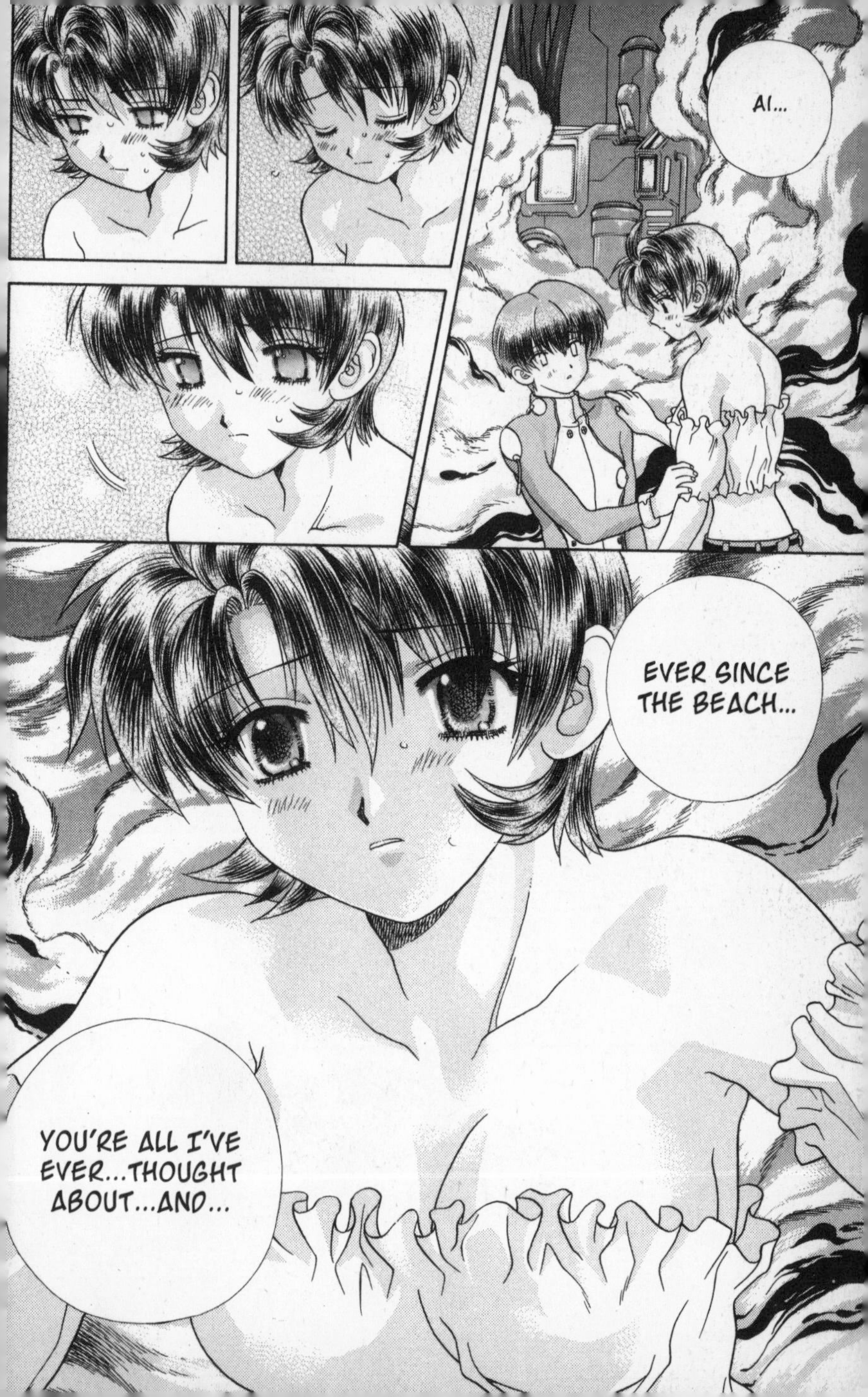
AI...
EVER SINCE THE BEACH...
YOU'RE ALL I'VE EVER...THOUGHT ABOUT...AND...

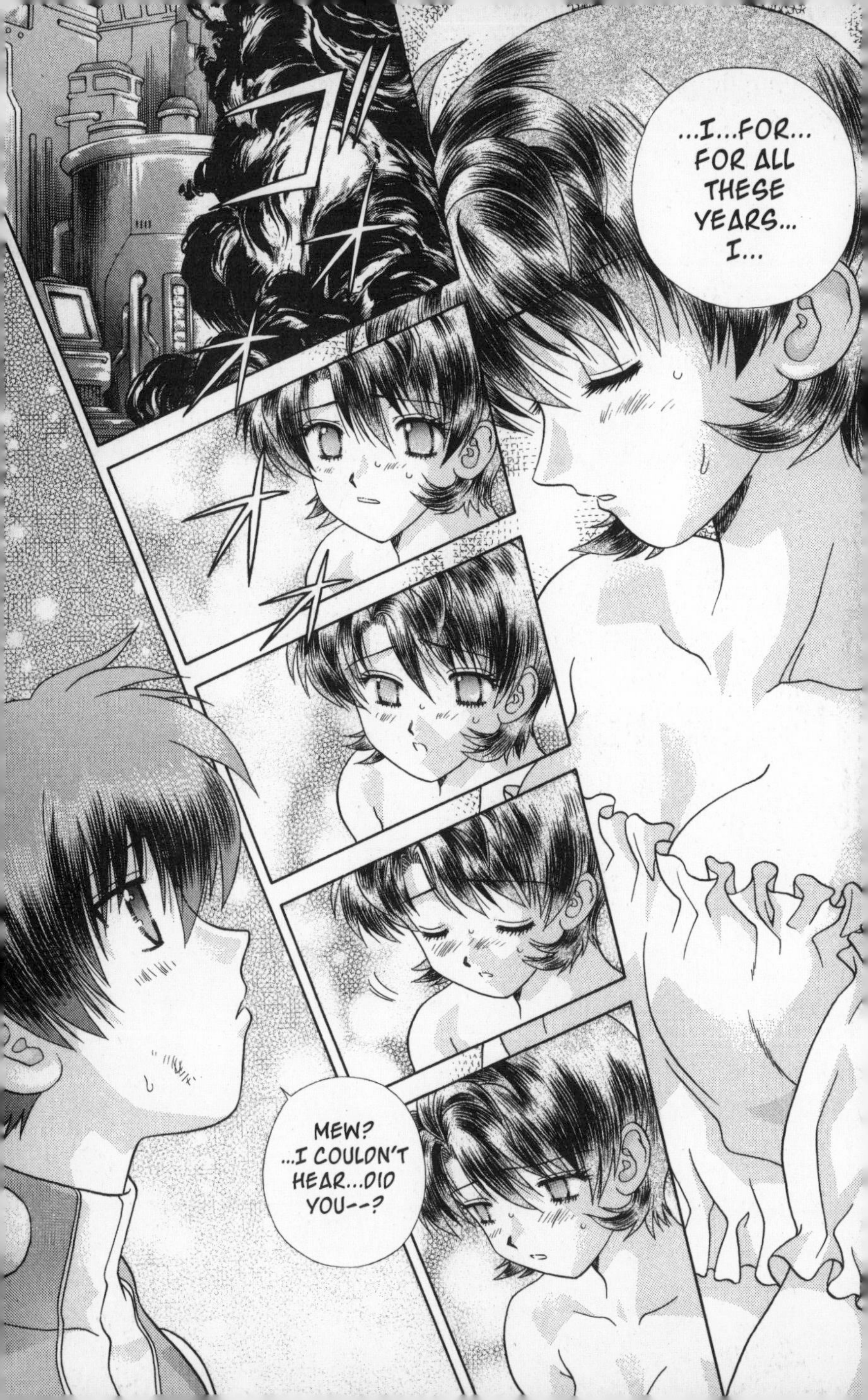
...I...FOR... FOR ALL THESE YEARS... I...
MEW? ...I COULDN'T HEAR...DID YOU--?

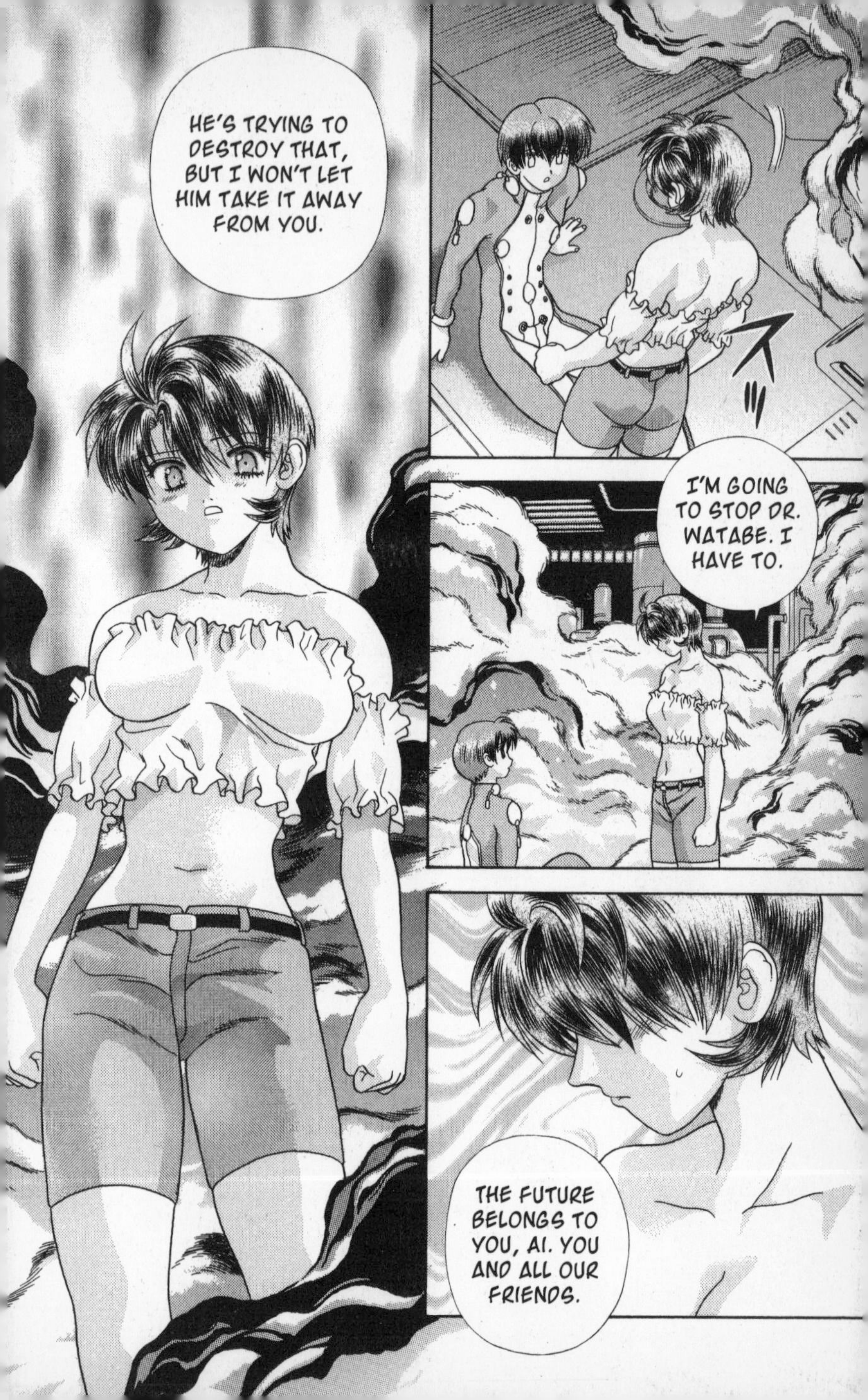
I'M GOING TO STOP DR. WATABE. I HAVE TO.
THE FUTURE BELONGS TO YOU, AI. YOU AND ALL OUR FRIENDS.
HE'S TRYING TO DESTROY THAT, BUT I WON'T LET HIM TAKE IT AWAY FROM YOU.

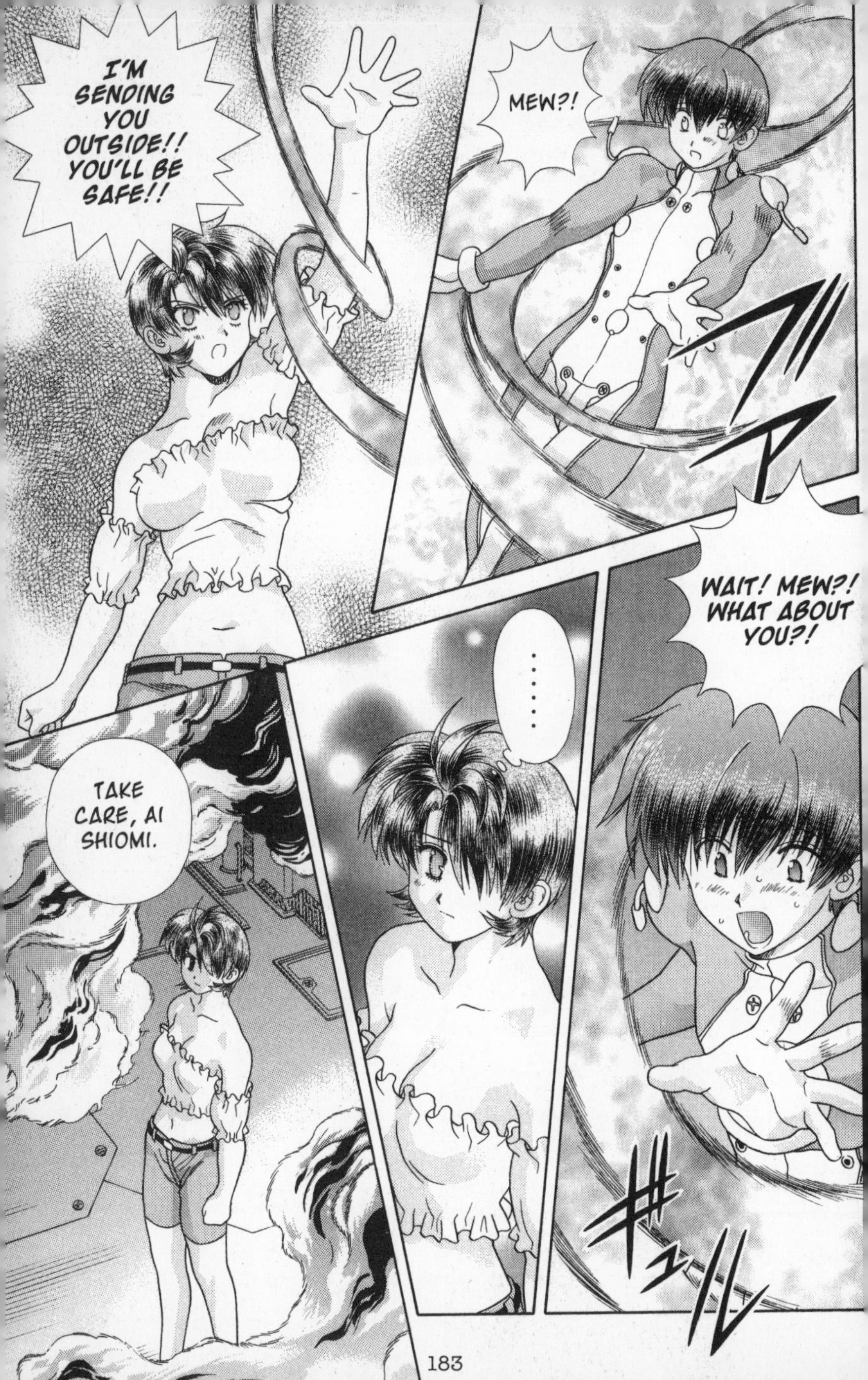
MEW?!
I'M SENDING YOU OUTSIDE!! YOU'LL BE SAFE!!
WAIT! MEW?! WHAT ABOUT YOU?!
......
TAKE CARE, AI SHIOMI.

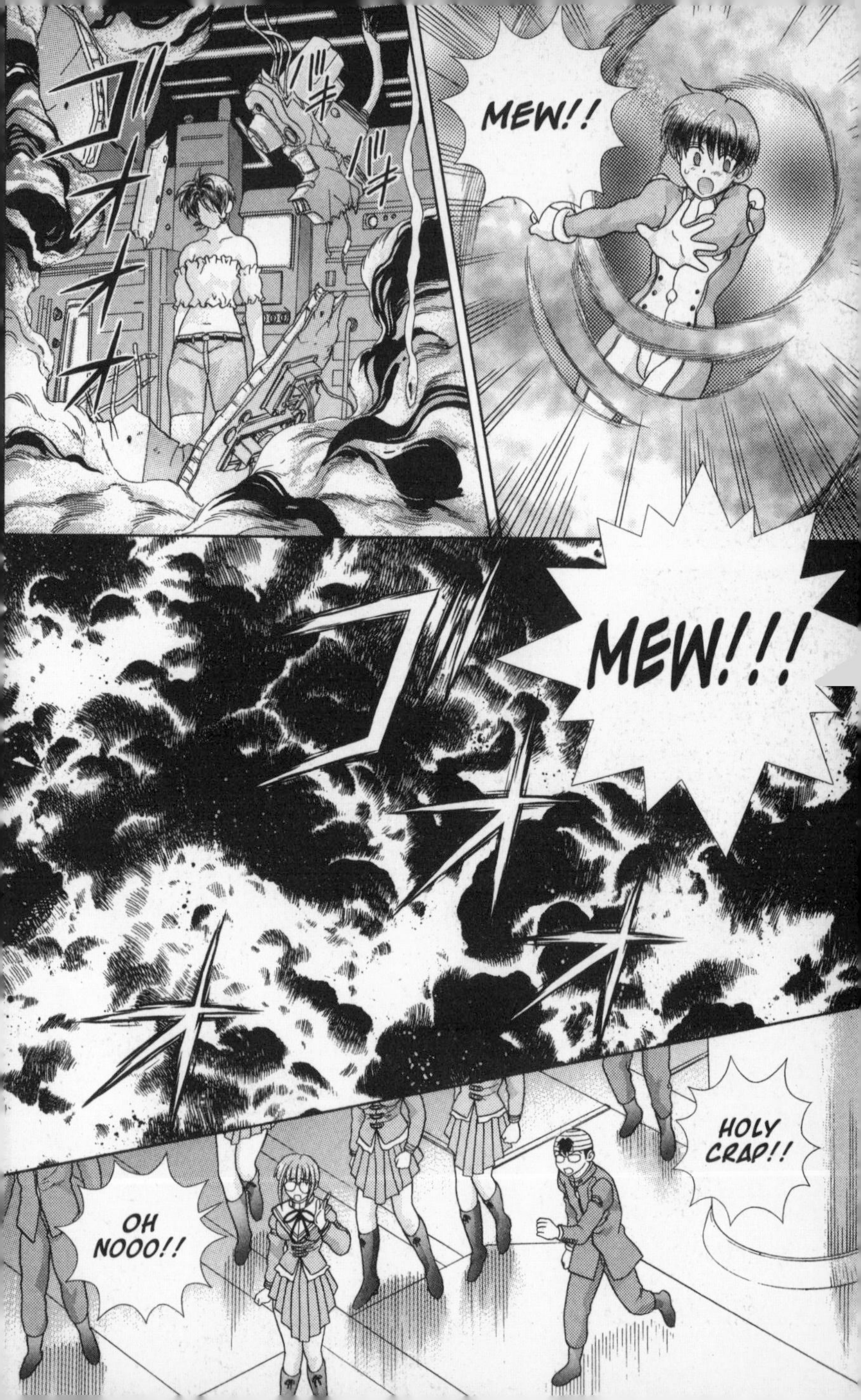
MEW!!
MEW!!!
HOLY CRAP!!
OH NOOO!!

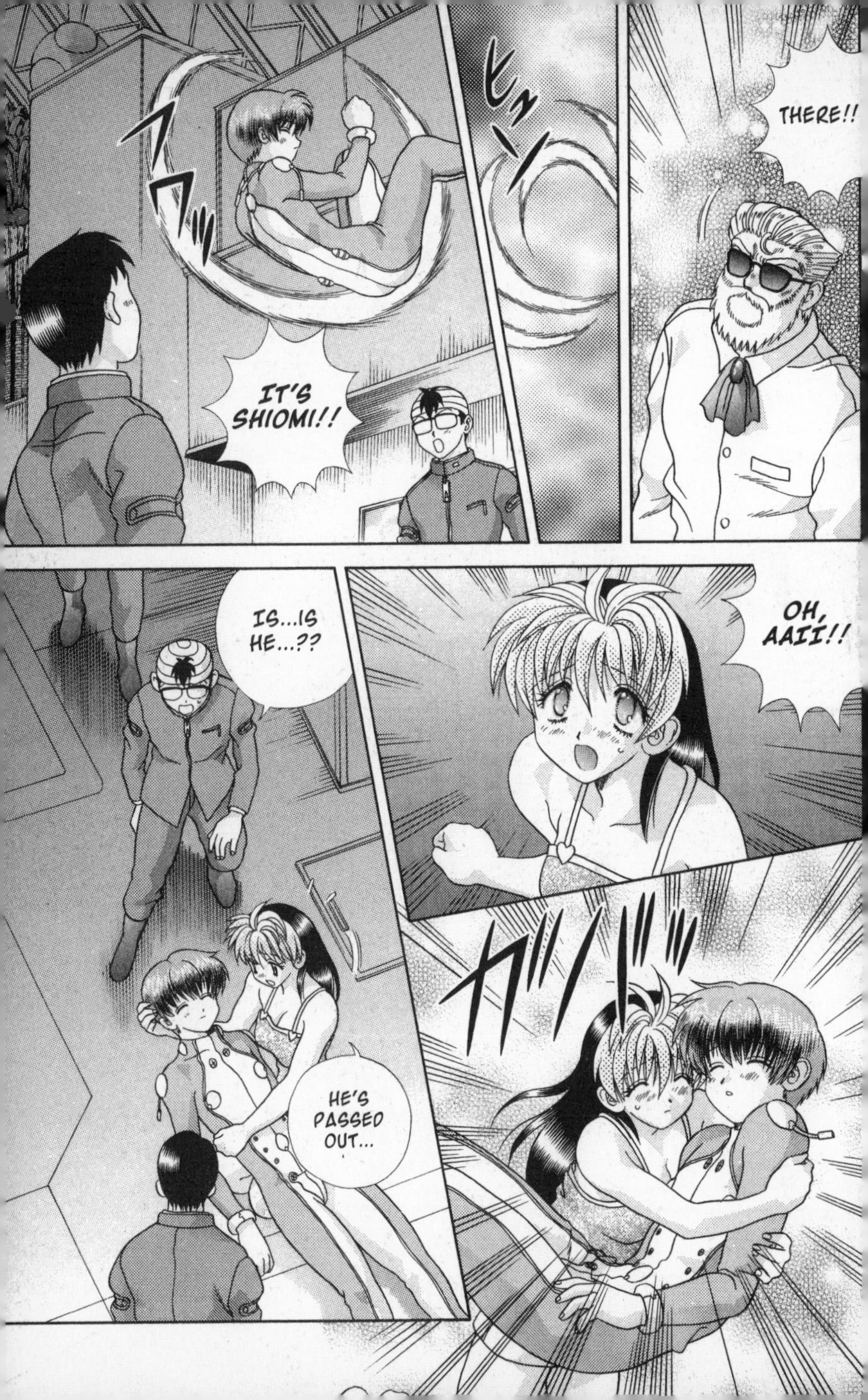
THERE!!
IT'S SHIOMI!!
OH, AAII!!
IS...IS HE...??
HE'S PASSED OUT...

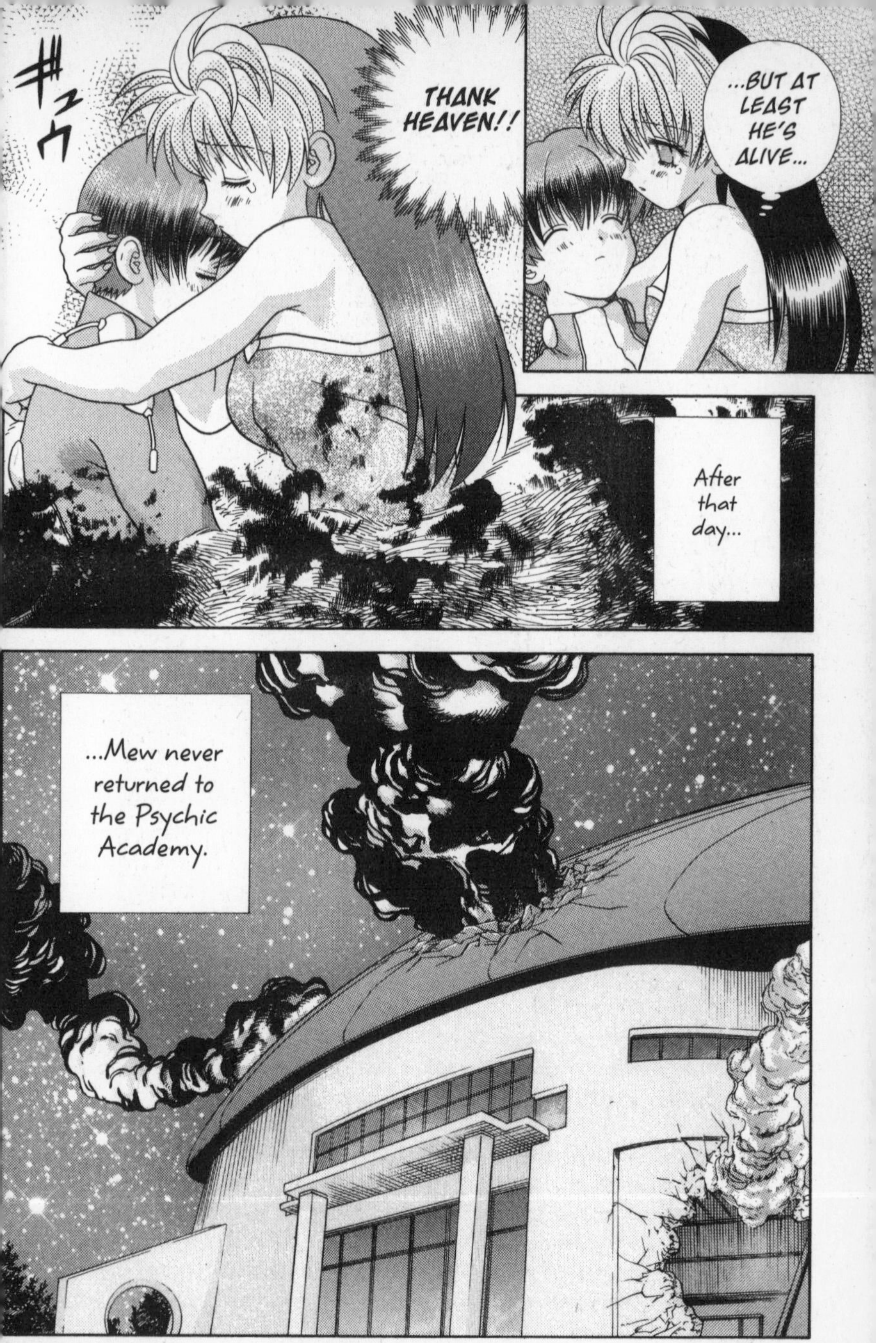
...BUT AT LEAST HE'S ALIVE...
THANK HEAVEN!!
ギュウ
After that day...
...Mew never returned to the Psychic Academy.

Psychic Academy 10 End

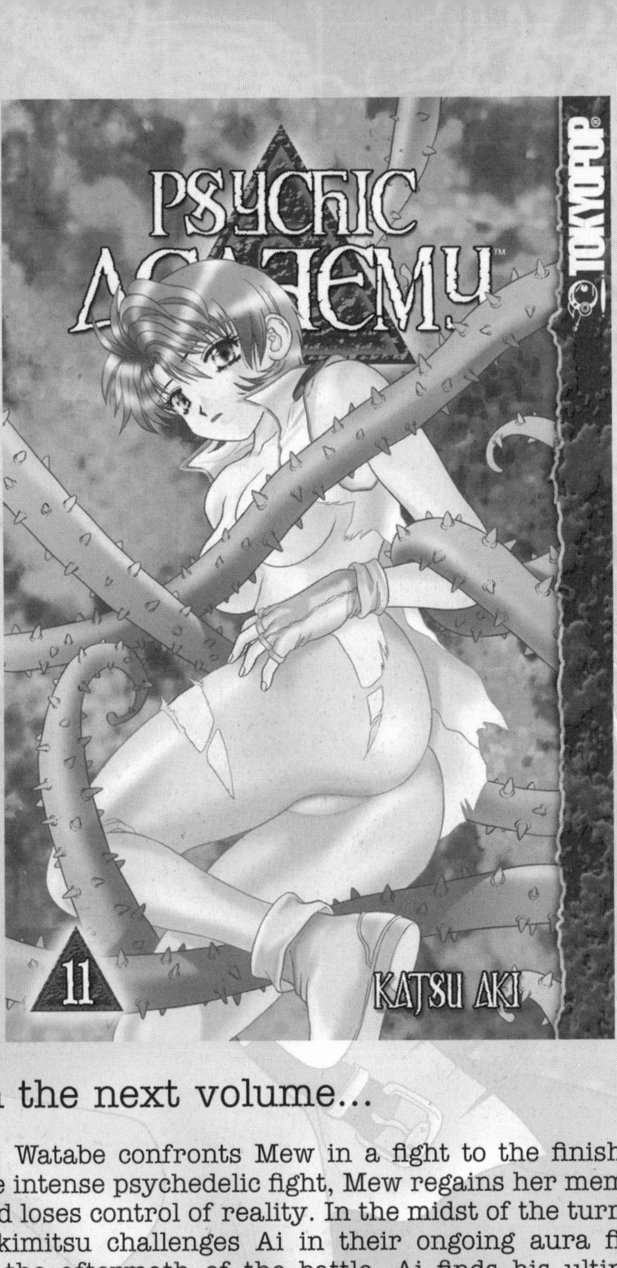
PSYCHIC ACADEMY
TOKYOPOP
11
KATSU AKI

In the next volume...

Dr. Watabe confronts Mew in a fight to the finish. In the intense psychedelic fight, Mew regains her memory and loses control of reality. In the midst of the turmoil, Tokimitsu challenges Ai in their ongoing aura fight. In the aftermath of the battle, Ai finds his ultimate purpose. Zerodyme and Ai must continue their mission against all odds.

TOKYOPOP PRESENTS
MANGA 漫画
THE NEW SIZZLING HOT
MANGA
MAGAZINE
ZELDA AND FRIEND FROM
WAR ON FLESH
©2005 Justin Boring, Greg Hildebrandt and TOKYOPOP
SIGN UP FOR FREE WWW.TOKYOPOP.COM

TOKYOPOP SHOP

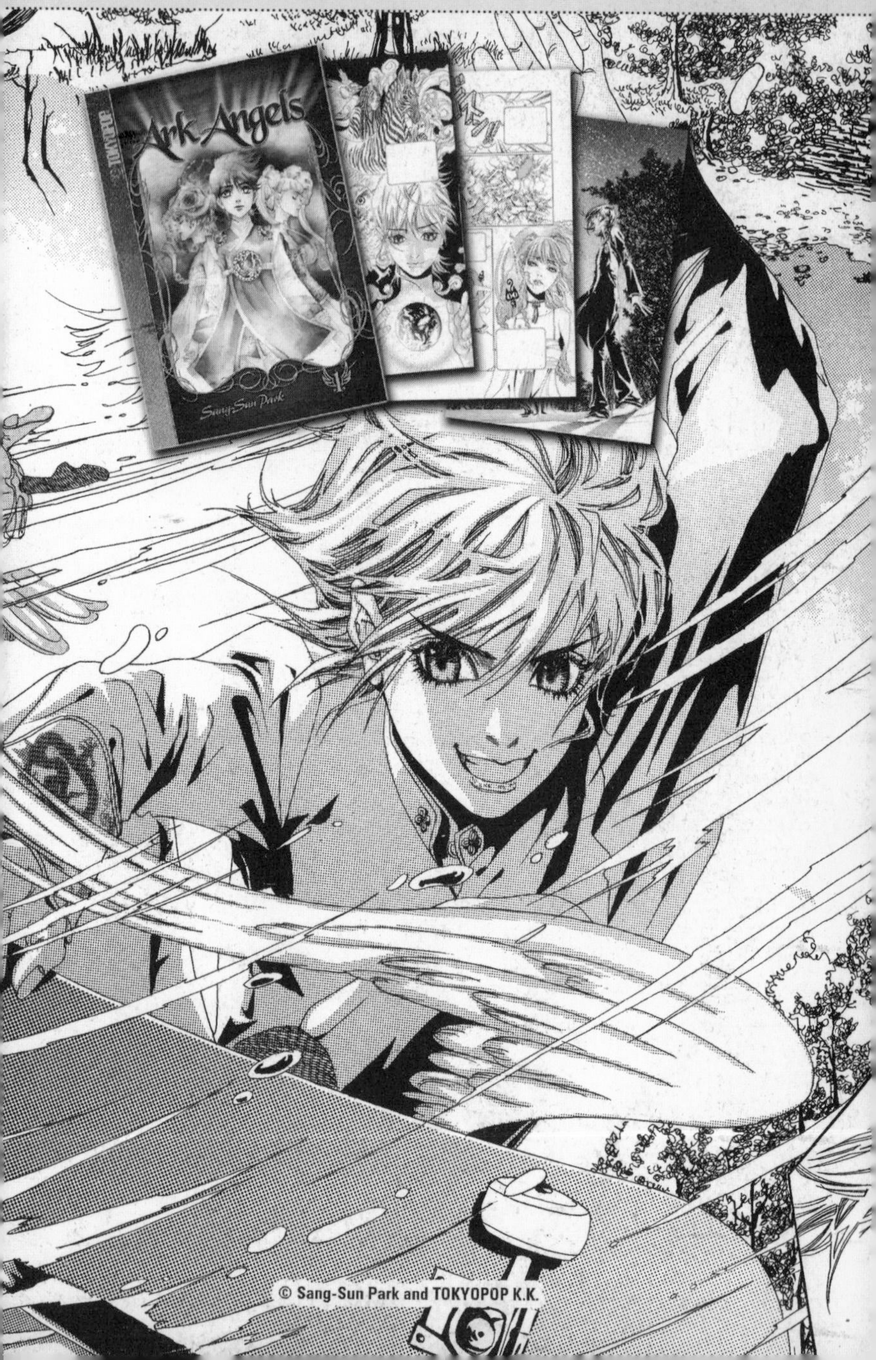
Ark Angels
TOKYOPOP
Sang-Sun Park
1

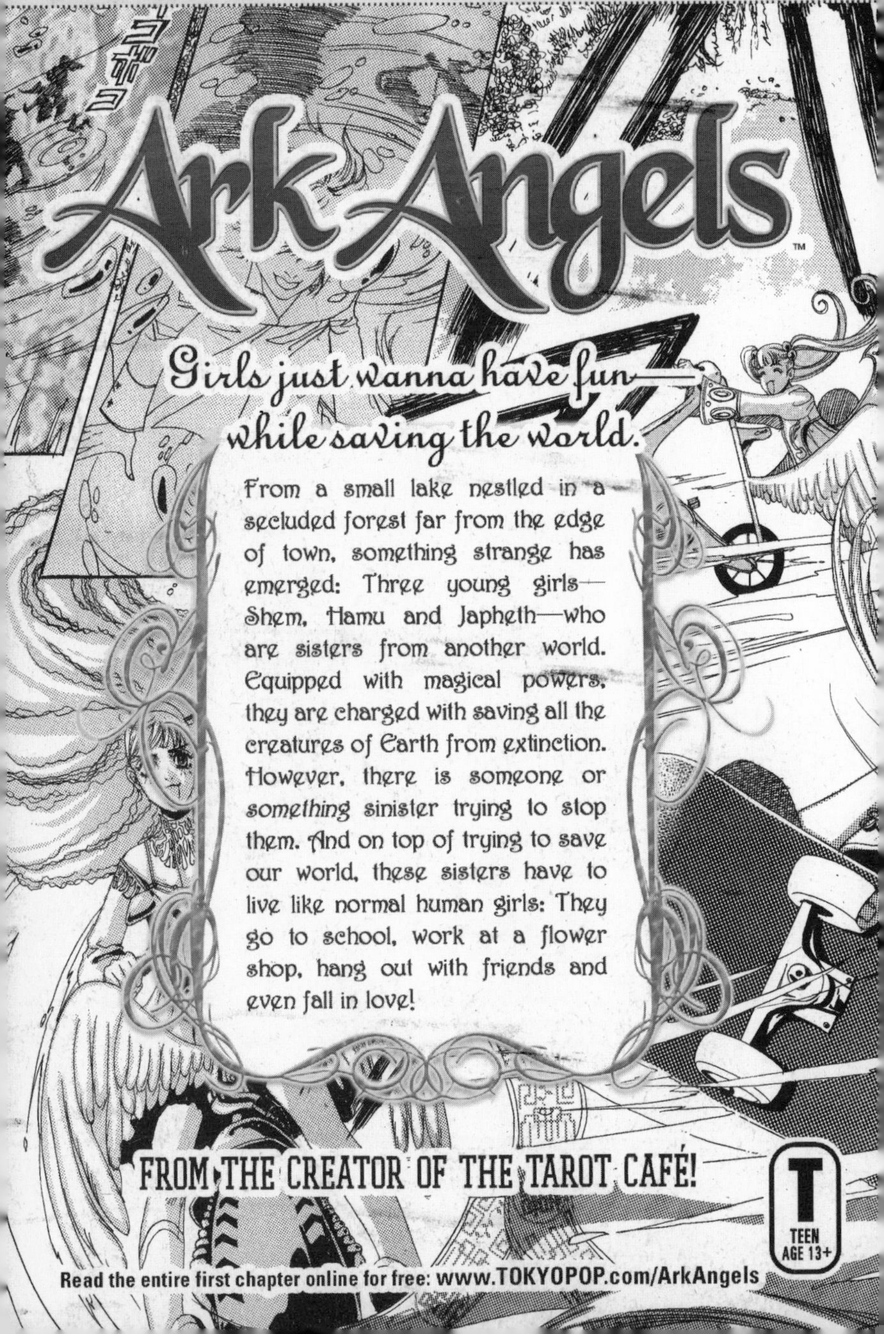
Ark Angels™
Girls just wanna have fun—while saving the world.
From a small lake nestled in a secluded forest far from the edge of town, something strange has emerged: Three young girls—Shem, Hamu and Japheth—who are sisters from another world. Equipped with magical powers, they are charged with saving all the creatures of Earth from extinction. However, there is someone or *something* sinister trying to stop them. And on top of trying to save our world, these sisters have to live like normal human girls: They go to school, work at a flower shop, hang out with friends and even fall in love!
FROM THE CREATOR OF THE TAROT CAFÉ!
T
TEEN AGE 13+
Read the entire first chapter online for free: www.TOKYOPOP.com/ArkAngels

STOP!

This is the back of the book.
You wouldn't want to spoil a great ending!

This book is printed "manga-style," in the authentic Japanese right-to-left format. Since none of the artwork has been flipped or altered, readers get to experience the story just as the creator intended. You've been asking for it, so TOKYOPOP® delivered: authentic, hot-off-the-press, and far more fun!

DIRECTIONS

If this is your first time reading manga-style, here's a quick guide to help you understand how it works.

It's easy... just start in the top right panel and follow the numbers. Have fun, and look for more 100% authentic manga from TOKYOPOP®!